Insurance Technology

Navigating the Innovation, Risk, and Future of Insurance

Insurance Technology

Navigating the Innovation, Risk, and Future of Insurance

Steven Haynes PhD, ARM
Associate Professor of Practice,
The University of Texas at Dallas

ELSEVIER

Academic Press is an imprint of Elsevier
125 London Wall, London EC2Y 5AS, United Kingdom
525 B Street, Suite 1650, San Diego, CA 92101, United States
50 Hampshire Street, 5th Floor, Cambridge, MA 02139, United States

For accessibility purposes, images in electronic versions of this book are accompanied by alt text descriptions independently provided by Elsevier, generated with the aid of AI. For more information, see https://www.elsevier.com/about/accessibility or Radarweg 29, 1043 NX Amsterdam, Netherlands.

Books and Journals published by Elsevier comply with applicable product safety requirements. For any product safety concerns or queries, please contact our authorised representative, Elsevier B.V., at productsafety@elsevier.com or Radarweg 29, 1043 NX Amsterdam, Netherlands.

Publisher's note: Elsevier takes a neutral position with respect to territorial disputes or jurisdictional claims in its published content, including in maps and institutional affiliations.

Notices

Knowledge and best practice in this field are constantly changing. As new research and experience broaden our understanding, changes in research methods, professional practices, or medical treatment may become necessary.

Practitioners and researchers must always rely on their own experience and knowledge in evaluating and using any information, methods, compounds, or experiments described herein. In using such information or methods they should be mindful of their own safety and the safety of others, including parties for whom they have a professional responsibility.

To the fullest extent of the law, neither the Publisher nor the authors, contributors, or editors, assume any liability for any injury and/or damage to persons or property as a matter of products liability, negligence or otherwise, or from any use or operation of any methods, products, instructions, or ideas contained in the material herein.

ISBN: 978-0-443-43972-8

For Information on all Academic Press publications
visit our website at https://www.elsevier.com/books-and-journals

Publisher: Peter Linsley
Acquisitions Editor: Peter Linsley
Editorial Project Manager: Surbhi Tyagi
Project Manager: Ashok Ravi
Cover Designer: Gopalakrishnan Venkatraman

Typeset by MPS Limited, Chennai, India

Last digit is the print number: 9 8 7 6 5 4 3 2 1

Contents

Instructor resources for this book are available on the Elsevier Educate platform and can be accessed by verified instructors at: https://www.educate.elsevier.com/book/details/9780443439728.

Acknowledgments

Writing a textbook is never a solitary endeavor. While my name may appear on the cover, this work is the result of numerous conversations, collaborations, and the support of colleagues, students, friends, and family who have influenced my thinking and sustained my efforts.

I am deeply grateful to my colleagues at the Naveen Jindal School of Management at The University of Texas at Dallas. Their encouragement and feedback have been essential in making this project possible. I would especially like to thank Robert, Carolyn, Hiro, Bill, Kelly, and Garrett for giving me the time and space to work on this project. Their insights were invaluable in helping me shape this book at the intersection of traditional insurance and emerging technology. To my mentor, Tony, thank you for your encouragement and guidance—you are truly a wonderful leader who inspires me to guide my students today.

This book would not have been possible without the encouragement of my students—both undergraduate and graduate—who continuously inspire me with their curiosity, creativity, and determination. Their questions, projects, and classroom discussions have challenged me to clarify my thinking and broaden the scope of this work, ensuring its relevance in both academic and industry contexts. To all my students throughout the years, thank you for reminding me that teaching is as much a privilege as it is a responsibility.

I would like to express my gratitude to my colleagues in the insurance and insurTech industries who shared their insights and experiences with me, whether through interviews, conference panels, or informal conversations. Their willingness to discuss the challenges and opportunities facing the insurance sector in the digital era has provided invaluable context for this book. I would especially like to thank Meredith and Nicole for their unwavering support and encouragement during some of my most challenging years of work.

I would like to express my heartfelt gratitude to my family for their patience, love, and encouragement, which supported me through countless hours of writing and research. To my wife, Alison, thank you for being my unwavering partner in every aspect of life. To my children, Jackson and Brenna, your love and laughter remind me every day why the work of creating safer and more resilient communities is so important. This book happened because you believed in me when I couldn't believe in myself.

To all who contributed in ways large and small—thank you. This book is dedicated to the students, professionals, and innovators who will carry the work of insurance technology forward, shaping a more resilient and equitable future.

CHAPTER

Introduction to insurance technology: history, drivers, and frameworks

1

CHAPTER OUTLINE

THE EVOLUTION OF THE INSURANCE INDUSTRY

Insurance dates back thousands of years and arises from a fundamental human need to manage and mitigate risks (Bernstein, 1996). Historical records indicate that early risk-sharing arrangements were practiced in ancient civilizations. For instance, maritime merchants in Babylonia around 1750 BCE developed basic marine insurance to protect against loss or damage during voyages (Vaughan & Vaughan, 2013). Similarly, Chinese traders around 3000 BCE employed simple risk-sharing techniques by distributing goods across multiple vessels to minimize potential losses (Bernstein, 1996). These early efforts highlight a fundamental principle of risk management: risk pooling which can lessen individual exposure to catastrophic losses, which continues to guide the insurance industry today (PWC, 2022).

Modern insurance, as we know it today, began to take shape in the coffee houses of 17th century London. Merchants, shipowners, and financiers gathered in these establishments to discuss maritime risks. One of the most notable coffee houses was Edward Lloyd's, which eventually became the foundation for Lloyd's of London, one of the most prominent and lasting global insurance markets.

In this early market, the underwriting process was formalized, which included structured risk assessments and the issuance of insurance policies. As the practice of

Insurance Technology. DOI: https://doi.org/10.1016/B978-0-443-43972-8.00002-X

underwriting became more sophisticated, the field of actuarial science emerged. This discipline focuses on calculating precise probabilities of various events, improving risk assessment, and policy pricing.

During the 18th and 19th centuries, the insurance industry experienced significant growth due to industrialization, urbanization, and the rapid expansion of global trade networks. Property and casualty insurance thrived during the Industrial Revolution by addressing new risks associated with factories, machinery, transportation infrastructure, and emerging business ventures (Swiss Re, 2017). At the same time, life insurance products became more popular as societies witnessed increased life expectancy, economic prosperity, and shifting cultural attitudes toward individual financial responsibility and family protection.

Despite the steady evolution of the insurance industry, the fundamental operations and distribution channels of insurance companies remained relatively stable throughout much of the 20th century. The traditional insurance model relied heavily on manual, paper-based processes. Underwriting was often lengthy and involved multiple layers of human evaluation. Claims settlement was cumbersome and slow, while inefficient legacy systems hindered policy administration. Insurance companies typically depended on networks of agents and brokers for product distribution, which limited direct customer interaction and slowed innovation in customer-facing practices (Stricker, 2023).

The latter part of the 20th century saw significant incremental improvements in the insurance industry, primarily due to advancements in computerization and digitization. Insurers began automating their internal processes, starting with mainframe computers in the 1960s and 1970s and later transitioning to more sophisticated client–server systems in the 1980s and 1990s (Yates, 1995). Although these advancements significantly reduced administrative burdens and enhanced data management, the core insurance model continued to rely heavily on traditional practices. The industry remained risk averse and often resistant to transformative change, ultimately lagging behind sectors such as banking, retail, and telecommunications regarding digital adoption and customer experience innovations.

In the early 21st century, traditional insurance models faced significant challenges. Demographic changes, evolving consumer expectations, and rapid technological advancements put pressure on these conventional approaches. Customers, who were used to seamless, digital-first experiences in other industries, started to demand similar interactions from insurers. They wanted faster claims processing, personalized product offerings, and transparent pricing structures (McKinsey & Company, 2021). Furthermore, insurers had to confront new and complex risks arising from globalization, climate change, cybersecurity threats, and increasing reliance on digital technology—risks that traditional actuarial methods could not handle.

Over the past decade, we have seen a significant rise in what is now known as "InsurTech." InsurTech refers to technology-driven innovations within the insurance industry, including digital distribution platforms, advanced analytics, blockchain-enabled smart contracts, Internet of Things (IoT) risk monitoring, and artificial intelligence (AI) applications in claims and underwriting processes (PWC, 2022). These advancements not only provide incremental improvements but also have the potential to create transformative changes in the conception, pricing, marketing, and servicing of insurance products.

Insurance technology startups have challenged established industry players using agile methodologies, cloud-native infrastructure, and customer-centric designs. These companies, such as Lemonade, Hippo, and Metromile in the United States and ZhongAn in China, have demonstrated the disruptive potential of technology in the insurance sector. They focus on simplifying policy language, automating claims settlements, and creating highly personalized risk models based on real-time data streams (World InsurTech Report, 2021).

Incumbent insurers are increasingly realizing the importance of digital transformation to stay competitive and maintain their relevance in the market. Traditional insurance companies are investing more in technology capabilities, forming partnerships with startups, launching innovation labs, and engaging in regulatory sandboxes to accelerate the development and implementation of innovative insurance solutions (Crocetta et al., 2023) Reinsurers have also joined this transformation by providing capacity and technical expertise to startups and innovation projects that may otherwise be challenging to scale.

While these technological advancements offer significant potential, they also introduce new challenges. Issues such as algorithmic bias in AI underwriting models, cyber vulnerabilities in digital distribution channels, and complex regulations across different jurisdictions make it difficult to adopt new technologies seamlessly. Furthermore, insurers must address cultural barriers within their organizations, including overcoming resistance to change, closing talent gaps, and fostering agile and innovative mindsets. Only by addressing these issues can they fully leverage the benefits of InsurTech innovations (Boston Consulting Group, 2022).

The insurance industry has transformed significantly from its early days of risk-sharing arrangements and London coffeehouses to a modern digital-first landscape. This evolution showcases the ongoing commitment to core principles—such as collective risk management, prudent financial governance, and actuarial precision—and the transformative changes brought about by technological advancements and evolving customer expectations. As insurance technology continues to develop, the industry is on the brink of a new era characterized not only by increased digital efficiency and enhanced customer experiences but also by greater access, improved transparency, and the potential for the democratization of risk management on a global scale.

WHAT IS INSURANCE TECHNOLOGY (INSURTECH)?

The term "InsurTech" is a combination of "insurance" and "technology." It broadly refers to the use of innovative digital technologies aimed at improving and transforming insurance industry operations. However, InsurTech goes beyond just updating technology or digitizing old processes; it fundamentally reshapes how insurers understand, distribute, and manage insurance products, customer relationships, and risk itself (PWC, 2022). InsurTech parallels the broader fintech movement in many ways, but there are distinct differences due to the insurance sector's unique nature, regulations, and cultural context.

At its core, InsurTech uses emerging technologies to create efficiencies, enhance customer experiences, develop innovative products, and broaden access to insurance coverage. This involves strategically utilizing technologies such as AI, machine learning, blockchain, big data analytics, cloud computing, and the IoT. These technologies do not operate in isolation; they interact and integrate to create robust platforms that can dynamically respond to changing market conditions, customer behaviors, and emerging risks (Crocetta et al., 2023).

The rise of InsurTech has been largely driven by changing consumer expectations. Today's consumers, who are used to digital-first interactions in retail, finance, and entertainment, increasingly demand the same intuitive and seamless experiences from their insurance providers. These customers seek transparency, personalization, ease of access, and quick responses—qualities that have traditionally been difficult to achieve in insurance due to manual processing, complex contracts, and intermediated distribution. InsurTech startups, such as Lemonade and Hippo, recognized early on that technology could address many of these pain points in the customer experience, leading to greater satisfaction, trust, and ultimately loyalty (Lemonade, n.d. and Hippo, 2025).

InsurTech companies focus on one or more of four core areas of insurance operations: distribution and customer engagement, underwriting and risk management, claims processing and settlement, and operational efficiency. Innovations in distribution primarily aim to improve how insurance products are sold and serviced. This includes digital marketplaces, direct-to-consumer mobile apps, embedded insurance within noninsurance platforms, and chatbots or digital assistants that enhance customer interaction. These platforms enable real-time quoting, policy issuance, and servicing, significantly simplifying what were once cumbersome processes. For instance, Lemonade's entirely digital platform allows customers to purchase renters' or homeowners' insurance within minutes through a mobile application, utilizing conversational AI to facilitate seamless interactions (World InsurTech Report, 2021).

Underwriting and risk management are some of the most complex areas for innovation in InsurTech. Traditionally, underwriting relied heavily on actuarial tables, historical claims data, and manual risk assessments. However, today's InsurTech startups use advanced machine learning algorithms, predictive analytics, and a variety of real-time data sources—such as telematics from vehicles and IoT-enabled devices in homes—to improve the accuracy and responsiveness of underwriting. By adopting these methods, insurers can better quantify and price risks in real time, resulting in personalized pricing models and more targeted coverage options (McKinsey & Company, 2021).

Claims processing, which is often seen as a major factor affecting customer satisfaction, is undergoing significant changes due to automation, digitization, and predictive settlement capabilities. Companies are utilizing technologies such as blockchain and smart contracts to streamline the verification and settlement of claims, dramatically reducing turnaround times. For example, blockchain-enabled parametric insurance products can trigger automatic payments based on predefined conditions, eliminating the need for manual claims investigations. This transformation enhances the speed of service and improves customer satisfaction through greater transparency (Deloitte, 2025).

Operational efficiency in the insurance sector is undergoing significant improvements due to advancements in InsurTech. Robotic process automation (RPA) and AI-driven tools streamline administrative tasks, including policy management, billing, compliance monitoring, and fraud detection. These innovations help reduce human error, lower operational costs, and enhance the overall speed of processes. In particular, advanced analytics and AI have proven highly effective in identifying fraudulent claims, which continue to pose a substantial cost burden on the global insurance industry (KPMG, 2021). Humans still need to detect fraud, as soft and hard fraud are often difficult to differentiate due to human behavior and perception.

While InsurTech shares some characteristics with the broader fintech sector, key differences are worth noting. Fintech typically focuses on transactional efficiency, financial inclusion, and disintermediation within banking and payment systems. In contrast, InsurTech deals with unique complexities related to insurance, such as long-term contractual obligations, complex actuarial calculations, stringent solvency regulations, and various types of risks beyond simple financial transactions.

Additionally, the nature of insurance requires a high level of trust, as customers pay premiums for coverage against uncertain future events. Therefore the technologies used in InsurTech must improve efficiency and enhance trust, transparency, and reliability (Boston Consulting Group, 2022).

Unlike fintech, which typically focuses on rapid transaction speeds and liquidity, InsurTech innovations need to balance speed and convenience while ensuring regulatory compliance, long-term risk stability, and accurate reserving. This requirement creates a distinct regulatory environment where innovations often undergo lengthy testing phases, regulatory sandboxes, and thorough compliance checks before being widely adopted.

Insurers that have been in the industry for a while increasingly realize that InsurTech is not just for startups; it has become a crucial part of their competitive strategies. Traditional insurance companies are investing more in digital transformation to keep up with agile startups and adopt innovative solutions that help them stand out in crowded markets. As a result, partnerships, acquisitions, and joint ventures between established insurers and new InsurTech firms have become more common. For example, Munich Re's Digital Partners has successfully connected startups' fast-paced nature with reinsurance capacity, allowing for quick market entry and the scalable launch of innovative products (World InsurTech Report, 2021).

While InsurTech offers great potential, its adoption faces several challenges. Integrating new technologies with legacy systems is often complex and costly. Many insurers encounter internal cultural resistance to rapid change, struggle to maintain regulatory compliance across various jurisdictions, and face risks associated with advanced technologies, such as algorithmic bias and cyber vulnerabilities.

Additionally, there is a persistent shortage of qualified talent who can effectively manage and implement these new digital capabilities—individuals with a combination of insurance knowledge, technological skills, and strategic agility.

The adoption of InsurTech continues to rise steadily. This growth is fueled by consumer demand, competitive pressures, technological advancements, and changing risk environments. As a result, the insurance industry increasingly sees technology-driven innovation as essential rather than merely beneficial. The successful insurer of the future will strategically leverage technology, embracing an agile, customer-centric, and data-informed approach. InsurTech is more than just a set of tools; it represents a fundamental rethinking of the insurance landscape, redefining who it serves and how effectively it can protect individuals, businesses, and society.

MARKET FORCES DRIVING DIGITAL CHANGE

The rise of InsurTech and the overall digitization of the insurance industry can only be understood by recognizing the key market forces driving these changes. These forces include shifts in consumer behavior, rapid technological advancements, evolving regulatory environments, and the emergence of new risks. Together, they put significant pressure on traditional insurers to adapt and innovate. In response, insurers worldwide are reevaluating their strategies and making substantial investments in digital infrastructure, customer-centric processes, and agile methodologies to stay relevant, competitive, and responsive to new demands.

One of the most significant market forces reshaping the insurance industry is the dramatic change in consumer expectations. Influenced by the seamless digital experiences of technology giants like Amazon, Google, and Netflix, today's customers expect similar frictionless, personalized, and transparent interactions from all service providers, including insurers. Modern consumers are digitally savvy, and their experiences in other sectors have raised their expectations for instant service, transparent pricing, customized offerings, and user-friendly interfaces. They have little tolerance for complexity, delays, or unclear pricing models traditionally associated with buying insurance (McKinsey & Company, 2021).

This shift is especially noticeable among younger demographics, such as millennials and Generation Z, who comprise an increasing share of the insurance-buying population. These groups prefer digital-first interactions, prioritize speed and simplicity, and often look for insurance solutions tailored to their lifestyles and values. For example, younger customers are increasingly attracted to usage-based and on-demand product coverage models that align with their specific needs and behaviors, rather than conventional standardized annual policies. Failing to meet these expectations may alienate a generation used to seamless, mobile-first, and personalized experiences, which could jeopardize long-term profitability and market relevance (Deloitte, 2025).

At the same time, technological advancements represent a significant force driving digital change in the insurance industry. The rapid pace of technological innovation, spurred by developments in AI, cloud computing, blockchain, big data analytics, 5G telecommunications, and the IoT, is transforming all facets of insurance operations. This includes underwriting, claims processing, distribution, and customer service (Crocetta et al., 2023). For instance, machine learning algorithms allow insurers to quickly and accurately analyze large datasets, offering new insights into risk assessment, customer behavior, and market trends. IoT devices such as telematics sensors in cars, wearable health monitors, and smart home technologies produce an unprecedented volume of real-time data. This empowers insurers to provide personalized, behavior-driven products that were unimaginable just a decade ago.

Blockchain technology is creating opportunities for increased transparency and trust in complex insurance processes. Its decentralized ledger approach enables real-time, verifiable transactions and automates claims processing through smart contracts. This significantly reduces administrative friction, fraud, and delays. Additionally, cloud computing infrastructure, along with open application programming interfaces (APIs), allows insurers to scale solutions quickly, integrate with external ecosystems, and innovate faster than was previously possible with traditional on-premise systems (Boston Consulting Group, 2022).

The third significant force reshaping the insurance industry is the evolving regulatory environment. Regulators worldwide recognize that while innovation is crucial for growth and market dynamism, it also brings new risks and challenges related to consumer protection, privacy, cybersecurity, and fairness. As a result, regulatory bodies are actively promoting balanced approaches by creating frameworks, such as regulatory sandboxes. These sandboxes allow insurers and startups to test new solutions in controlled environments with reduced compliance burdens. Examples of proactive regulatory responses to foster innovation while protecting consumer interests include the United Kingdom's Financial Conduct Authority (FCA) Sandbox, Singapore's Monetary Authority (MAS) Sandbox, and the National Association of Insurance Commissioners' innovation initiatives in the United States (FCA, 2022).

Insurers must navigate a complex regulatory environment that includes varying jurisdictional requirements and stringent data protection laws, such as the European Union's General Data Protection Regulation (GDPR). Additionally, emerging guidelines are focusing on algorithmic fairness and transparency. Regulators increasingly scrutinize technologies like AI-driven underwriting models and automated decision-making processes for potential bias and ethical considerations. Compliance with these evolving standards is becoming essential for competitiveness, not just a regulatory obligation. As a result, insurers are compelled to adopt strong data governance practices, transparent algorithmic models, and comprehensive risk management frameworks.

Another key driver of digital transformation is the evolving nature and complexity of global risks. Emerging threats—such as climate change, cyber risk, pandemics, geopolitical uncertainty, and systemic economic disruptions—pose challenges of unprecedented magnitude. Traditional actuarial methods and historical data models are often insufficient for effectively managing these new types of risks. As a result, insurers are increasingly adopting advanced modeling techniques, predictive analytics, and real-time data collection to quantify better, understand, and mitigate these risks. For example, climate-related risks have prompted insurers to adopt geospatial analytics, satellite imaging, and parametric insurance solutions that utilize real-time environmental data to trigger coverage responses (Swiss Re, 2025).

Cyber risk, driven by our increasing reliance on digital technology, is a critical area that requires technological innovation in the insurance sector. Cyberattacks' frequency, sophistication, and economic impact have grown significantly, prompting insurers to adopt advanced cybersecurity technologies, enhanced risk modeling, and customized cyber insurance offerings.

Forward-thinking insurers are creating real-time risk assessment tools, proactive threat detection systems, and predictive underwriting models designed to address dynamic cyber threats. Those insurers that fail or refuse to adapt to these rapidly evolving risks could face serious challenges, as their ability to accurately price, reserve, and manage claims may become increasingly compromised (Marsh & McLennan, 2021).

Venture capital investment and strategic partnerships are crucial in shaping digital transformation within the insurance sector. Over the past decade, venture capital firms, private equity investors, and established insurers have invested billions of dollars in InsurTech startups worldwide, highlighting the financial community's recognition of the sector's transformative potential. These investments have allowed startups to rapidly scale their innovations, offering agile, customer-centric products and distribution strategies that challenge traditional insurers.

To enhance their agility and foster rapid innovation, many incumbent insurers partner with or acquire startups to incorporate external innovations into their core operations. Companies like Munich Re's Digital Partners and AXA's Venture Partners exemplify this trend, facilitating technology integration through capital investment, mentoring, and access to global insurance distribution channels (World InsurTech Report, 2021).

The market forces are urging insurers to speed up their digital transformation journeys or face the risk of becoming obsolete. Insurers best positioned for future leadership will be those who can anticipate and adapt to these forces. This involves integrating advanced technologies into their core operations, aligning regulatory compliance with innovation, embracing customer-centric product design, and effectively managing increasingly complex risk landscapes. Ultimately, these forces are not merely temporary pressures; they represent enduring realities reshaping the insurance industry's identity, strategy, and operations.

THE INSURTECH ECOSYSTEM

The rapid growth and development of insurance technology, known as InsurTech, can be better understood by examining the diverse and dynamic ecosystem surrounding it. Unlike traditional models, where insurers often operated in isolation, the modern InsurTech landscape is marked by an interconnected network of stakeholders. This includes established insurers, innovative startups, regulatory authorities, technology providers, venture capitalists, reinsurers, academic institutions, and various intermediaries. Together, these participants create a collaborative yet competitive environment that drives ongoing innovation, market expansion, and improved customer experiences throughout the insurance industry.

At the heart of this ecosystem are the InsurTech startups. These agile, technology-driven companies are typically founded to disrupt established processes or enhance specific aspects of insurance operations. This can involve digital distribution, improved underwriting accuracy, claims automation, or innovative product offerings (Guo et al., 2025; Musaigwa & Netswera, 2025; Bhattacharya et al., 2025; BCG, 2025). Startups like Lemonade, Oscar Health, Hippo, and ZhongAn exemplify this new wave of companies, challenging traditional insurers by providing digital-first, customer-centric platforms. These platforms prioritize user experience, efficient claims processing, and transparent, flexible product structures. Often, these startups utilize advanced analytics, AI, and mobile technologies to fundamentally reimagine traditional insurance processes, offering policyholders simpler interactions and personalized insurance products.

The InsurTech ecosystem encompasses more than just startups. Established insurance companies play a crucial role as partners and competitors. Aware of the transformative potential of InsurTech, traditional insurers are adopting various strategies to integrate innovation into their operations. Some have created internal innovation labs or digital garages—such as Aviva's Digital Garage and AXA's Kamet Ventures—to foster new ideas and encourage entrepreneurial thinking within their organizations. Others have opted for strategic partnerships, joint ventures, or acquisitions to incorporate emerging technologies and capabilities into their core operations quickly. An example of this approach is Munich Re's Digital Partners initiative, which offers startup partners access to the reinsurer's substantial capital resources, technical expertise, and global distribution channels.

Reinsurers play a crucial role in the InsurTech ecosystem by enhancing scalability and stability. Beyond their traditional function of providing risk capacity and financial backing, reinsurers increasingly become channels for innovation. Swiss Re and Munich Re support InsurTech startups through dedicated innovation units, venture capital arms, and strategic partnerships. By utilizing their extensive underwriting experience, data resources, and global presence, reinsurers assist startups in navigating regulatory challenges, scaling products more quickly, and reaching broader markets. This mutually beneficial relationship allows reinsurers to gain first-hand exposure to cutting-edge technologies and innovative business models, ultimately boosting their competitive edge and long-term sustainability (Swiss Re, 2025).

Another essential player in this ecosystem is the venture capital community. Venture investors have recognized the significant growth potential in the insurance sector and have invested billions of dollars into InsurTech startups over the past decade. Firms, such as Andreessen Horowitz, Accel, SoftBank, and Sequoia Capital, have funded numerous high-profile startups, significantly accelerating innovation within the industry (World InsurTech Report, 2021). These investments enable startups to develop and scale their innovations and demonstrate confidence in the industry's broader digital transformation, attracting additional talent and resources to insurance technology ventures.

Technology providers are a crucial part of the InsurTech ecosystem, supplying the digital infrastructure, tools, and services needed to drive innovation in this field. Companies like Amazon Web Services, Microsoft Azure, and Google Cloud offer essential cloud computing capabilities that support agile product development, swift deployment, and global scalability. Additionally, other technology firms provide specialized solutions, including blockchain platforms for smart contracts, machine learning software for predictive analytics, and IoT sensors for real-time risk assessment. These providers assist insurers and startups by fostering rapid experimentation, lowering infrastructure costs, and delivering robust, scalable platforms to securely and efficiently manage increasing volumes of data (McKinsey & Company, 2021).

Regulatory authorities play a vital role in the InsurTech ecosystem. Due to the complex regulatory landscape of the insurance industry, active engagement with these regulatory bodies is essential for fostering sustainable innovation.

Regulatory sandboxes, such as those established by the United Kingdom's FCA, Singapore's MAS, and various US state regulators, are excellent examples of proactive regulatory involvement. These sandboxes offer controlled environments where InsurTech innovations can be tested with real customers while facing fewer regulatory constraints. This approach balances consumer protection and the encouragement of technological advancement (FCA, 2022).

Furthermore, by actively participating in the ecosystem, regulators can better understand emerging risks and technologies. This ultimately supports informed policymaking and the development of favorable regulatory frameworks.

Academic and research institutions play a dynamic role in the ecosystem by providing foundational research, thought leadership, and talent development. Universities and specialized research centers often collaborate with insurers and InsurTech firms to explore areas such as AI, behavioral economics, cybersecurity, climate risk, and advanced analytics. These partnerships facilitate knowledge exchange, create talent pipelines, and enhance innovation capabilities within the broader insurance industry. Moreover, academic institutions frequently support the ecosystem by hosting innovation hubs, incubators, and accelerators that nurture early-stage startups and foster entrepreneurial expertise among students and professionals (KPMG, 2021).

The ecosystem includes various intermediaries and facilitators, such as accelerators, incubators, and innovation networks. Accelerators like Plug and Play Insurtech, Lloyd's Lab, and Startupbootcamp InsurTech help early-stage startups connect with insurers, reinsurers, and venture investors (Lloyd's, 2020). They provide mentorship, funding opportunities, and structured support programs. These organizations often act as essential gateways for startups entering the broader insurance market, assisting them in refining their business models, navigating regulatory complexities, and developing scalable products aligned with industry needs. Additionally, innovation networks and industry consortia, such as InsurTech NY and InsTech London, further enhance connectivity, knowledge exchange, and collaboration among diverse stakeholders (InsurTech NY, n.d.; InsTech, n.d.).

The interconnected InsurTech ecosystem is constantly evolving, marked by a dynamic balance of collaboration and competition, often referred to as "coopetition" Incumbents and startups, insurers and reinsurers, and technologists and regulators all play dual roles as both partners and rivals. Each entity seeks to harness opportunities and address challenges within the shifting digital landscape. These complex relationships drive continuous innovation, challenge traditional industry boundaries, and support broader sector transformation.

HOW INSURANCE TECHNOLOGY ADDS VALUE

The insurance industry's swift adoption of technology, exemplified by the growth of InsurTech, goes beyond mere modernization. It signifies a strategic shift to enhance value throughout the insurance value chain. This added value is reflected in improved customer experiences, increased operational efficiencies, accurate risk assessments, and innovative products. Insurance technology enhances value clearly and significantly, fundamentally transforming how insurers interact with policyholders, partners, and regulators.

One of the main ways insurance technologies add value is by significantly enhancing customer experience and engagement. Traditional insurance transactions are often marked by complexity, cumbersome paperwork, and a lack of transparency, leading to consumer frustration and distrust. Digital solutions, especially mobile-first interfaces, automated chatbots, and self-service platforms, simplify the customer journey—from the initial policy purchase to ongoing account management and claims settlement.

Companies like Lemonade and Oscar Health exemplify this approach by offering intuitive and user-friendly digital platforms that allow customers to quickly and easily quote, bind, and manage their insurance products. Insurers can interact with policyholders more effectively by utilizing conversational AI and natural language processing. They can respond to inquiries instantly and process straightforward claims in real time, often within minutes (World InsurTech Report, 2021).

Enhanced digital interactions allow for unprecedented levels of personalization. Advanced analytics and machine learning algorithms process large volumes of customer data, ranging from basic demographics to detailed behavioral patterns. This analysis enables insurers to offer highly customized insurance solutions. For example, usage-based auto insurance utilizes telematics data to provide policyholders personalized pricing that reflects their driving habits. This level of precision improves customer satisfaction and encourages safer behaviors, ultimately reducing loss ratios and the frequency of claims (McKinsey & Company, 2021).

Insurance technology significantly enhances value by increasing operational efficiencies and addressing the significant challenges that traditional insurance companies often face. Legacy systems, manual workflows, and siloed processes have historically created bottlenecks, inflated administrative costs, and resulted in higher error rates. Technology-driven automation, especially RPA, AI-driven workflows, and cloud-based platforms, greatly streamlines and accelerates underwriting, policy issuance, claims processing, and compliance management processes. These innovations reduce overhead costs, minimize human errors, and free valuable personnel from repetitive administrative tasks, allowing them to focus more on complex problem-solving and engaging with customers.

Automation in claims processing has become a valuable application of technology in the insurance industry. Insurers that use AI algorithms and predictive analytics can quickly assess the validity of claims, estimate their severity, and initiate automated payments with minimal manual intervention. This streamlined claims process greatly improves customer satisfaction, as policyholders receive timely payouts when needed. Additionally, it helps reduce operational costs and minimizes the risk of fraud (Deloitte, 2025).

Insurance technology plays a crucial role in detecting and preventing fraud, which remains a persistent and costly challenge for the industry. Fraudulent claims cost insurers billions of dollars annually, affecting profitability and increasing consumer premiums. Innovations in InsurTech, using AI and big data analytics, allow quicker and more accurate identification of patterns that indicate fraudulent behavior compared to traditional manual reviews.

Predictive modeling tools analyze claims data in real time, utilizing machine learning algorithms to detect anomalies and proactively flag suspicious activities. By identifying potential fraud early in the claims process, insurers can save significant amounts of money and protect legitimate customers from increased premiums that result from fraud-related losses (KPMG, 2021).

Moreover, insurance technology adds significant value by enhancing risk modeling with precision and dynamism. Traditionally, insurance underwriting depended heavily on historical loss data and actuarial tables to determine policy prices. This often led to generalized and inflexible products that did not accurately reflect individual risk profiles. However, advanced analytics, IoT devices, geospatial data, and predictive modeling allow insurers to analyze risks in real time. This capability offers dynamic pricing models and personalized coverage options tailored to individual circumstances or unique risk exposures. For instance, property insurers increasingly use geospatial analytics and satellite imaging to assess climate-related risks in real time. This enables them to adjust coverage and premium pricing based on immediate environmental factors (Swiss Re, 2025).

The widespread adoption of IoT technology has significantly transformed risk management. IoT sensors installed in vehicles, homes, and commercial properties continuously collect data on behaviors, environmental conditions, and the health of assets. These data allow insurers to proactively identify risks, alert policyholders to potential issues, and even prevent losses before they happen. By implementing these proactive risk mitigation strategies, insurers can significantly reduce the frequency and severity of claims, resulting in improved profitability and greater policyholder satisfaction.

One important area where insurance technology adds significant value is in product innovation and market expansion. Insurers that effectively leverage technology can now develop new, customized products that address market segments that have been previously underserved. For example, parametric insurance uses clearly defined triggers and automated payouts based on measurable events like earthquake magnitude or rainfall. This provides straightforward, rapid-response coverage, especially for catastrophic risks and agricultural insurance needs. Microinsurance products designed for emerging markets or gig economy workers—often enabled through mobile payment platforms and digital distribution—extend insurance access to populations previously excluded from traditional coverage due to high costs or complex processes (World InsurTech Report, 2021).

Technology allows insurers to seamlessly integrate their insurance offerings into broader consumer and business ecosystems, a concept known as embedded insurance. This approach directly incorporates coverage into purchasing goods or services, such as automatically bundling travel insurance with flight bookings or offering warranty protection within e-commerce platforms. This provides consumers with convenient and contextually relevant coverage precisely when needed. Such strategies significantly simplify the insurance purchasing process, enhance acceptance rates, and create new revenue streams for insurers (Crocetta et al., 2023)

From an internal organizational perspective, insurance technology offers significant value by enhancing regulatory compliance and governance. The complex regulatory environment, strict consumer protection laws, and evolving data privacy standards place immense pressure on insurers to maintain detailed compliance records, audit trails, and governance procedures. InsurTech tools, such as blockchain-enabled smart contracts and AI-driven compliance platforms, automate and streamline these compliance processes, reducing human error and increasing transparency. These technologies enable insurers to remain compliant across various jurisdictions, quickly adapt to regulatory changes, and uphold consumer trust through clear transparency and accountability.

Insurance technology creates value by making insurance more accessible and promoting financial inclusion. Digital-first models help eliminate barriers to entry, reduce administrative costs, and simplify complex processes, allowing insurers to provide affordable and accessible coverage to populations that have been historically underserved. Mobile platforms and digital distribution channels have greatly improved insurance accessibility in emerging markets, giving millions of previously uninsured individuals access to essential coverage. This democratization of insurance represents a social benefit and opens up significant new market opportunities for insurers ready to embrace innovative, digitally enabled distribution strategies (Crocetta et al., 2023)

Technology enhances value by improving crisis response and resilience planning. Insurers that utilize real-time data analytics, predictive modeling, and flexible digital platforms can react more swiftly and effectively to catastrophic events, such as natural disasters, pandemics, or cyber incidents. These tools bolster operational resilience, strengthen communication with policyholders during crises, and enable quick and efficient claims settlements when policyholders need the most support.

Integrating technology into insurance operations represents a significant evolution toward customer centricity, efficiency, responsiveness, and precision, rather than just a superficial change. The diverse innovations offered by InsurTech—such as digital customer engagement, advanced risk modeling, claims automation, fraud detection, product innovation, regulatory compliance, and democratization—collectively redefine how value is created within the insurance industry. Insurers that effectively leverage these technologies gain a competitive advantage and significantly enhance the insurance experience. This, in turn, strengthens customer relationships and improves the overall resilience of the industry for years to come.

RISKS, CHALLENGES, AND BARRIERS TO ADOPTION

The transformative potential of InsurTech is well recognized, but the industry's journey toward integrating technology and fostering innovation comes with several notable risks, challenges, and obstacles. Successfully adopting and implementing insurance technology requires insurers to navigate a complex landscape, which includes limitations imposed by legacy infrastructures, cultural resistance, regulatory uncertainties, cybersecurity threats, talent shortages, and ethical concerns. Identifying and proactively addressing these challenges is crucial to fully harnessing InsurTech's benefits.

One of the most significant obstacles to the widespread adoption of InsurTech is the outdated technology infrastructure prevalent in the traditional insurance industry. Many established insurers still depend on legacy core systems and fragmented databases designed decades ago for different operational needs. These systems are often monolithic and inflexible, limiting insurers' ability to integrate new digital tools, advanced analytics, or real-time data streams. Efforts to add new technologies to this outdated infrastructure frequently lead to high integration costs, complex technical workarounds, and increased operational risks (Boston Consulting Group, 2022).

Legacy technology complicates data management, which is crucial for modern insurance operations. Issues such as data silos, inconsistent data formats, and limited system interoperability hinder insurers' ability to extract valuable insights and utilize advanced analytical capabilities. Additionally, maintaining outdated infrastructure consumes significant IT resources, diverting investments from innovation initiatives. Although modernization is essential, it requires substantial capital investment, careful planning, and ongoing organizational commitment—conditions not always easily met by insurers facing pressures from quarterly earnings or conservative investment strategies (Crocetta et al., 2023).

A related but distinct challenge is the widespread cultural resistance found in many insurance organizations. The insurance industry, historically risk averse, is grounded in conservative and methodical approaches that prioritize predictability and careful risk evaluation. This ingrained cultural conservatism often conflicts with the agile, iterative, and experimental mindset needed for technology-driven innovation. As a result, organizational inertia, fear of disruption, and skepticism toward new technology can hinder digital transformation efforts. Employees accustomed to traditional methods may resist adopting new technologies out of concerns about job displacement, skill obsolescence, or uncertainty regarding their future roles (Deloitte, 2025).

Overcoming cultural resistance requires intentional and ongoing leadership efforts. It involves clear communication about the strategic importance of innovation, the establishment of psychologically safe environments that encourage experimentation, and comprehensive change management programs. If cultural barriers are not addressed explicitly and systematically, insurers may face stalled adoption and limited internal support, and ultimately, they may fail to achieve the intended benefits of InsurTech.

The complexity of the regulatory environment poses a significant challenge for the insurance industry. InsurTech adoption often faces regulatory ambiguity and inconsistencies because insurance is heavily regulated worldwide. For example, innovative products like usage-based insurance, blockchain-enabled smart contracts, and AI-driven underwriting algorithms may not have clearly defined regulatory frameworks, leading to uncertainty regarding compliance obligations. Additionally, regulatory discrepancies across different jurisdictions further complicate matters, making it especially difficult for insurers operating internationally to consistently implement technology-driven innovations (World InsurTech Report, 2021).

Emerging technologies, such as AI, bring forth ethical and fairness concerns, particularly regarding algorithmic bias, data privacy, and the transparency of automated decision-making. Regulators are increasingly scrutinizing insurers' use of AI to prevent discriminatory pricing, protect customer privacy, and ensure transparency. As a result, insurers must navigate these changing ethical and regulatory landscapes carefully. They should engage proactively with regulators, invest in compliance codesign practices, and adopt transparent governance models to mitigate potential legal, reputational, and operational risks (McKinsey & Company, 2021).

Cybersecurity threats pose a significant risk in the insurance industry's digital transformation. As insurers adopt cloud computing, IoT connectivity, and mobile-first distribution strategies, their exposure to cyber risks significantly increases. Cyberattacks—such as ransomware, phishing, and sophisticated data breaches—can inflict serious financial, operational, and reputational harm on insurers. Those managing large volumes of sensitive customer data must consistently invest in cybersecurity infrastructure, advanced threat detection systems, and effective response plans. However, even with these advanced security measures, vulnerabilities cannot be eliminated, which requires insurers to remain vigilant and continuously balance technological innovation with security needs (Marsh & McLennan, 2021).

Integrating new technologies, such as IoT devices and third-party data sources, can introduce vulnerabilities in the supply chain and increase cybersecurity risks. Therefore insurers need to adopt comprehensive cybersecurity risk management practices. This includes incorporating risk assessments into innovation initiatives from the very beginning, continuously updating threat intelligence, and developing rapid incident response capabilities.

A significant yet often overlooked barrier to the adoption of InsurTech is the talent scarcity. Integrating advanced technologies into insurance operations demands specialized skills, especially in data science, software engineering, cybersecurity, and digital product management. These skills are frequently in short supply within the insurance labor market. As a result, insurers often face challenges in attracting, retaining, and effectively utilizing professionals proficient in cutting-edge technologies, agile methodologies, and digital product development. Additionally, the competition for skilled technical professionals from industries like technology, fintech, and consulting further complicates these efforts, driving up compensation expectations and making talent acquisition more difficult (KPMG, 2021).

Skill gaps are present among current employees who do not have adequate training and experience with digital technologies and agile processes. Insurers risk significant capability mismatches without organized upskilling initiatives, internal training programs, or partnerships with educational institutions. This limitation can hinder technology adoption's speed, effectiveness, and scale.

The adoption of InsurTech raises important ethical and social issues. Automated decision-making and AI-driven underwriting can unintentionally reinforce or exacerbate biases present in historical data. This can result in discriminatory outcomes or unfair pricing for vulnerable customer segments. Insurers must carefully evaluate their data inputs, modeling methods, and the transparency of their algorithms to avoid causing unintended harm or discrimination. It is essential to communicate transparently about how automated decisions are made and to establish clear accountability frameworks. This approach helps maintain consumer trust and ensures compliance with regulatory standards (Swiss Re, 2025).

Economic and market-driven factors, such as costs and uncertainties regarding return on investment (ROI), play a significant role in the adoption of InsurTech. Although technology offers substantial long-term benefits, the initial investments required can be considerable, creating barriers, especially for smaller insurers with limited resources. Moreover, quantifying the benefits of technology in traditional financial terms—like immediate ROI or payback periods—can be difficult, as many InsurTech initiatives provide strategic advantages rather than immediate financial returns. Consequently, gaining buy-in from leadership, justifying capital expenditures, and demonstrating early value can be challenging, which may slow adoption timelines or limit investments in promising innovations (Boston Consulting Group, 2022).

Successfully adopting insurance technology involves overcoming several significant barriers, including limitations of legacy infrastructure, cultural resistance, regulatory uncertainty, cybersecurity threats, talent shortages, ethical risks, and economic uncertainties. To address these challenges proactively, insurers must engage in comprehensive strategic planning, establish robust risk management frameworks, make sustained investments in modernizing their infrastructure, actively collaborate with regulatory bodies, implement systematic talent development initiatives, and foster deliberate cultural transformation efforts. By navigating these challenges effectively, insurers can position themselves to survive the digital transformation and thrive in the future insurance landscape driven by technology.

INTERDISCIPLINARY NATURE OF INSURANCE TECHNOLOGY

Insurance technology, commonly called InsurTech, requires a combination of multiple disciplines and areas of expertise. Unlike traditional insurance operations, which have historically focused primarily on actuarial science, finance, and compliance, modern insurance solutions necessitate integration across various fields, including data science, behavioral economics, software engineering, law and regulation, cybersecurity, and human-centered design (HCD). This interdisciplinary collaboration is beneficial and essential for insurers aiming to innovate, stay competitive, and effectively serve increasingly sophisticated customer bases.

At its core, the insurance industry relies on actuarial and financial principles. Actuarial science, which combines statistics, mathematics, and economics, is the foundation for risk assessment and product pricing. However, modern advancements in data analytics and machine learning have greatly expanded the methodologies used in actuarial work. This evolution requires actuaries to collaborate with data scientists and software engineers closely. Actuaries now work extensively with these technical experts, utilizing advanced computational tools, machine learning algorithms, and real-time data sources to improve traditional models. This integration enhances the accuracy of risk modeling, allows for greater product customization, and improves underwriting precision beyond what was previously possible with historical data alone (Society of Actuaries, 2021).

Data science has become essential in the operations of the insurance industry. As the industry increasingly relies on predictive analytics, AI, and large-scale data integration, there is a growing demand for professionals skilled in data manipulation, algorithm development, and statistical modeling. Insurance technology depends heavily on these data science capabilities to gain insights into consumer behavior, detect fraud, model predictive claims, and assess risks dynamically.

Data scientists analyze vast amounts of structured and unstructured data from various sources, including telematics, IoT sensors, and social media. They transform raw data into actionable insights crucial for insurers' strategic and operational decision-making processes (McKinsey & Company, 2021).

Software engineering is a crucial interdisciplinary component of InsurTech, connecting theoretical insights from actuarial and data sciences with practical, scalable solutions. Software engineers are key in transforming innovative concepts and predictive models into secure, robust, and user-friendly digital products and platforms. They are responsible for developing customer-facing applications, claims management systems, real-time quoting platforms, and integrated data pipelines that implement advanced analytical models. Additionally, software engineering practices—including agile methodologies, continuous integration and deployment, and cloud-native architectures—enable insurers to innovate quickly, iterate on their solutions, and adapt to changing customer demands and competitive pressures (Boston Consulting Group, 2022).

Behavioral economics offers a vital interdisciplinary perspective in the field of insurance technology. While actuarial science and data analytics provide the quantitative basis for pricing and risk assessment, behavioral economics enhances our understanding of customer behavior, decision-making biases, and psychological factors that influence how consumers interact with insurance products.

Insights from behavioral economics aid insurers in designing user-friendly interfaces, optimizing digital customer journeys, and creating products that align with policyholder preferences and cognitive tendencies. Key behavioral principles—loss aversion, framing effects, and default settings—are increasingly integrated into digital platforms. This integration improves customer engagement, encourages positive behaviors, and boosts overall satisfaction (Thaler & Sunstein, 2008).

Legal and regulatory expertise is equally important in the interdisciplinary field of InsurTech. The insurance sector, known for being one of the most highly regulated industries worldwide, faces the ongoing challenge of navigating complex and evolving legal frameworks, particularly when adopting new technologies. Legal professionals, compliance officers, and regulatory experts collaborate closely with technology teams to ensure that innovations comply with often fragmented regulatory standards, including data privacy laws like GDPR, consumer protection guidelines, and industry-specific regulations.

Additionally, legal teams are essential in developing contractual frameworks for emerging technologies, managing liability risks associated with AI and automation, and contributing to policy discussions around technology-driven ethical issues. These issues include fairness, transparency, and accountability in algorithmic decision-making (World InsurTech Report, 2021).

Cybersecurity is a crucial interdisciplinary component of InsurTech, combining information technology, risk management, and regulatory compliance. As digitization and interconnectedness increase, so does the exposure to cyber risks, making comprehensive cybersecurity practices essential. Cybersecurity specialists work alongside software engineers, data scientists, compliance professionals, and risk managers to integrate security measures into every stage of product development. This collaborative approach ensures that security is not an afterthought but is integral to InsurTech platforms, from the initial design and coding phases to deployment and ongoing monitoring. Insurers increasingly rely on cyber expertise to protect sensitive data, address vulnerabilities, and maintain operational resilience in the face of evolving cyber threats (Marsh & McLennan, 2021).

The interdisciplinary nature of insurance technology includes principles of HCD. HCD focuses on empathy, usability, and intuitive interactions, prioritizing the customer's experience in technological innovation. Designers work together with engineers, behavioral economists, and product specialists to develop digital platforms that are accessible, transparent, and user-friendly. This collaboration ensures that even the most advanced technologies remain understandable and meaningful to the end user. For instance, HCD principles inform the creation of claims automation tools, allowing for precise, empathetic, and responsive interactions during potentially stressful claims processes. This approach enhances overall customer trust and satisfaction (IDEO, 2021).

Academia and research institutions are vital in fostering interdisciplinary partnerships within the InsurTech sector. Universities and specialized research centers act as incubators for new knowledge, innovative methodologies, and a fresh talent pool. Insurers are increasingly collaborating with academia through joint research projects, internships, and innovation hubs. They leverage insights from various fields, including economics, computer science, actuarial science, law, and psychology. These partnerships promote continuous learning, enhance the innovation capabilities of insurers, and enable a deeper exploration of emerging risks, ethical concerns, and technological trends that will shape the insurance industry's future (KPMG, 2021).

The intersections of various disciplines define the unique character of modern insurance technology. InsurTech is not just about digital transformation; it fundamentally integrates multiple perspectives—such as actuarial analysis, data-driven insights, behavioral understanding, legal clarity, cybersecurity measures, and empathetic design—to create comprehensive, responsive, and effective insurance solutions. Insurers embracing this interdisciplinary approach are better equipped to adapt to technological changes and actively shape the industry's future. By synthesizing diverse expertise, these insurers can innovate effectively, manage complex risks, anticipate consumer needs, and successfully navigate an evolving regulatory landscape.

FRAMEWORKS TO UNDERSTAND THE INNOVATION LANDSCAPE

Innovation in the rapidly evolving insurance sector can feel complex and chaotic without clear frameworks to help understand and navigate the landscape. Insurers face challenges such as technology adoption, shifting customer preferences, regulatory changes, and competitive pressures. They need structured analytical tools to interpret, prioritize, and manage their innovation initiatives.

Several well-established theoretical frameworks have proven valuable in helping insurance organizations understand and manage innovation. These frameworks—including disruptive innovation theory, diffusion of innovation theory, digital maturity models, Gartner's hype cycle, and innovation portfolio management—provide essential guidance for insurers operating in a digitally driven marketplace.

One of the most influential and widely discussed frameworks for innovation is Clayton Christensen's disruptive innovation theory. Introduced in 1997, Christensen's framework explains why well-managed and successful companies often fail when faced with innovative newcomers that employ radically different business models or technologies (Christensen, 1997). According to Christensen, disruptive innovations typically emerge in underserved or overlooked market segments, which are initially seen as inferior or unprofitable by established companies. However, these innovations improve rapidly over time, capture larger market shares, and can ultimately disrupt entire industries.

Applying disruptive innovation theory to the insurance industry reveals that established companies initially underestimated early InsurTech startups. These startups were often seen as targeting small market segments, offering niche products, or lacking initial profitability. For instance, early offerings in parametric and microinsurance were considered marginal and irrelevant to traditional insurance practices. However, these innovations quickly proved their ability to scale and efficiently meet the needs of previously underserved customer segments, disrupting traditional market dynamics.

Insurers that embrace disruptive innovation theory are better equipped to proactively identify emerging threats, strategically engage with potentially disruptive entrants, and adapt quickly to changing market conditions. This proactive approach allows them to avoid merely reacting to disruptions after they have occurred (Christensen, Raynor, & McDonald, 2015).

Another important framework for understanding innovation in insurance is Everett Rogers' diffusion of innovation theory. In 2003 Rogers proposed a structured model that explains how new ideas, products, and technologies spread throughout societies and markets. This model categorizes adopters into distinct segments: innovators, early adopters, early majority, late majority, and laggards. Different levels of risk tolerance, attitudes toward innovation, and decision-making behaviors characterize each segment. By understanding this diffusion curve, insurers can strategically introduce innovative products, manage adoption timelines, and prioritize specific market segments for targeted communication and distribution strategies.

Within the InsurTech sector, the diffusion of innovation theory explains how new technologies—such as telematics-based auto insurance, digital health monitoring wearables, and blockchain-enabled smart contracts—transition from niche markets of tech-savvy early adopters to broader mainstream acceptance. Understanding this progression enables insurers to tailor their product launches, customer engagement strategies, and educational campaigns to meet the specific needs of different adopter segments, which can significantly enhance adoption rates and market penetration. Furthermore, the theory emphasizes the importance of strategically engaging influential early adopters and opinion leaders who can drive wider adoption through peer influence, social proof, and word-of-mouth recommendations (Rogers, 2003).

Digital maturity models provide a valuable framework for insurers navigating technological transformation. These models help organizations evaluate their current technological capabilities and guide them systematically toward digital excellence. Typically, digital maturity frameworks assess multiple dimensions, including technological infrastructure, strategic alignment, talent and skills readiness, cultural adaptation, and customer centricity. This assessment helps gauge an insurer's preparedness for digital innovation. Notable examples of these frameworks include Deloitte's digital maturity model and Boston Consulting Group's digital acceleration index (Deloitte, 2025).

Utilizing digital maturity models enables insurers to benchmark their performance against peers, pinpoint specific capability gaps, prioritize resource allocation, and create clear, actionable roadmaps for digital transformation. For example, an insurer may discover significant shortcomings in customer-facing digital engagement or back-office automation. This could lead to targeted investments in chatbots, cloud-native platforms, or process automation tools. Furthermore, digital maturity frameworks encourage insurers to take a comprehensive, enterprise-wide approach to technological transformation instead of relying on isolated, project-based methods. This fosters strategic coherence and enhances coordinated innovation management (Boston Consulting Group, 2022).

Gartner's Hype Cycle is a widely used framework for understanding emerging technologies in the insurance industry. This model outlines the typical trajectory of new technologies, starting with the initial "innovation trigger," followed by a rapid rise to the "peak of inflated expectations." This is often followed by the inevitable decline into the "trough of disillusionment," before finally reaching the "plateau of productivity" (Perri, 2022). This cycle provides insurers with essential context for assessing the maturity of technologies, managing expectations around innovation investments, and determining optimal timing for strategic entry points or adoption decisions.

Blockchain technology in the insurance sector has notably progressed along Gartner's hype cycle. This journey began with initial enthusiasm and inflated expectations regarding rapid disruption. However, it was followed by disillusionment due to challenges surrounding scalability and integration. Eventually, the focus shifted toward emerging practical use cases demonstrating sustained value.

Understanding this trajectory helps insurers avoid prematurely abandoning promising technologies and encourages them to practice strategic patience, set realistic expectations, and engage in structured experimentation. Insurers who apply Gartner's framework can better time their investments, manage their innovation portfolios adaptively, and maintain a strategic commitment to potentially transformative innovations, even in the face of short-term setbacks (Perri, 2022).

The concept of innovation portfolio management provides insurers with structured methodologies to balance their innovation investments across various categories and risk profiles. This approach, popularized by Nagji and Tuff in 2012, categorizes innovation projects into three main groups: core (incremental), adjacent, and transformational. Core innovations focus on improving existing products or processes. Adjacent innovations explore related markets or segments, while transformational innovations aim to create entirely new markets or disrupt established business models.

Using a portfolio approach in insurance enables organizations to strategically allocate resources, manage innovation risks, and balance short-term returns with long-term strategic goals. For instance, an insurer might maintain a portfolio that includes incremental innovations—such as process automation or enhancements to online customer service—adjacent innovations, like expanding into embedded insurance distribution channels, and transformational innovations, such as blockchain-based parametric products or decentralized insurance models. By maintaining balanced portfolios, insurers can systematically pursue diverse opportunities, mitigate risks through diversification, and sustain steady innovation momentum across different time horizons and risk levels (Nagji & Tuff, 2012).

Insurers increasingly incorporate HCD frameworks into their innovation processes. This approach prioritizes customer empathy, usability, and intuitive interactions as core principles of innovation. HCD frameworks, which stem from design thinking methodologies popularized by IDEO and Stanford, emphasize the importance of iterative experimentation, customer feedback integration, and continuous adaptation to users' real-world needs and experiences. By embedding HCD principles into their innovation strategies, insurers can ensure that technological advancements resonate with users, enhance policyholder satisfaction, and foster meaningful customer relationships.

Insurers using HCD methods often conduct thorough user research, empathy mapping, rapid prototyping, and iterative user testing while developing digital products. This approach ensures that innovations tackle real customer pain points effectively, simplify interactions, and provide clear user value. As a result, it significantly improves adoption rates and customer retention (IDEO, 2021).

In conclusion, successfully navigating the complex innovation landscape within the insurance industry requires structured and multidimensional frameworks that can interpret technological trends, market dynamics, customer behaviors, and organizational readiness. Insurers that effectively utilize frameworks such as Christensen's disruptive innovation theory, Rogers' diffusion of innovation theory, digital maturity models, Gartner's hype cycle, innovation portfolio management, and HCD methodologies are better equipped to proactively manage innovation risks, allocate resources strategically, improve their competitive position, and maintain meaningful customer relationships. Ultimately, these frameworks enable insurers to respond to technological changes and shape them proactively, positioning themselves as leaders and innovators in an increasingly dynamic and digitally driven insurance marketplace.

ROADMAP OF THIS TEXTBOOK

This textbook, *Insurance Technology: Navigating the Innovation, Risk, and Future of Insurance*, offers thorough coverage of the key technological innovations transforming the modern insurance industry. Each chapter is thoughtfully designed to provide graduate students, undergraduate learners, industry practitioners, regulators, and innovators with fundamental insights, practical frameworks, and actionable knowledge essential for navigating and leading the rapidly evolving digital insurance landscape.

This chapter (Chapter 1) provides a crucial foundation by detailing the insurance industry's evolution, defining InsurTech, and examining the ecosystem, market forces, interdisciplinary elements, and frameworks essential for managing innovation. Readers will finish this introductory chapter prepared to engage deeply with the more specialized content that follows.

Chapter 2 examines how blockchain technology has the potential to transform insurance operations. It covers the basics of blockchain, provides examples such as using smart contracts for claims management, discusses coding and implementation considerations, and addresses regulatory implications. The chapter offers clear guidance on how to adopt blockchain technology in the insurance sector.

Chapter 3 focuses on the innovation of parametric insurance, discussing its theoretical foundations, trigger mechanisms, technical considerations, data integration, and important applications in climate, agriculture, and catastrophic risks. This chapter enables readers to understand parametric products' unique advantages, limitations, and market potential.

Chapter 4 delves into machine learning and AI, highlighting how these technologies revolutionize underwriting, claims processing, customer interactions, and fraud detection. The chapter discusses key AI methodologies, the mathematics underpinning them, ethical considerations, and issues of transparency and interpretability. It also addresses the regulatory compliance frameworks essential for responsible AI adoption.

In Chapter 5, readers delve into regulation, ethics, and responsibility in insurance technology. The chapter highlights current regulatory trends and global compliance standards, such as GDPR and National Institute of Standards and Technology (NIST), while addressing the ethical implications of InsurTech innovations. Readers gain valuable insights into managing ethical risks and regulatory obligations in the face of technological advancements, emphasizing the crucial role of RegTech.

Chapter 6 explores decentralized insurance and the role of the IoT. It discusses decentralized models, including peer-to-peer insurance, decentralized autonomous organizations, and coverage based on embedded smart contracts. The chapter also focuses on IoT-driven data collection, real-time underwriting, automated claims processing, and the regulatory and ethical considerations that come into play.

Chapter 7 addresses the significant challenges insurers encounter due to heightened digital connectivity. Readers will delve into cyber threat modeling, relevant regulatory standards (such as ISO 27001 and NIST), the cyber risk insurance market, and the incident management strategies essential for effective cybersecurity governance.

Chapter 8 offers insights into how extensive data sources—such as telematics, wearables, social media, and geospatial analytics—can create personalized and predictive insurance solutions. The chapter emphasizes the importance of data governance, the ethical use of analytics, the challenges of technology integration, and the need to foster a data-driven organizational culture.

Chapter 9 delves into digital transformation in the insurance sector, providing strategic guidance for effectively managing transformational change. It covers digital maturity assessments, API and microservice ecosystems, cloud-native architectures, strategies for managing cultural change, and best practices for implementing transformation within traditional insurance environments.

Chapter 10 focuses on bridging the gap between innovative concepts and their practical, scalable implementation. It discusses innovation labs, regulatory sandboxes, funding structures, strategies for overcoming internal and external barriers, methods for measuring innovation effectiveness, and ways to build sustainable organizational capacity for innovation.

Chapter 11 offers valuable insights into the evolving professional opportunities and organizational frameworks that define careers in insurance technology. This chapter helps readers understand key roles within InsurTech firms, the essential skill sets required for various positions, and the career paths available to technology-oriented insurance professionals. It also outlines the typical organizational structures found in digitally driven insurance companies.

At the end of this textbook, you will find additional resources including a comprehensive Glossary of Insurance Technology Terms, a practical Case Study Compendium, Sample Code Snippets for blockchain and machine learning applications, and a detailed Regulatory Map that summarizes important global policies and standards. These materials provide valuable guidance and reference tools to support a deeper understanding and practical application of the concepts discussed.

This textbook is designed for both sequential learning and modular reference. Graduate students and professionals will benefit from in-depth discussions on regulatory frameworks, advanced analytics methodologies, cybersecurity considerations, and the practical aspects of implementing innovation. Undergraduate students will find foundational explanations, accessible case studies, and organized content that support their initial exploration of insurance technology. Industry leaders, innovation managers, regulators, and entrepreneurs will gain valuable strategic insights, enabling informed decision-making and effective strategic planning in the face of technological disruption.

By combining academic theory, industry insights, practical case studies, and interdisciplinary knowledge, this textbook aims to equip readers with the skills, perspectives, and strategic understanding needed to lead and succeed in the dynamic, digitally driven future of insurance.

AI DISCLOSURE

During the preparation of this work, the author(s) used Grammarly to improve readability and to correct grammatical mistakes. After using this tool/service, the author(s) reviewed and edited the content as needed and take(s) full responsibility for the content of the publication.

REFERENCES

BCG. (2025). How insurers can supercharge their strategy with artificial intelligence. Boston Consulting Group.

Bhattacharya, S., Castignani, G., Masello, L., & Sheehan, B. (2025). AI revolution in insurance: bridging research and reality. (Review article on AI in insurance).

Boston Consulting Group. (2022). *The rise of InsurTechs: The digital disruption of insurance*. https://www.bcg.com/publications/2022/digital-transformation-in-insurance.

Crocetta, F., Payne, C., Manchester, P., & Vermeulen, P. (2023). How insurers can realize value through digital transformation. EY. https://www.ey.com/en_gl/industries/financial-services/emeia/digital-transformation-can-unlock-value-for-insurers.

Bernstein, P. (1996). Against the gods: The remarkable story of risk. New York: John Wiley & Sons.

Christensen, C. M. (1997). *The innovator's dilemma: When new technologies cause significant firms to fail*. Harvard Business Review Press.

Christensen, C. M., Raynor, M., & McDonald, R. (2015). What is disruptive innovation? *Harvard Business Review*, *93*(12), 44–53.

Deloitte. (2025). *Digital Insurance Maturity 2025: Meeting customer expectations requires hybrid distribution and digital channels*. Deloitte Digital.

FCA. (2022). *Regulatory Sandbox*. FCA. https://www.fca.org.uk/firms/innovation/regulatory-sandbox.

IDEO. (2021). *The field guide to human-centered design*. IDEO.org. https://www.designkit.org/resources/1.

Guo, J. Yang, L. Zhou, X. & Jiang, G. (2025). The impact of big data technology application on the technical efficiency of insurance firms: empirical evidence from Chinese insurers. *Finance Research Letters*, *86*, 108828.

Hippo Insurance. (2025). Customer Reviews. https://www.hippo.com/reviews.

InsurTech NY. (n.d.). About Us. InsurTech NY. https://www.insurtechny.com/about-us/.

InsTechLondon/InsTech (global). (n.d.). Home—InsTech. https://www.instech.co/.

KPMG. (2021). *Future of InsurTech: The paradigm shift*. https://home.kpmg/xx/en/home/insights/2021/10/the-future-of-insurtech.html.

Lemonade, Inc. (n.d.). The secret behind Lemonade's instant insurance. https://www.lemonade.com/blog/secret-behind-lemonades-instant-insurance.

Lloyd's. (2020). *Ensuring a sustainable, resilient future*. https://www.lloyds.com/news-and-insights/market-news/sustainable-insurance.

Marsh, & McLennan. (2021). *Risk resilience report: Emerging risks and the need for adaptive risk management*. Marsh McLennan.

McKinsey & Company. (2021). *The future of insurance: Driving innovation and growth through technology*. https://www.mckinsey.com/industries/financial-services/our-insights/the-future-of-insurance.

Musaigwa, M., & Netswera, F. (2025). Transforming insurance: The impact of digital technologies on operations and processes. *International Journal of Applied Research in Business and Management*, *6*(1).

Nagji, B., & Tuff, G. (2012). Managing your innovation portfolio. *Harvard Business Review*, *90*(5), 66–74.

Perri, L. (2022). What's New in the 2022 Gartner Hype Cycle for Emerging Technologies. https://www.gartner.com/en/articles/what-s-new-in-the-2022-gartner-hype-cycle-for-emerging-technologies. (Accessed 10 July 2023).

PWC. (2022). *Top insurance industry issues in 2022*. https://www.pwc.com/gx/en/industries/financial-services/insurance.html.

Rogers, E. M. (2003). *Diffusion of innovations* (5th ed.). Free Press.

Society of Actuaries. (2021). *The future of the actuarial profession in a digital world*. https://www.soa.org/resources/research-reports/2021/future-of-actuarial-profession/.

Stricker, L. (2023). The future of insurance intermediation in the age of platforms. *Journal of Risk and Financial Management*, *16*(9), 381. https://doi.org/10.3390/jrfm16090381.

Swiss Re Institute. (2025). *Global property and casualty (P&C) insurance market has increased efficiency, capacity and resilience*. Press release.

Thaler, R. H., & Sunstein, C. R. (2008). *Nudge: Improving decisions about health, wealth, and happiness*. Yale University Press.

Vaughan, E. J., & Vaughan, T. M. (2013). *Fundamentals of Risk and Insurance* (11th ed). John Wiley & Sons.

World InsurTech Report. (2021). *Capgemini and Efma's global report on insurance innovation*. https://worldinsurtechreport.com.

Yates, J. A. (1995). Application Software for Insurance in the 1960s and Early 1970s. *Business and Economic History*, *24*(1), 123–134.

CHAPTER

Digital transformation in the insurance sector

2

CHAPTER OUTLINE

Insurance Technology. DOI: https://doi.org/10.1016/B978-0-443-43972-8.00007-9

INTRODUCTION TO DIGITAL TRANSFORMATION

The insurance industry is at a pivotal moment, facing significant changes. Traditionally seen as conservative and heavily regulated, the sector is now experiencing a radical transformation as it embraces digital advancements. This shift goes beyond adopting new technologies; it fundamentally redefines how insurers interact with customers, assess risk, deliver products, and organize their operations. In an age characterized by rapid technological progress, evolving consumer expectations, and increasingly complex risks, digital transformation has become a crucial necessity rather than an optional upgrade.

Digital transformation refers to integrating digital technologies across all business areas, leading to fundamental changes in how organizations operate and deliver value to their customers (Westerman et al., 2014). It goes beyond simply automating existing processes or transitioning to online platforms; it involves redesigning core capabilities and business models with a focus on data, connectivity, and customer-centric innovation.

Unlike digitization, which is the process of converting analog information into digital form, and digitalization, which involves using digital technologies to enhance business processes, digital transformation is a systemic and strategic process that impacts every part of the insurance value chain (Henriette et al., 2016).

Several macroeconomic and technological factors are driving this transformation. On the demand side, digital-native consumers now expect seamless, personalized, real-time interactions, similar to those provided by technology companies like Amazon, Apple, and Google. On the supply side, the emergence of artificial intelligence (AI), cloud computing, the Internet of Things (IoT), blockchain, and big data analytics has created new opportunities for risk modeling, fraud detection, customer engagement, and operational efficiency (Bharadwaj et al., 2013). These technologies are not merely complementary tools but enablers of entirely new business models, such as usage-based insurance (UBI), on-demand coverage, and parametric payouts.

The competitive landscape in the insurance industry is evolving. InsurTech startups, free from outdated infrastructure, are quickly developing and launching digital-first products that challenge traditional insurers' market share. Large technology companies are also entering the insurance sector through embedded offerings and platform partnerships. This combination of competition and innovation pressures legacy insurers to modernize their systems, reorganize their workforce, and embrace more agile operating models (Gimpel et al., 2018).

Digital transformation is increasingly connected to risk management. As the volume and speed of data rise, there are greater opportunities for real-time underwriting, dynamic pricing, and proactive claims handling. However, the growth of digital capabilities also brings new risks, including cybersecurity threats, data privacy breaches, and algorithmic bias. These risks need to be managed through strong governance and regulation.

The COVID-19 pandemic acted as a global stress test for the digital readiness of various industries. Insurance companies with strong digital capabilities were able to transition to remote operations, automate claims processing, and assist customers through virtual channels. In contrast, those lacking these capabilities experienced significant service disruptions, increased regulatory scrutiny, and damage to their reputations. The crisis highlighted the importance of digital resilience and accelerated the adoption of digital technologies throughout the sector (McKinsey & Company, 2020).

This chapter examines digital transformation in the insurance sector from strategic and technological perspectives. It explores the key drivers of change, the core technologies that enable transformation, and how insurers are reengineering their value chains—from underwriting and product design to claims management and customer service. Additionally, the chapter addresses the organizational, regulatory, and ethical dimensions of transformation, emphasizing how to assess digital maturity and what the future looks like for digitally advanced insurers.

This chapter's ultimate theme is that digital transformation is not a one-time project but a continuous process that demands vision, investment, and cultural change. For insurers who are ready to adapt, the benefits include improved efficiency and competitiveness and the chance to redefine the role of insurance in a digital society.

DRIVERS OF DIGITAL TRANSFORMATION IN INSURANCE

Various forces, including internal strategic pressures and broader changes in technology and society, drive digital transformation in the insurance sector. Understanding these drivers is crucial for grasping why insurers are urgently rethinking their business models, operational structures, and customer engagement strategies. No single factor is solely responsible for the rapid adoption of digital initiatives; instead, industry-specific challenges, evolving customer expectations, and external disruptions have sparked a significant era of change.

CHANGING CONSUMER EXPECTATIONS

The primary and most noticeable factor driving digital transformation is the changing behavior of customers. Tech-savvy consumers, particularly millennials and Generation Z, expect experiences that are seamless, intuitive, and mobile first. They have become accustomed to on-demand services, real-time updates, and personalized product recommendations from companies like Netflix, Uber, and Amazon. These expectations now influence the financial services and insurance sectors, where customers desire increased transparency, self-service options, and quicker claims resolution (PwC, 2017). Traditional insurance models, characterized by extensive paperwork, unclear pricing, and lengthy processing times, are increasingly out of sync with these evolving expectations.

The demand for personalized insurance products is increasing. Consumers are no longer content with generic coverage; they seek insurance solutions tailored to their individual behaviors and risk profiles. This shift has led to UBI, pay-as-you-drive auto policies, and health insurance plans that integrate data from wearable devices. Without digital transformation, insurers find it nearly impossible to provide this level of granularity and responsiveness to customer needs (Accenture, 2019).

COMPETITIVE PRESSURE AND MARKET DISRUPTION

InsurTech startups have emerged as strong competitors to traditional insurance companies. These nimble, technology-driven firms often focus on specific areas, such as digital distribution, claims automation, or customer experience, and excel at utilizing data, cloud platforms, and machine learning (ML) to provide innovative products and services. Companies like Lemonade, Metromile, and Root have introduced new models for underwriting and customer engagement and shown that low-cost, high-efficiency operations are possible through automation and AI (KPMG, 2021).

The increasing presence of nontraditional competitors intensifies this disruption. Technology giants like Amazon, Google, and Apple have started to enter the insurance market, mainly through partnerships and embedded offerings. Their advanced data ecosystems, strong customer relationships, and expertise in platform business models provide them with a strategic advantage in distribution and personalization. For traditional insurers, these developments pose a significant challenge that requires a digital response.

ADVANCES IN TECHNOLOGY

Rapid advancements in foundational technologies are allowing insurers to achieve what was previously unimaginable. The widespread availability of big data and improvements in data storage and processing power have made real-time analytics possible. AI and ML are now enabling predictive modeling, automated fraud detection, and chatbot-driven customer service. Additionally, cloud computing provides a flexible and scalable infrastructure, reducing reliance on costly legacy systems. Meanwhile, IoT devices—such as telematics sensors, smart home monitors, and wearable health trackers—are supplying insurers with valuable, real-time behavioral data that can be utilized for dynamic underwriting and pricing (Deloitte, 2024).

These technological advancements are not just incremental; they are revolutionary. They enable insurers to transition from reactive to proactive risk management, shift from static to dynamic pricing models, and move from batch processing to real-time engagement. As a result, insurance companies become more responsive, efficient, and focused on their customers.

OPERATIONAL INEFFICIENCIES AND COST PRESSURES

Traditional insurers experience significant internal inefficiencies, such as siloed data systems, manual processing, and outdated IT infrastructure. These issues lead to higher operational costs, slower time-to-market, and less-than-optimal customer experiences. Digital transformation provides a way to streamline processes, enhance agility, and reduce overhead costs. For instance, robotic process automation (RPA) can automate repetitive administrative tasks, allowing employees to focus on higher-value activities. Additionally, cloud-based platforms facilitate the faster deployment of new products and services, while integrated data ecosystems eliminate silos and enhance decision-making (Capgemini, 2020).

Cost pressure is another significant factor affecting the industry. Higher interest rates and reduced profit margins have prompted many insurers to pursue operational efficiencies to maintain profitability. Digital transformation offers tools that can help reduce claims leakage, minimize fraud, and optimize customer acquisition costs, making it both a strategic and financial necessity.

REGULATORY EVOLUTION AND DIGITAL COMPLIANCE

Regulation is often considered a constraint; however, evolving regulatory frameworks increasingly promote digital innovation. For instance, introducing regulatory sandboxes has permitted insurers to test new technologies in a controlled environment, without the full weight of regulatory requirements. Moreover, regulations surrounding electronic signatures, digital identity, and data sharing, such as Europe's Payment Services Directive 2 (PSD2), have enabled insurers to transition more of their services online (World Economic Forum, 2021).

Digital compliance is an essential factor to consider. As regulators increasingly require stronger governance over data handling, cybersecurity, and algorithmic transparency, insurers must invest in digital tools that facilitate compliance. The digitization of regulatory processes, often called RegTech, allows for real-time monitoring and automated reporting, which helps reduce compliance risks and costs.

THE COVID-19 ACCELERATION EFFECT

The COVID-19 pandemic acted as a catalyst for digital transformation in the insurance sector. With lockdowns, remote work, and social distancing, there was an urgent need for digital channels, automated claims processing, and virtual customer service. Insurers who had already started their digital journeys were better equipped to adapt, while those lagging behind had to accelerate their transformation efforts under pressure. The pandemic underscored the importance of digital resilience and showed that customer loyalty increasingly depends on the ability to provide seamless digital interactions (McKinsey & Company, 2020).

CORE TECHNOLOGIES POWERING TRANSFORMATION

Both strategic needs and the maturation and convergence of several key technologies drive digital transformation in the insurance sector. These advancements enable insurers to reimagine underwriting, streamline operations, enhance customer engagement, and provide more personalized, proactive, and responsive services. Importantly, these innovations do not function in isolation; they often work together. For example, AI processes IoT data on a cloud platform to create powerful synergies throughout the insurance value chain. This section explores the most impactful technologies shaping the digital insurance landscape.

CLOUD COMPUTING AND INFRASTRUCTURE AGILITY

Cloud computing has become essential for the digital transformation of insurance companies. Insurers can achieve greater scalability, flexibility, and cost efficiency by transitioning from on-premise legacy systems to cloud-based environments. Public, private, and hybrid cloud models enable insurers to deploy applications more rapidly, store large volumes of structured and unstructured data, and facilitate collaboration among teams in different geographic areas. Most importantly, cloud platforms support the integration of advanced analytics, AI, and third-party application programming interfaces (APIs)—tools crucial for maintaining a competitive edge in the digital landscape (Gartner, 2023).

Cloud adoption significantly improves business continuity and resilience. During the COVID-19 pandemic, insurers that had embraced cloud solutions found it easier to transition to remote operations. This shift allowed them to maintain service levels while ensuring employee safety. Additionally, cloud platforms facilitate continuous integration and deployment, enabling insurers to iterate and enhance their digital offerings quickly.

ARTIFICIAL INTELLIGENCE AND MACHINE LEARNING

AI and ML are among the most transformative technologies in the insurance industry. These technologies enable insurers to extract insights from complex datasets, automate decision-making, and enhance risk modeling. In underwriting, AI models evaluate thousands of data points, such as driving behavior and geospatial climate data, to assess risk profiles more accurately than traditional actuarial methods. In claims processing, ML models identify anomalies that may indicate fraud, while natural language processing (NLP) tools can read and categorize policyholder statements, repair estimates, and legal documents in seconds (Wüthrich, 2020).

Beyond automation, AI facilitates personalization on a large scale. Insurers can implement dynamic pricing based on real-time behaviors, suggest customized coverage options, and utilize chatbots that comprehend customer sentiment and intent. However, deploying AI requires strong governance to address issues related to algorithmic bias, model drift, and the need for explainability.

INTERNET OF THINGS

The rise of IoT devices, which include telematics sensors in vehicles, smart thermostats in homes, and wearable fitness trackers, has transformed how insurers gather and utilize data. Instead of relying solely on historical data or fixed underwriting criteria, insurers can now use real-time behavioral data to assess and price risk more accurately. This advancement has led to the creation of new insurance products, such as pay-as-you-drive, UBI, and wellness-incentivized health plans (He, Zhang, & Huang, 2019).

For example, in auto insurance, IoT-based telematics can monitor driving speed, braking habits, and location data to adjust premiums dynamically and encourage safe driving behavior. In property insurance, smart sensors can detect water leaks, fire hazards, and unauthorized entry, enabling insurers to provide proactive risk mitigation services. These capabilities reduce the number of claims and enhance customer engagement by positioning insurers as partners in risk prevention rather than just providers of indemnity.

ROBOTIC PROCESS AUTOMATION

RPA involves using software robots to automate high-volume, rule-based tasks that previously needed human input. RPA is especially useful in policy administration, claims intake, compliance checks, and back-office reconciliation in the insurance industry. For instance, bots can automatically extract data from scanned documents, fill out forms, initiate workflows, and update records across various systems (Deloitte, 2024).

RPA offers several advantages, including faster processing times, fewer human errors, and cost savings. Most importantly, RPA acts as a bridging technology, enabling insurers to modernize their operations without completely replacing legacy systems. When combined with AI, RPA transforms into intelligent automation, which can manage more complex tasks and make contextual decisions.

BLOCKCHAIN AND SMART CONTRACTS

Although it is still in the early stages of adoption, blockchain technology holds significant promise in claims verification, fraud prevention, and reinsurance settlements. The decentralized and immutable nature of blockchain ledgers guarantees data integrity. Additionally, smart contracts—self-executing programs on the blockchain—can automate the validation of coverage and the processing of payments based on predefined conditions (Mills, 2019).

In parametric insurance, a smart contract can be programmed to automatically trigger a payout when a specific threshold is reached, such as a certain level of rainfall or seismic activity. This process relies on verified data from an oracle. Additionally, in reinsurance, blockchain platforms can streamline multiparty transactions and enhance transparency, which helps reduce administrative overhead and settlement delays.

Despite ongoing challenges like scalability, regulatory uncertainty, and interoperability, adoption is expected to increase. Blockchain will likely become a more significant element in digitally transformed insurance ecosystems as these issues are resolved.

LOW-CODE/NO-CODE DEVELOPMENT PLATFORMS

Insurance companies are increasingly using low-code and no-code platforms to keep up with the fast pace of digital innovation. These tools allow users with little programming experience to design applications, automate workflows, and create customer interfaces using a simple drag-and-drop approach. For insurers, business teams can quickly prototype and launch digital products without relying on lengthy IT development cycles (Forrester, 2022).

Low-code platforms are especially effective in creating customer onboarding journeys, agent dashboards, and quote-to-bind workflows. When integrated with enterprise-grade capabilities, they help connect legacy systems with new digital front ends, speeding up time-to-market and promoting cross-functional collaboration.

DIGITAL TRANSFORMATION ACROSS THE INSURANCE VALUE CHAIN

Digital transformation goes beyond isolated initiatives or specific departments within insurance organizations. It signifies a comprehensive evolution that affects every stage of the insurance value chain—from product development and distribution to underwriting, claims processing, and customer engagement. Each value chain segment offers opportunities to utilize digital technologies to improve agility, efficiency, and customer focus.

UNDERWRITING AND RISK ASSESSMENT

Underwriting, which was once primarily based on actuarial models and historical loss ratios, has been significantly transformed by digital technologies. Insurers today are utilizing alternative data sources, such as social media activity, credit behavior, and real-time IoT data, to obtain a more detailed understanding of individual and commercial risk profiles (Guo and Lamberton, 2021). Advanced ML algorithms allow for dynamic risk segmentation and automated decision-making, reducing underwriting cycles from days to minutes.

Behavioral data has the potential to be highly transformative. For example, in auto insurance, telematics enables underwriting based on actual driving behavior instead of relying on demographic proxies. In health insurance, wearable devices collect biometric data to assess risk and encourage preventive health behaviors. This data-driven approach supports more equitable pricing models, which could help increase access for underserved populations.

Additionally, automation platforms facilitate straight-through processing (STP) for straightforward policies, allowing underwriters to concentrate on complex or high-value accounts. The transition to real-time, data-driven underwriting improves fraud detection and enhances portfolio risk management.

PRODUCT INNOVATION AND DEVELOPMENT

Digital transformation allows insurers to quickly adapt to new risks and shifting consumer demands by offering innovative products. Integrating digital platforms, real-time data feeds, and mobile interfaces enables the development of usage-based, on-demand, and parametric insurance models (EY, 2020).

UBI charges premiums based on the actual usage patterns of policyholders, such as the number of miles driven or hours operated. On-demand insurance lets consumers activate coverage for specific events or periods through mobile apps. On the other hand, parametric insurance relies on predefined triggers—like rainfall, wind speed, or seismic activity—rather than traditional claims assessments, enabling rapid payouts.

Digital tools enhance product lifecycle management by enabling a more agile approach. Insurers can rapidly prototype, test, and refine products based on customer feedback and behavioral analytics. This iterative, customer-focused strategy contrasts with the traditional multiyear product development timelines and highlights the increasing impact of design thinking in the insurance industry.

DISTRIBUTION AND SALES

Digital transformation has significantly changed the distribution of insurance products. Traditional agent-based models are being enhanced and, in some instances, replaced by digital channels, aggregators, and embedded insurance partnerships. Consumers increasingly opt to research, compare, and purchase insurance online, often without human interaction (Accenture, 2019).

Digital platforms facilitate omnichannel engagement strategies that combine self-service portals, mobile apps, chatbots, and call centers. This approach ensures continuity and personalization across different customer touchpoints, which enhances customer satisfaction and increases conversion rates. Additionally, embedded insurance—where coverage is seamlessly integrated into other purchases, such as airline tickets or e-commerce transactions—is emerging as a dominant trend, particularly in property and travel insurance.

For agents and brokers, digital tools improve productivity by providing automated quoting, customer relationship management integration, and real-time lead management. Insurers that equip their intermediaries with mobile tools, predictive analytics, and customer insights are more likely to maintain a competitive advantage in hybrid distribution models.

CLAIMS MANAGEMENT AND LOSS ADJUSTMENT

Claims management is a crucial yet traditionally inefficient function in the insurance industry. Digital transformation offers the opportunity to streamline this process, minimize fraud, and improve the customer experience. Insurers are implementing AI-driven triage systems, computer vision tools, and RPA to speed up claims handling and enhance accuracy (McKinsey & Company, 2020).

In auto insurance, policyholders can upload photos of vehicle damage using a mobile app. AI algorithms analyze these images, assess the severity of the damage, and generate repair estimates in just a few seconds. Similarly, in health and property insurance, AI scans and interprets claims documents, medical codes, and contractor invoices to identify anomalies and verify information.

Digital platforms facilitate self-service claims initiation and real-time tracking, enhancing transparency and customer trust. On the back end, blockchain solutions are being tested for multiparty claims verification and payment reconciliation, particularly in reinsurance and catastrophe claims.

The advantages of transforming digital claims extend beyond just speed and cost savings. They also encompass enhanced fraud detection, improved loss ratios, and increased customer satisfaction. As insurance companies continue to automate the claims process, the role of human adjusters is shifting toward handling exceptions, conducting complex assessments, and advocating for customers.

CUSTOMER ENGAGEMENT AND SERVICE

One of the most noticeable aspects of digital transformation is customer service. Insurers are not only evaluated based on the coverage they provide but also by the quality and convenience of their customer interactions. Today, digital engagement strategies include 24/7 chatbots, mobile apps, personalized content, and AI-driven recommendation engines (PwC, 2021).

Insurers are using customer data and behavioral analytics to provide timely and relevant interactions, such as renewal reminders, policy recommendations, and risk alerts. By utilizing sentiment analysis and NLP, companies can identify customer dissatisfaction and respond proactively.

Customer portals and mobile applications have become standard by providing features such as policy viewing, payment processing, document uploads, and real-time claims updates. These tools minimize friction, enhance transparency, and empower customers to manage their insurance relationships on their terms.

Personalization in the insurance industry is making significant strides thanks to AI. Insurers can now customize policy options, pricing, and communication styles to align with individual preferences. This transition from a transactional approach to a more relational engagement is transforming insurers into partners in risk management and life planning, rather than just commoditized service providers.

ORGANIZATIONAL TRANSFORMATION

Digital transformation in the insurance industry goes beyond technology; it represents a fundamental shift within organizations. Successfully integrating digital capabilities necessitates changes in company culture, leadership structure, talent strategy, and decision-making processes. Traditional insurance companies, which often operate with hierarchical management systems and isolated business units, must adopt agility, experimentation, and cross-functional collaboration. In this environment, organizational transformation is both a prerequisite for and a result of digital innovation.

EVOLVING LEADERSHIP ROLES

As insurers implement digital strategies, the traditional roles of executive leadership are changing significantly. Chief information officers (CIOs) are shifting from merely overseeing infrastructure to becoming strategic partners who guide digital innovation and efforts to monetize data. The emergence of the chief digital officer (CDO) highlights the increasing recognition that digital transformation goes beyond the IT department; it requires involvement across the entire organization, impacting areas such as marketing, underwriting, customer service, and compliance (Bharadwaj et al., 2013).

In more digitally mature organizations, CIOs and CDOs often collaborate to align technology roadmaps with broader strategic goals. At the same time, chief risk officers and chief compliance officers are increasingly responsible for overseeing the governance of digital technologies, including algorithmic decision-making systems and cloud security protocols. These expanded responsibilities require leadership teams to develop a strong understanding of digital operations and promote alignment across various functional areas.

Board governance is evolving. Directors are now expected to have digital literacy and to evaluate investments in emerging technologies not only for return on investment (ROI) but also for strategic alignment, risk exposure, and ethical considerations.

AGILE METHODOLOGIES AND INNOVATION CULTURE

To address the challenges of faster product development cycles and evolving customer expectations, insurance companies are moving away from traditional linear "waterfall" development models to adopt agile methodologies. Agile approaches emphasize iterative development, cross-functional teams, and continuous feedback, enabling organizations to experiment, pivot, and adapt in real time (Rigby, Sutherland, & Noble, 2018).

Implementing agile at scale often necessitates fundamentally reorganizing team structures and decision-making processes. Cross-disciplinary squads—including members from IT, product development, underwriting, compliance, and marketing—are empowered to manage their backlogs and key performance indicators (KPIs). This decentralization improves responsiveness but also demands effective coordination mechanisms and cultural buy-in.

Innovation labs and digital accelerators have become essential drivers of transformation within organizations. These internal units are specifically designed to explore new technologies, collaborate with InsurTech companies, and test prototypes focused on customer needs. By establishing safe spaces for experimentation, insurers can effectively manage the risks associated with innovation while also developing their internal capabilities.

Fostering an innovative culture goes beyond simply changing organizational charts or job titles. It requires reshaping employee incentives, encouraging risk-taking, and creating a psychologically safe environment for sharing bold ideas. Leaders must demonstrate curiosity and openness while establishing feedback loops that reward experimentation, even when the outcomes are uncertain.

TALENT TRANSFORMATION AND SKILL DEVELOPMENT

The digital transformation significantly impacts workforce strategy in the insurance industry. Traditional roles, such as underwriters, claims adjusters, and agents, are being enhanced or replaced by new positions emphasizing data science, user experience (UX) design, cybersecurity, and cloud architecture (World Economic Forum, 2020). Insurers face the challenge of recruiting individuals with these skills and reskilling current employees whose expertise is still valuable in a digital environment.

Learning and development programs are being restructured to incorporate modules on digital literacy, agile workflows, and analytics. Insurers collaborate with universities, bootcamps, and online learning platforms to expedite skill acquisition. Additionally, internal mobility programs enable employees to transition into digital roles, fostering cross-functional knowledge and enhancing employee retention.

There is an increasing emphasis on diversity, equity, and inclusion (DEI) in digital talent strategies. Diverse teams are more likely to identify user pain points, design inclusive products, and detect algorithm biases. Therefore DEI is a social imperative and a strategic driver of innovation.

MANAGING LEGACY SYSTEMS AND TECHNICAL DEBT

One of the most significant obstacles to digital transformation in the insurance industry is the continued dependence on legacy IT systems. Many insurers rely on outdated core platforms that are costly to maintain, challenging to integrate, and not designed to meet the demands of real-time data processing or API connectivity (McKinsey & Company, 2020). These systems often support essential functions, making their replacement a risky and expensive process.

Organizations must strategically decide whether to modernize, replace, or encapsulate their systems using middleware and cloud layers. The "two-speed IT" model, which allows legacy systems to support core functions while new digital capabilities are developed alongside, provides a transitional approach. However, this model can also lead to fragmentation and increased complexity.

Technical debt refers to the accumulated cost of using outdated, inefficient, or unscalable technology, and it needs to be actively managed. Neglecting this can reduce profit margins, stifle innovation, and increase the firm's exposure to operational and cybersecurity risks. To effectively reduce technical debt while facilitating transformation, it is essential to develop strategic technology roadmaps, establish clear architectural principles, and prioritize investments with discipline.

CHANGE MANAGEMENT AND ORGANIZATIONAL RESILIENCE

The human aspect of digital transformation is crucial and should not be ignored. Change management is vital in helping employees understand, accept, and embrace new technologies and work methods. Effective change management includes clear communication, inclusive planning, access to training resources, and established channels for feedback.

Resistance to change can derail even the most well-planned transformation programs, whether from fear of becoming obsolete, loss of control, or skepticism. Leaders need to show empathy, offer support, and communicate a compelling vision of why digital transformation is essential, not only for improving efficiency or staying competitive but also for ensuring long-term relevance and enhancing customer value.

Resilience is a crucial attribute for organizations undergoing digital transformation. The COVID-19 crisis demonstrated that insurers with flexible infrastructure, distributed workforces, and digital customer channels were more successful in maintaining operations and adapting to uncertainty. Organizational resilience is fostered through technology and agile leadership, adaptable workforces, and a culture that emphasizes learning.

DIGITAL ECOSYSTEMS AND PLATFORMS

The emergence of digital ecosystems represents one of the most significant shifts in the insurance industry's evolution. Traditionally, insurers operated within relatively closed systems, characterized by proprietary data, rigid processes, and siloed functions that defined service delivery limits. Today, the competitive advantage lies not in creating isolated capabilities but in harnessing interconnected networks of digital stakeholders, such as technology providers, data platforms, customer-facing businesses, regulatory entities, and competitors. These digital ecosystems are transforming the definition of insurance, how it is delivered, and the roles of those who provide it.

PLATFORMIZATION OF INSURANCE

Platform-based business models in insurance take vision from technology giants like Amazon and Apple, which create value by facilitating interactions among user groups on a shared infrastructure. In the insurance sector, this translates to a digitally orchestrated platform where various participants interact through standardized protocols and interfaces, including agents, customers, third-party service providers, reinsurers, and developers (Van Alstyne et al., 2016).

This model enables insurers to operate not only as risk underwriters but also as platform orchestrators. For example, ZhongAn, China's first digital-only insurer, provides a modular API-based architecture that allows third-party applications to integrate insurance services across various consumer touchpoints, including travel booking sites and e-commerce platforms (Capgemini and Efma, 2021). This approach transforms insurance into a background service that seamlessly integrates into users' digital lives.

The "platformization" of insurance fosters innovation by leveraging ecosystem synergies. For instance, an insurer can combine behavioral analytics from a fitness app, financial health scores from a neobank, and smart home sensor data—all through APIs. This integration of diverse data streams enables the creation of hyperpersonalized policies and predictive risk services, which would be unattainable in a closed, monolithic environment.

EMBEDDED INSURANCE: FRICTIONLESS COVERAGE AT THE POINT OF NEED

Embedded insurance represents a dynamic and commercially viable approach to ecosystem integration. Unlike traditional insurance models, which require consumers to search actively and purchase coverage, embedded insurance integrates protection directly into the customer's transaction process. This makes it nearly invisible yet immediately relevant. Doing so significantly reduces friction and increases access to insurance, particularly for underserved or digitally native populations (Téllez & Dietz, 2022).

For example, online travel bookings can include insurance coverage for delayed flights or lost baggage. Freelancers using gig platforms like Upwork or Fiverr can add short-term income protection or liability coverage while actively working on gigs. In auto sales, insurance quotes can be integrated into the digital checkout process, allowing for prefilled information and instant binding of coverage.

This model requires insurers to expand their focus beyond just policies and premiums. They need to design flexible, context-aware products that are easily distributed online. Additionally, this approach demands strong API infrastructures, cloud-native core systems, and a thorough understanding of the customer journey within the partner ecosystem.

Embedded insurance significantly shifts the control to the platform partner that manages the customer relationship. Insurers that do not adapt to risk are becoming unnoticed back-end providers. In contrast, some may evolve into "insurance-as-a-service" platforms, offering distribution partners the embedded protection needed to stand out in the market.

THE OPEN INSURANCE MOVEMENT AND DATA PORTABILITY

Open insurance is a developing concept driven by regulatory requirements and market demand. It parallels the evolution of open banking in the financial services sector. Open insurance seeks to establish an interoperable framework that allows customer-permissioned data to be securely shared among insurers, fintech companies, aggregators, and third-party developers through APIs (OECD, 2021).

The implications of this shift are substantial. Open insurance promotes greater competition, innovation, and transparency by providing access to information about policies, claims history, pricing, and customer preferences. It also empowers consumers to make more informed decisions and lowers the costs of switching between providers.

European regulators are exploring frameworks for open insurance that prioritize both innovation and privacy, building on the foundations of the General Data Protection Regulation and the success of the PSD2 in the banking sector. For insurers, this shift involves investing in API gateways, identity management systems, and consent architecture and ensuring data interoperability.

Open insurance ecosystems facilitate new services like policy wallets, digital ID integration, and unified dashboards that consolidate protection products across various categories, including life, property, auto, and health insurance. As the infrastructure develops, insurers may begin to compete based on the performance of their APIs and the usability of their ecosystems, in addition to traditional factors such as pricing and underwriting strength.

STRATEGIC PARTNERSHIPS AND CROSS-SECTOR COLLABORATION

Digital ecosystems flourish through collaboration. Instead of trying to dominate every customer interaction or data channel, insurers are forming partnerships with companies across various industries to enhance their services and expand their reach. These collaborations can vary from technology integrations to comprehensive joint ventures.

For example, Munich Re's collaboration with Google Cloud provides AI-powered risk modeling services for commercial clients. Meanwhile, Allianz has partnered with ride-sharing companies to offer embedded coverage for passengers and drivers in various countries. Additionally, partnerships with smart device manufacturers allow home insurers to provide real-time risk mitigation, such as leak detection and fire alerts, thereby creating value beyond claims payments.

Successful alliances necessitate transparent governance, aligned incentives, and a mutual understanding of roles within the ecosystem. Strategic factors to consider include cobranding, revenue sharing, ownership of customer data, and compliance with overlapping regulatory requirements. Companies that excel in partner management will be better positioned to transition from isolated insurers to integrated service hubs.

MANAGING COMPLEXITY: INTEROPERABILITY, SECURITY, AND GOVERNANCE

Digital ecosystems present immense opportunities, but they also bring about additional complexities. Each partner, platform, and data feed adds a new layer of cyber risk, operational failure, or legal liability. To effectively manage this complexity, insurers must invest in middleware, microservices architecture, and robust data orchestration tools to handle diverse inputs in real time.

Cybersecurity is a primary concern for insurers. As data is exchanged between partners, APIS must be encrypted, authenticated, and monitored for anomalies. Insurers must comply with various data localization and privacy laws when integrating into global ecosystems. The cybersecurity challenge is particularly significant for most insurers due to the lack of visibility between their third-party hosts and the insured parties.

Effective governance of the ecosystem is crucial. Platform owners must identify who is allowed to participate, the conditions for participation, and how conflicts will be resolved. For instance, can a partner customize the underwriting logic or pricing engines? Who is responsible for a fradulent claims or data breach? The answers to these questions are typically found in the "platform constitution," which outlines the rights and responsibilities within the ecosystem (Evans & Schmalensee, 2016).

Effective internal governance is essential. Participation in the ecosystem involves various functions, including product development, legal, IT, marketing, and compliance. Successfully coordinating these stakeholders is crucial for fostering innovation while minimizing risk exposure for the company. This skill is one of the most important competencies in the toolkit of a digital insurer.

METRICS, KEY PERFORMANCE INDICATORS, AND RETURN ON INVESTMENT OF DIGITAL TRANSFORMATION

Digital transformation in the insurance sector involves substantial investments in both capital and organization, typically extending over several years and impacting various business units. Due to the scope and complexity of these initiatives, insurers are under increasing pressure to quantify the value generated from their digital investments. Evaluating success goes beyond traditional financial metrics; it requires a deeper understanding of operational performance, customer engagement, innovation maturity, and risk management. This section examines the frameworks, metrics, and strategic considerations that insurers should utilize to effectively track digital transformation and communicate the ROI to internal and external stakeholders.

THE CHALLENGE OF MEASURING DIGITAL RETURN ON INVESTMENT

Measuring ROI in digital transformation is particularly difficult because of its intangible benefits, extended time frames, and effects spanning various functions. Unlike traditional capital projects with clear endpoints, digital initiatives evolve iteratively, with returns evident over time through increased agility, improved decision-making, and greater customer loyalty (Westerman et al., 2014).

Many insurers tend to overlook the indirect benefits of adopting digital technologies. For instance, automation can reduce operating expenses while enhancing service reliability and ensuring compliance with regulations. Likewise, data analytics capabilities may not immediately increase underwriting margins, but they can create long-term value by facilitating better risk selection and product personalization.

Thus traditional ROI formulas must be modified to capture a portfolio perspective on benefits. The focus should transition from short-term payback periods to strategic empowerment and long-term competitive advantage.

CORE CATEGORIES OF DIGITAL KEY PERFORMANCE INDICATORS

To create a robust performance framework, insurers should align KPIs with the strategic objectives of their digital transformation. These typically fall into several interconnected categories:

1. Customer Experience and Engagement
   - Net Promoter Score (NPS): Measures customer willingness to recommend the insurer, serving as a proxy for satisfaction and loyalty.
   - Customer Effort Score: Evaluates how easily customers can interact with digital channels (e.g., quote generation, claims submission).
   - Digital adoption rates: Tracks the percentage of customers using digital portals, apps, chatbots, or embedded insurance features.
   - First contact resolution: Assesses the percentage of inquiries resolved in a single interaction through digital means.
2. Operational Efficiency
   - Straight-through processing rate: Indicates the proportion of transactions or claims handled entirely by automation without manual intervention.
   - Average claims cycle time: Measures the time between claim initiation and resolution, especially in digitally enhanced workflows.
   - Underwriting turnaround time: Reflects the time to issue a policy postapplication.
   - Cost per policy/claims: Helps assess the financial efficiency of digital operations.
3. Innovation and Digital Maturity
   - Percentage of revenue from digital channels or new digital products.
   - Number of digital partnerships or ecosystem integrations launched.
   - Time to market for digital product development cycles.
   - Cloud adoption metrics and API usage frequency.
4. Data and Analytics Capabilities
   - Percentage of decisions informed by advanced analytics or ML models.
   - Data quality scores and availability of real-time dashboards.
   - Model performance indicators (e.g., precision, recall, area under the curve) for underwriting, pricing, or fraud detection algorithms.
5. Risk and Compliance
   - Cyber incident frequency and response time.
   - Compliance adherence in digitally enabled processes.
   - Audit findings tied to digital transformation initiatives.

LINKING METRICS TO STRATEGIC OBJECTIVES

Not all KPIs hold the same importance. Their value comes from their ability to monitor progress toward clearly defined strategic goals, such as entering a new market segment, enhancing product personalization, or minimizing operational risk. Insurers must align their KPIs with transformation priorities and routinely assess whether these metrics remain relevant as their strategies evolve (Kane et al., 2015).

For instance, a transformation initiative focused on customer centricity might prioritize NPS, digital adoption, and personalization capabilities. Conversely, an initiative centered on operational efficiency might emphasize STP rates, cloud infrastructure scalability, and automation cost savings.

Balanced scorecards and objectives and key results (OKR) methodologies are commonly used to connect digital KPIs with broader business outcomes. These tools enable alignment across departments and promote accountability for long-term transformational outcomes.

COMMUNICATING DIGITAL VALUE TO STAKEHOLDERS

Effectively communicating the value of digital transformation is essential for maintaining executive sponsorship, securing future investments, and managing stakeholder expectations. This communication should balance visionary goals with tangible evidence of progress.

Dashboards and performance reports should be customized for their intended audience. It is essential for board members and investors to focus on strategic impact, market differentiation, and risk management, rather than technical implementation details. In contrast, operational leaders benefit more from detailed KPIs and trend analyses that aid resource allocation and workflow improvements.

Storytelling is essential for demonstrating digital ROI. Utilizing case studies, user testimonials, and pilot results can help turn abstract concepts into concrete examples. For instance, instead of just presenting vague automation metrics, sharing that a chatbot resolves 80% of inquiries within 5 minutes and reduces call center workload by 40% tends to have a more substantial impact.

AVOIDING COMMON PITFALLS IN MEASUREMENT

Insurers often face challenges when measuring digital transformation. A common problem is the tendency to focus solely on vanity metrics, such as app downloads or page views, without connecting them to meaningful outcomes like conversion rates, customer retention, or operational savings.

Another challenge is fragmented measurement. Digital transformation encompasses marketing, operations, compliance, IT, and customer service. Without shared ownership of KPIs, efforts can become disjointed and challenging to scale.

Many companies overlook the complete costs of transformation, such as cultural change, process redesign, and opportunity costs. A thorough approach should include financial and nonfinancial indicators and systems for monitoring unintended consequences, like algorithmic bias or data privacy risks.

CASE STUDIES AND BENCHMARKS OF DIGITAL INSURANCE TRANSFORMATION

Real-world case studies provide essential insights into how insurers implement digital transformation strategies. They also offer valuable benchmarks for organizations at various stages of their digital journeys. Although no two transformations are the same, each being influenced by factors such as market position, regulatory environment, and technological maturity, specific common patterns can be identified. This section explores notable examples from global insurers and InsurTech companies to illustrate how digital transformation occurs in practice, the measurable outcomes achieved, and the challenges faced.

AXA: A GLOBAL APPROACH TO DIGITAL REINVENTION

AXA, one of the world's largest insurance and asset management groups, has implemented a comprehensive digital transformation strategy focusing on internal operations, customer experience, and external partnerships. Acknowledging the constraints of its legacy infrastructure, AXA has made significant investments to modernize its IT systems. This includes deploying cloud-based platforms and standardizing its digital architecture across various markets (AXA Group, 2020).

A key aspect of AXA's transformation was the establishment of AXA Next, a dedicated innovation unit focused on developing new business models, digital health services, and partnerships with startups. As part of its initiatives, AXA Next launched the Health Keeper app in Spain, which combines fitness tracking, telemedicine, and wellness incentives into one cohesive digital platform. The success of this program highlighted how digital services can enhance customer loyalty and generate new revenue streams.

AXA adopted ecosystem thinking by partnering with Uber to provide integrated rideshare insurance and with Alibaba to codevelop products designed for Chinese consumers. These collaborations demonstrate the company's strategy of integrating insurance into everyday digital experiences.

LEMONADE: A BORN-DIGITAL INSURTECH

Lemonade, founded in 2015, is a prime example of a fully digital insurance model. Built on a cloud-native infrastructure powered by AI, Lemonade provides renters, homeowners, pet, and term life insurance products through a seamless digital experience. The company's business model challenges traditional insurance practices by incorporating behavioral economics and an AI-driven claims process to foster trust and transparency (Lemonade, 2021).

A key element of Lemonade's digital transformation is its AI bot, Maya, which can underwrite insurance policies in under 90 seconds. Claims are managed by another AI named Jim, who can approve simple claims in less than 3 minutes without human intervention. This automation has reduced administrative overhead, enabled competitive pricing, and created a customer experience that feels intuitive and responsive.

Lemonade's "Giveback" model is also noteworthy because it donates unused premium revenue to charities selected by policyholders. Although this aspect is not inherently digital, the digital infrastructure allows for the necessary transparency and tracking to implement this model effectively at scale. Lemonade's use of real-time data analytics, behavioral science, and ML demonstrates how digital-native companies can fundamentally rethink risk and pricing.

PING AN: ECOSYSTEM POWERHOUSE IN ASIA

Ping An Insurance, headquartered in China, is recognized as one of the leading digital insurers in the world. Its evolution from a traditional insurance company to a comprehensive digital ecosystem spanning multiple industries sets Ping An apart. Its platforms encompass insurance, banking, health technology, smart city infrastructure, and real estate, all interconnected through shared data and AI infrastructure (KPMG, 2021).

The company's OneConnect platform provides cloud services, AI tools, and blockchain infrastructure to Ping An's subsidiaries and external financial institutions. Through this platform, Ping An has launched services such as Good Doctor, a telemedicine and health management app with over 300 million users, and the Auto-Owner App, which offers vehicle inspection, claims, and roadside assistance. AI and big data power both of these services.

Ping An's ecosystem model lowers acquisition costs, enhances risk segmentation, and fosters long-term customer loyalty. This strategy represents a bolder vision of digital transformation, where the insurer evolves into a digital lifestyle orchestrator, integrating risk services across various domains.

UNITED SERVICES AUTOMOBILE ASSOCIATION: DIGITAL TRANSFORMATION ROOTED IN MEMBER CENTRICITY

The United Services Automobile Association (USAA) is a US-based insurer that serves military members and their families. It has consistently ranked among the top performers in digital experience. USAA's transformation journey focuses on providing omnichannel access, automating customer service, and integrating robust data to ensure members receive seamless, personalized service (Forrester, 2022).

USAA's mobile app enables users to file claims using voice commands, capture accident scenes with augmented reality, and interact with AI-powered chatbots. The company has also invested in NLP to automate email and chat service interactions, significantly reducing response times.

USAA stands out due to its user-centered design philosophy. The company prioritizes digital initiatives based on member feedback, and its agile development practices enable quick adaptation to emerging needs. This emphasis on user experience and disciplined technology governance has established USAA as a benchmark for digital excellence in a highly regulated and competitive industry.

COMMON SUCCESS FACTORS AND BENCHMARKS

Across these case studies, several success factors emerge:

- Customer-Centric Design: Digital leaders prioritize customer needs and build solutions that reduce friction and enhance transparency.
- AI and Automation at Scale: Top performers have integrated ML, NLP, and RPA into core processes like underwriting, pricing, and claims.
- Cloud-Native Infrastructure: Flexible, scalable IT infrastructure is a prerequisite for rapid innovation and API-based ecosystem integration.
- Ecosystem Partnerships: Strategic alliances allow insurers to expand their capabilities and distribution without building everything in-house.
- Data-Driven Culture: High-performing organizations treat data as a strategic asset and invest in platforms, talent, and governance to extract actionable insights.

These benchmarks are a reference for other insurers as they evaluate their transformation journeys. While digital maturity differs significantly across the industry, these examples demonstrate that having clear strategies, aligned organizations, and disciplined execution can unlock substantial value through digital transformation.

FUTURE OUTLOOK FOR DIGITAL INSURANCE

The digital transformation in the insurance sector is set to accelerate, driven by rapid technological advancements, changing consumer expectations, and the increasing complexity of environmental, social, and geopolitical issues. The insurance industry is expected to undergo significant changes in the future, moving beyond minor improvements to transformative shifts that redefine how we approach risk protection. This section offers a forward-looking perspective on what is to come, including developments in technologies, business models, customer relationships, and the essential role of insurers in society.

INSURANCE AS AN EMBEDDED AND INVISIBLE SERVICE

One of the most significant changes is the shift toward embedded insurance products seamlessly integrated into other services and platforms. Shortly, consumers may not even realize they are purchasing insurance, as it will become a natural feature of digital experiences such as booking travel, buying vehicles, or using financial technology applications. These embedded models rely heavily on real-time data exchange, contextual risk assessment, and agile digital infrastructure.

The shift toward invisibility does not mean that insurers will play a lesser role; in fact, it will demand stronger collaboration with ecosystem partners, improved underwriting accuracy, and the ability to fulfill needs in real time. Insurers will transition from product-focused vendors to essential back-end enablers of digital commerce and lifestyle continuity.

AI-DRIVEN RISK ANTICIPATION AND PREVENTION

The next generation of AI in insurance will go beyond automation and analytics to focus on anticipatory risk management. Instead of simply responding to claims, insurers will take on the role of proactive risk advisors. They will identify potential threats before they occur and assist customers in mitigating those risks.

AI models are evolving from making predictions based on past data to focusing on causal inference and counterfactual forecasting. They will utilize complex simulation techniques to explore how risks could develop under different conditions. For instance, insurers might simulate climate scenarios at the asset level or model how policyholders behave during economic downturns to improve the pricing of long-term liabilities.

Personal risk mitigation will also evolve. AI assistants may help individuals make safer health or financial decisions in real time, with insurance coverage adjusting dynamically based on those choices. This shift could blur the line between insurance and personalized digital coaching.

SYNTHETIC DATA AND PRIVACY-ENHANCED ANALYTICS

As privacy regulations become stricter and public concern over data usage grows, the future of insurance analytics will depend on privacy-preserving technologies. Techniques such as synthetic data generation, homomorphic encryption, differential privacy, and federated learning will be essential for developing models that maintain confidentiality while still providing valuable insights.

This trend will be crucial in health, cybersecurity, and behavioral insurance, where valuable data is highly sensitive. Insurers establishing trustworthy AI ecosystems—characterized by transparency, compliance, and security—will gain a significant advantage in attracting customers and obtaining regulatory approval.

THE QUANTUM SHIFT AND CYBER-PHYSICAL CONVERGENCE

Over a longer time frame, quantum computing has the potential to transform actuarial science and portfolio optimization by addressing complex problems that are currently too difficult to solve. Quantum algorithms could facilitate almost instantaneous pricing for reinsurance, enhance cryptographic risk modeling, and improve systemic stress testing for global catastrophe events.

The ongoing expansion of cyber-physical systems, such as smart grids, autonomous vehicles, and connected factories, will create new insurable risks. Insurers must develop expertise in these areas, underlining events that combine physical damage with digital factors. As a result, new insurance policies may be created to cover issues like algorithmic failures, neural implants, and decentralized robotic fleets.

This convergence will require a new definition of liability, causality, and risk assessment frameworks, potentially resulting in entirely new lines of insurance and regulatory oversight mechanisms.

CLIMATE RESILIENCE AS A CORE INSURER FUNCTION

Climate change will not only impact catastrophe models; it will transform the insurer's social contract. In the coming decades, insurers must act as enablers of climate resilience, helping vulnerable populations and economies adapt.

This future includes:

- Microinsurance platforms deliver parametric protection to smallholder farmers through mobile devices.
- Climate-risk underwriting is baked into mortgage origination systems.
- Environmental, social, and governance–aligned investment portfolios that incentivize green infrastructure.
- Risk pooling consortia for nations facing existential weather risks.

As the public sector struggles to adapt, insurers may become default risk aggregators for climate volatility, collaborating with nongovernmental organizations, reinsurers, and governments in new public–private partnerships.

REIMAGINING REGULATION AND ETHICS IN THE DIGITAL CENTURY

Ultimately, the future of digital insurance will be influenced as much by regulatory innovation as by technological advancements. Regulatory sandboxes and adaptive compliance frameworks must evolve to keep pace with the speed and complexity of digital product development.

Ethical considerations—especially regarding AI transparency, algorithmic bias, and digital inclusion—will become issues at the board level. As insurers take on increased data stewardship and influence on behavior, new standards for explainability, accountability, and consent will emerge.

Educational institutions and industry organizations will be crucial in cultivating the ethical understanding to guide this transformation responsibly. The insurance professionals of tomorrow will require proficiency in underwriting and finance, ethics, data governance, and interdisciplinary collaboration.

CONCLUSION AND STRATEGIC TAKEAWAYS

The insurance industry is undergoing a significant transformation driven by digital technologies that impact all aspects of its operations, from underwriting and claims management to customer experience and distribution. This chapter has explored the complex nature of digital transformation, examined emerging platforms and ecosystem dynamics, outlined performance measurement frameworks, and provided real-world examples and future trends. As the sector continues to embrace digitization, several key strategic insights emerge that are important for insurers, regulators, educators, and technologists to consider.

DIGITAL TRANSFORMATION IS STRATEGIC, NOT JUST TECHNOLOGICAL

Digital transformation is often misunderstood as merely a series of technology upgrades, such as cloud migration, mobile applications, or automating outdated processes. In truth, a strategic necessity reshapes a company's value proposition, operating model, and organizational culture. The most successful transformations weave digital technologies into the organization's very fabric, aligning them with its purpose, prioritizing customer centricity, and fostering long-term resilience.

The implications for insurers are clear: transformation initiatives must be led at the C-suite level, supported by governance structures that cross IT silos and anchored in a clear vision of the future insurance business model.

ECOSYSTEMS WILL DEFINE THE COMPETITIVE LANDSCAPE

In the next decade, competition in the insurance industry will increasingly occur between ecosystems rather than individual companies. Traditional insurers must choose whether to become ecosystem orchestrators—developing platforms and establishing standards—or to participate as value-adding contributors. Both strategies require openness, technical agility, and strategic partnerships across various sectors.

Ecosystem readiness will rely on developing scalable APIs, strong data-sharing protocols, and interoperable platforms that provide value across health, finance, mobility, and smart home sectors.

MEASUREMENT AND ACCOUNTABILITY MUST EVOLVE

Measuring digital initiatives' ROI can be challenging using traditional financial methods. Companies should take a comprehensive view of their digital investments, emphasizing cost savings and factors like agility, customer lifetime value, and resilience against disruptions. Tools such as balanced scorecards, OKRs, and innovation accounting can provide valuable frameworks for aligning stakeholders and tracking progress.

Embedding transparency in digital performance—through customer feedback loops, data analytics, and KPI dashboards—into transformation efforts from the outset ensures accountability and promotes iterative learning.

FUTURE SUCCESS DEPENDS ON TALENT AND CULTURE

Technology can be obtained, but cultural change is the real differentiator in digital transformation. Organizations that promote experimentation, flatten hierarchies, encourage digital literacy, and incentivize cross-functional collaboration are more likely to succeed. This is especially crucial in a risk-averse industry like insurance, where innovation must exist alongside regulatory compliance and fiduciary responsibility.

Investing in digital talent is crucial, especially in data science, cyber risk, and UX design. Additionally, upskilling traditional insurance professionals to thrive in a digital-first environment is equally important.

THE ROLE OF EDUCATORS AND POLICYMAKERS

Academic institutions, professional associations, and regulators all play crucial roles in facilitating digital transformation. It is essential to update curricula to reflect the current realities of the insurance industry, incorporating case studies, technical literacy, ethical reasoning, and policy frameworks. Regulators should strive to balance innovation with consumer protection by creating flexible sandboxes and adopting adaptive rulemaking approaches. Collaborating effectively, these stakeholders can create a mature and ethically sound insurance sector ready to meet societal needs amidst increasing complexity and new risks.

AI DISCLOSURE

During the preparation of this work the author(s) used Grammarly to improve readability and correct grammatical errors. After using this tool/service, the author(s) reviewed and edited the content as needed and take(s) full responsibility for the content of the publication.

REFERENCES

AXA Group. (2020). *Annual report 2020.* https://www.axa.com/en/about-us/annual-report

Accenture (2019). Technology Vision for Insurance 2019: Success for insurers in the emerging post-digital world. Accenture. https://www.accenture.com/us-en/insights/insurance/technology-vision-insurance.

Bharadwaj, A., El Sawy, O. A., Pavlou, P. A., & Venkatraman, N. V. (2013). Digital business strategy: Toward a next generation of insights. *MIS Quarterly*, *37*(2), 471–482. https://doi.org/10.25300/MISQ/2013/37:2.3.

Capgemini (2020). World Insurance Report 2020. https://www.capgemini.com/mx-es/wp-content/uploads/sites/24/2020/09/Capgemini-World-Insurance-Report-2020.pdf.

Capgemini & Efma. (2021). World InsurTech Report 2021: Unprecedented access to capital investment fuels InsurTech and BigTech maturity and customer adoption. https://www.capgemini.com/us-en/news/world-insurtech-report-2021/.

Forrester. (2022). *The US customer experience index rankings*. https://go.forrester.com/.

Deloitte. (2024). 2025 global insurance outlook: Evolving industry operating models to build the future of insurance https://www.deloitte.com/us/en/insights/industry/financial-services/financial-services-industry-outlooks/insurance-industry-outlook-2025.html.

Evans, D. S., & Schmalensee, R. (2016). *Matchmakers: The new economics of multisided platforms*. Harvard Business Review Press.

Gartner, Inc. (2023). Gartner says cloud will become a business necessity by 2028. Gartner https://www.gartner.com/en/newsroom/press-releases/2023-11-29-gartner-says-cloud-will-become-a-business-necessity-by-2028.

Gimpel, H., Hosseini, S., Huber, R., Probst, L., & Röglinger, M. (2018). Structuring digital transformation: A framework of action fields and its application at a financial service provider. *Journal of Information Technology Theory and Application (JITTA)*, *19*(1), 31–54.

Guo, Y. J., & Lamberton, C. (2021). When does sharing stigmatize? Saving money (vs. seeking variety) through access-based consumption. *Frontiers in Psychology*, *12*. https://doi.org/10.3389/fpsyg.2021.778290.

He, D., Zhang, Y., & Huang, J. (2019). Usage-based insurance pricing with telematics data. *Risks*, *7*(1), 1–17. https://doi.org/10.3390/risks7010017.

Henriette, E., Feki, M., & Boughzala, I. (2016). Digital transformation challenges. *Proceedings of the 49th Hawaii international conference on system sciences (HICSS)*, *1*, 10. https://doi.org/10.1109/HICSS.2016.63.

KPMG. (2021). *Ping An: Leading innovation through technology*. https://home.kpmg/xx/en/home/insights/2021/11/ping-an-case-study.html.

Lemonade. (2021). *Annual benefit corporation report*. https://www.lemonade.com/blog/benefit-corporation-2021/.

McKinsey & Company. (2020). *COVID-19: Implications for the insurance industry*. https://www.mckinsey.com/industries/financial-services/our-insights/covid-19-implications-for-insurers.

Kane, G. C., Palmer, D., Phillips, A. N., Kiron, D., & Buckley, N. (2015). Strategy, not technology, drives digital transformation. *MIT Sloan Management Review and Deloitte University Press*. https://sloanreview.mit.edu/projects/strategy-drives-digital-transformation/.

Mills, D. (2019). Blockchain technology and smart contracts: Disrupting the insurance industry. *Journal of Insurance Regulation, National Association of Insurance Commissioners (NAIC)*, *38*(2), 1–25. https://sloanreview.mit.edu/projects/strategy-drives-digital-transformation/.

Organisation for Economic Co-operation and Development (2021). Open insurance: Assessing the potential and policy implications of insurance data sharing. *OECD Publishing*. https://doi.org/10.1787/7c291d57-en.
Price water house Coopers. (2017). Global FinTech report 2017: Redrawing the lines — FinTech's growing influence on financial services. *Global FinTech Survey 2017.*
Price water house Coopers. (2021).Global Digital Trust Insights Survey 2021 https://www.pwc.ch/en/publications/2020/ch-Digital-Trust-Insights-Survey-2021-report.pdf.
Rigby, D. K., Sutherland, J., & Noble, A. (2018). Agile at scale. *Harvard Business Review*, *96*(3), 88–96. https://hbr.org/2018/05/agile-at-scale.
Téllez, J. L., & Dietz, M. (2022).The future of financial inclusion: Leveraging digital innovation to expand access and reduce inequality https://documents.worldbank.org/en/publication/documents-reports/documentdetail/12345/the-future-of-financial-inclusion.
Van Alstyne, M. W., Parker, G. G., & Choudary, S. P. (2016). Pipelines, platforms, and the new rules of strategy. *Harvard Business Review*, *94*(4), 54–62. https://hbr.org/2016/04/pipelines-platforms-and-the-new-rules-of-strategy.
Westerman, G., Bonnet, D., & McAfee, A. (2014). *Leading digital: turning technology into business transformation*. Harvard Business Review Press.
World Economic Forum. (2021). Good data: Sharing data and fostering public trust and willingness (White Paper). https://www3.weforum.org/docs/WEF_Good_Data_Sharing_Data_and_Fostering_Public_Trust_and_Willingness_2021.pdf.
World Economic Forum. (2020). The future of jobs report 2020. World Economic Forum. https://www3.weforum.org/docs/WEF_Future_of_Jobs_2020.pdf.
Wüthrich, M. V. (2020). Machine learning in individual claims reserving. *SSRN Electronic Journal.* https://doi.org/10.2139/ssrn.3520734.

CHAPTER

Big data and analytics in insurance

3

CHAPTER OUTLINE

Insurance Technology. DOI: https://doi.org/10.1016/B978-0-443-43972-8.00006-7

INTRODUCTION TO BIG DATA IN INSURANCE

In today's digital economy, data has emerged as one of the most valuable strategic assets, transforming the foundations of nearly every industry. In the insurance sector, data serves as a historical record of claims and customer interactions and increasingly acts as a predictive tool for pricing, underwriting, fraud detection, and product innovation. "Big data" refers to datasets defined by their immense volume, rapid generation and processing speed, and diverse structure. These datasets often surpass the capabilities of traditional data management tools for storage, analysis, and visualization (Mayer-Schönberger & Cukier, 2013). This shift has transformed the insurance industry, encompassing everything from underwriting to claims, into a data-intensive ecosystem where analytical capabilities are crucial for gaining a competitive advantage.

The insurance industry has traditionally relied on data to assess risk and predict future outcomes. However, conventional actuarial methods focused mainly on structured, historical data collected from standardized forms and internal processes. While these methods are reliable, they operate within the limits of relatively small datasets, static risk models, and manual interpretation. The advent of big data represents a significant shift in this approach. Today, insurers are increasingly able to gather and analyze vast and diverse data streams, such as real-time driving behavior, satellite imagery, biometrics, and social media interactions. This capability allows them to create detailed, dynamic, and personalized risk profiles (McKinsey & Company, 2018).

Advancements in technology partly drive this shift. Developments in data storage, distributed computing, cloud platforms, and parallel processing have enabled insurance companies to utilize terabytes and even petabytes of data in near real time. Machine learning (ML) and artificial intelligence (AI) innovations have further accelerated this transformation, allowing insurers to identify complex patterns and anomalies that traditional statistical models might overlook (Brynjolfsson & McAfee, 2014). These tools are being used to improve pricing accuracy and streamline claims processing, detect fraud, assess climate risk, forecast customer churn, and develop personalized strategies.

Big data has a transformative impact that goes beyond improving operational efficiency. It has fundamentally changed how insurers interact with customers, moving the industry from a retrospective, transactional model to a more proactive, real-time service approach. With data collected from wearable health devices, telematics systems in vehicles, and behavioral analytics on digital platforms, insurers now have unprecedented insights into policyholders' day-to-day activities and preferences. This shift allows for dynamic pricing models, such as usage-based insurance (UBI), and enables insurers to offer customized products, incentives for risk-reducing behaviors, and on-demand services (PwC, 2020).

While big data holds great potential for the insurance industry, its integration presents several challenges. Key concerns include data privacy, algorithm fairness, regulation compliance, and the ethical implications of using surveillance for risk assessment. Additionally, many traditional insurance companies face structural and cultural hurdles that hinder the effective implementation of big data strategies. Addressing these issues often requires modernizing IT infrastructure, breaking down departmental data silos, retraining staff, and meeting increasing expectations regarding data transparency and governance (EY, 2021).

As competition grows and new InsurTech companies disrupt traditional value chains, leveraging big data becomes increasingly important. Insurers that invest in scalable data infrastructure, integrate analytics into their decision-making processes, and adopt ethical guidelines for data usage will be better equipped to foster innovation, enhance customer experiences, and comply with evolving regulatory standards. In contrast, those that fail to do so may struggle to compete in a marketplace that is becoming more data driven and customer focused.

SOURCES AND TYPES OF DATA IN INSURANCE

Today's insurance industry relies on a broader and more diverse range of data sources than ever. Traditionally, insurers based their underwriting, claims, and pricing decisions on structured internal data, such as application forms, actuarial tables, historical claims records, and demographic profiles. However, the digital age has introduced many alternative data types and sources, many of which are unstructured, high frequency, and dynamic. Understanding the variety of these data types is essential for grasping the transformative power—and complexity—of modern insurance analytics.

Structured data is the backbone of traditional insurance operations. This type of data consists of well-organized datasets that fit easily into relational databases, including information about policyholders, claims amounts, premium history, billing records, and underwriting classifications. Structured data allows insurers to maintain historical baselines, calculate loss ratios, forecast premiums, and comply with regulatory reporting requirements. Since these datasets are usually generated and managed internally, insurers have established robust systems and controls to ensure accuracy, auditability, and consistency across different business units.

The emergence of unstructured and semistructured data has significantly enhanced the analytical capabilities of insurers. Unstructured data consists of information that does not fit traditional database formats, including images, videos, audio recordings, emails, social media content, and free-text customer feedback. On the other hand, semistructured data, such as XML or JSON logs generated from digital interactions or mobile applications, possesses some organizational features that need to be transformed before being analyzed. These types of data provide insurers with valuable insights into customer sentiment, behavior, and emerging risk signals that might otherwise remain unnoticed (Chen et al., 2012).

An increasing number of data sources are now being integrated into insurers' analytical systems. One significant category is telematics and sensor data, which is particularly common in the auto and health insurance sectors. Telematics devices installed in vehicles can track driving behavior in real time, monitoring factors such as speed, acceleration, braking, mileage, and use time. This data supports UBI models, where policyholders are rewarded for safe driving habits or penalized for risky behaviors (Litman, 2015). Similarly, wearable fitness trackers, smartwatches, and mobile health apps allow life and health insurers to gather biometric data—including heart rate, activity level, sleep patterns, and caloric intake—which provides a real-time, behavior-based insight into personal health risks (Baig, GholamHosseini, & Connolly, 2013).

An increasingly important source of information comes from geospatial and satellite data. Insurers utilize satellite imagery and drone footage to evaluate property risk before underwriting, monitor flood zones and areas prone to wildfires, and verify claims following natural disasters. Remote sensing enables insurers to enhance the accuracy of catastrophe models and reduce fraud by confirming loss events at specific geographic locations (Kunreuther & Michel-Kerjan, 2009). This is particularly relevant in commercial and agricultural insurance, where the locations of assets and exposure to environmental risks can vary significantly across extensive geographic areas.

Social media and digital behavioral data have become increasingly valuable for insurers. They analyze social media platforms and web browsing patterns to infer lifestyle factors, interests, and potential fraud indicators. For instance, publicly available information can verify claims, assess risk behaviors, or identify significant life events such as marriage, travel, or job changes. While this data provides rich context, it raises ethical and legal questions regarding consent, fairness, and relevance, especially in underwriting decisions (Pasquale, 2015). Consequently, many insurers use this data for marketing and engagement purposes rather than risk classification.

Third-party consumer data enhances insurers' internal datasets. This data includes credit reports, public records, property valuations, vehicle registration databases, and criminal background checks. One of the most common applications of this data is credit-based insurance scoring, particularly in auto and homeowners insurance. Research has demonstrated a correlation between credit history and claims frequency (Monaghan, 2000). While this approach is practical for predictive modeling, credit and socioeconomic data have attracted regulatory scrutiny due to their potential to reinforce bias or create inequities, especially when transparency or mechanisms for recourse are limited.

Weather and climate data play a crucial role in property and catastrophe insurance risk modeling. Insurers use real-time weather feeds and historical climate models to predict storm paths, droughts, and heat waves, which helps improve risk pricing and disaster preparedness. Additionally, climate projection models allow insurers to evaluate long-term risks associated with rising sea levels, wildfire zones, and changing precipitation patterns. This information informs strategic decisions regarding coverage availability, reinsurance needs, and capital reserves (Surminski, 2014).

Internal behavioral and engagement data, such as clickstream logs, chat transcripts, call center metadata, and app usage patterns, enable insurers to monitor customer interactions and improve service delivery. These data sources allow insurers to personalize their offerings, identify signs of customer dissatisfaction, and implement retention strategies. For instance, ML algorithms can recognize a pattern of behaviors that may indicate a risk of customer churn, allowing insurers to intervene with tailored offers or outreach campaigns before the customer decides to leave (Ngai et al., 2009).

These data sources indicate a significant change in the amount and detail of information available to insurers. Insurers are no longer restricted to static, one-time declarations or periodic updates; they can now access continuously updated, multidimensional profiles of individuals, assets, and external conditions. While this wealth of information presents powerful opportunities for enhancing risk assessment and customer experience, it also introduces new challenges. These include managing data quality and interoperability, ensuring ethical use, and compliance with regulations. As insurers increasingly rely on nontraditional data, transparent data governance, informed consent, and risk-aware analytics practices become crucial to the industry's digital transformation.

BIG DATA INFRASTRUCTURE AND TECHNOLOGIES

Insurance companies must invest in modern, scalable, and integrated data infrastructures to fully harness big data's potential. These systems act as the technological backbone for advanced analytics, enabling everything from real-time decision-making in underwriting to large-scale simulations of catastrophic loss events. Unlike traditional IT architectures, big data infrastructures prioritize flexibility, speed, and scalability, built around static relational databases and batch reporting processes. This approach allows insurers to manage increasingly diverse datasets and implement analytics on a larger scale.

The data lake is at the core of big data infrastructure, a centralized repository designed to ingest, store, and organize vast amounts of raw, semistructured, and unstructured data. Unlike data warehouses, which require data to be cleaned and structured before storage, data lakes enable organizations to capture data in its original form, preserving its richness and detail. This architecture is particularly beneficial for insurers, as it facilitates a wide range of analytical applications, such as detecting claims fraud, modeling natural disasters, and segmenting customers, without predefined schemas, which could restrict analytical flexibility.

To effectively process and extract value from large datasets, insurers rely on distributed computing frameworks that can handle massive workloads in parallel across clusters of machines. One of the first such systems was Apache Hadoop, which offered a reliable method for splitting data into smaller chunks and processing them using the MapReduce programming model. However, as data science demands became more complex and latency requirements became stricter, Apache Spark emerged as a preferred platform. Spark enables in-memory processing, significantly reducing computation time for iterative algorithms used in ML, statistical modeling, and risk simulations. For an insurance company performing hundreds of simulations per second to assess reinsurance exposure or pricing volatility, Spark offers the performance advantage necessary to compete in real-time environments.

Data in the insurance sector comes in various forms, including structured policyholder records, streaming telematics, and free-form notes submitted through mobile apps. Insurers are increasingly adopting NoSQL databases to handle this diversity, which provide schema-less data storage solutions designed for flexibility and speed. Popular platforms such as MongoDB, Cassandra, and HBase enable insurers to manage unstructured data, like video surveillance footage, social media feeds, or geolocation data, on a large scale. For example, an insurer using satellite imagery to validate property claims after a natural disaster would find traditional SQL systems inadequate regarding agility and scalability.

The cloud computing revolution has become vital to digital insurance strategies, complementing storage and processing capabilities. Major cloud platforms like Amazon Web Services (AWS), Microsoft Azure, and Google Cloud Platform provide flexible compute and storage resources that enable insurers to scale their infrastructure based on demand. This flexibility is essential during events that lead to increased data processing needs, such as natural disasters, pandemics, or cyberattacks. Additionally, cloud services enhance geographic redundancy, improve disaster recovery, and streamline the deployment of data-intensive applications, including pricing engines, chatbot services, and AI-driven claims triage systems.

As insurers shift toward real-time business models, streaming data pipelines are becoming essential. Tools like Apache Kafka, AWS Kinesis, and Azure Event Hubs enable insurers to ingest and process high-velocity data streams from Internet of Things (IoT) sensors, mobile devices, and customer interaction logs. For example, an auto insurer can collect second-by-second telematics data from thousands of vehicles. Real-time analysis of this data allows for dynamic risk scoring, immediate fraud detection, and timely customer messaging. Streaming biometric data from wearable devices in the health insurance sector can trigger alerts, recommendations, or even pricing adjustments based on individuals' wellness behaviors. This creates a continuous, responsive, and personalized data loop.

These systems depend on effective extract, transform, and load (ETL) processes to move and clean data throughout the pipeline. In traditional insurance environments, data from core systems—such as claims management, customer relationship management, and policy administration—must be integrated and enhanced before it can support analytics. Modern ETL tools, like Apache NiFi, Talend, and Informatica, have evolved to handle batch and streaming data, enabling scalable ingestion, transformation, and real-time validation. This capability is especially crucial in regulatory contexts, where data lineage, traceability, and audit readiness are essential.

As the volume of data increases, the importance of data quality, metadata management, and governance controls also rises. Inaccurate, outdated, or poorly labeled data can undermine the validity of predictive models and violate compliance requirements. To address these issues, insurers implement data quality management platforms that profile data, monitor anomalies, and flag inconsistencies before they affect decision-making. Additionally, metadata repositories and data catalogs help standardize definitions across departments, allowing actuaries, data scientists, and underwriters to work from a consistent information foundation.

Insurers increasingly adopt containerization and orchestration technologies to facilitate agile model deployment and microservice architectures. Tools like Docker and Kubernetes enable data science teams to deploy models into production environments quickly and reliably. For instance, an ML model that predicts claims severity can be containerized, version controlled, and deployed across multiple regions with automated scaling policies. This ensures its availability even during peak processing periods. This approach promotes reproducibility and compliance with model governance protocols and allows for the seamless rollback of faulty versions if any anomalies are detected.

Big data infrastructure must prioritize both interoperability and security. Many insurers incorporate data from external vendors, reinsurers, government databases, and third-party application programming interfaces (APIs). To ensure secure and reliable data exchange, it is essential to implement well-designed APIs, encryption, and access control mechanisms. Additionally, as insurers face increasingly complex regulatory requirements—including General Data Protection Regulation (GDPR), California Consumer Privacy Act, and evolving AI governance rules—they must integrate auditability, privacy by design, and explainability directly into their technology frameworks.

Building and maintaining big data infrastructure in the insurance industry goes beyond a mere technical endeavor. It is a strategic driver for innovation, customer focus, and operational efficiency. With capabilities spanning high-throughput processing, real-time analytics, model deployment, and regulatory compliance, an insurer's ability to effectively manage and utilize data at scale will increasingly determine its relevance in a digitized, risk-intensive economy.

DESCRIPTIVE, PREDICTIVE, AND PRESCRIPTIVE ANALYTICS IN INSURANCE

The increasing availability of diverse data sources and advanced computational tools has significantly changed how insurers derive value from data. Insurance organizations are moving beyond merely reporting past events. They are now adopting various analytics, from descriptive to predictive to prescriptive, to guide their strategies, enhance automation, and provide customer-focused solutions. Each type of analytics serves a specific purpose, collectively fostering a more agile and data-driven approach to risk management and operational decision-making.

DESCRIPTIVE ANALYTICS: UNDERSTANDING THE PAST AND PRESENT

Descriptive analytics involves summarizing historical data to provide insights into past behavior and current operational conditions. In the insurance industry, descriptive analytics forms the foundation for dashboards, performance reports, and visualization tools that actuaries, underwriters, and executives use to monitor key performance indicators (KPIs). These KPIs include claims frequency, loss ratios, and customer retention rates (Davenport & Harris, 2007).

Traditional descriptive tools have progressed from simple spreadsheet models to advanced business intelligence platforms like Tableau, Power BI, and Qlik. These tools allow users to visualize multidimensional data across various regions, product lines, or periods, aiding in performance monitoring and trend identification. For instance, a claims analyst might use descriptive dashboards to compare historical claims costs across different geographies or identify seasonal property loss patterns. These insights help inform decisions about resource allocation, staffing, and reinsurance.

In customer analytics, descriptive methods assist insurers in gaining insights into their policyholders and how they engage with the organization. Metrics such as Net Promoter Score, policy conversion rates, and service touchpoints are commonly monitored to assess customer satisfaction and identify opportunities for improving engagement (Mayer-Schönberger & Cukier, 2013). While descriptive analytics primarily focuses on historical data, it lays the groundwork for more advanced, forward-looking analyses.

PREDICTIVE ANALYTICS: ANTICIPATING FUTURE OUTCOMES

Descriptive analytics focuses on explaining past events, while predictive analytics aims to forecast future occurrences. Using statistical models and ML algorithms, predictive analytics allows insurers to anticipate various events, such as claims, policy lapses, fraudulent activities, and customer churn (James et al., 2013). These models analyze historical data to identify patterns and relationships that can be applied to future situations.

In underwriting, predictive models are employed to estimate the likelihood of claims occurrence and severity based on policyholders' attributes, behaviors, and external indicators. For instance, auto insurers utilize telematics data to categorize drivers into various risk levels by analyzing average speed, braking intensity, and the time of day they travel. Similarly, health insurers may use biometric and lifestyle information to predict the risk of developing chronic diseases, which helps them create personalized wellness plans and set risk-adjusted premiums.

Claims departments utilize predictive models to effectively manage incoming claims by categorizing them according to the likelihood of severity, litigation risk, or fraud probability. This approach optimizes the allocation of adjuster resources, speeds up the processing of straightforward claims, and highlights high-risk cases that require further investigation. Similarly, customer service teams employ churn prediction models to identify policyholders at risk of leaving. This enables them to conduct proactive outreach campaigns that enhance customer retention (Ngai et al., 2009).

Different modeling techniques are used in predictive analytics based on the problem being addressed. Logistic regression is commonly employed for binary classification tasks, such as distinguishing between claims and no claims. Decision trees and random forests are popular choices as they provide interpretable, nonlinear models that accurately represent complex relationships.

For larger and high-dimensional datasets, gradient boosting machines, like XGBoost and LightGBM, and deep learning architectures can offer greater accuracy. However, these techniques often have a trade-off in interpretability, a crucial factor in regulated environments such as insurance (Kuhn & Johnson, 2013).

Data preparation plays a crucial role in predictive modeling. Insurers need to manage missing data, normalize variables, and address class imbalance, which is often encountered in fraud detection scenarios where the positive class (fraudulent claims) is rare.

To ensure the model's generalizability, it is important to validate it using cross-validation and holdout datasets. Performance metrics like accuracy, precision, recall, area under the curve–receiver operating characteristic, and F1 score are essential for guiding model selection and refinement.

PRESCRIPTIVE ANALYTICS: RECOMMENDING OPTIMAL ACTIONS

Prescriptive analytics is the most advanced level of data-driven decision-making. It predicts future outcomes and recommends specific actions to achieve desired results. Prescriptive models use optimization algorithms, simulation techniques, and decision rules to assist with dynamic pricing, portfolio allocation, resource scheduling, and personalized policy recommendations (Bertsimas & Kallus, 2020).

Prescriptive analytics can optimize premium pricing in commercial insurance by identifying the most profitable pricing points for various customer segments. This analysis considers market demand, regulatory constraints, and competitor behavior. In personal insurance, insurers utilize prescriptive tools to recommend cross-sell or upsell opportunities. These tools select the most relevant product offers based on customer profiles and historical buying patterns.

Prescriptive analytics plays a crucial role in catastrophe risk modeling. Reinsurers use stochastic models to simulate millions of potential natural disaster scenarios, assessing the financial impact across geographic portfolios. Optimization algorithms are then employed to determine the ideal reinsurance structure that minimizes risk while maximizing capital efficiency. Similar methods are applied in capital modeling under the Solvency II and Own Risk and Solvency Assessment frameworks to identify the most resilient capital allocations in adverse scenarios (Swiss Re Institute, 2021).

Prescriptive models play a crucial role in helping claims departments devise optimal response strategies based on expected claims outcomes, available resources, and service-level agreements. For instance, a prescriptive model might recommend expediting low-severity claims through straight-through processing in a high-volume claims environment. In contrast, it would suggest routing more complex or suspicious claims to human adjusters for thorough review. These recommendations are increasingly integrated into decision-support systems and AI-enabled platforms, enabling frontline staff to make data-driven decisions without interpreting the underlying models in real time.

Ethical and regulatory considerations play a crucial role in prescriptive analytics. Since these models often impact financial decisions and eligibility outcomes, insurers must prioritize transparency, fairness, and accountability in their model logic. Explainable AI (XAI) tools are increasingly integrated into prescriptive systems to support this. These tools justify model recommendations, which are essential for compliance with regulatory frameworks such as GDPR and the New York State Department of Financial Services guidelines for AI in financial services (Wachter et al., 2018).

INTEGRATING THE ANALYTICS SPECTRUM

Descriptive, predictive, and prescriptive analytics are not isolated stages but interdependent components of a broader analytics maturity model. Descriptive analytics identifies patterns and anomalies, predictive analytics forecasts outcomes based on those patterns, and prescriptive analytics determines the best responses to those forecasts. Leading insurers create integrated analytics platforms that facilitate smooth transitions between these stages. Robust data pipelines, model governance frameworks, and cross-functional analytics teams support these platforms.

The business value of the analytics continuum is evident. Insurers that effectively adopt advanced analytics capabilities can lower loss ratios, enhance customer retention, identify emerging risks more quickly, and speed up innovation cycles. Achieving these benefits involves more than just deploying algorithms; it necessitates a thoughtful strategy that aligns analytics with organizational goals, develops talent, and integrates analytics into everyday decision-making processes.

ACTUARIAL SCIENCE AND THE EVOLUTION OF DATA ANALYTICS

Actuarial science has long been the analytical foundation of the insurance industry. Traditionally based on mathematical statistics, probability theory, and financial modeling, actuarial methods have allowed insurers to forecast losses, set premiums, and maintain solvency with precision. For decades, the profession has concentrated on structured data analysis using established methodologies such as survival models, generalized linear models (GLMs), credibility theory, and stochastic simulations. However, the rise of big data and ML has started to transform the actuarial toolkit, prompting actuaries to adapt, evolve, and rethink their roles within increasingly data-driven organizations (Frees et al., 2014).

The actuarial function has traditionally depended on aggregated datasets and established assumptions. For example, pricing models typically utilize a limited set of rating variables—such as age, gender, zip code, and claims history—to estimate loss costs and determine premium adequacy. These models were transparent, interpretable, and well understood by both regulators and industry professionals. However, they had limitations, particularly in their ability to capture nonlinear interactions, behavioral nuances, or high-dimensional feature spaces (Antonio & Plat, 2014).

Today, due to the widespread availability of detailed, real-time data and advanced modeling tools, insurers can enhance traditional actuarial models by incorporating data science techniques. For instance, a predictive model that utilizes telematics data can analyze hundreds of variables related to driving behavior, such as acceleration patterns, harsh braking events, time of day, and average speed. This approach generates risk scores that are significantly more precise than those derived solely from demographic variables. ML algorithms like random forests, gradient boosting, and neural networks can effectively model these complex relationships without relying on predefined distributional assumptions, leading to improved predictive performance in certain situations (Henckaerts et al., 2022).

While ML offers significant capabilities, its integration into actuarial practice comes with challenges. A key concern is the trade-off between accuracy and interpretability. Traditional actuarial models are designed to be transparent and explainable, which is essential for regulatory compliance, internal audits, and effective communication with customers. In contrast, ML models often act as "black boxes," making decisions that are hard to deconstruct or justify to stakeholders who lack a technical background. This has led to a growing demand for XAI methods that illuminate model decision processes, highlight the importance of variables, and indicate the confidence level of predictions, especially in applications related to pricing fairness, claims denials, and risk classification (Wüthrich, 2020).

One significant shift is the expansion of sources for actuarial data. Nowadays, actuaries are not only working with structured policy and claims data but are also engaging with semistructured and unstructured information. This includes data from social media sentiment, customer service transcripts, health app data, and geospatial imagery. These new data sources demand different analytical techniques and enhanced data engineering capabilities. Consequently, actuarial teams are increasingly collaborating with data scientists, software engineers, and IT architects to create comprehensive pipelines for data acquisition, transformation, modeling, and deployment (Richman, 2021).

The evolution of the actuarial profession has significantly changed the educational landscape for aspiring actuaries. Professional organizations like the Society of Actuaries and the Casualty Actuarial Society have updated their credentialing requirements to include essential skills in programming, predictive modeling, and data analytics. As a result, actuarial students are now expected to be proficient in tools such as R, Python, SQL, and ML libraries, in addition to traditional subjects like finance, probability, and risk theory. Furthermore, continuing education programs are increasingly emphasizing emerging topics, including AI governance, ethics in modeling, and the implications of big data for insurance equity (CAS, 2020).

The rise of big data does not make traditional actuarial methods obsolete. Instead, it promotes a hybrid approach combining the statistical rigor, familiarity with regulations, and long-term solvency perspective of actuaries with modern data science's flexible, pattern-seeking capabilities. For instance, GLMs are crucial in ratemaking and reserving, mainly when used alongside credibility theory and Bayesian updates. Actuaries can also enhance these models by integrating ML-based risk scores or adding interaction terms identified through data-driven exploration (Frees et al., 2014).

Actuaries provide a valuable perspective on model governance and risk calibration. Their training focuses on conservative assumptions, long-term risk assessment, and capital adequacy. This outlook helps balance the short-term optimization goals often emphasized in ML models. Therefore actuaries are crucial in ensuring that advanced analytics enhance predictive accuracy while aligning with the fiduciary and societal responsibilities within the insurance industry (Wüthrich, 2020).

In reserving and capital modeling, actuaries increasingly use simulation-based models, such as bootstrapped reserves, dynamic financial analysis, and capital adequacy forecasting, on platforms that can handle larger datasets and higher processing loads. These models use distributed computing frameworks that can run thousands of stochastic scenarios. This capability improves stress testing, better tail risk estimation, and more effective reinsurance strategy design. As solvency regulations focus more on risk sensitivity and scenario-driven approaches, actuarial leaders must ensure thorough model validation, backtesting, and documentation.

Integrating actuarial science and data analytics is not about replacing the other; rather, it is about how they can complement each other. Actuaries should adopt data science tools and approaches, including agility, experimentation, and computational scalability, while still upholding the discipline, governance, and ethical standards that define their profession. Organizations that successfully combine these capabilities will be in the best position to develop analytics functions that are technically advanced, trustworthy, auditable, and strategically aligned.

USE CASES ACROSS THE INSURANCE VALUE CHAIN

Big data and analytics play a crucial role throughout all functions of an insurance company. Their value spans the entire insurance value chain, from product design and underwriting to claims management, marketing, and customer service. By integrating data-driven intelligence at each stage, insurers can optimize their operations, transform engagement strategies, improve loss ratios, reduce fraud, and enhance customer satisfaction.

UNDERWRITING: RISK SELECTION AND PRICING PRECISION

Underwriting has traditionally relied on actuarial risk models that use static variables like age, occupation, and claims history. However, with access to high-frequency behavioral data, underwriting is becoming more dynamic and tailored to individuals. Auto insurers, for example, now utilize telematics data to create UBI models. These models analyze real-time driving behavior, including acceleration, braking, cornering, and phone usage, which provides detailed insights into driving risk (Litman, 2015). By replacing demographic indicators with behavioral data, insurers can offer more personalized premiums and incentivize safer driving habits.

In property insurance, underwriters utilize satellite imagery, aerial drone footage, and geospatial data to evaluate building conditions, surrounding vegetation, and proximity to natural hazards such as flood zones or areas prone to wildfires. These tools help underwriters enhance the accuracy of risk classification and set more appropriate pricing in regions affected by climate variability (Kousky & Kunreuther, 2020). In commercial insurance, underwriters increasingly depend on predictive models that analyze business risks using financial statements, employee turnover rates, litigation history, and even customer reviews from the internet.

CLAIMS: AUTOMATION, FRAUD DETECTION, AND TRIAGE

Claims analytics is one of the most advanced big data applications in the insurance industry. Predictive models are commonly employed to evaluate the severity of claims, the likelihood of litigation, and the risk of fraud as soon as a claims is received. For instance, when a motor claims is submitted, image recognition algorithms can assess the extent of damage based on uploaded photos. Natural language processing (NLP) tools can also extract pertinent information from free-text descriptions to prioritize claims for review or expedite processing (He et al., 2019).

Fraud detection, particularly within the insurance industry, greatly benefits from using anomaly detection algorithms, network analysis, and unsupervised ML techniques. These models can identify outliers by analyzing claims patterns, submission timings, provider behaviors, and policyholder profiles. Claims that exhibit suspicious characteristics, such as multiple injuries treated by the same medical provider or patterns indicative of staged accidents, are flagged for further investigation by special investigation units. Additionally, ML enhances the ability to detect previously unknown fraud patterns, thereby improving detection rates and increasing the efficiency of investigation resources (Viaene et al., 2002).

Triage models are employed to enhance resource allocation. High-complexity claims, likely to involve litigation or significant payouts, are directed to experienced adjusters. In contrast, straightforward claims can be processed automatically. This approach ensures that skilled expertise is applied where it is most needed, while automation helps improve processing times and customer satisfaction.

MARKETING AND DISTRIBUTION: PERSONALIZATION AND LEAD OPTIMIZATION

In marketing, big data allows for hyperpersonalization of insurance offerings and enhances customer acquisition processes. Predictive models identify potential customers who are most likely to engage, based on demographics, online behavior, lifestyle indicators, and previous interactions. These insights help tailor messaging, delivery channels, and product bundles effectively. For instance, an insurer targeting small business owners may segment its audience according to business type, geographic location, digital engagement, and past claims data. This approach enables customized coverage recommendations and optimized outreach strategies (Ngai et al., 2009).

Analytics also improves the evaluation of channel performance. Multitouch attribution models track the customer journey across various touchpoints—email, digital ads, and call centers—and assign value to each interaction. By identifying which channels yield the best return on investment for different segments, insurers can optimize their marketing expenditures and prioritize distribution strategies.

Additionally, chatbots and digital agents, powered by NLP, are increasingly utilized to engage with customers in real time. They provide quotes, answer frequently asked questions, and collect prospect data, all contributing to broader analytics platforms.

CUSTOMER SERVICE: JOURNEY ANALYTICS AND SENTIMENT DETECTION

Customer service has traditionally been reactive, primarily responding to incoming requests or complaints. However, advancements in data analytics now allow for a proactive approach. Customer journey analytics track every interaction across various channels—including web, mobile, call centers, and claims portals—enabling insurers to identify points where customers disengage, areas where they experience difficulties, and gaps in service. These insights improve user experience, interface design, and service delivery workflows (Davenport & Harris, 2007).

Sentiment analysis tools evaluate emails, call transcripts, and chatbot interactions to identify signs of dissatisfaction, urgency, or the risk of customer churn. These insights allow insurers to take immediate action by escalating service issues, offering personalized solutions, or starting retention campaigns. For example, if a customer expresses frustration about delays in claims processing, sentiment algorithms can generate alerts for customer success teams, enabling them to address the issue before it worsens.

Insurers use AI-driven voice analytics during live service calls to assess emotional tone, detect compliance issues, and uncover coaching opportunities for agents. These tools provide real-time suggestions and postcall analysis to enhance service consistency and customer satisfaction.

PRODUCT DEVELOPMENT: BEHAVIOR-BASED AND MODULAR INSURANCE

Analytics has significantly changed how insurers develop and refine their products. Rather than creating static, one-size-fits-all policies, insurers now leverage data to design modular, usage-based, or event-triggered products that cater to individual needs. For instance, in travel insurance, insurers can provide on-demand policies that activate when a customer crosses a geographic boundary, which is detected via GPS. In gig economy insurance, coverage can be turned on or off based on whether the individual is actively working (e.g., delivering, driving, or freelancing) (PwC, 2020).

Consumer analytics—encompassing voice-of-the-customer data and social listening—is crucial in product design. Insurers use this information to identify emerging needs and address dissatisfaction with existing offerings. For instance, as climate anxiety grows and natural disasters become more frequent, there is an increasing demand for parametric products. These products provide automatic payouts triggered by measurable external events, such as earthquakes or hurricanes, instead of relying on traditional claims-based assessments.

Analytics supports A/B testing for product features, pricing structures, and bundling options. By experimenting with different plan designs across digital channels, insurers can identify the combinations that maximize conversions, customer lifetime value, or satisfaction metrics.

REINSURANCE AND CAPITAL MANAGEMENT: PORTFOLIO OPTIMIZATION

Reinsurers and large insurance companies utilize advanced analytics to manage portfolio risk and allocate capital effectively. Catastrophe modeling plays a key role, simulating millions of disaster scenarios and quantifying potential losses across various regions and product lines. These models incorporate historical loss data, meteorological projections, construction metadata, and exposure concentration to estimate probable maximum losses. This process helps insurers assess their reinsurance needs, establish risk appetites, and meet solvency requirements (Swiss Re Institute, 2021).

ML enhances capital allocation decisions by predicting efficiency across product lines, geographic regions, and customer segments. Scenario analysis, stochastic simulations, and stress testing assist insurers in adhering to regulatory capital thresholds while optimizing returns on capital.

DATA GOVERNANCE, REGULATION, AND ETHICS

In an insurance marketplace characterized by rapid digital transformation, the widespread adoption of big data analytics has outpaced traditional governance and ethical practices. While technological tools have advanced quickly, institutional frameworks for responsible data governance—particularly within complex, cross-functional organizations—have often failed to keep pace. This has created a growing divide between technically possible and ethically sound, strategically sustainable, or socially acceptable. To bridge this gap, insurers must take a comprehensive approach to data governance that includes compliance, trust, effective organizational design, and long-term risk management.

THE EXPANDING SCOPE OF DATA GOVERNANCE IN INSURANCE

Modern data governance in the insurance sector goes beyond data quality and system integration concerns. It requires a strategic framework defining roles, responsibilities, standards, and processes for collecting, classifying, protecting, and utilizing data. As insurers gather and act on data from diverse sources, such as customer behavior, third-party APIs, real-time sensors, and social media platforms, the scope of governance must adapt to ensure interoperability, accountability, and traceability on a large scale.

A robust data governance framework typically includes:

- Data ownership and stewardship models that assign responsibility for specific datasets, enabling accountability and escalation mechanisms
- Data catalogs and dictionaries that standardize terminology across the enterprise, reducing misinterpretation in cross-departmental initiatives
- Access controls and usage policies that delineate how data may be used by internal teams, contractors, and automated systems
- Lineage tracking tools that record how data moves, transforms, and is used to produce model outputs or business decisions

These capabilities are fundamental for insurers handling sensitive policyholder data, product-specific regulatory requirements, and essential pricing or reserving models. Furthermore, governance frameworks must be flexible and designed to adapt as technologies, regulations, and consumer expectations change.

ETHICAL IMPLICATIONS OF PREDICTIVE AND BEHAVIORAL DATA

Ethics becomes particularly important when insurers move from evaluating traditional risk factors like age or occupation to modeling behaviors using real-time and often invasive data sources. Tools like telematics, wearables, and smartphone sensors provide powerful means to customize policies for individuals, but they also bring up significant concerns regarding autonomy, fairness, and surveillance.

For example, consider an auto insurer that uses telematics to reward low-risk drivers with discounts. Does this mean that night-shift workers, who drive during "high-risk" hours due to their job, might be penalized for circumstances beyond their control? Similarly, if a health insurer encourages wearable fitness trackers, how will it handle those who opt out because of privacy concerns or health limitations? These examples highlight an important issue: when analytics prioritize statistical outcomes, they may fail to consider fairness, intent, or the complexities of individual situations (Barocas & Selbst, 2016).

Predictive analytics has the potential to reinforce historical inequities. When data reflects past biases, such as those found in underwriting decisions, marketing strategies, or claims approvals, it can perpetuate these biases in algorithmic form. Without careful design and oversight, this may result in unjust discrimination disguised as statistical efficiency. As a result, insurers should prioritize algorithmic fairness auditing as an essential governance function, assessing how their models perform across various demographic and socioeconomic groups.

MODEL GOVERNANCE AS A RISK CONTROL FUNCTION

Model governance is increasingly seen as a part of operational risk management. As predictive models and AI tools are used more for essential business functions, such as underwriting automation, fraud detection, and pricing optimization, they become vital to the company's control environment. A model that consistently misclassifies customers, underestimates risk, or wrongly denies legitimate claims can lead to regulatory penalties, legal action, or damage to the company's reputation.

Best practices in model governance include:

- Clear approval and documentation protocols for model deployment, including version history, assumptions, and limitations
- Validation and backtesting regimes that compare model predictions to real outcomes, flagging drift or unexpected behavior
- Sensitivity and scenario testing to identify failure points, edge cases, or unintended consequences
- Ongoing performance monitoring with automated alerts for anomalies or degrading accuracy

Insurers need to adopt these practices for actuarial models and ML and AI systems, which can evolve in response to new data. Unlike static models, ML systems can change their behavior over time, creating new challenges in documentation, reproducibility, and explainability. Therefore governance frameworks must include model lifecycle management that tracks not just the development of these models but also their deployment, feedback loops, and the impact of decisions made using these models.

CROSS-FUNCTIONAL ETHICS COMMITTEES AND ESCALATION PROTOCOLS

Ethical governance is most effective when integrated into cross-functional decision-making. Leading insurance companies are forming AI ethics committees or data ethics boards that include stakeholders from various departments, such as analytics, legal, compliance, marketing, risk management, and consumer advocacy. These committees evaluate high-impact models, data partnerships, and customer-facing analytics programs using an ethical perspective, assessing risks related to privacy invasion, ambiguous consent, and social equity implications.

These organizations often conduct prelaunch ethical impact assessments and structured reviews similar to privacy impact assessments or red-teaming exercises used in cybersecurity. When ethical concerns emerge, such as customer backlash against dynamic pricing models or controversial data usage, formal escalation protocols offer governance channels for addressing, adjusting, or withdrawing the affected practices.

By institutionalizing ethical deliberation, insurers advance from simply complying with regulations to proactively designing ethics, ensuring that their analytics programs align not only with legal requirements but also with stakeholder values and social responsibility.

TRUST AS A STRATEGIC ASSET

Trust is becoming increasingly important in the data economy. Consumers are now more aware of how their data is used and are more skeptical of decisions made by opaque automated systems. A single high-profile incident, such as an AI system denying coverage based on misunderstood data, can damage brand reputation and lead to regulatory scrutiny.

Insurance companies that excel in data ethics are establishing trust as a key competitive advantage. Transparent data practices, clear opt-in options, user-friendly consent management tools, and the ability to explain decisions in straightforward language are now essential for success. Research indicates that consumers are more inclined to share their data when they understand how it will be used and believe it will be used to benefit them fairly (Acquisti, Brandimarte, & Loewenstein, 2015).

As the analytics landscape changes, the most successful insurers will be those who combine advanced analytical techniques with ethical considerations. They will not only focus on what their models can predict but also on what they should predict, along with how those predictions are viewed, managed, and explained. By taking these factors into account, they can strengthen customer relationships, avoid regulatory pitfalls, and cultivate organizational cultures that promote innovation with integrity.

ORGANIZATIONAL STRATEGY AND DATA-DRIVEN CULTURE

The value of big data in insurance goes beyond just technology or analytics platforms; it lies in an organization's ability to integrate data-driven thinking into its strategy, structure, and culture. Although many insurers have invested significantly in analytics capabilities, few have achieved widespread transformation across the enterprise. The gap between potential and actual performance often results from organizational inertia, siloed thinking, or a misalignment between analytics functions and business objectives. Organizations need a clear strategic commitment, visionary leadership, and cultural changes at all levels to become a truly data-driven insurer.

STRATEGIC ALIGNMENT: FROM ANALYTICS AS A PROJECT TO ANALYTICS AS A CORE CAPABILITY

In many organizations, data initiatives often start as isolated projects, such as marketing pilots, dashboards for finance, or predictive models for claims. While these efforts may lead to short-term successes, they frequently struggle to scale or to influence the overall enterprise strategy. Analytics needs to evolve from a supporting role into a core strategic capability embedded throughout the entire value chain to create a lasting impact.

This shift starts with leadership. Senior executives must position data as a strategic asset and view analytics as a driver of innovation, rather than just a tool for efficiency. The CEO and the C-suite should regularly review analytics outcomes alongside financial metrics, integrating data insights into strategic planning, performance management, and investment decisions. When data and analytics are limited to back-office or IT functions, they often struggle to influence high-level direction and do not attract the necessary resources and attention to scale effectively (LaValle et al., 2011).

Achieving strategic alignment involves establishing clear value outcomes for analytics. Whether the objective is to improve underwriting accuracy, reduce fraud losses, enhance customer experience, or accelerate product innovation, analytics initiatives must be linked to measurable business goals. These objectives should be documented in KPIs and monitored through data governance frameworks to ensure accountability and promote continuous improvement.

BUILDING CROSS-FUNCTIONAL COLLABORATION

A common barrier to achieving analytics maturity is the presence of organizational silos. In traditional insurance companies, actuaries, underwriters, marketers, and claims professionals often work in isolation, resulting in limited data sharing and collaboration. Analytics can help break down these barriers by introducing shared data models, enterprise platforms, and customer-centric insights across different departments.

Insurers must build cross-functional collaboration into their operating models to capitalize on these opportunities. This can take several forms:

- Analytics centers of excellence: Central teams that house data scientists, data engineers, and analytics translators, offering services and tools to business units
- Federated analytics models: Each department maintains its embedded analytics team while aligning with enterprise standards and platforms
- Cross-functional squads or pods: Agile teams composed of analytics and business staff, codeveloping use cases and ensuring rapid iteration

Effective collaboration requires a shared language. Business users must grasp fundamental analytics concepts, such as model performance metrics and data hierarchies. Meanwhile, data professionals must understand the operational realities and constraints specific to the insurance industry. This mutual understanding can be fostered through shared training programs, team colocation, and cross-training initiatives that enhance empathy and fluency across different domains (Mayer-Schönberger & Cukier, 2013).

EMPOWERING TALENT AND UPSKILLING THE WORKFORCE

No analytics strategy can succeed without the right talent. However, the insurance industry continually struggles to attract and retain data scientists, engineers, and analytics leaders. This challenge is partly due to competition from tech firms and startups and partly to the perception of insurance as risk averse or slow moving.

Insurers must prioritize the development of a modern data workforce by recruiting new talent and upskilling current employees. This requires establishing clear career paths for data roles, providing incentives for skill enhancement, and supporting certifications in ML, data engineering, and data visualization. Equally important is the need to train nontechnical staff—including underwriters, adjusters, and product managers—in data literacy. This training will empower them to interpret dashboards, query datasets, and effectively collaborate with analytics teams (Harris, 2012).

A commitment to talent involves empowering frontline decision-makers with the right tools and autonomy. Advanced analytics should be accessible beyond specialized teams and support real-time decision-making throughout the organization. This necessitates deploying user-friendly tools, integrating models into core systems, and assuring that the outputs are interpretable, trustworthy, and aligned with business workflows.

ESTABLISHING A DATA-DRIVEN CULTURE

One of the most challenging yet crucial aspects of transforming into a data-driven organization is cultural change. To embrace analytics, organizations must cultivate a mindset of curiosity, promote evidence-based decision-making, and encourage openness to experimentation. These cultural attributes often conflict with traditional insurance practices, which have typically prioritized personal judgment, historical precedent, and a conservative approach to regulation.

Leadership is essential in promoting data-driven behavior. When executives ask questions based on data, share dashboards during town hall meetings, and celebrate successful analytics initiatives, they communicate the importance of data. Incentive structures should reward evidence-based thinking rather than relying solely on intuition or seniority. Additionally, analytics teams should be recognized for their contributions to business outcomes, not just for the technical complexity of their work.

Fostering a culture focused on learning also involves accepting failure and the need for iteration. Analytics projects typically entail uncertainty, experimentation, and the need for adjustments. Organizations must recognize that not every model will yield perfect results and that refinement is a natural part of the process. Implementing agile methodologies, rapid prototyping, and feedback loops can help instill this mindset and alleviate the fear of making mistakes.

Data culture is founded on trust—in the data, the systems, and the people who utilize them. Insurers must prioritize data accuracy, model explainability, and ethical safeguards to establish this trust. Employees must be confident that analytics will enhance their roles rather than replace them, and that insights will be used to improve outcomes instead of being used for micromanagement or punishment.

Creating a data-driven culture and strategy is not just a technical transformation; it also involves significant changes in human behavior and organizational structure. Success in this area requires alignment among leadership, governance, talent, and values. When executed effectively, it allows insurers to fully leverage the power of big data, not merely as a predictive tool but as a catalyst for agility, innovation, and a customer-centric approach.

CHALLENGES IN BIG DATA ADOPTION

While big data offers significant potential for the insurance industry, its adoption is not without challenges. Many insurers are torn between the desire to become data driven and the reality of outdated infrastructure, cultural resistance, talent shortages, and regulatory constraints. Transitioning from traditional actuarial models and isolated data warehouses to real-time analytics ecosystems and AI-driven decision-making presents numerous technical, organizational, and ethical hurdles. Understanding and addressing these challenges is crucial to fully realizing the benefits of significant data initiatives and avoiding expensive mistakes.

LEGACY SYSTEMS AND INTEGRATION COMPLEXITY

One of the most significant barriers to the adoption of big data is the presence of legacy IT systems. Many insurance companies, especially those with long histories, rely on mainframe architectures, siloed databases, and monolithic core systems not designed to meet the speed, scale, or flexibility required by modern analytics platforms. These outdated systems often store data in incompatible formats, lack real-time processing capabilities, and require manual intervention for basic reporting tasks.

Integrating big data tools, such as data lakes, streaming analytics platforms, and ML environments, with legacy systems can be technically complex and resource intensive. Data often needs to be extracted, transformed, and loaded through custom-built pipelines, which increases operational risks and maintenance overhead. Additionally, some core systems may not support API integrations or metadata tagging, limiting the accessibility and interpretability of the underlying data. Organizations typically require a phased modernization strategy that balances innovation with business continuity, regulatory compliance, and cost control to address these challenges.

DATA SILOS AND FRAGMENTED OWNERSHIP

Insurers encounter not only technical fragmentation within their systems but also organizational silos that hinder data flow and harmonization. Business units—including claims, underwriting, marketing, and finance—often collect and manage data independently, using varying definitions, formats, and access controls. These silos create challenges in building a unified view of customers, developing company-wide models, and extracting insights from cross-functional datasets.

Even when central data platforms are implemented, the absence of clear data ownership and stewardship can lead to inconsistent standards, duplicated efforts, and unresolved data quality issues. For instance, a customer's name and contact details may appear differently across various systems, resulting in mismatched records, communication errors, or inaccurate risk assessments. Therefore establishing robust data governance—with defined roles, shared taxonomies, and accountability for stewardship—is crucial to overcoming these structural challenges.

TALENT SHORTAGES AND SKILL GAPS

Successful implementation of significant data initiatives depends on a specialized workforce with expertise in statistics, computer science, business analytics, and insurance industry knowledge. However, attracting and retaining this talent is a significant challenge for many insurance companies. Data scientists and data engineers are in high demand across various industries, and the insurance sector is often perceived, whether justly or unjustly, as a less dynamic or technologically advanced career option compared to fintech, healthtech, or consumer tech industries.

Even when data professionals are successfully recruited, skill mismatches among existing staff can hinder project execution. For example, actuaries may not have experience with unstructured data or cloud-native tools, while underwriters may be unfamiliar with predictive modeling concepts. Additionally, business leaders may struggle to interpret data visualizations or ask the right analytical questions. To bridge these gaps, organizations must invest in ongoing training, encourage cross-disciplinary collaboration, and create incentives that reward continuous learning and experimentation.

DATA QUALITY AND TRUSTWORTHINESS

As insurers gather data from a broader range of diverse and decentralized sources, such as IoT devices, third-party vendors, and user-generated content, the risk of poor data quality increases significantly. Incomplete, outdated, or inconsistent data can harm model performance, distort insights, and introduce unintended bias into decision-making processes. For instance, if telematics data is lost or corrupted due to a device malfunction, a driver may be unfairly penalized in a UBI program.

The lack of transparency in data provenance, especially regarding external vendors or purchased datasets, can result in compliance issues and undermine stakeholder confidence. Without clear documentation outlining how data was collected, validated, and labeled, insurers may find it difficult to explain or defend their analytics-driven decisions, particularly under regulatory scrutiny. To build trust in the analytic process, it is essential to establish data quality benchmarks, implement lineage tracking tools, and maintain regular auditing protocols.

ETHICAL AMBIGUITY AND REPUTATIONAL RISK

Advanced analytics in the insurance industry often involves ethical dilemmas, particularly when algorithms impact pricing, eligibility, or claims processing. Customers might not realize that their behavioral data is being used to evaluate their risk, or they may feel uneasy about the level of surveillance that comes from real-time tracking or analysis of social media. Even if predictions are technically accurate, they can provoke adverse reactions if they seem unfair, opaque, or dehumanizing (Zuboff, 2019).

For instance, if an ML model identifies a higher risk among individuals from specific neighborhoods, based on proxy variables related to socioeconomic status, this could result in a disparate impact or accusations of digital redlining. While such outcomes may not necessarily violate written laws, they can harm a company's reputation, trigger regulatory investigations, and diminish customer trust. Therefore ethics and fairness should be integrated into the design and implementation of analytics programs, along with clear pathways for addressing emerging concerns.

RESISTANCE TO CHANGE AND CULTURAL INERTIA

Even in organizations that acknowledge the strategic importance of big data, cultural resistance can hinder its adoption. Employees may worry that automation will make their jobs obsolete or that data-driven performance monitoring will result in micromanagement. Managers used to making decisions based on intuition or experience might see analytics as an intrusion or a threat to their authority. These subtle and informal cultural dynamics can significantly slow down or undermine transformation efforts.

Effective change management is essential to overcome inertia in adopting big data practices. Leaders must communicate the purpose and value of these initiatives. They should provide training and support while involving staff in developing analytics tools to ensure usability and foster buy-in. Achieving quick wins and demonstrating business value, such as creating a model to reduce fraud or speeding up quote turnaround, can help build momentum and validate the effort.

Adopting big data in the insurance industry presents both human and strategic challenges and technical ones. Although the tools and technologies are becoming increasingly advanced, achieving success requires a comprehensive approach incorporating system modernization, governance, talent development, and ethical considerations. Organizations that recognize and proactively address these challenges with foresight and humility will be in a much better position to harness the full potential of data-driven innovation in today's competitive and regulated environment.

THE FUTURE OF DATA ANALYTICS IN INSURANCE

The insurance industry is evolving from a traditionally conservative, actuarial-based system into a dynamic, real-time ecosystem focused on digital risk assessment. Data analytics is becoming increasingly vital for competitive differentiation and operational resilience as this shift occurs.

In the future, the role of data analytics in insurance will be shaped not only by new technologies but also by how insurers manage to balance innovation with ethical responsibility, regulatory compliance, and customer trust. Several transformative trends are expected to influence the next decade of analytics in the insurance sector.

REAL-TIME ANALYTICS AND EVENT-DRIVEN DECISION-MAKING

One of the most significant changes on the horizon is the transition from historical analysis to real-time, event-driven analytics. As insurers begin to integrate streaming data from telematics devices, connected homes, wearable health monitors, and innovative commercial equipment, the ability to assess and respond to risk immediately becomes a strategic necessity.

Real-time underwriting could adjust premiums dynamically based on driving behavior, physical activity, or environmental conditions. Sensor data could trigger claims automatically, like a burst pipe alert from a smart home system, initiating preemptive damage mitigation services even before a customer files a report. These use cases require real-time data ingestion and low-latency analytics pipelines, edge computing capabilities, and intelligent automation frameworks that can scale and adapt as events unfold.

Insurers that develop these capabilities will transition from reactive service models to proactive risk partners, able to predict and prevent losses instead of merely indemnifying them.

EXPLAINABLE ARTIFICIAL INTELLIGENCE AND TRUSTWORTHY MODELING

As ML models are increasingly integrated into essential insurance functions, such as pricing, claims assessment, and fraud detection, there is growing demand for greater transparency and explainability in the decision-making processes driven by algorithms. Regulators, customers, and internal stakeholders are all pushing for this clarity. As a result, we are seeing the emergence of a new generation of tools and techniques designed for XAI.

Future analytics platforms are expected to incorporate built-in model interpretability features. This will enable business users to understand the outcomes of a model and grasp the reasoning behind those outcomes. Techniques such as Shapley Additive Explanations values, Local Interpretable Model-Agnostic Explanations, and counterfactual analysis will likely become standard elements in analytics workflows. These advancements will assist insurers in meeting regulatory requirements and defending their decisions in legal or reputational situations.

We are expected to see a greater focus on algorithmic fairness auditing, where models are regularly assessed for bias, disparate impact, and unintended consequences. Insurers that excel in this area will minimize regulatory risks and gain a competitive edge through ethical branding and increased consumer trust.

FEDERATED LEARNING AND PRIVACY-PRESERVING ANALYTICS

To address growing data privacy concerns and stricter regulations, the future of analytics will increasingly adopt privacy-preserving technologies, such as federated learning, differential privacy, and homomorphic encryption.

Federated learning enables insurers to develop ML models using decentralized datasets, such as those owned by partner organizations, reinsurers, or international subsidiaries, without transferring or centralizing the underlying data. This approach fosters collaborative innovation while reducing data leakage and compliance risks.

Differential privacy adds mathematical noise to analytical outputs, safeguarding individual identities even within aggregated datasets. Homomorphic encryption, while still computationally intensive, has the potential to enable insurers to analyze encrypted data without the need for decryption. This advancement could allow for secure analytics in sensitive health or life insurance areas.

These innovations will enable insurers to balance personalization and privacy, allowing for detailed insights while maintaining ethical standards and regulatory compliance.

HYPERPERSONALIZATION AND PRODUCT INNOVATION

With more detailed behavioral data and advanced segmentation algorithms, the future of insurance products will be hyperpersonalized, modular, and based on usage.

Instead of fixed annual policies, insurers will increasingly provide real-time coverage that adjusts according to the insured individual's behavior, preferences, and context.

Think about auto insurance that deactivates when the vehicle is parked, or travel insurance that only activates during a confirmed trip. Health plans driven by wearable technology might adjust premiums according to weekly fitness trends. Additionally, cyber insurance could modify coverage based on the current security status of a commercial client's network.

These innovations will be driven by predictive analytics, dynamic pricing engines, and real-time behavioral modeling. Customer-facing applications will support them with transparency, incentives, and self-service options. The underwriting process will become invisible to consumers, seamlessly integrated into digital experiences across retail, employment, travel, and lifestyle platforms.

ARTIFICIAL INTELLIGENCE–ENHANCED CLAIMS AND FRAUD MANAGEMENT

In the claims process, AI will take on a more autonomous role, shifting claims from simply a documentation task to a verification process. Visual AI will evaluate vehicle or property damage through photos and videos submitted by customers. NLP systems will analyze customer statements, while geospatial analytics will verify the environmental context of the loss.

Integrating blockchain technology can improve fraud prevention by creating immutable, time-stamped records of transactions, policy conditions, and claims history. This approach provides a shared source of truth among insurers, customers, and regulators. As a result, it can reduce cycle times, enhance customer satisfaction, and lower loss adjustment expenses, particularly in high-volume sectors like auto and home insurance.

Future claims models will be self-learning, continually updating based on actual outcomes, behavior patterns, and recognized fraud typologies. Additionally, they will be adaptive, capable of escalating complex cases to human adjusters while handling routine claims entirely through automation.

CONVERGENCE WITH ENVIRONMENTAL AND SOCIAL RISK MODELING

As climate change, demographic shifts, and economic instability transform the risk landscape, future analytics capabilities must incorporate environmental, social, and macroeconomic data into traditional actuarial models. Factors like wildfire risk, coastal flooding, pandemics, and migration trends will become essential elements of underwriting and reinsurance strategies.

Advanced geospatial analytics, remote sensing technologies, and scenario simulation platforms enable insurers to assess their exposure to climate events at a detailed parcel level. Additionally, analyzing social media sentiment and monitoring public policy will help insurers anticipate regulatory and consumer behavior changes. These capabilities will drive insurers to shift from assessing individual-level risks to forecasting system-level risks, where the resilience of their portfolios depends on comprehending interconnected vulnerabilities.

EVOLVING ROLES AND NEW ORGANIZATIONAL MODELS

The future of data analytics will transform the internal structure of insurance organizations. We can expect to see a blending of roles among actuaries, data scientists, product designers, and IT professionals. Cross-functional teams will work together, sharing responsibility for analytics' development, deployment, and governance.

The chief data officer's role is expected to broaden in scope and influence, transforming into a strategic advisor to the CEO and the board on issues such as data monetization and regulatory technology. Model governance committees will establish formal oversight of AI-driven decision-making systems, while ethical review boards will play a significant role in product development and vendor evaluation.

The most advanced insurance companies will adopt analytics-as-a-platform models. This approach will equip internal users with self-service tools, reusable data assets, and model marketplaces that help reduce time to value and foster experimentation. The key pillars of analytics maturity will be speed, scalability, and trust in this environment.

The future of data analytics in insurance goes beyond making better predictions; it transforms how insurers think, operate, and create value. It involves integrating data into the very core of the organization while managing a world that is increasingly uncertain, complex, and ethically challenging. Insurers that successfully lead this transformation will excel in traditional metrics and shape the future of insurance in a digitally connected society.

CONCLUSION AND KEY TAKEAWAYS

The transformation of the insurance industry through big data and analytics is not just a theoretical concept but a present and rapidly evolving reality. Insurers use data to change how they approach various aspects of their business, including underwriting practices, claims handling automation, and personalizing customer experiences. By leveraging data, companies fundamentally redefine how they measure, price, and manage risk. However, the effectiveness of these powerful tools and technologies relies on organizations using them wisely, ethically, and strategically.

This chapter emphasizes that data analytics in insurance is no longer limited to actuaries or IT departments; rather, it is an essential capability across the entire organization. This capability spans various areas, including operations, strategy, customer engagement, regulatory compliance, and product design. To thrive in this evolving landscape, insurers must align their analytics efforts with business objectives, modernize their infrastructure, and cultivate a culture prioritizing evidence-based decision-making.

Strong data governance has been a recurring theme throughout this discussion. As insurers manage larger volumes of sensitive and diverse data, ensuring quality, transparency, and traceability becomes foundational for operational effectiveness and building trust with regulators and customers. Ethical concerns, especially regarding algorithmic fairness and behavioral surveillance, highlight the necessity for thoughtful model governance and a commitment to responsible innovation.

We also explored the changing role of actuarial science, which is evolving alongside new data science methodologies. Rather than being replaced, actuaries are increasingly collaborating with ML professionals. They bring their extensive domain knowledge and expertise in risk calibration to hybrid models that achieve a balance between accuracy and interpretability.

To successfully adopt analytics, organizations must make structural and cultural changes. Leadership must actively support a transformation toward data-driven decision-making. It is also essential to prioritize the development of talent and to break down silos between departments, encouraging collaboration around shared data and customer-focused goals. Organizations that establish agile, cross-functional analytics environments will be better equipped to take advantage of new opportunities and respond to external challenges.

Data analytics is not simply a technological upgrade but a profound shift in how insurers understand risk, create value, and serve society. As the industry moves into this new era, the challenge is not just to build more powerful models but to use them wisely, with clarity, fairness, and foresight.

AI DISCLOSURE

During the preparation of this work the author(s) used Grammarly to improve readability and correct any grammatical mistakes. After using this tool/service, the author(s) reviewed and edited the content as needed and take(s) full responsibility for the content of the publication.

REFERENCES

Acquisti, A., Brandimarte, L., & Loewenstein, G. (2015). Privacy and human behavior in the age of information. *Science*, *347*(6221), 509–514. https://doi.org/10.1126/science.aaa1465.

Antonio, K., & Plat, R. (2014). Micro-level stochastic loss reserving for general insurance. *Scandinavian Actuarial Journal*, *2014*(7), 649–669. https://doi.org/10.1080/03461238.2012.759424.

Baig, M. M., GholamHosseini, H., & Connolly, M. J. (2013). A comprehensive survey of wearable and wireless medical sensor systems. *Sensors, 13*(5), 5740–5797. https://doi.org/10.3390/s130505740.

Barocas, S., & Selbst, A. D. (2016). Big data's disparate impact. *California Law Review*, *104*(3), 671–732. https://doi.org/10.2139/ssrn.2477899.

Bertsimas, D., & Kallus, N. (2020). From predictive to prescriptive analytics. *Management Science*, *66*(3), 1025–1044. https://doi.org/10.1287/mnsc.2018.3253.

Brynjolfsson, E., & McAfee, A. (2014). The second machine age: Work, progress, and prosperity in a time of brilliant technologies. W. W. Norton & Company.

Casualty Actuarial Society (CAS). (2020). CAS continuing education policy and emerging issues in actuarial science. Casualty Actuarial Society. https://www.casact.org/education.

Chen, H., Chiang, R. H. L., & Storey, V. C. (2012). Business intelligence and analytics: From big data to big impact. *MIS Quarterly*, *36*(4), 1165–1188. https://doi.org/10.2307/41703503.

Davenport, T. H., & Harris, J. G. (2007). *Competing on analytics: The new science of winning*. Harvard Business Review Press.

Ernst & Young (EY). (2021). How insurers can accelerate digital transformation and build resilience. EY Global. https://www.ey.com/en_gl/insurance/how-insurers-can-accelerate-digital-transformation-and-build-resilience.

Frees, E. W., Derrig, R. A., & Meyers, G. (2014). *Predictive modeling applications in actuarial science: Volume 1, Predictive Modeling Techniques*. Cambridge University Press.

Harris, J. G. (2012). Data-driven talent: Creating the analytics capability. *Journal of Business Strategy*, *33*(3), 20–28. https://doi.org/10.1108/02756661211224954.

He, W., Zhang, Z., & Huang, Y. (2019). Modeling telematics data to assess driving behavior in usage-based insurance. *Transportation Research Record*, *2673*(3), 240–250. https://doi.org/10.1177/0361198119828073.

Henckaerts, R. J., Antonio, K., & Verbelen, R. (2022). Boosting insights into loss reserving: A machine learning approach. *Insurance: Mathematics and Economics*, *102*, 30–45. https://doi.org/10.1016/j.insmatheco.2021.12.005.

James, G., Witten, D., Hastie, T., & Tibshirani, R. (2013). *An introduction to statistical learning: With applications in R*. Springer.

Kousky, C., & Kunreuther, H. (2020). Addressing affordability in the National Flood Insurance Program. *Journal of Extreme Events*, *7*(1). https://doi.org/10.1142/S2345737620500014.

Kuhn, M., & Johnson, K. (2013). *Applied predictive modeling*. Springer.

Kunreuther, H., & Michel-Kerjan, E. (2009). At war with the weather: Managing large-scale risks in a new era of catastrophes. https://mitpress.mit.edu/9780262514090/at-war-with-the-weather/.

LaValle, S., Lesser, E., Shockley, R., Hopkins, M. S., & Kruschwitz, N. (2011). Big data, analytics, and the path from insights to value. *MIT Sloan Management Review*, *52*(2), 21–32.

Litman, T. (2015). Evaluating vehicle travel reduction strategies. *Transportation Research Record: Journal of the Transportation Research Board*, *2531*, 14–22. https://doi.org/10.3141/2531–02.

Mayer-Schönberger, V., & Cukier, K. (2013). *Big data: A revolution that will transform how we live, work, and think*. Houghton Mifflin Harcourt.

McKinsey & Company. (2018). Insurance 2030: The impact of AI on the future of insurance. McKinsey & Company. https://www.mckinsey.com/industries/financial-services/our-insights/insurance-2030-the-impact-of-ai-on-the-future-of-insurance.

Monaghan, J. (2000). Casualty Actuarial Society Forum, Winter (2000), 87–139.

Ngai, E. W. T., Xiu, L., & Chau, D. C. K. (2009). Application of data mining techniques in customer relationship management: A literature review and classification. *Expert Systems with Applications*, *36*(2), 2592–2602. https://doi.org/10.1016/j.eswa.2008.02.021.

Pasquale, F. (2015). The Black Box Society: The secret algorithms that control money and information. Harvard University Press.

PricewaterhouseCoopers. (2020). Top insurance industry issues in 2020. https://www.pwc.com/us/en/industries/financial-services/library/top-insurance-industry-issues.html.

Richman, R. (2021). Data science in insurance: Where actuaries fit in. *The Actuary*. https://theactuarymagazine.org.

Surminski, S. (2014). The role of insurance in reducing direct risk: The case of flood insurance. *International Review of Environmental and Resource Economics, 7*(3–4), 241–278.

Swiss Re Institute. (2021). *Natural catastrophes in 2020: Secondary perils in the spotlight*. Swiss Re. https://www.swissre.com/institute.

Viaene, S., Derrig, R. A., Baesens, B., & Dedene, G. (2002). A comparison of state-of-the-art classification techniques for expert automobile insurance claim fraud detection. *Journal of Risk and Insurance*, *69*(3), 373–421. https://doi.org/10.1111/1539-6975.00030.

Wachter, S., Mittelstadt, B., & Russell, C. (2018). Counterfactual explanations without opening the black box: Automated decisions and the GDPR. *Harvard Journal of Law & Technology*, *31*(2), 841–887.

Wüthrich, M. V. (2020). Bias detection and mitigation in insurance pricing. *European Actuarial Journal*, *10*(2), 481–504. https://doi.org/10.1007/s13385-020-00240-0.

Zuboff, S. (2019). *The age of surveillance capitalism: The fight for a human future at the new frontier of power*. PublicAffairs.

CHAPTER

Artificial intelligence and machine learning in insurance

4

CHAPTER OUTLINE

Insurance Technology. DOI: https://doi.org/10.1016/B978-0-443-43972-8.00014-6

INTRODUCTION TO MACHINE LEARNING IN INSURANCE

Machine learning (ML) fundamentally transforms how industries utilize data, automate decisions, and navigate uncertainty, with particularly significant implications for the insurance sector. As insurers encounter increasing pressure to provide personalized services, assess risk in real time, and minimize operational costs, ML presents the tools necessary to move beyond traditional statistical modeling and adopt a data-driven approach to intelligent automation. Specifically, ML empowers insurers to derive insights from structured and unstructured data, uncover complex patterns without explicit programming, and generate real-time predictions at scale (Jordan & Mitchell, 2015).

ML is a branch of artificial intelligence (AI) that enables systems to learn from experience and improve their performance over time based on data without explicitly reprogramming. The key principle of ML is generalization, which allows an algorithm to identify patterns and make predictions about new, unseen data based on insights gained from previous examples (Hastie et al., 2009). This generalization ability distinguishes ML from traditional rule-based systems and actuarial methods, which depend on predefined assumptions and explicit formulations.

ML has proven effective in addressing various specific challenges in the insurance industry. These include identifying potentially fraudulent claims, segmenting customers for underwriting and marketing, predicting the severity of claims, optimizing pricing strategies, and automating routine tasks like document classification and chatbot-assisted claims intake (Crosman, 2017). The true value of ML lies not just in improving efficiency but also in its adaptability—its ability to evolve as new data becomes available continuously. This adaptability is essential in markets subject to dynamic risks such as climate change, telematics, cyber threats, and shifts in consumer behavior.

The shift toward ML in the insurance industry is primarily driven by the massive increase in the volume and variety of available data. While traditional insurance models have primarily relied on structured, tabular data—such as age, location, and vehicle type—modern ML models can utilize multiple data sources. These sources include text (e.g., claims narratives), images (such as photos of vehicle or property damage), sensor outputs (from telematics or wearable devices), and geospatial information. This transformation has been supported by the overall growth of big data infrastructure, advancements in cloud computing, and access to powerful open-source ML libraries like Scikit-learn, TensorFlow, and PyTorch.

The increasing use of ML in the insurance industry reflects significant changes in understanding risk and value. Traditional actuarial modeling is still crucial for setting rates and managing capital but has typically been linear, generalized, and heavily reliant on assumptions. This approach often simplifies complex data, leading to a potential underestimation of uncertainty and a failure to capture subtle interactions within the data. In contrast, ML excels in high-dimensional, nonlinear environments, allowing it to uncover hidden relationships and learn from sparse signals (Bishop, 2006). For instance, instead of assuming that claims frequency is solely related to age or ZIP code, ML models may identify nonlinear effects or interactions that provide a more accurate assessment of individual-level risk.

While ML offers many benefits, it is not a cure all. In the insurance industry—characterized by regulatory oversight, ethical standards, and trust-based relationships—models must be interpretable, auditable, and fair. There are valid concerns about algorithmic bias, data privacy, and overfitting, especially with complex models like deep neural networks. Therefore integrating ML into insurance requires careful consideration of data science, industry knowledge, and risk governance.

This chapter provides an in-depth exploration of ML within the context of insurance technology. It begins by laying out the mathematical foundations of ML, which include linear algebra, calculus, probability, and optimization. Next, it presents the most commonly used ML techniques, covering both supervised and unsupervised learning and emerging areas such as reinforcement learning (RL) and deep learning.

We will then delve into feature engineering, model evaluation, and performance validation. We will also discuss interpretability and explainability, which are crucial for regulatory compliance and model governance.

Lastly, we will examine real-world applications of ML in claims processing, underwriting, marketing, and risk assessment. The chapter will conclude by evaluating emerging trends, limitations, and ethical challenges that will likely influence the future of ML in the insurance industry.

MATHEMATICAL FOUNDATIONS OF MACHINE LEARNING

Understanding ML involves more than just being familiar with algorithms or software libraries; it requires a solid understanding of the mathematical principles that underpin learning systems. These principles provide the foundation for how models interpret data, reduce errors, generalize to new examples, and achieve optimal performance. This section will explore four key mathematical domains essential to ML: linear algebra, calculus, probability and statistics, and optimization theory. We will focus on the foundational theory and the practical applications of these tools in insurance analytics and modeling.

LINEAR ALGEBRA: REPRESENTING AND TRANSFORMING DATA

Data is at the core of every ML model, and linear algebra serves as the framework for understanding it. Data points are typically represented as vectors, while datasets can be viewed as matrices. In this context, each row corresponds to an observation (such as a customer or policy), and each column represents a feature (such as age, income, or vehicle type).

In linear regression, the fundamental equation is:

$$y = X\beta + \epsilon$$

where:

- y is the outcome vector (e.g., claims amount).
- X is the design matrix of features (e.g., customer data).
- β are the coefficients to be estimated.
- ϵ is the error term.

Matrix operations such as transpose, inverse, and dot product are used to solve for β, often using the normal equation:

$$\beta = (X^T X) - {}^1X^T y$$

Linear algebra is crucial in dimensionality reduction techniques such as principal component analysis (PCA). In PCA, eigenvectors and eigenvalues are utilized to identify the directions of maximum variance, allowing data to be projected into a lower-dimensional space. This is particularly important in the insurance industry, where models may incorporate hundreds of risk variables.

CALCULUS: LEARNING THROUGH OPTIMIZATION

Calculus, especially differential calculus, is essential in training ML models. Many learning algorithms focus on minimizing a loss function, quantifying the discrepancy between a model's predictions and the actual outcomes. For example, a commonly used loss function in linear regression is the mean squared error (MSE).

$$L(\beta) = 1/n\sum i = \ln(yi - y^\wedge i)^2$$

To minimize this function, we calculate its gradient, which indicates the direction in which the function increases most rapidly. The opposite direction represents where the loss decreases—this is the path taken during gradient descent, a key optimization strategy.

Gradient descent updates parameters iteratively:

$$\theta_{t+1} = \theta_t - \eta\nabla_\theta L(\theta)$$

where:

θ are the model parameters (e.g., weights in a neural network).

η is the learning rate.

$\nabla_\theta L$ is the gradient of the loss concerning the parameters.

In deep learning, backpropagation uses the chain rule of calculus to calculate gradients through the layers of a neural network.

PROBABILITY AND STATISTICS: MODELING UNCERTAINTY

Insurance fundamentally involves managing uncertainty, with probability theory offering a framework for modeling this uncertainty. ML heavily relies on probabilistic reasoning, which is crucial for understanding data distributions and modeling predictions.

In supervised learning, we often model the conditional probability:

$$P(y|x)$$

which represents the likelihood of an outcome y (e.g., claims = yes/no) given features x (e.g., age, policy duration, prior claims).

Probabilistic models include:

- Naive Bayes, which applies Bayes' theorem assuming feature independence
- Logistic regression, which models:

$$P(y = 1|x) = 1/1 + e^{-x^{T}\beta}$$

Insurance applications also make use of the following:

- Poisson regression for claims frequency modeling
- Gamma distributions for modeling claims severity
- Bayesian inference for credibility theory and updating beliefs in dynamic settings

These tools play a crucial role in model calibration and performance evaluation, especially for assessing the likelihood of rare events like catastrophic claims or fraud.

OPTIMIZATION: FINDING THE BEST MODEL

Optimization serves as the mathematical backbone of learning. Whether minimizing error in linear regression or maximizing the margin in support vector machines (SVMs), ML fundamentally revolves around optimization problems.

Key concepts include:

- Objective function: What the model seeks to minimize or maximize (e.g., loss function)
- Constraints: Conditions that must be satisfied (e.g., nonnegative weights)
- Convexity: A property of functions that ensures a single global minimum

Stochastic gradient descent (SGD) is a commonly used algorithm for training large-scale models. Unlike traditional gradient descent, which computes gradients using the entire dataset, SGD updates weights using small random batches of data, thereby enhancing computational efficiency.

Regularization is an important optimization technique to prevent overfitting by adding a penalty term to the objective function.

- L1 regularization (Lasso) adds $\lambda\sum|\beta i|$ encouraging sparsity.
- L2 regularization (Ridge) adds $\lambda\sum\beta i^2$, shrinking weights toward zero.

These techniques are particularly beneficial for high-dimensional insurance data, where models may include dozens or hundreds of variables, many of which could be redundant or have weak predictive power.

CONNECTING MATHEMATICS TO INSURANCE PRACTICE

These mathematical foundations play a crucial role in how insurers build, interpret, and implement ML models. For example:

- Linear algebra enables insurers to preprocess and model complex, multivariate datasets.
- Calculus and optimization support the iterative refinement of pricing and claims models.
- Probability theory forms the basis of risk modeling, capital reserve estimation, and catastrophe forecasting.
- Regularization and loss minimization ensure that models generalize well and comply with regulatory standards for solvency and capital adequacy.

Together, these disciplines facilitate the design of predictive, scalable, and auditable models that enhance modern underwriting, claims analysis, customer engagement, and risk segmentation.

KEY MACHINE LEARNING ALGORITHMS AND TECHNIQUES

At the core of ML are algorithms that identify patterns from data to make predictions or reveal structures. These algorithms can be broadly classified into several categories: supervised, unsupervised, semisupervised, reinforcement, and deep learning methods. Each category is designed for specific problems and is based on mathematical principles that affect how models are trained, optimized, and interpreted.

This section introduces the most commonly used ML algorithms in various categories, explains their functioning, and emphasizes their practical applications in insurance, including claims analytics, customer segmentation, underwriting, and fraud detection.

SUPERVISED LEARNING

Supervised learning is the most widely used type of ML in the insurance industry. It involves training a model on labeled data, where the input features and the output target variables are known.

Linear regression models a linear relationship between input features x and a continuous output variable y. Its form is:

$$y = x^T\beta + \epsilon$$

The coefficients β are estimated by minimizing the MSE. In the insurance industrv, linear regression is frequently utilized to predict claims amounts, customer lifetime value, or premium elasticity.

Logistic regression models the probability that an outcome belongs to a specific class. It is commonly used for binary classification problems such as fraud detection:

$$P(y = 1|x) = 1/1 + e^{-x\top\beta P}$$

The model is trained using maximum likelihood estimation, and regularization techniques (either L1 or L2) are often employed to prevent overfitting.

A decision tree organizes data by recursively splitting it based on the values of different features to make predictions. For instance, in a claims adjuster model, the tree might split the data by accident type, severity, and the number of prior claims. The algorithm chooses splits that minimize impurity, using metrics like the Gini index or information gain. Note: Decision trees are interpretable and useful in underwriting but prone to overfitting.

A random forest is a collection of decision trees, each trained on a bootstrap sample with a selection of features chosen at random. Final predictions are determined by a majority vote in the case of classification or by averaging for regression tasks. Random forests are resilient to noise and frequently outperform individual models, particularly in high-dimensional insurance data, such as customer segmentation or predicting the risk of multiple claims.

SVMs identify the hyperplane that optimally separates data points into different classes by maximizing the margin between them. For nonlinear problems, kernel methods, such as radial basis function or polynomial kernels, are utilized to project data into higher-dimensional spaces.

SVMs are used in insurance for early fraud detection and risk classification but are less interpretable than tree-based methods.

UNSUPERVISED LEARNING

Unsupervised learning identifies patterns in data without labeled outputs, making it valuable for exploratory analytics and segmentation tasks.

K-means clustering divides observations into k-clusters by minimizing the within-cluster sum of squares. It is utilized to identify customer segments based on attributes like policy tenure, claims frequency, and coverage type.

The algorithm:

1 Initializes k-centroids
2 Assigns each point to the nearest centroid
3 Updates centroids as the mean of assigned points
4 Repeats until convergence

Hierarchical clustering creates a dendrogram of nested clusters without defining the number of clusters beforehand. It effectively identifies natural groupings in data, such as regional claims behaviors or correlated product preferences.

PCA is a technique for reducing dimensionality. It transforms correlated variables into a smaller set of uncorrelated principal components. PCA identifies the directions, called eigenvectors, along which the data varies the most. In insurance, PCA reduces feature space in high-dimensional models, such as telematics data or text analysis of claims narratives.

SEMISUPERVISED AND REINFORCEMENT LEARNING

In semisupervised learning, models are trained using a small amount of labeled data alongside a large volume of unlabeled data. This approach is particularly beneficial in the insurance sector, where labeled data, such as confirmed fraud cases, is often limited, while unlabeled transaction data are abundant.

RL is a learning method by interacting with an environment to maximize cumulative rewards. It is an emerging area in the insurance sector, particularly for dynamic pricing and portfolio optimization.

Markov decision processes consists of:

- States (e.g., customer status)
- Actions (e.g., offer retention discount)
- Rewards (e.g., premium collected)
- Transition probabilities

The goal is to learn a policy that maximizes expected rewards over time.

Q-learning is a model-free RL algorithm that learns the value of action-state pairs. It updates a value function iteratively.

$$Q(s,a) \leftarrow Q(s,a) + \alpha[r + \gamma \max a' \, Q(s',a') - Q(s,a)]$$

Q-learning can be applied to adjust claims-handling workflows dynamically or optimize multipolicy retention offers.

DEEP LEARNING

Deep learning involves neural networks with several layers that can learn complex, high-dimensional representations. These models require substantial datasets and are computationally intensive, but they provide state-of-the-art performance across various domains.

Feedforward neural networks (FNNs) are the simplest type of neural network. Each neuron calculates a weighted sum of its inputs, applies a nonlinear activation function (such as rectified linear unit or sigmoid), and transmits the result to the next layer. The backpropagation algorithm is employed to update the weights using gradient descent.

FNNs are utilized in various applications, including pricing, fraud detection, and loss prediction, where the relationships between features are complex.

Convolutional neural networks (CNNs) are primarily used for image data. CNNs apply filters to detect patterns like edges or shapes. In insurance, they are used for:

- Damage assessment from car/property images
- Aerial imagery analysis for disaster exposure

Recurrent neural networks (RNNs) are designed for sequence data (e.g., time series). They maintain a memory of past inputs. Long short-term memory networks, a type of RNN, are used for:

- Forecasting claims over time
- Customer interaction modeling

Transformers were initially developed for natural language processing (NLP); transformers (e.g., Bidirectional Encoder Representations from Transformer [BERT], Generative Pretrained Transformer [GPT]) are now being applied to insurance for analyzing:

- Claims narratives
- Customer service transcripts
- Policy documents

They use attention mechanisms to capture relationships between all words in a sentence, enabling accurate document classification and summarization.

Autoencoders reduce data to low-dimensional representations and can detect anomalies (e.g., in claims). Generative adversarial networks (GANs) can synthesize new data for scenario testing and augmentation.

CHOOSING THE RIGHT TECHNIQUE IN INSURANCE CONTEXTS

The problem type, data availability, model interpretability, and regulatory constraints influence the choice of algorithm. For example:

- Logistic regression is popular because of its simplicity and ease of interpretation.

- Random forests and gradient boosting provide impressive performance on tabular data, often requiring minimal preprocessing.
- Neural networks and transformers are gaining traction in claims image analysis and document classification, where the complexity of the data warrants their advanced capabilities.

In the insurance industry, an ML model's success is determined by its accuracy and how well it aligns with business goals, the quality of data it utilizes, its interpretability, and its adherence to compliance requirements.

DATA PREPROCESSING AND FEATURE ENGINEERING

ML models are only as effective as the quality of the data they are based on. Before training an algorithm, collecting, cleaning, transforming, and structuring the data is crucial to enhance the model's ability to learn meaningful patterns. In the insurance industry—where datasets are frequently large, fragmented, and contain sensitive information—data preprocessing and feature engineering are essential steps that significantly influence the success or failure of a predictive model.

This section outlines essential techniques for preparing insurance data for modeling, addressing both statistical and domain-specific challenges. We also present strategies for engineering features that improve model performance and interpretability.

DATA COLLECTION AND INTEGRATION IN INSURANCE

Insurance data comes from various sources, both internal and external. Internally, insurers collect data from policy applications, claims reports, billing systems, and customer service interactions. Externally, they may utilize:

- Third-party data vendors (e.g., credit scores, vehicle reports)
- Geospatial and environmental datasets (e.g., flood zones, weather)
- Internet of Things (IoT) and telematics devices (e.g., driving behavior sensors)
- Public databases (e.g., court records, demographics)

A typical insurance dataset includes:

- Structured data: Numerical/categorical fields (e.g., premium, deductible, zip code)
- Unstructured data: Free-text claims narratives, images, PDF forms
- Time-series data: Policy renewals, payment history, telematics logs

Effective ML starts by consolidating various sources into a unified analytical dataset, where each row represents an entity (such as a policyholder or a claims), and the columns represent features.

HANDLING MISSING DATA

Missing data commonly occurs in insurance due to incomplete forms, system migrations, or inconsistent reporting. Strategies for managing missing values include:

- Deletion: Removing rows or columns with excessive missingness. This can introduce bias if not handled carefully.
- Imputation.
- Mean/median imputation for numerical variables.
- Mode imputation for categorical features.
- Predictive imputation using models like k-nearest neighbors or regression.
- Missing-indicator method: Adding a binary feature indicating whether a value is missing.

In insurance datasets, missing values are often informative. For example, a missing driver's license number may correlate with fraudulent activity. Thus missing values should be viewed as gaps and potential signals.

OUTLIER DETECTION AND TREATMENT

Outliers can distort model training, especially in models sensitive to distance metrics (e.g., k-nearest neighbors, SVMs). Common sources of outliers in insurance include:

- Catastrophic losses (e.g., large fire claims)
- Fraudulent entries (e.g., inflated vehicle damage)
- Data entry errors

Detection methods include:

- Z-scores: Standardize features and flag values beyond a threshold (e.g., ± 3).
- Interquartile range method: Identify values outside 1.5× the interquartile range.
- Model-based approaches: Use clustering or isolation forests to detect anomalies.

Sometimes, outliers should be capped (winsorized) or transformed using logarithmic scales, especially for heavily skewed loss distributions.

DATA NORMALIZATION AND SCALING

Many ML algorithms assume that data features are on similar scales. Normalization ensures that each feature contributes proportionally to the model's objective function.

Common techniques:

- Min-Max Scaling: Transforms features to a [0, 1] range
- Z-Score Standardization: Centers features around zero with unit variance
- Log Transformation: Compresses long-tailed distributions, often used for claims amounts

Normalization is essential for distance-based algorithms and neural networks, where features on different scales can lead to unstable convergence.

ENCODING CATEGORICAL VARIABLES

Insurance data often includes various categorical variables, such as policy type, region, and vehicle make. To train models effectively, these categories must be converted into numerical formats.

Here are some common encoding methods:

- One-hot encoding: This method creates binary columns for each category, representing the presence or absence of a category.
- Ordinal encoding: This method assigns integers to ordered categories. For example, vehicle usage can be encoded as personal (0), commercial (1), and fleet (2), reflecting their hierarchy.
- Frequency or target encoding: This approach replaces categories with their occurrence frequency or average target value. It benefits high-cardinality features, such as zip or product codes.

When utilizing tree-based models like random forests or XGBoost, one-hot encoding is often unnecessary, as these algorithms can handle categorical splits natively.

FEATURE SELECTION TECHNIQUES

Not all features in a dataset provide the same level of information. Feature selection is a crucial process that helps reduce noise, improve model performance, and enhance interpretability. There are several techniques for feature selection:

- Filter methods: These methods use statistical criteria—such as correlation or mutual information—to select the most informative features.
- Wrapper methods: These techniques evaluate model performance based on different subsets of features. An example of this is recursive feature elimination.
- Embedded methods: These methods perform feature selection during the model training process. One example is Lasso regression, which applies a penalty to irrelevant variables.

In the insurance industry, reducing the feature set is particularly beneficial for regulatory reporting and internal audits, where it is essential for models to be easily explainable.

FEATURE ENGINEERING IN INSURANCE APPLICATIONS

Feature engineering is the process of creating new and informative variables from raw data. This step is crucial for determining the effectiveness of a model, especially in complex domains like insurance, where relationships can be nuanced. Here are some examples of engineered features:

- Ratios: Claims-to-premium ratio, loss frequency per policy year
- Temporal variables: Time since the last claims, seasonal risk of events (e.g., storm risk during hurricane season)
- Geospatial features: Distance to the coast, urban versus rural classification, flood zone indicators
- Interaction terms: Combining features to capture nonlinear effects (e.g., age multiplied by vehicle type)

Modern tools such as feature stores, automated feature extraction libraries, and domain-specific transformations (like the International Organization for Standardization symbols and exposure modifiers) are increasingly becoming vital in actuarial and pricing workflows.

PRACTICAL CONSIDERATIONS AND PITFALLS

While preprocessing and feature engineering can be powerful tools, there are several pitfalls to avoid:

- Data leakage: This occurs when information about the target variable inadvertently appears in the input features. For example, using claims payouts to predict claims severity can lead to skewed results.
- Overengineering: Creating an excessive number of features can lead to overfitting, where the model performs well on training data but poorly on unseen data. This can also create issues with interpretability.
- Misaligned granularity: Combining data at different levels of detail, such as claims-level and policy-level data, without appropriate aggregation can lead to misleading insights.

Effective data preprocessing requires a blend of domain expertise, statistical rigor, and careful validation. It is essential to ensure that the features improve predictive power while also adhering to business logic and regulatory compliance.

MODEL EVALUATION AND VALIDATION TECHNIQUES

After training an ML model, the next crucial step is to evaluate its performance, not only on the training data but also on new, unseen data that reflects real-world scenarios. Without thorough validation, models may experience overfitting (performing well on training data but poorly in production) or underfitting (failing to grasp the underlying patterns in the data).

In the insurance industry, where models often assist with pricing, risk segmentation, or regulatory reporting, model validation must be both quantitatively robust and operationally dependable. This section introduces common evaluation metrics, validation strategies, and practical considerations specific to insurance contexts.

TRAIN-TEST SPLIT AND CROSS-VALIDATION

The first step in model evaluation is separating the available data into different subsets:

- Training set: Used to fit the model
- Validation set (optional): Used for tuning hyperparameters
- Test set: Used to estimate out-of-sample performance

A typical allocation might assign 60%–70% of the data for training, while the remaining portion is set aside for testing. This division can introduce variance due to sampling randomness, particularly in smaller datasets.

To address this, various cross-validation techniques are employed:

- k-Fold cross-validation: The dataset is divided into k-folds. The model is trained n times, with each fold being used once as the validation set while the remaining folds are used for training. The average performance across all folds is then taken as the evaluation score.
- Stratified k-Fold: This method ensures that each fold maintains the same class distribution as the entire dataset, which is especially beneficial for imbalanced datasets, such as those used in fraud detection.
- Leave-one-out cross-validation: This is an extreme form of cross-validation where each individual observation is used once as a test set while the remaining observations form the training set. While this method can provide very accurate results, it is also computationally intensive.

Cross-validation is commonly used for tuning hyperparameters in algorithms such as XGBoost, logistic regression (with regularization), and SVMs.

CLASSIFICATION METRICS

Classification metrics are applicable when the target variable is categorical (e.g., fraud = yes or no, policy renewal = yes or no).

Accuracy or the proportion of correct predictions:

$$\text{Accuracy} = (\text{TP} + \text{TN})/(\text{TP} + \text{TN} + \text{FP} + \text{FN})$$

However, accuracy can be misleading in imbalanced datasets (e.g., 98% accuracy when 98% of claims are legitimate).

Precision: Of all predicted positives, how many were correct?

$$\text{Precision} = \text{TP}/(\text{TP} + \text{FP})$$

Recall (Sensitivity): Of all actual positives, how many did we correctly identify?

$$\text{Recall} = \text{TP}/(\text{TP} + \text{FN})$$

F1 score is the harmonic mean of precision and recall:

$$F1 = 2 \cdot (\text{precision} \cdot \text{recall})/(\text{precision} + \text{recall})$$

A confusion matrix is a 2×2 table that displays true and false positives and negatives, providing a comprehensive overview of model performance.

The receiver operating characteristic (ROC) curve graphs the true positive rate against the false positive rate at various thresholds. The area under the curve quantifies performance, where a value of 1.0 indicates perfect accuracy and 0.5 suggests random guessing. In the context of insurance fraud detection or churn prediction, precision-recall curves are often more insightful than ROC curves, particularly due to class imbalance issues.

REGRESSION METRICS

Regression metrics are used when predicting continuous values (e.g., claims amount, premium, customer lifetime value).

Mean absolute error (MAE):

$$\text{MAE} = \ln \sum i = \ln |yi - y\text{^}i|$$

MSE:

$$\text{MSE} = \ln \sum i = \ln |yi - y\text{^}i|^2$$

Root mean squared error (RMSE): Warning is more sensitive to large errors.

$$\text{RMSE} = \text{SqRt(MSE)}$$

R^2 (coefficient of determination): Proportion of variance explained by the model.

In actuarial models for severity or pricing, Gini coefficients and lift charts are used to measure performance ranking and assess business impact.

MODEL CALIBRATION AND RELIABILITY

High prediction accuracy does not always indicate that a model's probabilities are trustworthy. It is crucial to have well-calibrated models in risk-sensitive fields such as insurance.

For example, if a model predicts a 20% claims probability, then about 20 out of 100 such cases should actually result in claims. Miscalibration can lead to:

- Underpricing or overpricing of policies
- Misallocation of capital reserves
- Poor customer experience due to false expectations

Calibration techniques include:

- Platt scaling (logistic regression applied to model scores)
- Isotonic regression (nonparametric calibration)
- Reliability diagrams (visual calibration assessment)

Calibration plays a crucial role in regulatory frameworks such as Solvency II and IFRS 17.

OVERFITTING, UNDERFITTING, AND MODEL ROBUSTNESS

A central objective of validation is to identify and reduce overfitting, which occurs when a model performs well on training data but struggles to generalize to new, unseen data.

- Overfitting: High accuracy on training data but poor accuracy on test data
- Underfitting: Low accuracy on both training and test data
- Ideal scenario: High performance on both datasets, demonstrating stable generalization

Techniques to manage overfitting:

- Regularization (L1, L2 penalties)
- Cross-validation
- Early stopping in neural networks
- Ensemble methods (e.g., bagging, boosting)
- Simplifying the model by reducing parameters or features

Model robustness is tested by:

- Evaluating out-of-time samples (e.g., future policy year)
- Stress testing with synthetic edge cases (e.g., very large claims)
- Examining sensitivity to missing or erroneous data

STATISTICAL SIGNIFICANCE AND CONFIDENCE INTERVALS

In regulated insurance environments, simply reporting performance metrics is not sufficient; insurers must also show that any improvements are statistically significant. To achieve this, they can use several methods:

- Hypothesis tests: Models can be compared using paired t-tests or nonparametric alternatives, such as the Wilcox test.
- Bootstrapping: This involves repeated sampling to create confidence intervals around the metrics.
- Model stability Checks: This tests models across multiple folds, time slices, or subgroups to ensure that results are consistent.

For instance, an insurer might demonstrate that a new claims model reduces MAE by 10%, with a 95% confidence interval of (8%, 12%). This provides a statistically robust justification for implementation.

Model validation is a critical process that combines technical necessity with business importance. In the insurance industry, where decisions can significantly influence profitability, regulatory compliance, and consumer trust, evaluation frameworks need to merge statistical precision with industry expertise. A well-validated model is one that not only shows strong performance on historical data but also adapts, provides explanations, and scales effectively in response to changing risk environments.

INTERPRETABILITY AND EXPLAINABILITY IN MACHINE LEARNING

As ML becomes increasingly integrated into the insurance industry, the issue of interpretability—understanding how and why a model reaches specific predictions—has shifted from a technical detail to a crucial business requirement. In a field built on trust, accountability, and regulation, opaque or "black-box" models pose significant challenges. Whether in underwriting, pricing, claims processing, or fraud detection, various stakeholders—including regulators, actuaries, customers, and company executives—are all seeking answers to a fundamental question: Why did the model make this decision?

Interpretability in ML refers to how easily a human can understand the inner workings of a model or its results. Some models, such as linear regression, logistic regression, and decision trees, are inherently transparent. In contrast, many of the most powerful models in modern ML—like random forests, gradient boosting machines, and deep neural networks—are often considered "black boxes." While these models can capture complex, nonlinear relationships in data and offer high predictive performance, their internal logic is usually difficult or impossible for end users to comprehend.

This disconnect presents risks for insurers. In pricing, regulators may require clear justifications for differences in premiums to ensure that rate setting is nondiscriminatory and based on sound actuarial principles. Customers may appeal decisions in claims processing and expect meaningful explanations for claims denial or reduced payouts. In underwriting, fairness and transparency are crucial when applications are declined or policy conditions are changed. In all of these situations, a lack of clarity can undermine trust, delay regulatory approvals, and expose insurers to legal issues or reputational damage.

To address this issue, the field of explainable AI (XAI) has rapidly developed, providing tools and frameworks designed to clarify complex models. These approaches can be divided into two main categories: interpretable-by-design models and post hoc explanation methods.

The first category includes models specifically designed for transparency, such as generalized additive models or monotonic gradient boosting machines, where the effects of different features are clearly defined and easy to visualize. The second category comprises techniques that explain the behavior of black-box models after the fact, offering approximations or insights into the model's operations without revealing every internal calculation.

One of the most widely used techniques for post hoc explanations is Shapley Additive Explanations (SHAP). Derived from cooperative game theory, SHAP assigns an importance value to each feature involved in a prediction, indicating how much that feature contributed to the outcome. For example, in a claims severity model, SHAP may reveal that a claimant's driving history increased the predicted payout by $1,200, while the low vehicle value decreased it by $300. These explanations are local, meaning they are specific to an individual prediction, but they can also be aggregated to gain insights into the overall behavior of the model across an entire portfolio. The strength of SHAP lies in its theoretical consistency and its ability to provide both the direction and magnitude of feature effects.

Another widely used method for interpreting ML models is Local Interpretable Model-Agnostic Explanations (LIME). This technique creates a simple, interpretable model around a specific prediction, such as linear regression. By making small changes to the input data and observing how the black-box model responds, LIME approximates the local decision boundary and highlights the most influential features in that specific case. This can be particularly useful for underwriters or claims adjusters who want to understand the reasoning behind decisions made for particular customers or claims. However, it is important to note that because LIME relies on random sampling and model simplification, it may be less stable and faithful compared to SHAP when it comes to explaining highly nonlinear models.

In addition to local explanation methods, global interpretability tools help stakeholders understand the overall structure of a model. Commonly used tools include feature importance charts, partial dependence plots (PDPs), and individual conditional expectation (ICE) plots. These tools illustrate how features influence predictions across the entire dataset. For example, a PDP may show that the predicted probability of churn increases sharply after a policyholder receives a third rate increase within 2 years. ICE plots offer more detailed insight by demonstrating how this effect varies among different customers.

While these techniques are useful, they do have limitations. They often depend on assumptions that may not be accurate when dealing with correlated insurance data, and they do not provide true interpretability. Additionally, as regulatory scrutiny increases, relying on post hoc tools may not be adequate to justify decisions, especially in sensitive areas like life insurance underwriting or auto pricing. Regulators are paying closer attention to how models handle sensitive variables and are requiring formal documentation showing how models are tested for bias, validated for stability, and designed to ensure fairness.

Regulatory frameworks such as the European Union's General Data Protection Regulation (GDPR) and the US Equal Credit Opportunity Act are converging around a key principle: individuals affected by algorithmic decisions should be able to understand and, when necessary, challenge those decisions. In response to this principle, many insurers are adopting governance practices incorporating explainability into the model development process. This includes creating model documentation, often referred to as "model factsheets," conducting regular audits, and maintaining internal model risk management teams responsible for reviewing, approving, and monitoring all production models.

In this broader governance framework, explainability is no longer merely a technical feature; it has become an essential aspect of risk management. Business units are increasingly interested in interpretable models. Underwriters need to trust the scores provided by predictive engines, while claims adjusters require clear logic for triage decisions. Executives must understand how ML impacts the customer experience. Moreover, customers demand transparency, especially in situations involving significant financial consequences. Simply stating, "The algorithm said so," is not only insufficient; it is unacceptable when explaining a premium increase or a claims denial.

As ML systems become increasingly integrated into insurance operations, the demand for clarity will only rise. A new wave of techniques is emerging to address this need, including interpretable neural networks, monotonic boosting frameworks, and fairness-aware modeling libraries. At the same time, insurers are adapting traditional modeling methods to enhance their flexibility and expressiveness, ensuring that predictive power does not compromise transparency.

Explainability is not just a technical requirement; it is a fundamental pillar for the ethical, legal, and commercial viability of ML in the insurance industry. By making complex systems understandable, insurers can ensure compliance, build trust, and develop models that not only perform well but also align with their core mission of protecting individuals in times of need.

MACHINE LEARNING APPLICATIONS IN INSURANCE

ML has quickly transitioned from being a proof of concept to becoming a key component in the insurance industry. It is being utilized across various areas, including underwriting, claims management, fraud detection, and marketing. By leveraging ML, insurers can extract valuable insights from complex datasets, automate decision-making processes, and tailor customer experiences. This section will delve into how insurers implement ML throughout their operations, featuring real-world examples and emerging use cases.

CLAIMS MANAGEMENT AND FRAUD DETECTION

Claims Prediction and Triage

One of the most impactful applications of ML is in claims prediction—forecasting claims frequency, severity, and potential litigation early in the process.

ML models can:

- Predict the likelihood of a claim following a quote or incident report.
- Classify claims by complexity to prioritize adjuster assignments.
- Forecast total incurred losses, aiding reserve estimation and capital planning.

For example, models that have been trained on historical claims data—such as information about claimants' demographics, types of claims, and details of incidents—can predict whether a new claim will result in settlement costs exceeding

$25,000. These predictions assist in efficiently allocating resources, automating the handling of low-severity claims, and identifying cases that need specialist review.

FRAUD DETECTION

Insurance fraud costs the US industry approximately $40–$60 billion each year. Traditional rule-based systems often struggle to identify new or subtle patterns of fraud.

ML enhances fraud detection by:

- Identifying anomalies using unsupervised learning or autoencoders
- Clustering suspicious claims into investigation queues
- Detecting synthetic identities in life and auto insurance applications
- Monitoring provider behavior in health insurance for upcoding or ghost billing

Supervised models, such as gradient boosting machines and neural networks, can be trained on labeled fraud cases and integrated into real-time workflows to flag suspicious activity as it happens. Importantly, XAI techniques (see the above section) are employed to provide justifications for alerts and to help prevent false accusations.

UNDERWRITING AND RISK ASSESSMENT

Traditionally, underwriters depended on actuarial tables and established rules. ML facilitates predictive underwriting, allowing models to simultaneously assess applicant risk based on numerous variables.

Applications include:

- Auto insurance: Using telematics data to predict crash risk based on driving patterns
- Property insurance: Modeling fire risk using satellite imagery, vegetation indexes, and building characteristics
- Life insurance: Predicting mortality using wearable data, lifestyle indicators, and electronic health records

By dynamically adjusting risk scores, ML enables underwriters to provide personalized pricing and facilitate streamlined approvals, particularly in direct-to-consumer channels.

GEOSPATIAL RISK MODELING

Insurers increasingly use satellite data, geolocation services, and Geographic Information System layers to assess climate-related and environmental risks:

- Predicting flood, hail, and wildfire exposure at the parcel level
- Monitoring property change over time via aerial imagery
- Incorporating real-time weather feeds into catastrophe response

ML facilitates the creation of composite risk scores and regularly updated hazard maps, which are particularly valuable for underwriting in high-risk areas or emerging markets.

CUSTOMER SEGMENTATION AND PERSONALIZATION

ML enables insurers to identify customer segments based on behavior and values rather than just broad demographic groups.

Using clustering and unsupervised learning, insurers can group customers based on:

- Product mix and purchase behavior
- Channel preference (digital vs. agent based)
- Risk tolerance and responsiveness to incentives
- Claim behavior and policy utilization

These segments help facilitate targeted communication, retention efforts, and modeling of customer lifetime value.

CHURN PREDICTION

ML is especially effective at predicting policyholder churn. Classification models can determine which customers are likely to lapse or switch carriers based on:

- Premium increases
- Claims history
- Service interactions
- Competitor marketing exposure

By understanding the factors that lead to customer churn, insurers can provide targeted retention offers, such as discounts and bundling, to the appropriate customers at the optimal time.

PRICING AND RATING MODELS

ML can enhance rating sophistication by:

- Modeling nonlinear interactions between variables (e.g., driver age × vehicle type)
- Incorporating external data like credit scores, traffic patterns, or lifestyle indicators
- Using advanced regression and tree-based models to improve generalized linear model–based pricing structures

For instance, rather than assuming a fixed increase in risk per year as vehicles age, a gradient-boosting model might uncover specific thresholds where the risk rises sharply (e.g., after 7 years), which can inform tiered pricing strategies.

It is crucial that pricing models adhere to actuarial fairness and regulatory requirements. Consequently, insurers frequently combine ML-driven segmentation with transparent base rate structures and interpretable modeling frameworks.

MARKETING, SALES, AND CUSTOMER ACQUISITION

ML is used throughout the insurance marketing funnel to:

- Score leads based on conversion probability
- Personalize email campaigns or website content using recommendation systems
- Allocate digital advertising budgets dynamically across platforms
- Optimize agent–customer matching in hybrid distribution models

Predictive modeling identifies each segment's most effective marketing channels and messages, thereby reducing customer acquisition costs and increasing conversion rates.

Embedded insurance models, such as travel or e-commerce insurance, use ML to identify context-sensitive offers, including weather-triggered coverage suggestions or event-based activation, like during wildfire season.

AUTOMATION IN CLAIMS AND POLICY SERVICING

ML also powers operational automation, especially in customer service and claims:

- NLP is used to extract structured data from:
  - Claims forms
  - Email/text communications
  - Call center transcripts
- Chatbots and virtual assistants, trained on historical support interactions, resolve common customer queries (e.g., "When will my claim be paid?").
- Document classification models route incoming documents to appropriate systems (e.g., medical records vs. police reports).
- Image recognition models assess vehicle damage from photos or videos and estimate repair costs.

This allows insurers to automate low-complexity claims and reduce turnaround time from days to minutes, improving both efficiency and customer satisfaction.

ACTUARIAL, FINANCIAL, AND RESERVING APPLICATIONS

Actuaries are now using ML to:

- Forecast claims development using time series and survival models
- Estimate incurred-but-not-reported claims via ensemble methods
- Simulate capital adequacy scenarios using stochastic ML models
- Support IFRS 17 and Solvency II compliance with granular claim–level projections

ML is not replacing actuarial judgment; rather, it is enhancing traditional tools with new methods to identify emerging risks, tail events, and complex dependencies.

CASE STUDIES

CASE STUDY: LEMONADE (UNITED STATES)

Lemonade is frequently regarded as a prototypical example of an "InsurTech-native" company—one that has integrated AI into almost every core function from the very beginning. Primarily focusing on renters, homeowners, and pet insurance, Lemonade has disrupted the traditional insurance model by utilizing deep learning, behavioral science, and automation to provide a faster and more responsive insurance experience.

At the core of its services is a ML-driven underwriting engine that analyzes customer responses during the onboarding process. This engine not only assesses risk but also examines subtle behavioral indicators—such as response time, keystroke patterns, and tone of language—that could suggest potential fraud. These factors are evaluated using NLP and deep learning models that have been trained on millions of anonymized interactions.

When a customer submits a claim, Lemonade's AI-based claims bot, known as "AI Jim," comes into action. The system reviews the claim and cross-references the data with past claims and policy details. If no red flags are raised, it can approve and pay the claim in under 3 minutes, all without human involvement. Behind the scenes, a triage algorithm assesses the legitimacy of the claim using text classifiers, document verification, and even facial recognition when videos are submitted as part of the process. Only claims that are suspicious or complex are directed to human adjusters.

Lemonade's approach showcases how a comprehensive AI architecture can reshape customer expectations, enhance operational efficiency, and generate new data flows. However, it also raises significant concerns regarding transparency, fairness, and regulatory compliance—especially in an environment where explainability and consent are under increasing scrutiny.

CASE STUDY: ALLIANZ (GLOBAL)

Allianz, one of the largest insurance groups in the world, has taken a leading position in using ML to address climate risk—an increasingly important concern for insurers in property and commercial lines. Acknowledging that traditional catastrophe models often depend on broad regional data and static hazard scores, Allianz has invested in creating a proprietary geospatial risk engine that utilizes advanced ML techniques.

This engine combines satellite imagery, weather simulations, urban development data, and historical loss records to assess exposure at a hyperlocal level. Instead of evaluating flood risk at the ZIP code level, the model analyzes specifics such as parcel-level elevation, proximity to waterways, drainage infrastructure, and recent land use changes. ML algorithms trained on this data uncover previously hidden patterns in loss occurrence and severity. This allows underwriters to better differentiate between adjacent properties that may have very different risk profiles.

These insights are incorporated into the workflows of commercial property underwriting, providing underwriters with access to dynamic risk maps and forecasts of climate impacts. For clients, this translates to more accurate pricing, customized coverage options, and in some cases, proactive recommendations for reducing exposure—such as relocating HVAC systems or investing in green roofs.

Allianz's geospatial ML platform illustrates how insurers can transition from reactive coverage to proactive resilience planning, presenting a convincing vision for the role of AI in an era of increasing climate volatility.

CASE STUDY: PROGRESSIVE INSURANCE (UNITED STATES)

Progressive has established itself as a technology-driven insurer, especially known for its adoption of telematics and usage-based insurance. Its flagship program, "Snapshot," collects real-time driving data from policyholders using mobile apps or plug-in devices. This data includes metrics such as acceleration, braking patterns, time of day, and mileage.

Behind the scenes, ML models analyze data to estimate each driver's relative risk profile. This analysis informs individualized premium adjustments. Instead of relying solely on proxies like age or vehicle type, Progressive employs regression models and decision tree ensembles to correlate actual driving behavior with the frequency and severity of claims. This approach enables a more personalized pricing model that rewards safer drivers and provides risk-based incentives for behavioral change.

The Snapshot program enhances customer engagement by incorporating feedback loops. Drivers receive real-time reports and safety tips that encourage them to adopt safer driving habits. Over time, Progressive has developed one of the largest behavioral driving databases in the world, which it continuously analyzes to improve its models and assess risk factors.

Progressive's use of ML is guided by clear regulatory frameworks and includes opt-in consent mechanisms. By blending transparency with innovation, the company has established itself as a leader in behavioral underwriting and real-time risk assessment. This positions Progressive as a trailblazer for other insurers looking to explore mobility-based insurance models.

CASE STUDY: AXA (EUROPE AND ASIA)

AXA has integrated ML into various aspects of its claims and customer service operations, aiming to reduce processing times and enhance consistency. A key innovation is the introduction of an AI-powered virtual assistant that utilizes NLP and computer vision to assist with vehicle and travel claims.

When a customer starts a vehicle claim, they are prompted to upload photographs of the damage through AXA's mobile app. These images are analyzed in real time using CNNs that are trained to identify types of damage, estimate repair costs, and verify the vehicle's identity. The system can detect surface-level damage, such as dents or broken lights, and correlate it with established repair cost ranges based on historical data from repair shops.

AXA's NLP system simultaneously analyzes both written and spoken claims narratives. It extracts structured data elements such as the accident location, time, and any third-party involvement. This automation aids in populating claims forms and also flags inconsistencies that could indicate fraud or need further investigation.

AXA's approach emphasizes the importance of multimodal AI, which integrates ML models that operate across text, images, and structured data sources. This method enhances customer experiences by delivering seamless interactions. Additionally, it shows how traditional insurers can increase automation while ensuring high service quality and adhering to regulatory compliance.

ML is no longer optional—it is foundational to modern insurance. When used responsibly, these models provide benefits such as more accurate pricing, faster service, reduced costs, and a more responsive and personalized customer experience. However, their implementation must be supported by strong governance, transparency, and ethical practices. This ensures that while we harness their predictive capabilities, we also maintain fairness and trust.

CHALLENGES AND LIMITATIONS OF MACHINE LEARNING IN INSURANCE

ML has revolutionized various aspects of insurance operations, but it comes with its own set of limitations. Behind the effectiveness of advanced predictive models are several practical, organizational, ethical, and technical challenges that can hinder their overall effectiveness and, in some cases, their acceptance. As insurers adopt data-driven decision-making, they must recognize the limitations of ML, especially in a highly regulated environment that relies on trust.

One of the most fundamental challenges in ML is ensuring data quality. The effectiveness of ML models relies heavily on the quality of the data used for training. In the insurance industry, data is often scattered across legacy systems, brokers, third parties, and customer self-entry portals, making it notoriously messy. Common issues include incomplete fields, inconsistent coding, and outdated formats. For example, claims narratives can vary significantly in tone and structure depending on the adjuster. Important details, such as the causes of losses, severity of injuries, or customer intentions, may be hidden within unstructured text or images, which require extensive preprocessing. If inaccurate or biased data is fed into a model without proper checks, it can result in flawed predictions that may unintentionally penalize or exclude certain groups.

The issue of model bias is closely related to the use of ML models. These models learn from historical data, which can unintentionally reinforce existing inequalities. For instance, a pricing model based on past underwriting decisions might replicate biases that put minority applicants at a disadvantage—even if variables like race or gender are excluded from consideration. Proxy variables such as zip code, education level, or occupation can still act as indirect indicators of these protected attributes.

This situation poses significant legal and ethical challenges in regions with stringent antidiscrimination laws, like the United States and the European Union. Insurers are, therefore required to conduct fairness audits and implement bias mitigation strategies. However, these fields are still developing, and there are currently no universally accepted standards in place.

Interpretability, as discussed in detail in the previous chapter, presents a significant challenge. While complex models like gradient boosting machines and deep neural networks often achieve higher predictive accuracy, they sacrifice transparency. In regulated industries, particularly in areas like pricing and claims, insurers are required to provide clear explanations for their decisions to both regulators and consumers. If a policyholder is denied coverage or faces a higher premium, they deserve a comprehensible rationale behind that decision. Without such explanations, trust diminishes, and insurers risk violating consumer protection laws. This situation creates a tension between technical performance and ethical responsibility, compelling insurers to find a balance between accuracy and accountability.

Regulatory uncertainty also contributes to the slow adoption of automated decision-making technologies. In many countries, laws related to areas such as data usage, digital contracts, and automated decision-making are still evolving. For instance, under the EU's GDPR, consumers have the right to contest decisions made by algorithms and request a human review. However, the definition of what constitutes a "fully automated decision" remains ambiguous. Similarly, regulators in states like California and New York are examining the use of external data sources, including social media, credit scores, and behavioral data, in pricing models. These uncertainties can make insurers hesitant to implement ML systems that, while innovative, may not align with existing regulatory frameworks.

In addition to legal compliance, organizations face the challenge of adopting ML. This technology requires new skill sets, including data science, software engineering, and statistical modeling, which may not have been present in actuarial or underwriting departments. As a result, there can be a disconnect between technical teams and business stakeholders, hindering implementation. Business leaders might find it difficult to interpret model outputs or may lack confidence in results that cannot be traced back to traditional logic. Therefore effective change management, training, and internal communication are essential for successfully integrating ML into the organization.

One limitation involves scalability and infrastructure. Developing a high-performing model in a controlled, offline environment differs significantly from deploying that model in a real-time, production-grade system. Integrating with policy administration systems, claims management platforms, or customer portals often requires substantial IT investment. Furthermore, once a model is deployed, it must be monitored for performance drift, which occurs when the model's accuracy declines over time due to changes in data distribution. For instance, a claims triage model trained prior to a major regulatory reform or natural disaster may no longer accurately reflect current patterns and may need retraining or recalibration. This necessitates robust monitoring pipelines and data versioning protocols.

Ethical concerns continue to influence the conversation about AI and insurance. Insurers have a long-standing social contract to provide protection during vulnerable times. The use of ML should honor this relationship by promoting fairness, transparency, and empathy. Automated systems that treat customers merely as data points risk dehumanizing the insurance experience. Additionally, as insurers begin to utilize nontraditional data sources—such as wearable devices, smart homes, and telematics—questions arise regarding data ownership, consent, and surveillance. Consumers may not fully understand how their data is used or may feel pressured to share sensitive information in order to receive better pricing. To maintain trust, it is essential to establish clear policies, informed consent mechanisms, and data governance standards.

In summary, although the potential of ML in the insurance industry is significant, its implementation comes with considerable challenges. Key factors such as data quality, fairness, explainability, legal compliance, organizational readiness, and ethical responsibility are essential in determining the success or failure of any ML initiative. Insurers looking to the future must invest not only in technical capabilities but also in building strong frameworks for governance, transparency, and stakeholder engagement. As ML becomes an integral part of the insurance sector, its long-term impact will rely not only on the accuracy of model predictions but also on the responsibility with which these models are designed, deployed, and maintained.

EMERGING TRENDS AND INNOVATIONS IN INSURANCE MACHINE LEARNING

As ML becomes more established in the insurance industry, a wave of new technologies and research frontiers is expanding the possibilities in risk modeling, customer interactions, and operational efficiency. Current applications, such as predictive underwriting and claims triage, have already demonstrated measurable value. However, the most transformative impacts may still be ahead. Innovations in automation, privacy-preserving analytics, real-time data processing, and hybrid modeling architectures are reshaping the landscape and creating new strategic opportunities for insurers.

One of the most significant developments in technology is the rise of automated ML or AutoML. AutoML platforms are designed to make data science more accessible by automating many of the time-consuming and technically complex steps involved in model development. These steps include feature selection, algorithm selection, hyperparameter tuning, and performance validation.

For insurers, AutoML serves as a powerful tool, enabling business analysts and actuaries to prototype predictive models quickly without requiring advanced programming skills. Additionally, it allows data science teams to accelerate the deployment of models while ensuring consistency and quality.

Companies like H2O.ai, DataRobot, and Amazon SageMaker now provide enterprise-ready AutoML tools, some of which are integrated into underwriting and customer analytics workflows. These systems not only enhance efficiency but also promote reproducibility and thorough documentation, making them particularly well suited for regulated environments.

There is a growing interest in federated learning, which is an approach to train ML models collaboratively across multiple organizations or data sources without sharing raw data. This method is particularly appealing in the insurance industry, where privacy regulations, competitive concerns, and fragmented data ownership often prevent insurers from pooling their datasets.

With federated learning, models are trained locally on each dataset, and only the learned model parameters are shared with a central server. This process allows for collaboration between companies, such as insurers and reinsurers or insurers and healthcare providers, without compromising data privacy.

Additionally, federated learning opens up opportunities for industry-wide insights on rare or emerging risks—such as cyber threats or pandemic patterns—where any single firm may lack enough data to develop a robust model on its own.

The rapid growth of real-time data from sensors, telematics, and connected devices is leading to the development of dynamic, context-aware models. These models can update predictions based on live data feeds, making risk assessments more responsive and personalized. For instance, a car insurance model could adjust a driver's risk score daily based on actual driving behavior, which is captured by a mobile app or onboard device. Similarly, property insurers are exploring IoT-enabled smoke detectors, water sensors, and environmental monitors that continuously provide feedback on risk exposure. These data streams facilitate usage-based pricing, event-triggered alerts, and proactive risk mitigation strategies. To implement such models, insurers need low-latency architectures and edge-computing capabilities. However, the benefits are significant, as this allows insurers to transition from reactive claims handling to preventive service models that reduce losses' severity.

An important area of advancement is the integration of NLP with insurance operations. While NLP has already been utilized in applications like chatbots and document classification, recent developments in large language models—such as BERT, GPT, and specialized transformer architectures—are now enabling the accurate analysis of complex insurance texts. This includes underwriting guidelines, claims narratives, legal contracts, and regulatory filings, which can be processed at scale to extract insights, identify inconsistencies, or generate summaries.

Some insurers are implementing NLP to develop "smart assistants" for underwriters and adjusters. These tools help surface relevant policy rules or similar historical cases during the decision-making process. Additionally, others are exploring the use of conversational AI for customer support, implementing systems that can handle multiturn dialogues and only escalate more complex queries to human agents.

As language models become increasingly powerful, it is essential to focus on model safety, prompt engineering, and bias mitigation. However, the potential productivity gains from these innovations are substantial.

The increasing availability of synthetic data is noteworthy. Synthetic datasets, which are generated using techniques like GANs, enable insurers to simulate new policyholder behaviors, loss scenarios, and claim patterns without risking the exposure of sensitive customer information. These datasets are valuable for stress-testing models, developing edge-case scenarios, or training systems in situations where real data is limited or restricted by regulations. For instance, insurers might use synthetic flood claim data to evaluate the stability of a new pricing model in response to changes in climate-related risks. While synthetic data cannot entirely replace real data, it serves as a flexible complement that enhances model resilience and encourages innovation while adhering to strict privacy requirements.

At the architectural level, there is a shift toward hybrid modeling frameworks that combine traditional actuarial techniques with ML. This includes generalized linear models that are enhanced by ML-derived interaction terms, credibility-adjusted loss forecasts that utilize ensemble outputs, and neural network architectures that are guided by established business logic. These hybrid models aim to leverage the strengths of both approaches—maintaining interpretability and regulatory compliance while also improving predictive accuracy and adaptability. For example, in reserving and capital modeling, actuaries are investigating how ML can improve triangle-based projections without compromising essential actuarial assumptions.

The convergence of ML and environmental, social, and governance objectives is becoming a strategic priority. Insurers are leveraging ML to assess climate-related risks, identify social vulnerability indicators, and evaluate commercial clients' sustainability performance. Models that quantify exposure to wildfires, floods, or extreme heat are being integrated into underwriting platforms, which enhances proactive resilience planning.

At the same time, insurers face pressure to ensure that their algorithms do not worsen inequality, exclude vulnerable populations, or reinforce discriminatory practices. As regulators and investors heighten scrutiny of ethical AI and responsible insurance practices, companies are investing in fairness-aware modeling, conducting bias audits, and engaging with communities. This approach aims to align innovation with positive social impact.

These trends indicate that the future of ML will not merely be a tool for optimization but will serve as a foundational element of modern insurance companies. From underwriting to claims processing, from actuary dashboards to customer mobile apps, intelligent models are becoming the essential link that facilitates real-time insights, adaptive decision-making, and personalized experiences. However, to fully harness these innovations' potential, insurers must adopt advanced technologies and invest in the organizational, legal, and ethical frameworks necessary to support trustworthy and human-centered AI.

CHAPTER SUMMARY

This chapter has examined the growing and changing role of ML within the insurance industry. We have explored everything from foundational mathematics to advanced applications, unpacking the algorithms, data pipelines, and decision systems that are transforming how insurers assess risk, engage with customers, and optimize operations. One key takeaway from this journey is that ML is not just a technical tool; it is a strategic capability reshaping insurance's future.

We started by establishing the mathematical foundations of ML, including linear algebra, calculus, probability, and optimization. These disciplines are essential to the logic and mechanics of learning systems. They are not merely academic concepts; they play a crucial role in important insurance functions such as pricing, reserving, risk classification, and forecasting. By understanding the mathematics involved, practitioners gain deeper insights into how models operate and greater confidence in assessing and enhancing them.

Building on that foundation, we explored the major families of ML algorithms: supervised, unsupervised, semisupervised, RL, and deep learning. Each of these families has distinct strengths and challenges. We examined how various methods, including linear models, decision trees, clustering techniques, neural networks, and advanced architectures such as transformers, are applied in real insurance workflows. These tools enable insurers to tackle a wide range of problems, including predicting claims, detecting fraud, pricing policies, managing portfolios, and segmenting customers.

We then focused on preparing the data, emphasizing the importance of preprocessing and feature engineering in developing effective and reliable models. Insurance data is often noisy, incomplete, and multidimensional. Careful data cleaning, transformation, and feature design can significantly impact the performance of a model, distinguishing a mediocre one from a high-performing one. Additionally, integrating domain knowledge into these steps ensures that the models remain interpretable and aligned with business objectives.

Model evaluation was presented as both a technical and strategic necessity. We discussed various metrics used in classification tasks, including accuracy, precision, recall, F1 scores, and ROC curves. Additionally, we explored metrics such as MAE, RMSE, and R^2 in the context of regression tasks. Importantly, we examined techniques to prevent overfitting, ensure model calibration, and validate models using cross-validation and statistical testing. For insurers subject to regulatory scrutiny, these evaluation practices are not just best practices—they are essential requirements.

Interpretability has become a central theme, particularly due to the legal and ethical implications of AI in the insurance industry. We examined the development of XAI techniques such as SHAP, LIME, and PDPs. These techniques enhance the transparency and accountability of complex models. In an industry where trust is essential, having the ability to explain how a premium is calculated, why a claim is denied, or how a risk score is assigned is crucial for both customer experience and regulatory compliance.

The chapter also highlighted practical applications throughout the insurance lifecycle, covering areas such as underwriting, pricing, claims automation, fraud detection, and customer retention. Real-world case studies demonstrated how ML is being used today to deliver measurable results. Notable examples include Lemonade's AI-driven claims processing, Allianz's geospatial modeling for climate risk, Progressive's pricing based on telematics data, and AXA's multimodal approach to claims automation.

While these technologies are highly effective, we also highlighted their limitations and challenges. Issues such as data quality, algorithmic bias, lack of transparency, regulatory uncertainty, and organizational readiness can impact the successful implementation of ML in the insurance sector. We emphasized the importance of model governance, ethical safeguards, and continuous monitoring to ensure that AI systems are fair, accountable, and aligned with human values.

As we look to the horizon, we observe emerging trends such as AutoML, federated learning, synthetic data, and the use of real-time sensor feeds. These innovations indicate a future where insurance becomes more adaptive, personalized, and predictive. However, they also require careful integration of legal, ethical, and operational frameworks to ensure that innovation does not outpace oversight.

In summary, ML is transforming the insurance industry—not as an isolated technology but as an integral component that enables smarter, faster, and more customer-focused decision-making. The insurers that will thrive in this new era will not necessarily be those with the most advanced algorithms, but rather those who combine technical proficiency with transparency, governance, and a comprehensive understanding of the risks and responsibilities associated with intelligent automation.

AI DISCLOSURE

During the preparation of this work the author(s) used Grammarly to improve readability and correct grammatical errors. After using this tool/service, the author(s) reviewed and edited the content as needed and take(s) full responsibility for the content of the publication.

REFERENCES

Bishop, C. M. (2006). *Pattern recognition and machine learning*. Springer.

Crosman, P. (2017). *Machine learning could boost insurers' profits by 30%. American Banker*. https://www.americanbanker.com/news/machine-learning-could-boost-insurers-profits-by-30.

Jordan, M. I., & Mitchell, T. M. (2015). Machine learning: Trends, perspectives, and prospects. *Science*, *349*(6245), 255–260. https://doi.org/10.1126/science.aaa8415.

CHAPTER

Decentralized insurance and the role of internet of things

5

CHAPTER OUTLINE

Insurance Technology. DOI: https://doi.org/10.1016/B978-0-443-43972-8.00001-8

INTRODUCTION: REDEFINING INSURANCE THROUGH DECENTRALIZATION

Institutions and intermediaries have historically shaped insurance, but it is now undergoing a significant transformation. For centuries, the industry has relied on centralized models where large firms underwrite pooled risks, collect premiums, manage claims, and maintain solvency through regulated capital reserves. These centralized insurers form the backbone of modern economies, protecting against uncertainty and financial loss. However, trust in these institutions has often fallen short of consumer expectations, particularly in a world increasingly characterized by transparency, speed, and digital empowerment.

Decentralized insurance represents a new risk-sharing and protection approach, leveraging distributed ledger technology, smart contracts, and peer-to-peer (P2P) coordination. Unlike traditional insurance models that rely on centralized companies, decentralized insurance aims to create a system of mutualization based on code, community governance, and algorithmic trust.

The potential benefits are significant: reduced costs, increased transparency, faster claims processing, and better access for those whom conventional insurance models have underserved. By minimizing or eliminating the role of intermediaries, decentralized systems seek to democratize access to insurance and establish more direct, data-driven relationships between those holding risk and the providers of capital (Schär, 2021).

Blockchain technology advancements have made this movement possible, which provides the necessary infrastructure to support decentralized, immutable, and trustless transactions. Smart contracts—self-executing code stored on a blockchain—automate policy terms and allow claims to be paid without human intervention, based on predefined conditions. These capabilities have led to the emergence of decentralized autonomous organizations (DAOs) that manage mutual risk pools with community governance and transparent rules encoded directly into their protocols (Buterin, 2014). In this context, insurance transforms from a product companies sell into a service orchestrated by decentralized communities.

Decentralization represents a technological change and a significant shift in philosophy and operations regarding how insurance has historically been understood. It challenges the traditional roles of insurers as financial intermediaries, claims adjudicators, and arbiters of risk. In this new framework, policyholders are viewed as stakeholders, coders take on the role of underwriters, and consensus algorithms function as risk evaluators.

However, these new roles come with their complexities. Issues related to solvency, regulatory compliance, ethical oversight, and governance structures are closely linked to the viability of this model. Additionally, while decentralization presents theoretical advantages such as disintermediation and lower administrative costs, it also introduces tangible risks. These risks include smart contract bugs, protocol manipulation, liquidity volatility, and legal uncertainties (Allen, 2020).

This model paves the way for more inclusive insurance options, particularly in areas where centralized insurance systems are either lacking or ineffective. In emerging markets, decentralized insurance protocols can provide micro-coverage for risks such as climate events, crop failures, or health issues. This is made possible through community engagement and mobile-first technologies. Global, censorship-resistant platforms allow risk-sharing to occur across different geographies and social divides, driven by principles of solidarity rather than corporate underwriting. In these situations, decentralized insurance is not merely about increasing efficiency; it serves as a potential leapfrog solution to the structural gaps in insurance coverage (Müller & Seitz, 2021).

The growth of decentralized finance (DeFi) has increased interest in decentralized insurance models, especially as on-chain assets and financial services create new types of risk. Protocols such as Nexus Mutual and Etherisc have emerged to cover issues like smart contract failures, oracle malfunctions, and exchange hacks—risks that traditional insurers often overlook. These protocols utilize blockchain-based mechanisms like staking, bonding curves, and governance tokens to fund risk pools, assess claims, and align incentives. Although still in the early stages and primarily focused on crypto-related risks, these models are beginning to explore real-world applications, such as travel insurance, flight delays, and crop protection.

A significant development in the evolution of decentralized insurance is the integration of Internet of Things (IoT) devices. These devices provide real-time, reliable data that can be used for dynamic risk assessment and automated claims processing. Connected sensors can measure rainfall, track vehicle telemetry, monitor home temperature, or detect wildfires. This data can be directly fed into smart contracts, triggering immediate payouts based on predefined objective criteria. The combination of IoT technology and a decentralized framework enables parametric insurance that is both seamless and scalable. However, this also raises important concerns regarding data privacy, the security of devices, and the governance of sensor infrastructure.

This chapter explores the architecture, applications, and implications of decentralized insurance. It begins by outlining the technological foundations, including blockchain mechanics, smart contracts, and tokenized governance. The chapter then examines the rise of DAOs in the insurance sector, along with P2P risk-sharing models and parametric designs made possible through IoT integration.

Regulatory and ethical considerations are discussed in detail, followed by a critical analysis of the benefits and limitations of this model. Finally, the chapter looks to the future of decentralized ecosystems, considering how these tools might reshape insurance both as a business and as a public good.

As insurance technology evolves, decentralization presents a disruptive force and a design alternative. It encourages us to rethink concepts of risk, protection, and community from the ground up. Whether it complements existing systems or challenges their dominance, decentralized insurance raises essential questions that the industry must address in the coming years.

FOUNDATIONS OF DECENTRALIZED INSURANCE

To grasp the concept of decentralized insurance, it is essential to understand the technological and conceptual foundations upon which it is built. These foundations include distributed ledger systems, smart contracts, token-based governance, and methods for trustless coordination. At its core, decentralized insurance leverages blockchain technology as a data repository and as the operating system for a novel form of institutional logic. This approach prioritizes transparency, automation, and community alignment over hierarchical authority and proprietary control.

BLOCKCHAIN INFRASTRUCTURE

The blockchain is at the core of any decentralized system. This cryptographically secure, append-only ledger enables a network of nodes to maintain a shared version of truth without centralized control. Blockchains allow data to be recorded tamper evidently, ensuring provenance and auditability for every transaction. In the insurance context, this technology enables policies, claims, and payment histories to be stored transparently, making them accessible to all participants in a verifiable format (Narayanan et al., 2016).

Public blockchains like Ethereum, Avalanche, and Solana are particularly well suited for decentralized insurance due to their programmability and composability. Unlike Bitcoin, which primarily focuses on asset transfer, these networks support Turing-complete smart contracts. This means they can execute arbitrary logic and respond to events on the blockchain. As a result, decentralized insurance protocols can embed underwriting logic, claims conditions, and payment execution directly into blockchain-based applications.

The decentralized nature of blockchain ensures that no single party can alter or censor transactions independently. This feature allows for trustless insurance protocols, where participants do not have to depend on a centralized entity to enforce contract terms or resolve disputes. Instead, the rules are embedded in smart contracts and enforced by the blockchain's consensus mechanisms.

SMART CONTRACTS AND AUTOMATION

Smart contracts are essential for the operation of decentralized insurance. They serve as digital agreements that automatically enforce their terms without the need for third-party intermediaries. For instance, a parametric crop insurance policy can be structured as a smart contract that receives rainfall data from a trusted oracle. The contract automatically issues a payout if the precipitation falls below a specified threshold during the growing season. Once deployed, the smart contract operates independently, eliminating the need for manual claims processing or discretionary judgment.

This automation provides several benefits. First, it lowers administrative costs, which often constitute a significant portion of traditional insurance premiums. Second, it speeds up the payout process, as claims can be verified and paid instantly based on objective criteria. Third, it minimizes opportunities for fraud, since smart contracts operate using publicly auditable inputs and predefined logic.

Smart contracts present several challenges despite their advantages. Their immutability, which enhances trust, also means that coding errors or logical mistakes can lead to unexpected results, such as losing funds or denying legitimate claims (Atzei, Bartoletti, & Cimoli, 2017). To address these issues, many decentralized insurance protocols conduct formal audits of their smart contract code and implement modular upgrade mechanisms governed by community votes or multisignature arrangements. However, the legal status of smart contracts remains debated in many jurisdictions, and disputes regarding their execution can raise new questions about liability and jurisdiction.

TOKENIZATION AND GOVERNANCE

Decentralized insurance often utilizes both automation and tokenization. Tokenization involves creating digital assets representing value, access rights, or governance privileges. Governance tokens enable participants to vote on important aspects, such as protocol upgrades, changes to underwriting parameters, and the allocation of reserves. Additionally, these tokens can function as financial instruments, offering rewards for activities like staking capital, participating in risk pools, or referring to new users.

This model turns policyholders into stakeholders, allowing them to have a say in the rules governing their coverage and giving them a share in the benefits of a well-managed protocol. Governance tokens are typically distributed through initial token offerings, liquidity mining, or as incentives for participating in risk-sharing. The value of these tokens can fluctuate depending on market conditions, the performance of the protocol, and user adoption. This creates economic feedback loops that align the community's behavior with the protocol's sustainability.

Tokenized insurance models introduce new liquidity dynamics. Users can sometimes exit a protocol by selling their tokens or redeeming their stake in a capital pool. This differs from traditional insurance, where capital is typically locked into reserves. The liquidity feature allows for more flexible participation but can also create capital flight risks, particularly during periods of high claims or market volatility.

Beyond governance, token models enable the creation of customized insurance instruments. Each policy or product can be represented as a nonfungible token (NFT) or a stream of recurring payments integrated into DeFi protocols. This flexibility allows decentralized insurance to connect with broader Web3 ecosystems, providing coverage for DAOs, NFT collectors, and cross-chain assets that traditional insurance methods might not cover.

ORACLES AND EXTERNAL DATA INTEGRATION

One limitation of smart contracts is that they cannot access off-chain data directly. To interact with real-world events, such as rainfall, crop yields, asset prices, or flight delays, decentralized insurance protocols rely on oracles. Oracles are systems that provide trusted external data to the blockchain. These can include centralized services, such as application programming interface (API) bridges, decentralized oracle networks like Chainlink, or hardware-integrated systems like IoT sensors connected through edge computing.

Oracles are crucial in parametric insurance, where claims are triggered by objective, measurable events rather than subjective evaluations. The quality and security of oracle systems are therefore essential for the credibility of decentralized insurance. If an oracle is compromised, manipulated, or simply inaccurate, the smart contract may process incorrect payouts, which can undermine trust and jeopardize the solvency of the protocol.

To ensure reliability, many protocols address this issue by utilizing multiple data sources, median voting mechanisms, or reputation-weighted oracle networks. Additionally, some are exploring using zero-knowledge proofs and secure multiparty computation to validate data while maintaining privacy. Developing robust and decentralized oracle systems is crucial for enabling innovation in decentralized insurance, but it also presents significant risks.

Decentralized insurance is built on several key components: blockchain technology, programmable automation, tokenized governance, and real-time data feeds. These elements work together to create a new risk transfer model that emphasizes openness, programmability, and values such as transparency, autonomy, and global accessibility. However, this foundation has its challenges. Smart contracts can fail, token values fluctuate, and data can be manipulated. The success of decentralized insurance will rely not only on the effectiveness of its tools but also on the strength of its governance, the engagement of its community, and its ability to adapt to real-world complexities.

DECENTRALIZED AUTONOMOUS ORGANIZATIONS IN INSURANCE

DAOs represent a significant shift from traditional insurance governance in the blockchain era. At their core, DAOs are community-governed entities that operate under transparent, predefined rules encoded in smart contracts. Unlike traditional insurers, which depend on centralized management teams and regulatory charters, DAOs are governed by token holders. These holders collectively propose, vote on, and implement policy decisions.

In the context of insurance, DAOs present a new model for mutualization, enabling the sharing of risks directly through code-based coordination mechanisms rather than through corporate intermediaries. These structures are typically fluid, borderless, and highly participatory, allowing insurance coverage to develop organically within decentralized communities with similar exposures or interests.

WHAT IS AN INSURANCE DECENTRALIZED AUTONOMOUS ORGANIZATION?

An insurance DAO is a blockchain-based organization that manages a risk pool and offers insurance-like services, including issuing coverage, assessing claims, and processing payouts through community involvement. Typically, these DAOs are organized around a treasury of digital assets, a governance token, and a set of smart contracts that automate essential functions. Token holders play a key role by proposing upgrades, allocating reserves, voting on claims, and setting underwriting parameters.

Governance mechanisms differ significantly among DAOs. Some employ quadratic voting, which allows smaller token holders to have a more balanced influence in decisions. Others use token-weighted voting, where decision-making power is directly proportional to the number of tokens owned. Additionally, more sophisticated DAOs have implemented reputation systems to ensure that experienced or long-term participants wield greater influence over critical decisions, such as fraud investigations or treasury disbursements.

Insurance DAOs often operate as informal collectives rather than registered legal entities, governed by rules established on the blockchain. This lack of formal legal status creates regulatory uncertainty, particularly regarding taxation, liability, and enforcement. Despite these challenges, DAO governance is considered a promising approach for creating community-oriented insurance, especially in environments where centralized oversight is untrustworthy or does not align with user needs (Wright & De Filippi, 2015).

CASE STUDY: NEXUS MUTUAL

One of the most well-known examples of a DAO-based insurance provider is Nexus Mutual, which was launched in 2019 on the Ethereum blockchain. Nexus Mutual offered "smart contract cover," a novel protection against DeFi protocol bugs and exploits. Instead of relying on traditional underwriting and actuarial modeling, Nexus uses a staking mechanism that allows members to lock tokens to express their confidence in the safety of a protocol—the more staked tokens, the lower the premium, reflecting a collective, market-based risk assessment.

Claims in Nexus Mutual are evaluated by community members who vote on their legitimacy. Members who vote honestly are rewarded, while those who frequently submit dishonest votes risk losing part of their stake. This incentive structure, though not perfect, aims to replicate the checks and balances found in traditional claims departments through a decentralized peer-review system.

Nexus Mutual has gradually expanded its range of products to include custody coverage, yield token coverage, and protocol-specific insurance. This makes it one of the most comprehensive on-chain insurance providers available. However, despite its success, the project has encountered several challenges. These include the scalability of claims assessments, slow adoption beyond DeFi-native risks, and ongoing debates regarding governance centralization as the protocol matures (Nexus Mutual, 2023).

OTHER DECENTRALIZED AUTONOMOUS ORGANIZATION–BASED INSURANCE MODELS

Other insurance DAOs have adopted various approaches. For instance, Etherisc is a protocol for creating decentralized insurance products rather than operating from a single risk pool. It offers a collection of templates and tools that enable communities or developers to launch their parametric insurance schemes, such as flight delay coverage or crop insurance. Unlike Nexus, Etherisc prioritizes modularity and openness, which allows for a greater diversity of insurance types and governance models (Etherisc, 2022).

InsurAce is a decentralized reinsurance platform that offers coverage across various protocols and blockchain networks while integrating with centralized DeFi aggregators. It combines DAO governance with delegated underwriting, enabling professional risk assessors to collaborate with token-holding voters. Some emerging hybrid models also allow the DAO to govern high-level policy and treasury functions while delegating specific claims or technical decisions to specialized working groups or service providers.

These examples demonstrate that DAO architecture is not a one-size-fits-all solution. Some protocols prioritize decentralization and openness, while others focus on operational efficiency and legal compliance. However, they are united by the belief that community governance can create more transparent, responsive, and equitable insurance systems, particularly in contexts where traditional regulatory frameworks are insufficient or untrusted.

OPERATIONAL AND LEGAL CHALLENGES

Despite their potential, DAOs encounter significant operational and legal challenges in the insurance sector. A primary concern is regulatory uncertainty. In most jurisdictions, insurance is a heavily regulated industry that requires licenses, capital reserves, solvency audits, and adherence to consumer protection laws. Many DAO-based insurance projects operate in legal gray areas, which raises questions about their legitimacy and the risk of regulatory enforcement.

Some DAOs have sought to address legal challenges by establishing structures such as cooperatives or limited liability foundations. These entities can engage with courts, hire employees, and have legal standing in disputes. In contrast, some DAOs maintain complete decentralization, arguing that no single entity controls the protocol, and thus no individual party is held responsible. However, regulators are increasingly scrutinizing these claims, particularly as DAOs expand in size and influence.

One significant challenge is scaling governance. While participatory voting is effective in small or highly engaged communities, it becomes less so as the user base grows. Issues like voter apathy, governance capture, and information asymmetry can undermine the quality of decision-making. Additionally, DAO voting often lacks the procedural safeguards in traditional governance, such as due process, appeals mechanisms, and protections for minority viewpoints. This absence can lead to potential abuse or exploitation.

Security is a significant concern for DAOs. Since they operate through smart contracts, they are susceptible to various threats such as exploits, flash loan attacks, and manipulation of governance. Several DAO-based insurance protocols have experienced technical failures or malicious governance actions, damaging user trust and underscoring the vulnerabilities of systems that rely solely on code. While audits, bug bounty programs, and multisignature controls are essential, they cannot eliminate all risks.

WHY DECENTRALIZED AUTONOMOUS ORGANIZATIONS STILL MATTER

Despite their risks, DAOs represent a significant experiment in reimagining insurance. They show that risk pooling and mutual protection can operate without centralized gatekeepers, and they frame insurance as a participatory public good rather than merely a commercial transaction. By doing this, DAOs encourage us to rethink how insurance is delivered and who has the authority to define the rules of financial protection.

For marginalized or underserved populations—those excluded from traditional insurance markets due to factors such as geography, income, or creditworthiness—DAOs present a potentially transformative alternative. They foster bottom-up innovation, promote solidarity-driven design, and enhance community-based risk resilience, free from the barriers and exclusions of conventional systems.

As regulatory clarity improves and DAO tooling becomes more sophisticated, we are likely to see the emergence of hybrid models that combine decentralized governance with professional risk assessment, legal compliance, and user-friendly interfaces. While these hybrids may not entirely replace traditional insurers, they will broaden the possibilities in digital insurance and establish new standards for transparency, accountability, and adaptability.

PEER-TO-PEER RISK-SHARING MODELS

P2P insurance is a significant link between traditional mutual insurance and the growing realm of decentralized risk pooling. While the concept is often linked to blockchain and digital platforms, its origins run much deeper. It is rooted in cooperative structures, fraternal societies, and community-based mutual aid networks that predate the establishment of institutional insurers. What sets today's P2P insurance models apart is using digital tools to scale, automate, and democratize these mutual principles in our interconnected world.

P2P insurance allows individuals or entities to form self-organized risk pools, where they agree to protect one another from specific types of loss. These groups establish their terms of engagement, share responsibility for claims, and—unlike traditional insurance—often reduce or eliminate the need for centralized intermediaries. P2P insurance, particularly within blockchain ecosystems, is more than an underwriting model; it represents a governance and cultural approach emphasizing community, transparency, and mutual trust.

HISTORICAL AND CONCEPTUAL FOUNDATIONS

The origins of P2P insurance can be traced back to the earliest cooperative societies and mutual benefit associations. Before the emergence of commercial insurance in the 18th and 19th centuries, local communities established informal arrangements to support members who suffered losses, whether due to fire, illness, or crop failure. These models relied on social capital and reputation rather than profit. Contributions were often voluntary, and payouts were made based on need rather than contractual obligations.

In the 19th century, formal mutual insurance companies emerged, establishing a new approach to insurance. The policyholders owned these organizations, which shared the risks and any surpluses. Mutual insurers typically focused on long-term sustainability and prioritizing member services rather than maximizing profits, which marked a significant contrast to shareholder-driven firms. Although many mutual insurance companies were eventually acquired or transformed into stock companies, the principle of collective responsibility remains a fundamental part of insurance history.

The digital age has sparked renewed interest in cooperative models of insurance. P2P insurance is increasingly used to describe platforms replicating mutual insurance logic through automation, smart contracts, and social networking tools. In this context, P2P insurance presents a traditional and modern model, grounded in established practices while reimagining the era of digital trust.

MODERN PEER-TO-PEER INSURANCE PLATFORMS

Modern P2P insurance platforms differ significantly in their structure and level of decentralization. Some operate within regulated frameworks and as licensed insurers, utilizing technology to manage claims and allocate premiums. In contrast, others implement fully decentralized models, acting as risk-sharing communities governed by code and consensus.

One well-known example is Friendsurance, a German platform launched in 2010. Friendsurance allows small groups of users to pool part of their premium contributions into a communal fund. This fund pays Minor claims, while a traditional insurer covers larger or excess claims. If the pool has low claims activity, participants receive a cashback bonus at the end of the year. This hybrid model ensures regulatory compliance while providing financial incentives for collective risk management and promoting responsible claims behavior.

Teambrella is another notable model that operates without a central insurer. In Teambrella, users form teams based on shared risk preferences and collectively fund each other's claims. The group votes on each claim, and contributions are tracked on a blockchain to ensure transparency. Instead of paying a premium upfront, users preauthorize funds that can be used for claims made by their peers. This structure blurs the line between traditional insurance and a social contract. While this approach emphasizes direct democratic control, it requires significant participant engagement and relies on a high degree of trust and cooperation.

In DeFi ecosystems, various structures that utilize token-based governance, bonded staking, and coordination through DAOs are being explored. In these models, automated market makers or bonding curves typically support peer risk pools, which dynamically adjust premiums based on the pool's capacity, expected loss ratios, and staking activity. Participants may earn governance tokens or yield incentives by providing capital and participating in decisions related to claims or underwriting policies.

MECHANICS OF PEER-BASED RISK POOLS

In both centralized and decentralized contexts, P2P insurance models typically rely on a few standard features:

- Risk pooling: Members contribute funds into a shared reserve, which is used to pay claims.
- Claims vetting: Claims may be evaluated by members, algorithms, or a hybrid of both. Peer voting mechanisms are often used to prevent fraud.
- Surplus distribution: If fewer claims are made than expected, surplus funds are redistributed to participants or rolled over into the next cycle.
- Governance mechanisms: Participants may vote on membership criteria, policy design, or dispute resolution rules, promoting participatory governance.

What makes these models appealing is the alignment of incentives among members. They benefit from lower claims costs and shared surplus distributions, which encourage them to act honestly, avoid unnecessary use of services, and monitor the integrity of other participants. This self-regulating dynamic contrasts with traditional models, where information asymmetries and adversarial claims processes can lead to friction and mistrust.

This model raises several concerns regarding group bias, exclusion, and governance fatigue. Peer voting can disadvantage marginalized members and potentially allow cliques to dominate decision-making. In larger groups, the decision-making becomes slower and less consistent. Additionally, without professional underwriters, there is a risk that the pricing models may be overly simplistic or underfunded, particularly during catastrophic events.

BENEFITS OF PEER-TO-PEER MODELS

Proponents of P2P insurance highlight several key advantages:

- Lower administrative costs: Automation and reduced need for intermediaries can lead to lower premiums.
- Faster claims: Peer-approved or algorithmically triggered payouts can reduce delays.
- Greater transparency: Blockchain-backed records and open voting processes promote trust.
- Incentive alignment: Participants have skin in the game and are less likely to file exaggerated or fraudulent claims.
- Community engagement: Shared ownership and governance can foster stronger loyalty and retention.

The benefits of P2P insurance are particularly significant in situations where there is low trust in traditional insurance providers or where current options provide insufficient or unaffordable coverage. For small businesses, gig workers, and those in informal sectors, P2P insurance may represent the only viable solution for risk protection.

LIMITATIONS AND CHALLENGES

Despite their appeal, P2P insurance models are not without flaws. Key limitations include:

- Scalability: Group-based decision-making and social cohesion are harder to maintain as networks grow.
- Adverse selection: Without actuarial expertise, groups may attract higher-risk members or misprice coverage.
- Governance risks: Participation may be uneven, and power can consolidate in active minorities.
- Regulatory uncertainty: Fully decentralized models often lack legal clarity, exposing participants to compliance risk or unenforceable claims.
- Liquidity stress: In catastrophe scenarios, P2P pools may not have sufficient reserves or reinsurance to remain solvent.

Many P2P platforms utilize hybrid architectures that combine decentralized governance with centralized infrastructure, professional actuarial input, or reinsurance support. These hybrid models provide a practical approach for innovation while maintaining the prudential safeguards established over decades of insurance regulation.

P2P insurance offers an intriguing alternative to traditional insurance models. By empowering individuals, fostering transparency, and rethinking how risk is shared,

P2P systems have the potential to redefine insurance in a decentralized world. While they may not completely replace conventional insurance providers, peer-based models introduce essential experimentation that could encourage established insurers to become more participatory, ethical, and adaptable in their approach.

INTERNET OF THINGS AND DECENTRALIZED INSURANCE

The combination of decentralized insurance and the IoT is one of the most transformative advancements in risk management. At its core, IoT refers to a network of interconnected devices—such as sensors, actuators, meters, and wearables—that collect, transmit, and act on data from the physical world. In traditional insurance contexts, IoT has already started to change underwriting, loss prevention, and claims processing. However, when combined with decentralized platforms and smart contracts, IoT does more than simply improve existing systems; it fundamentally redefines how risk is measured, monitored, and resolved.

The IoT has the potential to significantly enhance decentralized insurance by providing reliable, real-time data that can trigger automatic payouts or streamline loss response mechanisms. This innovation addresses a critical limitation of traditional insurance: the delays and subjectivity involved in claims assessment. In centralized systems, claims processing often relies on paperwork, adjuster visits, and lengthy validation periods. These factors contribute to increased costs, inefficiencies, and frustration for policyholders. In contrast, decentralized insurance models leverage IoT to facilitate instant, data-driven decisions that minimize fraud, eliminate subjective judgment, and enhance transparency.

Imagine a smart contract created to insure homes against flood damage. Unlike traditional indemnity insurance, which requires proof of damage, an investigation into its cause, and negotiations over coverage, a decentralized system can streamline this process. For instance, a water-level sensor installed in a basement can directly transmit data to the blockchain. If the water-level exceeds a predetermined threshold, such as rising above 6 inches, the smart contract will automatically trigger a payout to the homeowner based on preagreed terms. This system eliminates the need for a claims process, removes the need to appeal to an insurer, and avoids any delays. In this model, the event itself serves as the claim.

This model is called parametric insurance, and its effectiveness is greatly improved by the IoT. In the past, parametric models depended on publicly available indices, such as weather reports and earthquake registries. Now, with IoT, insurance can be based on highly localized and personalized data. For example, a vineyard in California can be insured against drought using soil moisture sensors, while a commercial refrigeration system can be monitored through real-time temperature trackers. Additionally, the risk of wildfires can be reduced by integrating air quality monitors and thermal imaging feeds. This detailed and specific data enables smarter underwriting and fairer pricing, allowing policies to be tailored to the actual conditions faced by the insured asset.

In a decentralized context, data is directly fed into smart contracts, self-executing code that operates on a blockchain and implements policy logic without human intervention. When the data reaches a specific threshold, the contract triggers a payout, records the event, and updates the system's state. Since the process is governed by code, it is both transparent and auditable by anyone in the network. This method significantly reduces administrative overhead and minimizes opportunities for disputes or manipulation, reinforcing one of the fundamental goals of DeFi: building trust through transparency.

The use of IoT in decentralized insurance faces several challenges. The most significant issue is data reliability. A decentralized smart contract cannot verify if an IoT sensor has been tampered with, miscalibrated, or damaged. If payouts are tied to sensor data, the integrity of that data becomes a crucial point of failure. This creates a dependency on trusted oracles, which act as intermediaries to validate and transmit real-world data to the blockchain. Although decentralized oracle networks like Chainlink aim to reduce reliance on single data sources, the overall system still requires mechanisms to verify and reconcile conflicting inputs.

One of the challenges facing the IoT is interoperability and standardization. The IoT ecosystem is fragmented, with devices produced by various vendors, each using different communication protocols and storing data in incompatible formats. For decentralized insurance protocols to scale effectively, they must integrate a wide range of sensors across different domains, such as homes, factories, farms, and vehicles, without requiring custom configurations for each specific use case. This necessitates the creation of universal data schemas, APIs, and decentralized identity (DID) standards that enable devices to be recognized and trusted across different blockchain ecosystems.

Security is a critical concern when it comes to IoT devices, which are often vulnerable to cyberattacks. If a sensor is compromised, it could produce false readings, potentially leading to fraudulent payouts or draining insurance reserves. Unlike traditional insurers, who can investigate and challenge suspicious claims, decentralized systems execute transactions automatically and typically offer no avenue for recourse. This highlights the necessity of device authentication, network security, and real-time anomaly detection as essential components of any insurance model that integrates IoT technology.

Despite the associated risks, the potential benefits are significant. Integrating IoT technology allows decentralized insurance to advance beyond basic coverage into predictive and preventive risk management. For instance, a decentralized policy that covers equipment breakdown could not only provide payouts upon failure but also receive early warning data from vibration sensors or thermal scans. This data could be transmitted through the blockchain to trigger preventive maintenance suggestions, distribute incentives for reducing risk, or even adjust pricing dynamically based on exposure levels.

The implications for sectors such as agriculture, climate resilience, and the gig economy labor are particularly significant. Smallholder farmers, who have often been underserved by traditional insurers due to high administrative costs and limited data visibility, can now access weather-indexed crop protection through decentralized applications that utilize remote sensors and satellite imagery. Rideshare drivers can also benefit from telematics-based coverage programs that automatically adjust premiums or activate benefits based on real-time behavior and exposure. In both cases, the IoT serves as the vital link between physical risk and digital enforcement.

A particularly effective application of IoT in decentralized insurance is wildfire detection and response. In regions prone to wildfires, such as California and Australia, sensors mounted on utility poles, homes, or drones can monitor changes in air temperature, particulate matter, and wind patterns. This data can be integrated into a decentralized insurance system that issues alerts, preauthorizes emergency expenditures, or triggers payouts if specific thresholds are exceeded. This model not only supports faster recovery but also encourages property owners to install and maintain sensors, creating a feedback loop that enhances collective resilience.

The integration of IoT data into decentralized governance models introduces new forms of algorithmic accountability. For instance, if a community DAO is responsible for a wildfire coverage pool, its members must consider the accuracy and availability of sensor data when designing payout rules and determining capital requirements. This situation creates opportunities for deeper civic engagement, where policyholders also act as data stewards and decision-makers. This represents an evolution of insurance from merely a financial contract to a community-based social system, supported by connected infrastructure.

In summary, the IoT provides decentralized insurance with the necessary tools to function in the physical world. By converting real-world conditions into verifiable digital data, IoT enables decentralized protocols to automate coverage, customize pricing, and extend their reach beyond theoretical financial risks to encompass actual experiences. The journey ahead calls for strong data governance, enhanced sensor reliability, and better integration with blockchain ecosystems, but the foundational elements are already established. As the boundaries between the digital and physical worlds continue to blur, IoT will not only support decentralized insurance but also make it a reality.

REGULATORY AND ETHICAL CONSIDERATIONS

As decentralized insurance becomes more popular within blockchain ecosystems and real-world applications, it enters a sector that has long been governed by regulation, fiduciary duty, and public accountability. Unlike most financial innovations, insurance operates within a framework of significant public interest. At its core, insurance serves as a social utility—a means of resilience, protection, and redistribution. Consequently, it is one of the most regulated financial sectors in nearly every jurisdiction, subject to strict capital adequacy requirements, licensing regulations, solvency supervision, and consumer protection mandates. The emergence of decentralized systems—governed by code instead of institutions—raises important questions about how these legal and ethical obligations can be fulfilled in a landscape where no single entity is officially in charge.

The most pressing regulatory challenge posed by decentralized insurance is the ambiguity regarding jurisdiction. Traditional insurers operate within specific national or regional boundaries, where they obtain licenses, undergo audits, and comply with local insurance regulations. In contrast, decentralized insurance protocols function as borderless digital entities. Their smart contracts are hosted on global blockchains like Ethereum or Solana, their users may be located in numerous countries, and their governance is spread among anonymous token holders whose identities and nationalities may be unknown. This leads to a fundamental question: Who, if anyone, can be held accountable when something goes wrong?

This ambiguity complicates enforcement. If a smart contract wrongly denies a claim or if a DAO mismanages its reserve funds, traditional legal remedies, such as suing an insurer in court or filing a complaint with a regulator, may not be effective or applicable. Furthermore, many insurance DAOs lack legal personality entirely, which raises questions about their ability to enter into contracts, be sued, or be required to disclose information. In the absence of a clearly identifiable party, regulators have limited tools to supervise or take action against these entities.

Some jurisdictions are starting to address this issue by requiring decentralized protocols that serve local residents to register as legal entities. For example, the Wyoming DAO law allows DAOs to register as limited liability companies, which provides them with legal recognition and protects individual members from personal liability. Additionally, some countries have proposed the concept of "on-chain compliance" obligations, where protocols must incorporate specific regulatory functions into their smart contracts. These functions could include solvency thresholds, dispute resolution mechanisms, or identity verification procedures. Although these initiatives are still in the early stages, they indicate a growing consensus that legal recognition should be accompanied by accountability in the underlying code.

Consumer protection and financial stability are equally important considerations. Insurance regulators are designed to prevent market failures, protect policyholders, and ensure that claims are paid. However, decentralized systems often lack essential features such as reserve requirements, reinsurance coverage, and stress-tested solvency models. In these systems, capital is pooled voluntarily, and withdrawals can be made instantly, which can lead to liquidity crises during periods of high claims. Without the safeguards typically found in traditional markets, such as insurance guaranty funds or central bank facilities, users of decentralized insurance protocols may face uncompensated losses if the system fails.

Ethical concerns emerge not only from regulatory gaps but also from the fundamental structure of decentralized risk sharing. Decentralized systems are typically built on libertarian principles of autonomy, disintermediation, and financial sovereignty. While these ideals can be empowering, they may also lead to ethical minimalism. The absence of a central authority often results in a lack of meaningful oversight.

For instance, if a parametric insurance policy pays out based on data from an IoT sensor that later turns out to be compromised, who is responsible for correcting the error? Additionally, if a DAO votes to reject a valid claim in order to protect its reserves, do its members have ethical responsibilities similar to fiduciary obligations?

These questions are not merely theoretical; they highlight the real consequences of algorithmic governance that lacks moral accountability.

Privacy is a critical issue in decentralized insurance systems that often depend on high-frequency data from IoT devices, wearables, or GPS tracking systems. These data streams are sensitive and can reveal personal information about an individual's movements, behaviors, or health status. When this data is used to determine policy pricing or trigger payouts, it raises important questions about informed consent, data ownership, and ethical considerations regarding surveillance.

Unlike centralized insurers, which must adhere to strict data protection laws like General Data Protection Regulation or Health Insurance Portability and Accountability Act, decentralized protocols may lack clear responsibilities or the means to comply with such regulations. This creates a growing tension between technological capabilities and ethical considerations.

Bias and fairness in decentralized insurance are topics that have not been fully explored. In theory, smart contracts operate impartially, executing rules without any discretion or bias. However, the data that informs these contracts can be significantly biased. For instance, using ZIP code–based pricing in home insurance could reinforce existing racial or economic inequalities. In a decentralized system, detecting and addressing these issues may be more challenging, particularly if the models are closed source or managed by a small group of token holders. Furthermore, the absence of appeals mechanisms or dispute resolution systems can disproportionately affect marginalized users who may lack the technical knowledge or resources to challenge automated decisions.

Additionally, governance introduces ethical challenges within insurance DAOs. In many cases, voting rights are granted based on the number of tokens held, which can reflect or exacerbate existing power imbalances. Wealthier users, institutional investors, or early adopters may have an outsized influence on premium pricing, coverage rules, and claims approval processes. This token-weighted governance model can compromise the democratic principles that decentralized insurance aims to uphold. Therefore the critical questions arise: How are decisions made, who gets to make them, and whose interests are ultimately being served?

To address these concerns, some decentralized insurance protocols are experimenting with hybrid models that incorporate compliance and ethics. These models include embedding ethical safeguards into smart contracts, such as requiring multisignature approvals for sensitive actions or implementing audit triggers when certain thresholds are surpassed. Additionally, some protocols are adopting human-in-the-loop systems, where community-elected review boards have the authority to override or pause automated processes in exceptional circumstances. Others are developing reputation systems and trust scores to encourage ethical behavior through transparency and peer accountability rather than relying on legal coercion.

The future of decentralized insurance will depend not just on technical advancements but also on ethical frameworks and open discussions with regulators.

Developers, users, regulators, and scholars must collaborate to create systems that respect the principles of decentralization while also addressing the responsibilities involved in managing societal risk. This requires us to go beyond simple compliance and engage with deeper questions: How can decentralized insurance promote equity and accessibility? How can communities self-govern without marginalizing vulnerable populations? What values should be integrated into our protocols, and who will make those decisions?

Decentralized insurance represents an ambitious experiment that questions our beliefs about trust, power, and responsibility. However, like all forms of insurance, its credibility will rely not only on the promises it makes but also on the protections it provides when people need them the most. The challenge ahead is to create resilient systems while ensuring that those systems remain accountable to the individuals and communities they are designed to serve.

BENEFITS AND LIMITATIONS OF DECENTRALIZED MODELS

Decentralized insurance has the potential to disrupt a centuries-old industry by reimagining how individuals share, manage, and mitigate risk. By utilizing blockchain technology, smart contracts, and community-based governance, these models offer a vision of insurance that is more transparent, efficient, and inclusive. However, this vision comes with trade-offs. The very features that make decentralized systems appealing—autonomy, automation, and openness—also expose them to risks, complexities, and operational challenges that need to be understood and addressed. The future of decentralized insurance will depend not only on its theoretical appeal but also on its practical viability and ethical implementation.

BENEFITS OF DECENTRALIZED INSURANCE

One of the most commonly cited advantages of decentralized insurance is its potential to lower costs and minimize administrative hurdles. Traditional insurers have multiple layers of operational overhead, including underwriting departments, claims adjusters, compliance officers, and distribution channels, all of which need to be financed through premium margins. In contrast, decentralized protocols automate many of these functions using smart contracts. Claims can be triggered and settled instantly using parametric inputs, underwriting rules can be embedded in code, and reserve management can be managed algorithmically. As a result, the system becomes leaner, promising to provide greater value to participants while reducing the inefficiencies associated with legacy insurers.

Another significant benefit of decentralized models is transparency. In these systems, all transactions, claims, and governance decisions are recorded on a public ledger. Participants can review how premiums are pooled, how reserves are managed, and how votes are cast on important protocol changes. This level of transparency sharply contrasts with the lack of openness often seen in centralized insurance companies, where pricing algorithms, claims approvals, and investment strategies are proprietary and unclear. For consumers who have historically been skeptical of insurance, decentralization provides an unprecedented level of institutional accountability.

Decentralized insurance promotes greater inclusivity by eliminating geographic, bureaucratic, and financial barriers. This approach can help serve populations that have historically been excluded from traditional insurance markets, such as smallholder farmers in the Global South, gig economy workers, and communities facing climate risks. P2P structures and DAO-based risk pools enable hyperlocal or community-specific coverage that is tailored to individual needs. Participants no longer have to wait for global reinsurers to acknowledge their risk profiles; instead, they can create their own systems governed by community consensus and access coverage on their own terms.

Closely related to inclusivity is the principle of programmability. Decentralized protocols are not limited by the rigid product templates of traditional insurers. They can create entirely new categories of coverage, such as cryptocurrency asset insurance, weather-based crop protection, parametric wildfire response, or NFT custody protection. These products can be deployed quickly, updated in real time, and integrated with other DeFi applications. As a result, decentralized insurance becomes part of a broader digital ecosystem where financial protection is embedded within the infrastructure of the internet itself.

Decentralized models present innovative incentives for ethical behavior. Users often become stakeholders by holding governance tokens, staking capital, or participating in claims reviews, which gives them a vested interest in maintaining the integrity of the system. This alignment of incentives can help reduce fraudulent behavior and promote responsible risk-taking. For instance, in protocols where capital providers vote on claims, honest voting can be rewarded with protocol fees or staking rewards. Therefore decentralization creates economic feedback loops that enhance trust and discourage exploitation.

LIMITATIONS AND TRADE-OFFS

Despite their potential, decentralized insurance models encounter significant limitations—technical, financial, social, and legal—that hinder their scalability and development.

A primary concern for the insurance industry is solvency and capital adequacy. Traditional insurers operate under strict solvency regulations that ensure reserves are sufficient to cover claims, even in extreme scenarios. In contrast, decentralized protocols often depend on voluntary capital contributions without actuarial oversight or reinsurance protection. During times of crisis, liquidity can diminish significantly, particularly if stakeholders or capital providers withdraw their funds in mass. Events such as flash crashes, smart contract hacks, or high-claims occurrences can lead to undercollateralization, leaving policyholders vulnerable. Without robust risk modeling, these systems risk falling into a cycle of boom and bust, which undermines long-term sustainability.

One significant challenge is regulatory fragmentation. Decentralized protocols operate across various countries and are therefore subject to overlapping and sometimes conflicting regulatory frameworks. A single platform might serve users in the United States, Europe, India, and sub-Saharan Africa, each with distinct definitions of insurance, licensing requirements, and consumer protection laws. This regulatory uncertainty discourages institutional adoption and could expose users to legal risks. Furthermore, as mentioned in previous sections, many DAOs lack legal personality, leading to a gap in liability. If a claim is unjustly denied, a contract fails, or a protocol is exploited, users may find they have limited recourse under existing laws.

Decentralized insurance also faces governance challenges. Many DAOs rely on token-weighted voting systems, where influence is proportional to wealth or early adoption. This can lead to governance capture, decision-making paralysis, or poorly informed outcomes. Voter turnout is often low, and the complexity of insurance decisions—ranging from actuarial design to fraud detection—makes it difficult to implement effective crowdsourced governance. Without professional oversight and institutional memory, these models can become vulnerable to short-term thinking and internal conflict.

Security is a significant concern in the realm of smart contracts. While they offer powerful functionality, they are also susceptible to bugs, exploits, and vulnerabilities arising from game theory. A single line of faulty code can potentially drain reserves or trigger cascading failures across DeFi integrations. Although code audits and formal verification techniques have improved, the risk of undiscovered exploits or attacks based on governance remains high. These risks are further heightened by composability, as many decentralized insurance protocols are interconnected within broader financial systems that share infrastructure and liquidity.

Even the widely praised transparency of decentralized insurance has its limitations. Although on-chain data is publicly available, understanding this data still requires technical knowledge and specialized tools. Additionally, privacy concerns can emerge when sensitive information, such as health records, location history, or financial behavior, is used to determine coverage pricing or trigger payouts. In a world with transparent ledgers, the use of privacy-preserving computation and zero-knowledge proofs is crucial, but these technologies are not yet commonly implemented in consumer-facing insurance applications.

The most significant challenge facing decentralized insurance is public understanding and trust. Insurance is already one of the least understood financial products, and introducing elements like blockchain, oracles, DAOs, and parametric logic adds complexity. For the average user, the potential benefits of decentralized insurance can be lost amid technical jargon, confusing user interfaces, and steep learning curves. To build trust on a large scale, we need not only improved infrastructure but also a cultural shift that makes decentralized insurance as intuitive and reliable as traditional insurance.

The benefits of decentralized insurance are significant: lower costs, improved transparency, broader inclusion, and faster innovation. However, these advantages do not arise automatically; they require active engineering, testing, and careful governance. At the same time, the limitations of decentralized systems are not insurmountable. With thoughtful design, better regulation, and the maturation of ecosystems, many of today's challenges could become tomorrow's solutions. The key is to balance idealism with realism—to create insurance systems that are not only innovative but also resilient, equitable, and capable of effectively managing risks.

THE FUTURE OF DECENTRALIZED INSURANCE ECOSYSTEMS

The concept of decentralizing insurance, which once seemed like a fringe idea within the broader blockchain movement, has now evolved into a serious proposal for the future of risk management. This transformation has been rapid but uneven. It started with simple parametric contracts and P2P risk pools, developed into complex platforms governed by DAOs, and is now moving toward integration with emerging technologies such as artificial intelligence (AI), decentralized identity, and the IoT. As the infrastructure of Web3 continues to mature and public expectations for transparency and autonomy increase, decentralized insurance ecosystems are set to play a crucial role in reshaping both the delivery and governance of financial protection.

Looking ahead, one of the most promising developments in the insurance industry is the convergence of AI and decentralized infrastructure. AI can significantly enhance the ability of decentralized insurance platforms to assess risk, detect fraud, and customize coverage. By using machine learning algorithms on anonymized claims histories, IoT data streams, and social data, decentralized protocols can provide personalized pricing and real-time loss modeling without the need for centralized underwriting teams. Additionally, smart contracts that are "AI-assisted" rather than static can dynamically adjust to emerging risks, such as climate variability or pandemic outbreaks, by utilizing streaming data and decentralized oracles.

The ongoing implementation of DID frameworks offers a solution to one of the most challenging issues in Web3 insurance: verifying user identities without compromising their privacy. DID systems allow individuals to prove specific attributes, such as age, location, or licensing status, without disclosing their full identity or creating centralized data repositories that could be vulnerable to breaches. This is particularly crucial in the insurance sector, where it is important to balance fraud prevention and regulatory compliance with ethical data management. When combined with verifiable credentials, DID will facilitate underwriting and claims processing based on proof rather than full disclosure, paving the way for new models of pseudonymous, reputation-based insurance.

The future will redefine what constitutes an insurable asset. Traditional insurance has always focused on physical risks such as fire, illness, accidents, and death. However, with the rise of DeFi and digital ownership, new categories of value have emerged: NFTs, DAO treasuries, digital identities, and tokenized real-world assets. These assets face different threats, including contract bugs, exploit risks, oracle failures, and market manipulation, which require customized coverage embedded within digital ecosystems.

In this new landscape, insurance will no longer be an external product; instead, it will be an invisible layer integrated into smart contracts, protocols, and platform logic. In this vision, the future of insurance is not just about policies—it is about functionality.

As embedded insurance models become increasingly common, interoperability will emerge as a key challenge and opportunity. Currently, decentralized insurance platforms function in disconnected silos, each with its own user base, reserve strategies, and claims processes. The future ecosystem will demand cross-chain liquidity, standardized claims frameworks, and interchangeable identity and reputation layers. Initiatives aimed at creating open insurance protocols—similar to the ERC token standards in Ethereum—will be vital for providing a seamless user experience and enabling composable risk products. These innovations will facilitate the smooth transfer of insurance across different blockchains, covering everything from on-chain digital risks to real-world events relayed through satellite-based oracles and IoT networks.

The regulatory environment is set to evolve, though unevenly and inevitably. As governments transition from reactive enforcement to proactive policy design, we can expect to see tailored regulatory frameworks for algorithmic insurance, particularly in jurisdictions that are eager to promote innovation. Regulatory sandboxes will broaden to include decentralized protocols, while global coalitions may strive to harmonize regulations for DAOs, data rights, and cross-border capital flows. Similar to the early days of the internet, the ultimate acceptance of decentralized insurance will rely not on avoiding regulation but on actively participating in its development through collaboration, experimentation, and transparency.

From a market perspective, decentralized insurance is unlikely to completely replace traditional insurers. Instead, a hybrid model is expected to emerge. Large insurance companies may adopt blockchain technology to improve back-office efficiency or automate claims processing. Meanwhile, new players might utilize full-stack decentralization to cater to underbanked populations or specific digital risks. Some platforms may operate with complete DAO governance, while others may integrate with licensed insurers through APIs or embedded finance partnerships. This coexistence will not be defined by ideological differences but will focus on practical alignment regarding user needs, capital efficiency, and regulatory compliance.

Another important area of focus is climate resilience and inclusive finance. Decentralized insurance is particularly effective in addressing the underinsurance of climate risks, especially in sectors such as agriculture, energy, and disaster relief. By utilizing satellite data, IoT sensors, and parametric smart contracts, these protocols can provide immediate crop failure insurance, wildfire alerts, or storm-triggered payouts in regions where traditional insurance is either unavailable or unaffordable. These innovative models not only reduce vulnerability but also promote climate adaptation, thereby empowering communities that have historically been excluded from global financial systems.

The cultural shift surrounding decentralized insurance is significant. It presents a new narrative that focuses on building resilience collectively rather than merely selling protection. This approach encourages users to become cocreators of their risk environment instead of being passive customers. Although this participatory ethos is still in its early stages and can be overshadowed by technical complexities or financial speculation, improvements in user experience, increased education, and the accumulation of success stories are likely to highlight core values such as transparency, fairness, and mutual accountability. These values may ultimately redefine society's expectations for risk institutions.

In this future, insurance is not merely a product you purchase, but a protocol you trust. It is not controlled by opaque institutions, but rather by communities that have a stake, a voice, and a sense of responsibility. Insurance doesn't just react to loss; it anticipates, prevents, and learns from it. The tools needed for this transformation—such as blockchain, the IoT, AI, and DAOs—are already available. What remains is the task of carefully building, governing, and evolving these systems with ethics and foresight.

Decentralized insurance is not a complete solution, but it is a compelling option that encourages us to rethink how we manage and share risk. As we face increasing systemic uncertainties and digital complexities, this reimagining of insurance may not only be timely but also necessary.

AI DISCLOSURE

During the preparation of this work the author(s) used Grammarly to improve the readability and correct grammatical mistakes. After using this tool/service, the author(s) reviewed and edited the content as needed and take(s) full responsibility for the content of the publication.

REFERENCES

Allen, D. W. E. (2020). Blockchain and the innovation of insurance. In D. W. E. Allen D. M. (2020). Powell (Eds.), *Handbook of blockchain, digital finance, and inclusion* (Vol. 1, pp. 395–410). Academic Press. https://doi.org/10.1016/B978-0-12-810441-5.00015-2.

Atzei, N., Bartoletti, M., & Cimoli, T. (2017). A survey of attacks on Ethereum smart contracts (SoK). Proceedings of the 6th international conference on principles of security and trust (164–186). Springer. https://doi.org/10.1007/978-3-662-54455-6_8.

Buterin, V. (2014). *DAOs, DACs, DAs and More: An incomplete terminology guide*. Ethereum Foundation Blog. https://blog.ethereum.org/2014/05/06/daos-dacs-das-and-more.

Etherisc. (2022). *Decentralized insurance protocol documentation*. https://docs.etherisc.com/.

Müller, K., & Seitz, C. (2021). Blockchain technology in insurance: Use cases and future applications. *Journal of Risk Finance*, *22*(3), 240–257. https://doi.org/10.1108/JRF-01-2020-0014.

Narayanan, A., Bonneau, J., Felten, E., Miller, A., & Goldfeder, S. (2016). *Bitcoin and cryptocurrency technologies: A comprehensive introduction*. Princeton University Press.

Nexus Mutual. (2023). *Whitepaper v2: A new mutual for the digital age*. https://nexusmutual.io/docs.

Schär, F. (2021). Decentralized finance: On blockchain-and smart contract-based financial markets. *Federal Reserve Bank of St. Louis Review*, *103*(2), 153–174. https://doi.org/10.20955/r.103.153–74.

Wright, A., & De Filippi, P. (2015). Decentralized blockchain technology and the rise of lex cryptographia. *Social Science Research Network*. https://doi.org/10.2139/ssrn.2580664.

CHAPTER

Blockchain and distributed ledger technologies in insurance

6

CHAPTER OUTLINE

Insurance Technology. DOI: https://doi.org/10.1016/B978-0-443-43972-8.00003-1

INTRODUCTION & LEARNING OBJECTIVES

The insurance industry has traditionally depended on centralized systems and complicated administrative processes, often resulting in inefficiencies, errors, and delays in service delivery. With the rise of emerging technologies, blockchain is one of the most transformative innovations in insurance operations. Blockchain is a decentralized and tamper-proof digital ledger that can help reduce fraud, streamline claims processing, and facilitate real-time policy execution through smart contracts.

This chapter examines the adoption of blockchain technology throughout the insurance value chain, from underwriting to claims settlement. It highlights how smart contracts—self-executing programs that run on blockchain—can provide automation and enhance trust in high-risk, high-volume environments. Additionally, we will explore practical platforms, development environments, and sample code to link technical capabilities with real-world industry use cases.

Whether you are a risk professional, technologist, or studying financial innovation, this chapter offers a clear and practical foundation for understanding the increasing role of blockchain in modern insurance.

BLOCKCHAIN FUNDAMENTALS

WHAT IS BLOCKCHAIN?

Blockchain is fundamentally a distributed ledger technology that enables data to be recorded, stored, and shared securely and immutably across multiple nodes (Nakamoto, 2008). Each record, referred to as a block, includes a set of transactions cryptographically linked to the preceding block, creating a continuous chain. Due to its decentralized and tamper-resistant nature, blockchain offers secure data validation and traceability, eliminating the need for a trusted third party.

Unlike traditional databases controlled by a central authority, blockchain technology distributes the ledger across a network of computers known as nodes. Each node keeps a complete copy of the ledger and uses consensus algorithms to validate new transactions. The most common consensus mechanisms include:

- Proof of work—Used by Bitcoin; energy-intensive but highly secure
- Proof of stake—Used by Ethereum 2.0; more energy efficient and scalable
- Practical Byzantine Fault Tolerance—Common in permissioned blockchains like Hyperledger Fabric, ideal for enterprise environments

Here's a more detailed and expanded version of the section:

KEY CHARACTERISTICS OF BLOCKCHAIN

Decentralization

Blockchain technology functions on a decentralized network of nodes, meaning no single entity or authority controls the data or the decision-making process. This structure eliminates the need for intermediaries, leading to more efficient and cost-effective transactions. In the insurance sector, decentralization builds trust among parties by reducing reliance on centralized institutions like brokers or underwriters.

Transparency

Blockchain offers a high level of transparency, as all transactions are recorded on a public ledger that all participants in the network can access. This open-access feature enables parties to verify and audit transactions in real time, which promotes accountability and helps reduce fraud. For the insurance industry, this is especially beneficial as it streamlines the claims process and helps verify the accuracy of data used in underwriting and risk assessment.

Immutability

Once a transaction is recorded on the blockchain, it becomes nearly impossible to alter or erase. This durability is ensured through cryptographic hashing and consensus algorithms, which maintain the integrity of the data. In the insurance industry, this immutability helps prevent fraud, as policy information, claims records, and contract terms cannot be tampered with or changed after they are confirmed. This ensures that all historical records remain intact.

Security

Blockchain employs advanced cryptographic techniques to secure data, ensuring that transactions are encrypted and authenticated before they are recorded. This process guarantees the privacy of sensitive information, such as personal data and financial records, while maintaining data integrity. In the insurance sector, blockchain's strong security features make it particularly effective for protecting customer data, preventing identity theft, and ensuring that financial transactions are safe and verifiable.

Blockchain technology's core attributes appeal to the insurance industry, where trust, transparency, and data accuracy are crucial for maintaining customer confidence, minimizing operational risks, and enhancing overall efficiency.

TYPES OF BLOCKCHAINS

Public blockchains (e.g., Ethereum, Bitcoin)

Public blockchains are open and permissionless networks that allow anyone to join, validate transactions, and participate in the consensus process. These blockchains are characterized by high transparency and decentralization, making them ideal for applications that require public access and visibility. In the insurance industry, public blockchains can be used for solutions accessible to the public, such as verifying policyholders' coverage or executing smart contracts in a decentralized manner.

Private blockchains (e.g., Hyperledger, Quorum)

Private blockchains are closed networks with restricted access, allowing only authorized participants, often managed by a central organization or consortium. These blockchains provide enhanced privacy and security, making them ideal for enterprise applications where confidentiality is crucial. In the insurance sector, private blockchains are commonly used for internal data sharing among stakeholders such as insurers, reinsurers, and brokers. They ensure that sensitive business information, such as underwriting criteria and claims history, remains secure and is only accessible to trusted parties.

Consortium blockchains (e.g., Blockchain Insurance Industry Initiative, R3 Corda)

Consortium blockchains are managed by a group of organizations rather than a single entity. They find a balance between decentralization and control, as decision-making power is shared among multiple institutions while maintaining a level of governance. In the insurance industry, consortium blockchains are often used for cross-company collaborations, such as claims processing, fraud prevention, and regulatory reporting. An example is B3i (Blockchain Insurance Industry Initiative), which brings together several large insurers and reinsurers to develop blockchain-based solutions for the industry.

The various types and features of blockchain enable insurers to create customized solutions that address their specific operational needs and regulatory requirements. For example, private or consortium blockchains can be tailored to comply with industry standards and regulations while facilitating secure and efficient information exchange among stakeholders. Whether streamlining claims management, automating underwriting processes using smart contracts, or improving fraud detection, blockchain offers a flexible and scalable platform for transforming the insurance industry.

INSURANCE USE CASES FOR BLOCKCHAIN

Blockchain technology is transforming the insurance industry by addressing longstanding inefficiencies and trust issues. Its decentralized and tamper-proof ledger and programmable features are reshaping essential functions such as underwriting, claims processing, and fraud detection. This section examines how blockchain applications are changing the insurance value chain, focusing on their practical impact and the development of industry standards.

CLAIMS MANAGEMENT AND AUTOMATION

Claims processing is one of the insurance industry's most costly and time-consuming functions. Traditionally, this process involves multiple handoffs and manual verification, with significant potential for disputes. Blockchain technology improves this workflow by creating a single, unchangeable record of events accessible to all stakeholders, including policyholders, insurers, reinsurers, and third-party administrators.

Smart contracts integrated into the blockchain can be programmed to release payments automatically when specific, predefined conditions are met. For instance, in the case of flight delay insurance, a blockchain-enabled smart contract can verify airline data from a trusted data oracle and initiate payment directly to the policyholder—eliminating the need for a formal claims submission. This approach enhances the customer experience, reduces administrative overhead, and speeds up the settlement process.

Automation is especially effective in parametric policies, where payout conditions are based on events rather than damages. In catastrophe insurance, smart contracts can automatically trigger a payout when wind speeds or seismic activity surpasses a specified threshold. This process eliminates the need for expensive loss assessments and reduces payment delays.

FRAUD DETECTION AND RISK PREVENTION

According to industry estimates, insurance fraud costs the global industry over $80 billion each year. Much of this fraud stems from duplicate claims, forged documents, and identity theft. Traditional methods of detecting fraud typically involve retroactive audits or advanced analytics performed on centralized datasets. However, these methods are often constrained by the quality and accessibility of the data.

Blockchain provides a fundamentally different approach by ensuring that every transaction—whether it involves submitting a claims, issuing a policy, or making a payment—is transparently recorded and time stamped on a shared, tamper-resistant ledger. When data is distributed across a network and validated using cryptography, the chances for data manipulation are significantly reduced.

For example, when a vehicle accident is recorded on a blockchain-based claims platform, the claims becomes immediately visible to other insurers in the consortium. This transparency prevents a policyholder from submitting the same claims to multiple insurers, a common opportunistic fraud. Additionally, integrating blockchain technology with AI-driven anomaly detection systems allows insurers to identify unusual patterns in near real time, flagging potentially suspicious behavior before funds are disbursed.

POLICY ISSUANCE AND LIFECYCLE MANAGEMENT

Policy creation, renewal, and management often involve several systems, third parties, and regulatory steps. Blockchain provides a more streamlined and transparent alternative by digitizing the entire lifecycle of the policy.

Digital policies stored on a blockchain can be:

- Issued instantly with verified identity credentials
- Programmed to automatically adjust coverage, notify customers, or trigger renewal options based on external events
- Accessible to customers at any time, with built-in data integrity guarantees

For example, a usage-based auto insurance policy could be connected to telematics data and implemented as a smart contract. When the policyholder's monthly mileage data is updated (automatically recorded through a GPS-enabled app), the premium can be recalculated and deducted based on the logic embedded in the smart contract—without requiring any action from the insurer or the customer.

This method enhances customer satisfaction, minimizes administrative errors, and facilitates new pricing models, particularly personalized and on-demand insurance.

IDENTITY VERIFICATION AND KNOW YOUR CUSTOMER COMPLIANCE

Know Your Customer (KYC) and antimoney laundering requirements substantially burden insurers, especially those operating across multiple jurisdictions. Whenever a customer engages with a new service provider—an insurer, bank, or healthcare provider—they generally have to repeat the same identity verification process.

Blockchain provides a decentralized solution through self-sovereign identity systems, allowing individuals to maintain control over their personal data in a secure digital wallet. Instead of repeatedly submitting documents, individuals can only grant access to their verified credentials when necessary. The insurer can validate the information through blockchain technology without storing sensitive documents.

This speeds up onboarding and improves privacy, data security, and regulatory compliance, especially under data protection laws like the General Data Protection Regulation (GDPR) and California Consumer Privacy Act.

REINSURANCE AND RISK SHARING

Reinsurance transactions involve complex layers of risk transfer, large datasets, and extensive reconciliation between ceding insurers and reinsurers. Delays in data sharing can lead to late or inaccurate payouts, which increases systemic risk.

Blockchain enables real-time risk data sharing and automated settlements between insurers and reinsurers. All parties can access a synchronized ledger that records policy details, claims activity, and payment status. Smart contracts can automatically activate reinsurance coverage when specific thresholds are reached in the primary insurer's portfolio.

A reinsurer could set up a smart contract that automatically initiates a payment when the total losses from a hurricane surpass a specified dollar amount. This amount would be verified using external catastrophe modeling platforms. This approach enhances capital efficiency and improves liquidity planning for both parties involved. Initiatives like the B3i are testing various use cases to develop a blockchain-based global ecosystem for reinsurance transactions.

PARAMETRIC INSURANCE AND EVENT-TRIGGERED PRODUCTS

Parametric insurance is designed to provide payments based on the occurrence of specific events rather than the assessed value of losses. For instance, a parametric policy for drought conditions may trigger a payment if rainfall drops below a certain threshold, as verified by satellite data.

Blockchain facilitates this model by integrating smart contracts with data oracles to automate the process. Oracles are reliable external data sources—like weather stations, satellite networks, or seismographs—that provide event data to the blockchain. Once a triggering event is confirmed, the smart contract automatically executes the payment.

This approach is particularly impactful in areas susceptible to natural disasters, as delays in indemnity-based claims can be critical for survival versus financial collapse. In several developing economies, blockchain-based parametric insurance has already been introduced to assist smallholder farmers facing climate risks.

MICROINSURANCE AND FINANCIAL INCLUSION

Over half of the global population cannot access formal insurance products, especially in low-income and rural areas. High administrative costs, limited distribution infrastructure, and lack of trust impede market penetration.

Blockchain helps solve these barriers by:

- Lowering operational costs through automation and decentralized processes.
- Facilitating mobile-based policy distribution in areas with high smartphone usage.
- Increasing transparency fosters trust among new insurance buyers.

A blockchain-based microinsurance initiative in Kenya provided pay-as-you-go crop insurance via mobile payments. When satellite feeds detected drought conditions, smart contracts initiated immediate payouts to enrolled farmers, creating a trustworthy, cost-effective solution for financial protection.

SMART CONTRACTS IN INSURANCE

Smart contracts are among the most revolutionary applications of blockchain technology in the insurance industry. Unlike traditional contracts that require manual intervention, administrative review, and often human arbitration, smart contracts are self-executing codes stored on a blockchain. When predefined conditions are met, they automatically perform specified actions—such as issuing a payout (Buterin, 2014). This section will explore how smart contracts work, their advantages in the insurance sector, and the limitations that must be considered for their real-world implementation.

UNDERSTANDING SMART CONTRACTS

The term "smart contract" was first introduced by cryptographer Nick Szabo in the 1990s to describe computerized transaction protocols that enforce the terms of an agreement. In today's blockchain ecosystems, smart contracts are essentially scripts written in programming languages such as Solidity (for Ethereum) or Go/JavaScript (for Hyperledger Fabric). These scripts are deployed on a blockchain and are immutable, meaning they cannot be changed once launched.

A smart contract operates similarly to a digital vending machine: it automatically performs an action when the correct inputs are provided. For example, when a user inserts the right amount of money, the vending machine dispenses a snack. In insurance, a smart contract might specify: "If the rainfall in a given region is less than 20 mm during the month of June, then pay $500 to the policyholder."

Once a trusted oracle verifies the rainfall data, the contract executes without further intervention.

This level of automation significantly decreases operational overhead, enhances accuracy, and establishes a new model of trustless interaction—one in which parties do not need to trust each other because the technology transparently enforces the rules.

APPLICATIONS IN INSURANCE OPERATIONS

Smart contracts can be integrated into nearly every phase of the insurance process. Some of the most notable applications include:

Policy issuance and underwriting

Smart contracts can incorporate policy terms and underwriting criteria into a digital agreement that activates only when the applicant meets certain conditions. For example, a life insurance policy could be initiated only if the applicant's verified health data falls within acceptable risk parameters. This approach enables insurers to:

- Reduce manual underwriting processes.
- Provide instant approval or dynamic pricing.
- Create more personalized and data-driven policies.

In peer-to-peer insurance models, smart contracts can distribute risk among users without needing a central insurer, enabling the creation of decentralized mutual insurance platforms.

Claims processing and settlements

The traditional claims process often experiences delays due to the need for documentation, verification, and negotiations. Smart contracts can significantly reduce this friction by automatically verifying event data and triggering payouts (Deloitte, 2016). A typical example is flight delay insurance: a smart contract linked to aviation databases can instantly compensate when a flight is delayed beyond a certain threshold.

This process benefits both insurance companies and policyholders. Insurers reduce processing costs and fraud exposure, while customers enjoy faster, more reliable payouts with less paperwork and ambiguity (Tapscott, D. & Tapscott, A., 2016).

Parametric insurance automation

Smart contracts are especially effective for parametric insurance, where payout conditions depend on objective and measurable events instead of loss assessments. For instance, in agricultural insurance, satellite data could activate a smart contract to pay a farmer when rainfall levels fall below a specific threshold, indicating a drought.

This method removes the necessity for human claims adjusters and provides immediate financial relief in urgent situations, enhancing policyholder satisfaction and retention.

INTERFACING WITH ORACLES

A significant challenge in implementing smart contracts is their reliance on external data to evaluate real-world conditions. To overcome this issue, they require intermediaries known as oracles. An oracle is a service that provides off-chain data—such as weather reports, stock prices, or flight statuses—into the blockchain.

Since blockchains are inherently closed systems that cannot access external information independently, oracles enable smart contracts to interact with the physical world. For insurance applications, oracles must be:

- Dependable, providing precise and secure data
- Redundant, sourcing from various channels to avoid manipulation
- Verifiable, promoting transparency and traceability

Oracles reintroduce a level of trust into the trustless blockchain system, and their proper selection and management are essential for maintaining the credibility of automated insurance products.

ADVANTAGES OF SMART CONTRACTS IN INSURANCE

The attractiveness of smart contracts comes from their capacity to create automated, transparent, and cost-efficient insurance processes. Key advantages include:

- Speed: Instant execution of contract terms upon condition verification.
- Cost savings: Reduction in administrative and legal costs.
- Transparency: Policyholders can review and verify contract logic on-chain.
- Immutability: Contract terms cannot be changed unilaterally after deployment.
- Auditability: All transactions are recorded on a distributed ledger, supporting compliance and dispute resolution.

These features strongly align with the industry's goals of improving efficiency and building customer trust.

LIMITATIONS AND CHALLENGES

Smart contracts have significant potential, but they also encounter various technical, legal, and operational challenges that must be overcome for widespread adoption in the insurance sector.

CODE IS LAW—BUT CODE CAN BE FLAWED

Smart contracts are only as reliable as the code they are written in. Bugs or vulnerabilities in the contract's logic can result in unintended consequences, such as unauthorized payments or systemic exploitation. Unlike traditional contracts, which can be interpreted and enforced by courts, a smart contract becomes final once executed—unless it is programmed to allow for dispute resolution or updates.

This strictness necessitates security audits and comprehensive testing before deployment, particularly for consumer-facing products.

REGULATORY AND LEGAL AMBIGUITY

Smart contracts challenge existing legal frameworks. Questions remain about:

- Who is liable if a smart contract fails?
- How do regulators ensure consumer protection when no human oversight is involved?
- Are smart contracts legally enforceable in court?

Regulators and legal scholars are currently examining these questions, but until there is more clarity, widespread adoption will probably be confined to low-risk or pilot programs.

INTEROPERABILITY AND INTEGRATION

Insurance companies typically use outdated IT systems and isolated databases. Incorporating blockchain and smart contracts into their existing infrastructures may require substantial investment in system redesign, employee training, and IT support.

Interoperability between blockchains continues to be a challenging issue. A smart contract on Ethereum may not easily interact with a policy ledger on Hyperledger unless it is bridged or redesigned.

BLOCKCHAIN CODING AND IMPLEMENTATION IN INSURANCE

Blockchain technology presents exciting theoretical possibilities, but its real value comes from practical applications. For insurance professionals, it is essential to grasp the capabilities of blockchain and the underlying structures and implementation in real-world scenarios. This section offers a foundational overview of the platforms, tools, and programming languages used in blockchain development, along with a sample smart contract relevant to the insurance industry.

While not every reader may become a blockchain developer, having a basic understanding of the involved technologies will enable professionals to work more effectively with technical teams, assess vendor solutions, and imagine new applications.

COMMON BLOCKCHAIN PLATFORMS USED IN INSURANCE

Blockchain platforms are primarily categorized into two types: public, which is open and decentralized, and permissioned, which is restricted and enterprise focused. Both kinds are utilized in the insurance industry, depending on specific business models and use cases.

Ethereum

Ethereum is the most widely used public blockchain for developing smart contracts. It features a Turing-complete programming language called Solidity, enabling developers to create complex agreements. Ethereum is particularly well suited for decentralized insurance applications, parametric products, and experiments with decentralized autonomous insurance organizations. However, its public nature could raise privacy and regulatory concerns for insurers managing sensitive data.

Hyperledger fabric

Hyperledger Fabric, developed under the Linux Foundation, is a modular and permissioned blockchain framework for enterprise environments. It provides fine-grained access control and supports private data collection, making it particularly suitable for insurers managing proprietary claims or underwriting data. Smart contracts in Hyperledger can be written in Go, Java, or JavaScript, offering flexibility for traditional IT teams.

Chainlink

Chainlink is a decentralized oracle network, not a blockchain itself. Its primary function is to provide off-chain data to smart contracts. In the insurance industry, Chainlink is commonly utilized to deliver reliable data such as weather information, market insights, and geolocation inputs for parametric and event-based contracts.

Corda and Quorum

These platforms serve financial institutions and are utilized in cross-border insurance and reinsurance applications. Their emphasis on privacy, scalability, and business logic customization makes them appealing for multiparty risk-sharing agreements.

DEVELOPMENT TOOLS AND LANGUAGES

Every blockchain platform has its ecosystem of tools and preferred development environments. For insurance applications, the most commonly used tools include:

- Solidity: The primary language for writing smart contracts on Ethereum. It's statically typed and influenced by JavaScript and C++.
- Remix IDE: A browser-based integrated development environment to write, test, and deploy Solidity contracts.
- Truffle suite: A robust development framework for Ethereum that includes tools for testing, migrations, and scripting.
- Ganache: A personal Ethereum blockchain used for development and testing.
- MetaMask: A browser wallet that enables users to interact with Ethereum-based applications, commonly used in prototypes and customer interfaces.

For enterprise blockchains like Hyperledger, developers use:

- Go or JavaScript for Chainlink (the equivalent of smart contracts)

- Docker containers to manage distributed nodes
- Kubernetes and Helm to scale deployments for more extensive networks

Sample Code: Parametric Insurance Smart Contract

Below is a simplified example of a smart contract written in Solidity for a parametric insurance policy that pays out when the temperature threshold is crossed. This is a common use case in crop and climate insurance.

```
// SPDX-License-Identifier: MIT
pragma solidity ^0.8.0;
contract ParametricInsurance {
  address public insurer;
  address payable to public policyholder;
  uint256 public premium;
  uint256 public payout amount;
  int256 public temperature threshold;
  bool public isActive;
  constructor(
  address payable_policyholder,
  uint256_premium,
  uint256_payoutAmount,
  int256_temperatureThreshold
  ) {
  insurer = msg.sender;
  policyholder =_policyholder;
  premium =_premium;
  payoutAmount =_payoutAmount;
  temperatureThreshold =_temperatureThreshold;
  isActive = true;
  }
  function triggerPayout(int256 currentTemperature) public {
  require(isActive, "Policy is not active.");
  require(currentTemperature <= temperatureThreshold, "Condition not
   met.");
  isActive = false; // Prevent re-use
  policyholder.transfer(payoutAmount);
  }
  // Function to fund the contract
  receive() external payable {}
}
```

How it works:

- The insurer initiates the contract, outlining the terms and funding arrangements.
- When a weather oracle reports a temperature below the threshold, the triggerPayout function can be invoked.
- The policyholder will receive an automatic payout if the required conditions are met.

This simplified model assumes interaction with a manual oracle for demonstration purposes. An automated oracle like Chainlink would generate the trigger in production environments.

CONSIDERATIONS FOR IMPLEMENTATION

Implementing blockchain in insurance environments requires more than coding. It also requires:

Security

Smart contracts are immutable. If a vulnerability exists in the code, it can be exploited indefinitely. Before deployment, all contracts must undergo formal audits, penetration testing, and bug bounty programs.

Compliance and integration

Any implementation of blockchain technology must adhere to industry regulations, including data protection laws like GDPR and insurance-specific requirements such as KYC protocols. Additionally, insurers must integrate blockchain with their current policy administration systems, often necessitating using application programming interfaces and middleware solutions.

Scalability and cost

Public blockchain transactions incur fluctuating gas fees based on network traffic. Insurers using Ethereum need to manage contract complexity carefully to reduce costs. In contrast, permissioned blockchains like Hyperledger provide better scalability and more predictable performance for enterprise applications.

CASE STUDY: REAL-WORLD BLOCKCHAIN IN INSURANCE

Although blockchain is still an emerging technology in the insurance industry, several companies and consortiums have already showcased its potential through live pilots and operational deployments. This section presents a real-world case study demonstrating how blockchain technology has enhanced transparency, automated insurance processes, and improved customer outcomes.

CASE STUDY: ETHERISC AND PARAMETRIC FLIGHT DELAY INSURANCE

Etherisc is a decentralized insurance protocol that has become a prominent example of innovation in blockchain-based insurance. It was created to illustrate how smart contracts and decentralized infrastructure can streamline the insurance value chain, beginning with one of the most common and frustrating issues travelers face: flight delays.

Background

Traditionally, flight delay insurance requires policyholders to file a claims after experiencing a delayed flight. This process is followed by a manual review conducted by the insurer. Customers may need to submit documentation, such as boarding passes or confirmation of the delay, and the claims can take weeks to be processed. The administrative effort can often exceed the payout amount for relatively low-value claims.

Etherisc aimed to fully automate the process by leveraging blockchain technology and oracles to create a parametric insurance product that would:

- Initiate coverage immediately.
- Monitor flight data in real time.
- Trigger automatic payouts for delays that exceed a specified threshold.

How it worked

The customer was provided with:

- The option to purchase insurance for a specific flight is available through Etherisc's user interface.
- Payments were made using cryptocurrency, and the policy terms were coded into a smart contract on the Ethereum blockchain.

Data Oracle Integration

- Flight status data was provided by Chainlink oracles, which monitored delay times using public aviation databases.
- The smart contract will be activated if the delay surpasses the policy's threshold, such as 45 minutes.

Automated Payout

- Once activated, the smart contract automatically processes the payout to the customer.
- The smart contract automatically transfers the payout to the customer's wallet—without needing claims submission or human approval.

Transparency and Trust

- All policy terms, execution history, and payout records were available on-chain, ensuring complete transparency and auditability.

IMPACT AND LESSONS LEARNED

The Etherisc model showcased how intelligent contract automation can significantly enhance the insurance process's speed, efficiency, and trust. Customers valued the straightforwardness of not needing to submit paperwork or dispute their eligibility. Additionally, insurers enjoyed reduced claims administration costs and a lower risk of fraud.

However, the deployment also highlighted essential challenges:

- Regulatory uncertainty hindered Etherisc's ability to scale in heavily regulated markets.
- Cryptocurrency volatility created barriers to consumer adoption and pricing stability.
- Limitations of smart contracts made it challenging to manage nuanced claims or accommodate exceptions.

Etherisc has led the development of blockchain-based products in areas like crop insurance, hurricane protection, and decentralized mutual aid.

OTHER REAL-WORLD EXAMPLES

Blockchain insurance industry initiative

B3i (N.D.), launched by major global insurers and reinsurers, aimed to streamline reinsurance contracts using Hyperledger Fabric. Their objective was to simplify the reconciliation and settlement processes among multiple parties in the event of a catastrophe. Pilot programs demonstrated significant reductions in administrative costs and faster settlement times.

AXA Fizzy

Before it was discontinued, AXA experimented with parametric flight insurance branded as "Fizzy." This platform utilized Ethereum smart contracts and promised automatic payouts if a customer's flight was delayed by more than 2 hours. This initiative showcased traditional insurers' early interest in applying blockchain technology.

Arbol

Arbol is a platform that provides weather insurance through blockchain-based parametric contracts. Its purpose is to safeguard farmers and agribusinesses from revenue losses caused by adverse weather conditions. By utilizing smart contracts and climate data oracles, Arbol can expand its insurance products into underserved markets where traditional underwriting methods are not feasible.

These examples illustrate that blockchain technology in insurance is progressing from concept to practical application. Although still in its early phases, this technology demonstrates its value in specialized fields such as parametric insurance, reinsurance, and operations that rely heavily on automation.

CHALLENGES AND LIMITATIONS OF BLOCKCHAIN IN INSURANCE TECHNOLOGY

While blockchain has significant potential to transform the insurance industry, its widespread adoption faces several challenges. Insurers and industry stakeholders need to understand these limitations when considering blockchain-based solutions.

SCALABILITY ISSUES

Scalability is one of the most significant challenges facing blockchain technology. Public blockchains, such as Bitcoin and Ethereum, have limitations in transactions throughout because of the time required to process and validate transactions. As more participants join the network and more data is recorded, these systems can become slower and less efficient. In the insurance industry, where transactions need to be processed quickly—such as in claims handling or underwriting—slow transaction times can undermine the effectiveness of blockchain-based solutions.

Private and consortium blockchains can help alleviate scalability concerns by limiting the number of participants and simplifying consensus protocols. However, they may still encounter performance issues when handling large transactions, hindering insurers' ability to scale their operations effectively.

REGULATORY AND COMPLIANCE CHALLENGES

The decentralized and transparent nature of blockchain presents regulatory and compliance challenges, especially in heavily regulated industries such as insurance. The insurance sector is subject to strict data protection and privacy regulations, such as the GDPR in the European Union. This immutable nature of blockchain could potentially conflict with these legal requirements.

In some jurisdictions, individuals have a "right to be forgotten," which allows them to request the deletion of their data from digital records. However, the immutable nature of blockchain technology contradicts this principle since once data is recorded, it cannot be changed or deleted. Furthermore, regulatory bodies may face challenges in monitoring blockchain systems. The absence of a central authority makes it more difficult to enforce regulations and track activities in real time.

Insurers must navigate regulatory hurdles by collaborating with regulators, ensuring blockchain applications comply with current laws, and creating solutions that protect privacy and data security while adhering to industry standards.

INTEGRATION WITH LEGACY SYSTEMS

Many insurance companies continue to rely on legacy systems, which can be complex, outdated, and incompatible with blockchain technology. Integrating blockchain with existing infrastructure can be costly, time-consuming, and technically challenging. Additionally, insurers may be hesitant to adopt blockchain solutions if they require a complete overhaul of their current systems or if the potential return on investment is uncertain.

The need for interoperability between blockchain technology and legacy systems is a significant barrier to adoption. Insurers must ensure blockchain can seamlessly communicate with their existing databases, claims management platforms, and other technology solutions. This may require the development of custom solutions or the implementation of hybrid systems.

DATA PRIVACY AND SECURITY CONCERNS

Although blockchain is known for its security, it is not free from privacy and security concerns. While the data stored on a blockchain is cryptographically secure, risks are still associated with exposing sensitive information. In public blockchains, all transactions can be seen by anyone on the network, which can compromise the confidentiality of personal or financial information.

Private blockchains offer greater control over data access but also raise concerns regarding data security and access control. Additionally, if a cyberattack targets a blockchain network, the repercussions could be significant, as a breach in a decentralized system could impact numerous stakeholders.

Insurers must thoroughly assess the security measures implemented for blockchain solutions to ensure they are sufficiently robust for handling sensitive insurance data.

HIGH ENERGY CONSUMPTION

Public blockchains, particularly those that use proof-of-work consensus mechanisms like Bitcoin, require significant computational power to validate transactions. This results in high energy consumption, raising environmental concerns. As sustainability becomes an increasingly important priority for businesses and regulators, insurers may experience public and regulatory pressure to reduce the environmental impact of their operations.

Alternative consensus mechanisms like proof of stake are more energy efficient but have not been widely adopted and still pose their own challenges. Insurers need to consider the environmental impact of blockchain technology and look for solutions to reduce energy consumption while maintaining performance and security.

LACK OF STANDARDIZATION

The blockchain industry is still in its early stages, and no widely accepted standards or protocols exist. This lack of standardization can result in fragmentation, where different insurers or service providers use incompatible blockchain solutions. Such fragmentation can hinder collaboration and interoperability, making it challenging for insurers to benefit from blockchain technology fully.

To tackle this issue, industry consortia like B3i strive to create shared standards for blockchain-based solutions in the insurance sector. However, the widespread adoption of these standards will take time, and insurers may encounter challenges as they navigate this evolving landscape.

RESISTANCE TO CHANGE

The insurance industry is typically conservative, with many organizations reluctant to adopt new technologies due to concerns about potential risks and costs. Introducing blockchain could disrupt existing business models, leading to resistance from stakeholders who prefer the status quo. Insurers may also encounter challenges in educating their workforce and customers about the benefits of blockchain technology and in persuading them to embrace it.

For successful blockchain integration in the insurance industry, insurers must implement change management, promote a culture of innovation, and showcase the concrete benefits that blockchain can provide in terms of efficiency, transparency, and trust.

SUMMARY

This chapter explores the fundamental concepts of blockchain technology and its potential applications in the insurance industry. We examine the key characteristics of blockchain—decentralization, transparency, immutability, and security—that make it an appealing solution for the insurance sector. These features can enhance operational efficiency, improve data accuracy, and foster greater trust among the parties involved.

We also examined the various blockchains—public, private, and consortium—emphasizing their respective advantages and applications in the insurance sector. Public blockchains offer open access, which can benefit insurance solutions aimed at the general public. In contrast, private and consortium blockchains provide greater control and security, making them ideal for enterprise-level and collaborative use cases.

The chapter also discusses the challenges and limitations associated with adopting blockchain technology. Insurers face significant obstacles such as scalability issues, regulatory hurdles, difficulties in integrating with legacy systems, and concerns over data privacy. Moreover, the absence of industry standards, high energy consumption, and resistance to change add to the complexity of achieving widespread blockchain adoption in the insurance sector.

In conclusion, blockchain can potentially transform the insurance industry, but successfully implementing it requires careful consideration of various challenges.

Insurers must strategically address these limitations and tailor blockchain solutions to their specific operational, regulatory, and customer needs. With thoughtful planning and collaboration, blockchain could become a powerful tool for modernizing the insurance landscape.

AI DISCLOSURE

During the preparation of this work the author(s) used Grammarly to improve readability and correct any grammatical mistakes. After using this tool/service, the author(s) reviewed and edited the content as needed and take(s) full responsibility for the content of the publication.

REFERENCES

B3i. (n.d.). *Blockchain Insurance industry initiative*. https://b3i.tech/.

Buterin, V. (2014). *A next-generation smart contract and decentralized application platform*. Ethereum White Paper. https://ethereum.org/en/whitepaper/.

Deloitte. (2016). *Blockchain applications in insurance*. Deloitte Center for Financial Services. https://www2.deloitte.com/.

Etherisc. (n.d.). *Decentralized insurance platform*. https://etherisc.com/.

Nakamoto, S. (2008). *Bitcoin: A peer-to-peer electronic cash system*. https://bitcoin.org/bitcoin.pdf.

Tapscott, D., & Tapscott, A. (2016). *Blockchain revolution: How the technology behind Bitcoin is changing money, business, and the world*. Penguin.

CHAPTER

Parametric insurance: innovations in trigger-based payouts

7

CHAPTER OUTLINE

Insurance Technology. DOI: https://doi.org/10.1016/B978-0-443-43972-8.00011-0

The insurance industry is transforming as it adapts to the increasing frequency and severity of global risks, including climate change, natural disasters, and systemic disruptions that challenge traditional indemnity-based models. In this context, parametric insurance has emerged as one of the most promising innovations in risk transfer. Unlike conventional insurance products, which require a detailed postevent loss assessment, parametric insurance provides payouts based on the occurrence of predefined events linked to measurable external parameters, such as rainfall, temperature, seismic activity, or wind speed (Weiss, 2021).

FROM INDEMNITY TO PARAMETRIC MODELS

Traditional insurance policies aim to compensate the insured for actual losses incurred. While this method provides flexibility and nuance, it also entails complex administrative challenges.

- Losses must be individually verified and appraised.
- Claims adjustment is subject to interpretation and negotiation.
- Payouts can be delayed by weeks or months.
- Administrative costs and fraud detection systems inflate overhead.

These challenges are heightened in large-scale disasters, rural or remote areas, and developing economies, where the infrastructure for handling claims may be limited. In contrast, parametric insurance defines the event, the index, and the payout structure in advance. This allows for policies that can be executed automatically with minimal human intervention.

Consider, for instance, a parametric hurricane policy designed for a coastal municipality. This contract specifies that if wind speeds recorded at a designated meteorological station exceed 120 mph, a payout of $5 million will be triggered. There is no requirement to assess actual property damage. The event data is obtained from reliable sources, such as National Oceanic and Atmospheric Administration (NOAA), and once validated, the contract will be executed.

Though conceptually straightforward, this model needs careful technical and actuarial design to ensure fairness, efficiency, and sustainability.

HISTORICAL CONTEXT AND EVOLUTION

Parametric insurance is not an entirely new concept. Its early versions emerged in the 1990s as weather derivatives, mainly utilized by energy companies to protect themselves against unfavorable temperature or precipitation conditions. However, with the advancement of satellite-based remote sensing, Internet of Things (IoT) devices, and enhanced climate modeling, the scope and reliability of parametric indices have significantly increased.

The key moments in its evolution include:

- 2003: The Chicago Mercantile Exchange introduced weather futures and options.
- 2007–12: Index-based crop insurance pilots launched across India, Ethiopia, and Kenya.
- 2014 onward: Emergence of blockchain-enabled parametric products (e.g., Etherisc).
- The 2020s: Growing integration with climate resilience finance, microinsurance, and decentralized insurance protocols.

Currently, parametric insurance is utilized by reinsurers, such as Swiss Re, national governments like Mexico through its catastrophe bond program, and non-governmental organizations (NGOs) that provide climate risk finance to vulnerable communities. This type of insurance is increasingly being integrated into blended financial structures, including sovereign risk pools and public–private partnerships.

THE LOGIC BEHIND PARAMETRIC DESIGN

The basic concept of parametric insurance is trigger-based coverage. A trigger event is linked to a specific metric—such as temperature exceeding 40°C, rainfall falling below 20 mm, or wind speeds surpassing 120 knots.

- Objective: Data must be observable and verifiable.
- Transparent: Policyholders and insurers understand what conditions lead to a payout.
- Measurable: The event is tied to a numerical value, not a subjective interpretation.
- Timely: The data source must be available shortly after the event to enable rapid response.

This structure allows quick and efficient payouts, often within a few days. From a risk management standpoint, it minimizes loss uncertainty and establishes an incentive-aligned mechanism for resilience. The insured party understands precisely what they are purchasing, while the insurer can better predict aggregate exposure.

This section discusses basis risk, a key concept of this chapter. Basis risk arises when an event that should trigger a payout occurs, but no actual damage is sustained (a false positive), or when damage does occur. Still, the index fails to trigger (a false negative). Such situations can lead to customer dissatisfaction and necessitate careful statistical calibration of the parametric model to minimize these risks.

RELEVANCE IN EMERGING RISK ENVIRONMENTS

Various global trends have led to an increased demand for parametric insurance. These trends are:

Climate volatility

Extreme weather events are becoming more frequent and severe. Traditional insurance has difficulty simultaneously assessing losses across large regions, mainly for risks like flooding, wildfires, and drought. Parametric models can provide rapid relief based on regional data inputs.

Speed of capital disbursement

Timing is crucial in areas prone to disasters. Governments and humanitarian organizations frequently depend on insurance to finance their emergency responses. Delayed payouts can mean the difference between stabilizing a region and allowing it to spiral into a crisis. Parametric payouts can be issued within 10–14 days, providing essential working capital when it is most needed.

Underserved markets

Parametric insurance can reach otherwise uninsurable individuals under traditional models. For example, smallholder farmers with irregular incomes and no formal credit histories can still purchase a weather-based policy that requires no loss documentation or claims processing infrastructure.

Integration with smart contracts

When integrated with blockchain technology, parametric insurance can utilize smart contracts for fully automated claims settlements by leveraging real-time data feeds. This approach minimizes transaction costs and the risk of fraud while improving transparency.

ACADEMIC AND TECHNICAL INTEREST

For actuaries, data scientists, and risk engineers, parametric insurance offers a compelling domain for quantitative modeling, data integration, and probabilistic forecasting. It raises questions such as:

- How do we construct a reliable index with minimal basis risk?
- What are the statistical trade-offs between simplicity, coverage precision, and scalability?
- How do we simulate the likelihood of trigger events across time horizons and climate scenarios?
- How should portfolios of parametric contracts be correlated, reinsured, or hedged?

Parametric insurance serves as both a practical tool and a platform for academic innovation in fields like applied statistics, geospatial analytics, and computational finance.

CORE COMPONENTS OF PARAMETRIC INSURANCE

Parametric insurance products comprise four key components: the trigger event, the index, the payout structure, and the data infrastructure that links these elements. Each component must be thoughtfully designed to ensure the policy functions reliably, reduces basis risk, and is actuarially sound. Unlike traditional insurance, where payouts depend on verifying losses, parametric policies rely on precise, predefined models that execute automatically in response to measurable inputs.

TRIGGER EVENT SPECIFICATION

The trigger event is at the core of every parametric insurance contract—the clearly defined condition that activates the policy's payout mechanism. This trigger must satisfy four essential criteria:

- Observable: The condition must be verifiable by a third party (e.g., temperature readings, rainfall totals, or wind speeds).
- Quantifiable: The condition must be tied to a specific numeric threshold (e.g., $\geq$100 mm rainfall in 24 hours).
- Time bounded: The trigger must occur within a predefined period (e.g., June 1–August 31, 2025).
- Location specific: The trigger should apply to a specific geographic area relevant to the insured exposure.

Triggers are generally established based on historical loss correlations, conditions statistically linked to insured damage. For instance, historical analysis may show that wind speeds surpassing 120 mph at a specific coastal location are associated with average commercial property losses exceeding $1 million. Consequently, a trigger can be set at this threshold, accompanied by a fixed payout structure.

Triggers can be binary (yes/no, e.g., earthquake magnitude $\geq$7.0) or graduated (where payouts increase in tiers as the parameter intensifies). Binary triggers simplify contract logic but are more vulnerable to basis risk at marginal values (e.g., magnitude 6.9 vs. 7.0).

INDEX CONSTRUCTION AND VALIDATION

The index serves as the reference dataset that quantifies the trigger event. In technical terms, an index is defined as a parametric function $I(x, t, l)$, where:

x = input variable (e.g., rainfall)
t = time interval (e.g., monthly total)
l = location (e.g., weather station coordinates or satellite grid cell)

The index must be:

- Statistically robust: Validated using historical time-series data.
- Predictively accurate: Strongly correlated with actual loss outcomes.
- Transparent and replicable: This is so that all parties can independently verify it.
- Resilient to manipulation or disruption, especially for products relying on real-time IoT or satellite data.

Indexes can be derived from:

- Ground-based sensor networks (e.g., World Meteorological Organization–certified weather stations)
- Satellite remote sensing (e.g., Moderate Resolution Imaging Spectroradiometer, Sentinel, Tropical Rainfall Measuring Mission)
- Model-derived data (e.g., ERA5 reanalysis, catastrophe models)
- Third-party platforms (e.g., NOAA, European Centre for Medium-Range Weather Forecasts, Japan Aerospace Exploration Agency, Swiss Re's CatNet)

Index design also involves spatial interpolation techniques, such as kriging or inverse distance weighting, to address data gaps. Additionally, data preprocessing must consider:

- Sensor calibration errors
- Missing data imputation
- Time resolution alignment (e.g., daily to monthly aggregation)

Actuarial teams frequently utilize copula models, generalized additive models, or machine learning algorithms to enhance the index's correlation with the observed claims data.

PAYOUT FUNCTION DESIGN

The payout function f(I) determines how much the insured receives based on the index value. This is essential for balancing risk transfer, affordability, and minimizing basis risk.

Three primary payout structures are commonly used:

1. Binary/Lump-Sum Payout
   f(I) = P, if I ≥ T0, otherwise f(I) = {P, if I ≥ T 0, otherwise}
   - Payout (P) is fixed.
   - Trigger threshold (T) defines the activation point.
   - Easy to implement but has high basis risk near the threshold.
2. Tiered Payouts
   f(I) = Pi, if Ti≤I<Ti+1 f(I) = P_i, if T_i ≤ I < T_{i+1}
   - The policyholder receives a payout corresponding to the severity band.
   - Improves basis alignment.
   - Requires careful statistical calibration and regulatory disclosure.

3. Linear or Piecewise-Linear Payout
   f(I) = α(I−T), where I≥Tf(I) = α(I − T), where I ≥ T
   - The payout increases continuously as the index rises above the trigger.
   - Allows proportional loss recovery.
   - It is best used when the index-loss correlation is strong and continuous.

Visualizing this as a loss curve enables insurers and policyholders to evaluate coverage accuracy.

DATA INFRASTRUCTURE AND ORACLES

Parametric products depend on reliable, secure, and tamper-resistant data infrastructure for execution. In blockchain deployments, oracles serve as the link between off-chain data sources and on-chain smart contracts.

There are three main categories of oracles:

- Inbound Oracles: Feed external data into the blockchain (e.g., Chainlink weather oracle).
- Consensus Oracles: Aggregate multiple data sources to reduce manipulation risk.
- Custom application programming interfaces (APIs): Directly query certified data feeds (e.g., from NOAA, Japan Meteorological Agency).

Key considerations for oracle selection include:

- Data integrity: Cryptographic proof, redundancy, and auditing
- Latency: How quickly data is available postevent
- Security: Resistance to tampering and distributed denial-of-service attacks
- Smart contract integration: Compatibility with platforms like Ethereum or Hyperledger

Parametric products typically follow a "trust but verify" model, ensuring that data is independently accessible to insurers, the insured, and regulators. High-quality oracles may utilize multisource aggregation, cryptographic signing, or decentralized autonomous data validation.

CONTRACT EXECUTION ARCHITECTURE

The contract architecture uses software logic to connect the index, trigger, and payout functions. For blockchain implementations, this involves:

- Smart contract deployment (e.g., on Ethereum or Polygon)
- Oracle data feed integration
- Escrow management for funds (ensuring liquidity)
- Automated audit logging and dispute mechanisms

Advanced platforms enable parametric portfolio bundling, where smart contracts represent indexed contract portfolios with pooled capital buffers. These can be reinsured or collateralized using insurance-linked securities.

DESIGN CONSIDERATIONS AND ACTUARIAL IMPLICATIONS

Creating effective parametric insurance products requires carefully balancing mathematical precision and practical reliability. The attraction of rapid, automated payouts is significant. Still, the success of these policies depends on several key factors: the development of indices, the calibration of thresholds, the modeling of correlated losses, and the assessment of basis risk. These actuarial components must be closely integrated to ensure that parametric contracts are operationally viable, fair, scalable, and sustainable across various market environments.

One of the most significant and commonly cited limitations of parametric insurance is basis risk—the risk that the payout from the policy does not correspond to the actual losses experienced by the policyholder (Clark & Decron, 2016). Basis risk can take several forms:

1. Spatial Basis Risk: This occurs when the data source used to trigger the policy (such as a weather station or satellite pixel) does not accurately reflect the conditions at the specific location of the insured.
2. Temporal Basis Risk: This arises when there is a mismatch between the period covered by the data collection and the actual timing of the loss.
3. Structural Basis Risk: This refers to situations where the indexed variable is a poor indicator of the underlying cause of the loss. For example, triggering a payment based solely on rainfall may not reflect the true loss if the actual damage was caused by flooding due to inadequate drainage or soil saturation.
4. Behavioral Basis Risk: This can occur when a policyholder perceives the policy as unfair, even if it operates as intended. This perception often stems from poor communication or a misunderstanding of the trigger conditions.

By understanding these various types of basis risk, stakeholders can better address potential gaps between policy payouts and actual losses.

Quantifying basis risk involves a thorough statistical analysis of the relationship between an index and historical loss outcomes. Actuaries typically assess this relationship using paired time-series data, including loss data (actual or modeled) alongside index values over a sufficiently long period. Common statistical tools for this analysis include linear regression, quantile regression, and copula-based models. These techniques help evaluate the degree of correlation and tail dependency between indexed events and financial loss.

Measures such as root mean square error or mean absolute error can calculate the difference between expected payouts and actual losses, with larger values indicating weaker alignment and higher basis risk. When loss data are not readily available, proxy variables—such as crop yields, insurance claims totals, or economic loss estimates from catastrophe models—may approximate the relationship between loss and the index.

The calibration of parametric triggers is closely related to basis risk, which involves defining the conditions and thresholds for when payouts occur. Calibrating a trigger is not just about choosing a simple round number or adhering to a regulatory benchmark; it requires a data-driven approach to optimize the payout function about expected loss behavior.

For instance, a rainfall index used in drought insurance may be based on the 30-day accumulated precipitation measured at a regional meteorological station. If historical loss data indicate that crop yields begin to decline significantly when rainfall falls below 40 mm, this threshold can serve as the baseline trigger. However, having a single threshold creates a binary outcome—either a payout or no payout—resulting in a stepwise payout behavior that can be frustrating for policyholders who fall near the threshold.

To mitigate this issue, many insurers implement tiered or continuous payout functions, such as piecewise-linear models, where the payout gradually increases as the index moves further from the threshold. This approach offers smoother and more predictable compensation for policyholders.

Optimizing the trigger threshold is typically done using simulation models or grid search algorithms. These methods assess various threshold values against historical datasets to minimize the absolute difference between observed losses and projected payouts. In this context, the chosen trigger should correlate strongly with losses and align with pricing targets, reinsurance structures, and customer expectations. Additionally, the optimization process must consider regulatory constraints, actuarial fairness, and the level of detail in the available data.

In addition to designing individual policies, actuaries must consider the spatial correlation of loss events across a region or portfolio. For example, suppose a drought index triggers payouts for numerous farmers within a single area. In that case, this creates a potential correlation risk that needs to be reflected in capital provisioning and reinsurance strategies. Actuaries typically use geostatistical techniques such as kriging, Gaussian process regression, and semivariogram analysis to model this spatial dependency. These methods help quantify how the index variable varies over geographic distances. By employing these tools, insurers can understand how quickly weather conditions change across space and determine whether a single data point, such as a weather station or satellite grid cell, accurately represents a larger area. Actuarial teams can then simulate portfolio loss scenarios using spatially correlated synthetic data to evaluate how frequently and severely correlated events could result in significant aggregate payouts.

The transition from exposure-based pricing to event-based modeling is a significant change in traditional underwriting for parametric products. Instead of evaluating a client's building characteristics, credit score, or loss history, parametric underwriting emphasizes the statistical frequency of the triggering event and its historical payout potential.

Premiums are calculated based on three main components: expected loss, risk load, and operational expenses. The expected loss is determined through historical simulations or synthetic data modeling. The risk load is designed to account for capital volatility and tail risk.

In many cases, Monte Carlo simulations or Latin hypercube sampling techniques are utilized to model the stochastic behavior of the index across thousands of years of synthetic weather or seismic conditions.

Insurers often utilize probabilistic catastrophe models (e.g., Risk Management Solutions, AIR, or Oasis) for risks related to catastrophic events—such as hurricanes, earthquakes, and wildfires. These models simulate the likelihood of parametric triggers over different return periods, allowing insurers to estimate key metrics like average annual loss, probable maximum loss, and tail value at risk. These estimates help determine the pricing structure and reinsurance layers. Advanced pricing methods also consider uncertainties related to climate patterns, changes in the frequency of events due to environmental conditions, and geopolitical shifts in exposure.

Parametric product structures face various design constraints beyond just statistics and actuarial logic. These constraints include technical issues, such as the resolution and latency of data feeds; operational challenges, such as claims liquidity and escrow funding; and user experience considerations, like clarity of coverage and transparency of payouts. In more sophisticated products, insurers may use hybrid structures—like dual-trigger contracts that are activated only when multiple conditions are met (e.g., both rainfall and soil moisture occurring)—or dynamic deductibles that adjust based on the behavior of policyholders. While these innovations enhance customization and align risks more closely, they also increase the complexity of obtaining regulatory approval and require a more significant effort in educating users.

In summary, the design of parametric insurance requires careful integration of statistical calibration, index modeling, correlation analysis, and financial structuring. It combines precision with artful balance, demanding that practitioners effectively navigate between risk transfer goals and the practicalities of data-driven contracts. When executed well, parametric insurance can produce transparent, scalable, and impactful products that address today's most urgent climate and catastrophe risks.

SMART CONTRACTS AND AUTOMATION IN PARAMETRIC PRODUCTS

Parametric insurance is characterized by its capacity to provide quick, rule-based payouts activated by measurable events. To achieve this level of automation, it is essential to integrate a strong data infrastructure with programmable logic. Smart contracts—self-executing scripts on blockchain platforms—allow parametric products to move from concept to practical application. They encode the policy's trigger conditions, data interfaces, and payout functions into unchangeable digital code.

At their core, smart contracts act as digital intermediaries that assess real-time data and perform actions without requiring manual intervention or claims adjusters. In parametric insurance, these contracts monitor an external data source—such as rainfall, temperature, or seismic activity—and execute a payment when the data meets the policy's predefined conditions. For example, a contract might be programmed to issue a $1,000 payout to a farmer if satellite-recorded rainfall over 30 days is below 40 mm. Once this condition is verified, the smart contract automatically releases the funds, resulting in a transparent, traceable, and tamper-resistant process.

The architecture of a smart contract consists of several key components. The first is the policy logic, which defines the rules for trigger conditions, payout amounts, and eligibility timeframes. Next is the data interface, which connects the contract to trusted external data sources through mechanisms known as oracles. Oracles are crucial because blockchain systems are closed environments that cannot access off-chain data without an external bridge. Regarding parametric insurance, oracles collect information from sources such as meteorological services, satellite imagery databases, or government seismic agencies. Once the data is gathered, the oracle transmits it to the blockchain, where the smart contract evaluates whether the trigger conditions are met.

Data interactions must be both secure and verifiable. Oracles can utilize single-source data feeds or multisource aggregation methods that compare readings from multiple providers to deliver a consensus value. This approach helps reduce the risk of tampering or corruption of the inputs. Leading platforms like Chainlink offer decentralized oracle networks that ensure data integrity through cryptographic signatures, redundant sources, and reputation-scoring systems. These measures are particularly crucial when smart contracts handle significant capital disbursements, such as in catastrophe or sovereign risk insurance.

Once a trigger event is verified, the contract executes the payout process, which typically involves transferring funds from an escrow wallet to the insured party's account. This payout must be prefunded through direct premium collection or risk-pooling mechanisms. In decentralized models, capital may come from liquidity providers, insurers, reinsurers, or decentralized autonomous organizations (DAOs). To guard against insolvency or shortfall scenarios, contracts can incorporate safeguards such as minimum capital thresholds, liquidity caps, and automated shutdowns if reserves drop below acceptable levels.

The workflow for a fully automated parametric insurance product follows a consistent sequence. When a user purchases a policy, they pay a premium, which is securely stored in an escrow wallet managed by the smart contract. This contract is deployed with specific parameters, including the trigger threshold, policy period, data source endpoint, and payout function.

During the policy period, an oracle actively monitors the relevant data stream—such as daily rainfall readings, wind speeds, or temperature highs. If the oracle reports that the trigger condition has been met or exceeded, the contract evaluates this condition, calculates the corresponding payout using the embedded function, and initiates the transfer of funds to the policyholder.

All these actions are recorded on the blockchain, providing an immutable audit trail that regulators, reinsurers, or third-party auditors can review.

While the automation provided by smart contracts offers significant operational efficiency, it also brings several technical and legal challenges. Once deployed, smart contracts are usually immutable, which means that any errors in logic or security vulnerabilities cannot be fixed unless upgrade mechanisms are integrated. Therefore insurers must subject smart contracts to thorough code audits, unit testing, and formal verification processes before deployment. This process includes simulation testing using historical data, security assessments with tools such as Slither or MythX, and peer reviews conducted by qualified blockchain developers.

Legal enforceability remains a complex issue in many jurisdictions. While smart contracts provide automated execution, they still need to be incorporated into or associated with a legal master agreement to ensure that they can be enforced in court. Regulatory frameworks differ in their definitions of "digital contracts," and many jurisdictions require clear disclosure to policyholders regarding how these contracts operate, including their potential limitations. Increasingly, hybrid models are being used, where smart contracts manage automation, while legal documents establish the governance framework and pathways for dispute resolution.

From a systems architecture perspective, advanced parametric insurance platforms are now being developed with a focus on composability and modularity. This approach allows for the creation of contracts that support nested coverage—such as policies triggered by both rainfall and soil moisture—or stacked coverages, where the payout from one policy can be used to pay the premium of another. These arrangements enable more precise risk segmentation and facilitate portfolio-level optimization strategies. Additionally, blockchain-native parametric products are increasingly being integrated with decentralized finance (DeFi) protocols. This integration allows premiums to be pooled in yield-bearing contracts, with the interest earned being used to fund reserves or lower costs for policyholders.

A promising direction for the development of on-chain insurance markets involves the buying, selling, and underwriting of parametric insurance policies entirely through decentralized applications. These markets can facilitate dynamic pricing, allow for the secondary trading of risk exposure, and ensure transparent capital flow, all managed via smart contracts. Underwriters can serve as liquidity providers in this system, earning returns based on premiums. The pricing of risk is determined in real time, taking into account event probability, available capital, and historical volatility.

While smart contract–based parametric products are advanced, they are not a one-size-fits-all solution. These products work best for risks that are objective, frequent, and backed by reliable data, where clear rules can be consistently applied. However, traditional insurance is often the better choice for more complex or subjective types of loss, such as liability claims, litigation, or gradual environmental degradation. On the other hand, for risks related to weather, climate, travel, and supply chains, the combination of parametric triggers and smart contract automation offers a scalable, transparent, and resilient solution.

REAL-WORLD USE CASES

Parametric insurance has moved beyond being just a theoretical concept; it is now actively used in various sectors and regions to overcome the limitations of traditional indemnity-based insurance. This is especially important in scenarios where speed, transparency, and scalability are crucial. From smallholder agriculture to municipal climate risk management, parametric models have facilitated quick financial relief by utilizing structured triggers and objective data. This section will explore real-world use cases, focusing on each implementation's design choices, data architecture, and actuarial implications.

AGRICULTURE AND CROP INSURANCE

Parametric insurance is widely recognized in the field of agricultural risk, particularly in areas where traditional crop insurance is not feasible due to challenges such as inadequate claims infrastructure, high administrative costs, or the lack of reliable loss data. In regions like sub-Saharan Africa, South Asia, and Latin America, various programs have effectively implemented weather-index insurance to safeguard smallholder farmers against the uncertainties of climate change.

The Kenya Agriculture Insurance Program, supported by the Kenyan government and reinsured by Swiss Re, utilizes satellite-derived rainfall data along with readings from ground-based weather stations to trigger payouts for drought events. This index is calibrated using historical yield data and specific rainfall thresholds that are relevant to the crops and regions involved. Farmers pay their premiums through mobile money, and when drought conditions are met, they receive automated payouts directly into their accounts. This system eliminates the need for local claims adjusters and facilitates scaling across thousands of geographically dispersed farmers.

The index is usually a cumulative measure of rainfall during a crucial phase of crop growth, such as germination or flowering. The triggers are structured in tiers to match different levels of rainfall deficit, with higher payouts for more severe drought conditions. These thresholds are determined using a decade or more of yield and weather data, which are analyzed through regression models or multivariate climate-yield response surfaces.

Despite its success, there are still challenges to address. One major issue is basis risk, which tends to be high in regions with few weather stations. Although satellite data is available worldwide, it may fail to capture local microclimatic variations, particularly in mountainous or diverse landscapes. Advanced geostatistical interpolation and downscaling techniques are often utilized to enhance the accuracy of indices.

NATURAL CATASTROPHE AND CLIMATE RISK INSURANCE

Parametric insurance has proven to be particularly valuable in managing catastrophe and climate risk transfer. During such events, traditional claims processes can become overwhelmed due to the high volume of claims or hindered by damage to infrastructure. Parametric products allow governments, municipalities, and NGOs to quickly access immediate funding when specific predetermined thresholds are met.

The Caribbean Catastrophe Risk Insurance Facility (CCRIF SPC, 2020) is a multicountry risk pool that offers parametric coverage for hurricanes, earthquakes, and excess rainfall to countries in the Caribbean and Central America. The trigger conditions for payouts are based on modeled storm parameters and real-time data from organizations such as the US Geological Survey and the NOAA. Payouts are made within 14 days of an event, providing a rapid cash injection for disaster response and recovery.

The underlying index model utilizes synthetic storm simulation along with location-specific exposure weighting to calculate modeled losses. Unlike basic single-parameter models, CCRIF's parametric structure incorporates spatial loss estimation based on factors such as storm track, wind field radius, and local exposure. When an event occurs, the model operates in real time to generate a deterministic loss estimate that determines the payout.

This system is highly effective in managing liquidity risk, but it does not fully cover all losses. Instead, it offers shock absorption capital, which helps to reduce fiscal volatility—an increasingly important concept in sovereign risk finance. Similar models are being investigated in Pacific island nations, Southeast Asia, and parts of Africa, where there is significant exposure to cyclones, tsunamis, and volcanic activity, yet insurance penetration remains low.

ENERGY, UTILITIES, AND BUSINESS CONTINUITY

In the energy sector, parametric insurance is used to guard against fluctuations in load due to temperature changes, volatility in renewable energy production, and disruptions in supply caused by climate factors. For example, energy distributors might purchase parametric coverage to protect against extreme temperatures that can affect heating or cooling demand.

These contracts are usually based on heating degree days (HDDs) or cooling degree days, which are derived from detailed weather data. For example, a utility company may seek insurance against the risk of average daily temperatures dropping below a certain threshold in a specific month, leading to increased heating costs that exceed what was forecasted. The insurer calculates payouts based on how much cumulative HDDs deviate from historical averages. Typically, the trigger data for these calculations is obtained from national meteorological services or real-time IoT sensors.

Renewable energy producers, especially those in the wind and solar sectors, are increasingly looking for parametric protection against revenue losses caused by weather anomalies. For example, a solar farm might establish a contract that activates if the average solar irradiance falls below a specific threshold, which could jeopardize revenue targets or debt service coverage ratios. This situation can be analyzed using historical irradiance data along with satellite-based solar forecasting models.

These products are often tailored for corporate buyers, with payouts structured to reflect operating loss thresholds, energy input costs, or contractual penalties. From an actuarial perspective, pricing these contracts requires multiyear weather normalization, production modeling, and financial sensitivity analysis.

ENVIRONMENTAL, SOCIAL, AND GOVERNANCE FINANCE AND DEVELOPMENT APPLICATIONS

A new area of growth for parametric insurance is in climate resilience, microfinance, and financial instruments linked to environmental, social, and governance (ESG) factors. Development banks, NGOs, and impact investors are increasingly integrating parametric insurance into their programs that focus on poverty reduction, food security, and disaster preparedness.

An example of an innovative initiative is ARC Replica, a parametric insurance program backed by the African Risk Capacity and international donors. This program provides insurance to countries facing extreme drought by utilizing rainfall data and food insecurity models. When specific trigger conditions are met, payouts are simultaneously released to both governments and their humanitarian partners. This approach allows for precoordinated response efforts to address the crisis effectively.

This model integrates parametric logic with forecast-based financing, enabling humanitarian actors to mobilize resources before or immediately after an event instead of waiting for traditional postdisaster assessments and funding cycles.

In the microfinance sector, parametric insurance is linked to loan repayment protection. Borrowers in vulnerable sectors, such as agriculture or fisheries, can receive debt forgiveness or an extension on their loans if certain climate-related triggers are activated. These contracts are usually designed with straightforward metrics, such as rainfall, temperature, or flood depth, and they are distributed through mobile platforms or included in group lending schemes.

These systems utilize low-cost satellite data, mobile identity verification, and automated mobile money transfers to expand their operations without relying on traditional claims infrastructure. Although premiums are often subsidized, it is essential for the data infrastructure and contract logic to comply with actuarial and legal standards concerning risk pooling, solvency, and consumer protection.

LESSONS LEARNED FROM REAL DEPLOYMENTS

Across all sectors, several recurring insights have emerged:

- Data fidelity and transparency are nonnegotiable. Poor-quality index inputs are the primary source of dissatisfaction and legal disputes.
- Stakeholder education is essential. Many consumers and policymakers misunderstand parametric insurance's structure, especially the concept of basis risk.

- Regulatory engagement must begin early. Parametric models challenge many jurisdictions' conventional licensing, reserve, and claims regulations.
- Customization drives value. Off-the-shelf parametric products often underperform compared to those tailored to local risks, exposures, and preferences.

These lessons continue to inform best practices in parametric design, including the use of hybrid models, adaptive triggers, and participatory index validation with communities and regulators.

REGULATORY, ETHICAL, AND PRACTICAL CHALLENGES

While parametric insurance has distinct operational and strategic benefits—including speed, transparency, and automation—it also faces a unique array of challenges that hinder its widespread adoption. These challenges include regulatory uncertainties, ethical concerns related to basis risk and data usage, and practical issues affecting consumer trust, integration with financial systems, and legal enforceability. This section examines these challenges from a multidisciplinary perspective, connecting regulatory frameworks, behavioral economics, and system design.

LEGAL AND REGULATORY CLASSIFICATION OF PARAMETRIC PRODUCTS

One of the fundamental challenges with parametric insurance is its ambiguous legal status in many jurisdictions. In traditional insurance, regulators require that an insured event results in a measurable economic loss, and the payout is directly linked to that loss. In contrast, parametric insurance pays out based on an objective index, acting as a proxy for loss rather than relying on a verified damage report. Although this approach is efficient, it raises a regulatory question: Is a parametric product truly considered insurance, or is it more akin to a derivative, warranty, or financial contract? The answer is not so obvious.

The classification of parametric contracts varies based on jurisdiction. In some countries, these contracts are considered insurance only if there is an insurable interest and evidence that the payouts are used to mitigate losses. Conversely, if parametric contracts are not clearly linked to a physical asset or are traded on secondary markets, they may be treated as derivatives.

In the United States, insurance regulation occurs at the state level, leading to significant differences in the definitions of permissible index-based products among states. Meanwhile, in the European Union, the Solvency II framework provides a risk-based capital guideline that accommodates parametric triggers, but insurers must still prove that their contracts adhere to essential legal and actuarial principles.

From a compliance perspective, insurers that offer parametric coverage must still adhere to traditional obligations, including licensing, solvency, capital adequacy, consumer protection, and reinsurance approval. If smart contracts are utilized, additional questions emerge regarding contract enforceability, jurisdiction, and the admissibility of code-based agreements in legal proceedings. Some regulators, such as the United Kingdom's Financial Conduct Authority and Bermuda's Monetary Authority, have started to provide guidance, but a standardized framework is still lacking.

BASIS RISK AS A CONSUMER PROTECTION ISSUE

From a technical standpoint, basis risk is a statistical artifact—an expected deviation between index and loss. But from a regulatory and ethical standpoint, basis risk is a consumer protection challenge. Policyholders often do not understand why they received no payout when they experienced real damage, or why they were compensated when no damage occurred. This disconnect can erode trust in the insurance mechanism, particularly in vulnerable populations with limited financial literacy.

To address this, insurers and regulators must invest in transparent product disclosures, informed consent protocols, and grievance mechanisms. Policy documents should clearly describe:

- The index source and its frequency of measurement
- The trigger threshold(s)
- The payout calculation method
- Potential scenarios where no payout would occur

Some programs now require codesign workshops with stakeholders before launch or publish simplified model results (e.g., payout simulation tables) to demonstrate expected policy behavior under historical event conditions. These steps improve alignment between technical design and customer expectations.

Further, third-party validation of indices, akin to credit rating agencies or accounting standards boards, could help ensure widely used triggers' statistical integrity and fairness. Regulators may also require ongoing monitoring of trigger performance to detect systemic bias or adverse selection patterns.

DATA PRIVACY, CONSENT, AND ALGORITHMIC ETHICS

Parametric products frequently rely on automated data collection from sensors, satellites, and personal devices, which can raise privacy and ethical concerns. For instance, if a microinsurance product uses mobile phone location data or digital wallet transactions to determine eligibility or trigger a payout, insurers must ensure compliance with data protection laws such as GDPR, CCPA, or similar regulations in emerging markets.

Key considerations include:

- Consent: Has the policyholder explicitly authorized the use of personal data?
- Transparency: Are the data source, frequency, and retention policy disclosed?

- Data minimization: Is only the data necessary for the policy being collected?
- Data sovereignty: Where is the data stored, and under whose legal jurisdiction?

When machine learning or artificial intelligence (AI) is utilized to calibrate trigger indices or predict payout probabilities, insurers need to ensure that the algorithms are nondiscriminatory, explainable, and auditable. It is especially important to maintain algorithmic transparency when coverage is denied or when payout amounts are calculated through complex modeling processes that those without expertise do not understand easily.

Some jurisdictions may require algorithmic impact assessments or mandate human oversight for high-stakes insurance decisions. Industry initiatives are starting to emerge to establish ethical guidelines for AI in the insurance sector. Many of these initiatives incorporate principles from responsible fintech and digital identity governance.

LEGAL ENFORCEABILITY OF SMART CONTRACTS

Smart contracts, often referred to as "contracts," are not universally acknowledged as legally binding documents. Their enforceability largely depends on how different legal systems interpret the concept of code as law. While many jurisdictions accept digitally signed contracts under electronic signature laws, such as electronic IDentification, Authentication, and Trust Services in Europe or Electronic Signatures in Global and National Commerce Act in the United States, the situation becomes more complicated when the agreement is fully embedded in code and executed automatically.

Key legal questions include:

- Does the policyholder understand the terms if they are expressed in code?
- Who is liable if the contract executes incorrectly (e.g., due to bad data or a bug)?
- Can a smart contract be challenged, amended, or rescinded?
- Where is legal jurisdiction established if the contract is distributed across multiple nodes?

Legal hybrid models are emerging in the insurance industry. Many insurers are now using smart contracts for performance automation while still relying on traditional paper or digital documents as legally binding agreements. These "dual-format" contracts enable the smart contract to execute transactions, while any disputes, modifications, and compliance issues are managed under conventional legal frameworks.

Standard-setting bodies and regulators are starting to address these concerns. For example, the International Association of Insurance Supervisors has recognized the importance of smart contracts in parametric microinsurance and is promoting regulatory sandboxes to test new implementations. However, there is a significant need for harmonized legal standards that connect traditional contract law with blockchain-based systems.

OPERATIONAL RISK AND SYSTEMS INTEGRATION

Implementing parametric insurance products, especially on a large scale, adds a level of operational complexity that is frequently underestimated. Even with the use of smart contracts and automated data collection, insurers need to integrate these systems with essential functions like underwriting, policy administration, claims reporting (when applicable), and reinsurance accounting.

Legacy systems often lack the flexibility to process real-time data or interact with smart contracts. Consequently, many parametric pilots are developed as standalone systems, which limits their potential for scalability and cross-selling. Over time, the value of parametric insurance will depend on insurers' ability to integrate these products into enterprise platforms, digital customer journeys, and third-party ecosystems, such as lenders, governments, and NGOs.

Operational risk also includes:

- System downtime or data feed disruption during critical events
- Oracle manipulation or corruption (especially for blockchain-linked products)
- Escrow liquidity mismatch, where insufficient funds are available to pay triggered policies
- Insider risk or programming errors, which may not be caught until after contract execution

Mitigation of these risks requires robust governance, including:

- Multisignature escrow controls
- Third-party oracle audits
- Code review and penetration testing
- Disaster recovery protocols and legal dispute frameworks

The growth of parametric insurance relies not only on data and algorithms but also on institutional trust and regulatory alignment. To achieve this, we must ensure legal clarity, establish data governance, and develop consumer protection frameworks that evolve alongside technological innovations. By tackling these systemic challenges, parametric insurance can scale effectively and fulfill its potential as a tool for climate resilience, financial inclusion, and advanced risk management.

INNOVATION AND THE FUTURE OF PARAMETRIC PRODUCTS

As global risk landscapes become increasingly volatile, climate sensitive, and rich in data, parametric insurance is set to evolve from a niche product into a fundamental component of modern risk transfer. The convergence of technologies—such as satellite sensing, AI, blockchain, and DeFi—is transforming the way risks are assessed, priced, and distributed. At the same time, significant shifts in areas like climate adaptation, sustainability-linked finance, and digital financial inclusion are generating new demand for fast, reliable, and scalable insurance solutions.

This section examines the cutting-edge advancements in parametric insurance, emphasizing the integration of technology, product modularity, distribution models, and its significance within global financial systems.

EMBEDDED AND PROGRAMMABLE INSURANCE-AS-A-SERVICE

One of the most important advancements in digital insurance is the emergence of embedded insurance—coverage that is seamlessly integrated into digital platforms, purchasing processes, or mobile applications. Parametric products, known for their simplicity, automation, and low-friction claims process, are particularly well suited for this approach. As APIs and microservices architectures continue to develop, insurers can implement parametric coverage discreetly in various contexts, such as::

- Travel bookings (e.g., automatic delay insurance at checkout)
- Agriculture platforms (e.g., crop input loans bundled with drought coverage)
- Logistics networks (e.g., shipment delay or cargo temperature breach insurance)
- Event platforms (e.g., rainfall coverage for concerts or outdoor festivals)

The future of this integration lies in programmable insurance, where policies adapt in real time based on behavior, location, or risk exposure. Smart contracts and event-driven architectures can enable dynamic coverage models. Examples include:

- A farmer's parametric coverage adjusts automatically as satellite normalized difference vegetation index (NDVI) readings change.
- A gig worker's weather-based income protection activates based on forecasted rainfall.
- A renewable energy developer's wind shortfall policy scales with seasonal production variability.

Advancements in real-time data analytics, IoT integration, and machine-readable policy logic are essential, along with legal frameworks that accommodate dynamically adjusting contracts.

DECENTRALIZED FINANCE, BLOCKCHAIN, AND DECENTRALIZED INSURANCE POOLS

The convergence of parametric insurance and DeFi signifies a significant transformation in the way risk capital is sourced, distributed, and managed. Blockchain platforms enable individuals to invest capital in decentralized risk pools. These pools are managed through smart contracts that handle the issuance, pricing, and payout of parametric insurance policies (Schär, 2021).

Projects like Etherisc, Arbol, and InsurAce are developing fully on-chain parametric insurance platforms where:

- Liquidity providers fund parametric risk pools and earn yield.
- Smart contracts monitor oracles and execute payouts without human intermediaries.
- DAO governance structures vote on policy parameters, underwriting criteria, and Oracle providers.

These platforms are particularly well suited for:

- Weather-based agriculture and energy hedging
- Index-linked natural catastrophe protection
- Livelihood coverage for informal workers and self-employed individuals

DeFi-native parametric products raise regulatory classification, capital adequacy, and data verification questions, but they also provide the opportunity to unlock global, permissionless access to insurance markets—particularly in underinsured economies.

Future directions in this field include reinsurance marketplaces, where parametric portfolios can be tokenized and traded; insurance yield protocols, which allow unused premiums to be invested for returns; and staking-based risk assessment, where underwriters can post capital against the models they develop.

ENVIRONMENTAL, SOCIAL, AND GOVERNANCE–LINKED RISK POOLS AND SUSTAINABILITY FINANCE

As capital markets increasingly prioritize ESG-aligned investing, parametric insurance provides a transparent, outcome-focused tool for climate adaptation, resilience finance, and impact measurement.

Development institutions and climate funds are increasingly structuring result-based financing models using parametric triggers. For example:

- A sovereign catastrophe bond linked to a rainfall index can be structured so that when a severe drought occurs, capital is released not only for recovery but also for climate-resilient infrastructure.
- Coastal cities vulnerable to sea level rise can collaborate to create a regional parametric flood risk pool, with payout parameters linked to both damage thresholds and green mitigation standards.
- Smallholder farmers using regenerative practices can be rewarded with discounted premiums through parametric index-based microinsurance platforms that incorporate soil moisture, vegetation cover, and land-use metrics from satellite data.

These products align climate mitigation and adaptation goals with market-based incentives, providing a clear path for insurers to support sustainable development goals while managing climate risks.

The clarity and verifiability of parametric triggers make them ideal for green bonds, climate-linked loans, and resilience-linked credit instruments, where financing depends on the achievement of specific climate metrics.

MICROINSURANCE 2.0 AND DIGITAL INCLUSION

Parametric insurance serves as the basis for a new wave of digitally delivered, inclusive microinsurance designed to reach billions of underserved individuals in rural, informal, or low-income economies. Historically, microinsurance has faced challenges with:

- High distribution costs
- Claims verification challenges
- Low renewal and satisfaction rates

Parametric products distributed through mobile platforms, community cooperatives, or agricultural technology ecosystems help eliminate many barriers. For instance:

- Policies can be purchased, funded, and paid out via mobile money.
- Satellite data or mobile-based sensor data can trigger coverage automatically.
- Gamified onboarding, voice bots, and local language interfaces can improve financial literacy and adoption.

These models are being tested in Africa, South Asia, and Latin America, frequently with support from climate funds or reinsurance resources provided by global organizations. Smart contracts help streamline operations by managing fund custody, payout processes, and claims finalization within a single digital workflow.

Innovative developments include weather-indexed credit scoring, which enhances access to loans based on participation in insurance, and "pay-as-you-grow" insurance, allowing micro-premiums to scale according to production or income flows.

DYNAMIC AND MULTIVARIATE TRIGGERS

Looking forward, the most advanced parametric products will move beyond single-variable models and include multivariate or compound indices. These can address multiple hazards, seasonal effects, and interacting risk factors. For example:

- A flood insurance policy could use rainfall, river discharge, and tidal levels to trigger payouts.
- An agricultural index might combine rainfall, NDVI, and soil temperature to better capture crop stress.
- A wildfire index could use wind speed, humidity, fuel dryness, and proximity to human infrastructure to trigger loss compensation.

Statistical modeling of these indices necessitates the use of machine learning techniques, such as ensemble methods, random forests, or neural networks, to effectively calibrate and validate the payout model. The acceptance of these more intricate indices by regulators will hinge on whether they can be clearly explained, audited, and simulated, ensuring that policyholders understand them and that insurers can adequately plan for solvency.

There is increasing interest in adaptive triggers that change over time based on predicted climate trends, behavioral patterns, or policyholder exposure. These developments could lead to long-duration parametric contracts that remain relevant as climate baselines shift and infrastructure evolves.

The future of parametric insurance depends on its integration of technology, transparency, and social utility. It is more than just a product category; it represents a new way of thinking about insurance in our data-driven, decentralized, and increasingly unpredictable world. Whether implemented through traditional insurance carriers, DeFi platforms, government pools, or environmentally and socially responsible financial instruments, parametric solutions provide the insurance industry with a powerful tool for adaptation, resilience, and financial inclusion.

SUMMARY

Parametric insurance represents a significant shift in how insurance contracts are structured, priced, and executed. Unlike traditional indemnity-based models, which depend on postloss assessment and human decision-making, parametric products offer predefined payouts based on measurable and objective trigger events. This approach allows for faster claims settlements, reduces administrative costs, and expands insurance access to underinsured populations and markets where traditional products may be unfeasible.

In this chapter, we explored the fundamental elements of parametric insurance, starting with an overview of its concepts and history and moving on to the technical design of triggers, indices, and payout structures. We highlighted the significance of basis risk as both an actuarial and ethical concern and discussed methods for calibrating indices, modeling correlations, and simulating spatial risks. Parametric underwriting necessitates a shift toward modeling event probabilities, which is supported by advanced analytics and long-term climate and hazard datasets.

We also explored how smart contracts and oracles can automate parametric execution, promoting transparency and decreasing dependence on manual processes. We highlighted the operational architecture of blockchain-based implementations and emphasized the importance of secure data pipelines in ensuring the reliability of automated payouts.

Real-world examples from agriculture, catastrophe finance, energy, travel, and development demonstrate the flexibility and scalability of parametric models across various sectors. These case studies highlight not only the technical foundations of successful implementations but also the practical factors influencing adoption, such as data availability, trust, regulation, and affordability.

In addressing the challenges, we highlighted the regulatory and ethical complexities related to legal classification, data governance, smart contract enforceability, and consumer protection. These factors emphasize the necessity for interdisciplinary collaboration among actuaries, technologists, legal scholars, and policymakers to scale parametric products responsibly.

In conclusion, we focused on the future by identifying key innovations such as dynamic triggers, ESG-linked resilience finance, decentralized risk pools, and embedded insurance delivery. As the insurance industry adapts to climate change, financial digitization, and systemic shocks, parametric models provide an effective and modular framework for next-generation risk transfer.

AI DISCLOSURE

During the preparation of this work the author(s) used Grammarly to improve readability and correct any grammatical mistakes. After using this tool/service, the author(s) reviewed and edited the content as needed and take(s) full responsibility for the content of the publication.

REFERENCES

Caribbean Catastrophe Risk Insurance Facility (CCRIF SPC). (2020). *Annual report 2020.* https://www.ccrif.org/.

Clarke, D., & Dercon, S. (2016). *Dull disasters? How planning ahead will make a difference.* Oxford University Press.

Schär, F. (2021). Decentralized finance: On blockchain- and smart contract-based financial markets. *Federal Reserve Bank of St. Louis Review*, *103*(2), 153–174. https://doi.org/10.20955/r.103.153–74.

Weiss, G. (2021). Parametric insurance: Closing the protection gap with trigger-based solutions. *Lloyd's Innovation Series*. https://www.lloyds.com/.

CHAPTER

Cybersecurity and privacy risks in insurance technology

8

CHAPTER OUTLINE

Insurance Technology. DOI: https://doi.org/10.1016/B978-0-443-43972-8.00005-5

INTRODUCTION TO CYBERSECURITY AND PRIVACY IN INSURANCE

Insurance has historically been a foundational element of modern economic stability, specializing in managing risks associated with physical assets, human health, and economic uncertainties (Rejda & McNamara, 2021). Traditionally, insurers concentrated on quantifying and mitigating tangible risks such as fire, theft, natural disasters, and medical events. However, the emergence of digital technology has significantly transformed this landscape, introducing new complexities related to data security and privacy (Biener, Eling, & Wirfs, 2015).

In recent decades, the landscape of the insurance industry has been profoundly transformed by digital innovation. The rise of online platforms, mobile applications, and data-driven underwriting methodologies has notably enhanced customer experiences, streamlined operational efficiencies, and facilitated more accurate risk modeling (Catlin, et al., 2017). Leveraging big data analytics, artificial intelligence (AI), telematics, and Internet of Things (IoT) devices, insurers are now equipped to predict and manage risks with unprecedented precision, paving the way for developing innovative insurance products and services. However, these advancements are accompanied by substantial challenges, including increased exposure to cybersecurity threats and the pressing need for robust data privacy safeguards (Deloitte, 2021).

Cybersecurity involves organizations' strategies and measures to safeguard their information systems, networks, and sensitive data from unauthorized access, disruption, exploitation, and destruction (Von Solms & Van Niekerk, 2013). Insurance companies are particularly vulnerable to cybercrime due to the large amounts of sensitive personal, financial, and medical information they collect. Consequently, they face ongoing threats from ransomware, phishing attacks, data breaches, and increasingly sophisticated cyberattacks aimed at financial gain or disruption (Marotta & McShane, 2018).

The issue of data privacy has become increasingly important alongside cybersecurity. Privacy encompasses protecting information from unauthorized access and the need for transparency and ethical management of how personal data is collected, stored, and processed (Solove & Hartzog, 2014). Today, consumers expect greater accountability and transparency regarding their personal information, especially in predictive analytics, automated decision-making, and targeted marketing. These expectations have led to the implementation of stringent privacy laws across the globe, including the European Union's General Data Protection Regulation (GDPR) and the California Consumer Privacy Act (CCPA). These regulations have significantly changed the compliance landscape for insurers (Tikkinen-Piri, Rohunen, & Markkula, 2018).

The relationship between cybersecurity and privacy poses significant challenges for insurers. On one hand, gathering and analyzing large amounts of consumer data allows insurers to customize products and enhance risk management. On the other hand, managing extensive personal data increases the compliance burden and heightens the potential reputational and financial risks associated with data breaches (Cavoukian, 2019). Additionally, the rapid adoption of cloud computing and third-party data management solutions adds further complexity, making it more difficult for insurers to maintain a strong cybersecurity stance (Zissis & Lekkas, 2012).

Insurers must view cybersecurity and privacy not just as regulatory requirements but as essential elements of their operational resilience and a source of competitive advantage. Failing to manage cybersecurity risks and privacy obligations effectively can result in severe regulatory penalties, loss of customer trust, costly litigation, and lasting damage to reputation (Romanosky, Hoffman, & Acquisti, 2014). On the other hand, insurers adopting proactive and integrated cybersecurity and privacy approaches can build customer trust, reduce operational vulnerabilities, and stand out in a competitive market.

This chapter intends to thoroughly examine the intersection of cybersecurity, privacy, and insurance technology. It will explore relevant laws and regulations, cybersecurity standards and frameworks, and practical risk management strategies.

Additionally, it will address the significant implications of emerging technologies, such as AI. By comprehensively addressing these topics, this chapter will equip current and future insurance professionals with the knowledge and insights needed to navigate the complex digital landscape securely, ethically, and effectively.

MAJOR CYBERSECURITY AND PRIVACY LAWS AND REGULATIONS

In response to the increasing prevalence of cybersecurity breaches and privacy concerns, governments worldwide have implemented comprehensive regulations. These regulations impose strict obligations on organizations, including insurers, due to the sensitive personal, financial, and health-related data they handle. The insurance industry, in particular, faces rigorous regulatory expectations to protect consumer privacy and ensure robust cybersecurity measures are in place (Biener, Eling, & Wirfs, 2015; Marotta & McShane, 2018).

GENERAL DATA PROTECTION REGULATION

Enacted by the European Union in 2018, the GDPR is one of the most influential privacy frameworks in the world (Tikkinen-Piri, Rohunen, & Markkula, 2018). The GDPR aims to protect the personal data of EU citizens by imposing obligations related to consent, transparency, data minimization, and accountability (Voigt & Von dem Bussche, 2017).

Under the GDPR, insurers must communicate how they use data, obtain explicit consent from individuals, facilitate requests for data access and erasure, and demonstrate compliance through thorough documentation (Tikkinen-Piri et al., 2018). Noncompliance with the GDPR can lead to penalties of up to €20 million or 4% of a company's global annual revenue, which can severely affect insurers financially and in terms of their reputation (Voigt & Von dem Bussche, 2017).

CALIFORNIA CONSUMER PRIVACY ACT AND CALIFORNIA PRIVACY RIGHTS ACT

Inspired by the GDPR, California enacted the CCPA in 2020, which was expanded by the California Privacy Rights Act (CPRA) in 2023 (Goldman, 2021). The CCPA and CPRA give consumers significant control over their personal information, including the right to access, delete, and restrict the use or sale of their data (Goldman, 2021). For insurers, compliance requires careful management of data requests, transparent disclosures about data handling practices, and effective consent management. California's approach is also influencing other states in the United States, leading to similar privacy initiatives and creating complex compliance environments for national insurers (Chander, Kaminski, & McGeveran, 2021).

HEALTH INSURANCE PORTABILITY AND ACCOUNTABILITY ACT

The US Health Insurance Portability and Accountability Act (HIPAA), enacted in 1996, establishes standards for protecting sensitive patient health information (Gostin, Halabi, & Wilson, 2018). HIPAA includes two main provisions: the Privacy Rule and the Security Rule.

The Privacy Rule outlines the acceptable uses and disclosures of protected health information (PHI) and requires explicit authorization for many of these disclosures (Gostin et al., 2018). The Security Rule specifies detailed security measures for electronic PHI, which include mandatory risk assessments, encryption of sensitive data, secure access management, and comprehensive employee training (McGraw, 2013).

Failing to comply with HIPAA can result in significant financial penalties and severe damage to a provider's reputation, making strong compliance essential for health insurers and related organizations (Gostin et al., 2018).

GRAMM–LEACH–BLILEY ACT

One significant regulation that impacts insurers is the Gramm–Leach–Bliley Act (GLBA), enacted in 1999 to govern how financial institutions, including insurers, handle consumers' financial data (Janger & Schwartz, 2002). The GLBA includes the Financial Privacy Rule, which requires insurers to disclose their information-sharing practices and provide consumers with options to opt out. Additionally, it features the Safeguards Rule, which mandates the implementation of comprehensive security programs to protect consumer data (Janger & Schwartz, 2002). To comply with the GLBA, insurers must maintain documented risk assessments, enforce encryption standards, and rigorously manage third-party vendors' security (Janger & Schwartz, 2002).

NEW YORK DEPARTMENT OF FINANCIAL SERVICES CYBERSECURITY REGULATION

In response to increasing cybersecurity threats, the New York Department of Financial Services (NYDFS) implemented the NYDFS Cybersecurity Regulation (23 NYCRR 500) in 2017. This regulation explicitly targets banks, insurers, and other financial entities (Skinner, 2019). It establishes various cybersecurity obligations, including regular risk assessments, vulnerability testing, incident response planning, and the mandatory appointment of a chief information security officer (CISO) (Skinner, 2019). The NYDFS framework has set a standard that influences cybersecurity expectations in other US states and globally, mainly due to New York's significant role in the global finance and insurance markets (Skinner, 2019).

INTERNATIONAL CYBERSECURITY AND PRIVACY REGULATIONS

International insurance companies face additional challenges when navigating cybersecurity and privacy laws worldwide. Australia's Privacy Act establishes strict standards for data management and requires breach notifications (Greenleaf, 2012). Similarly, Singapore's Personal Data Protection Act and Canada's Personal Information Protection and Electronic Documents Act provide clear guidelines for data transparency, accountability, and consumer consent (Greenleaf, 2012; Scassa, 2020). To comply with these international standards, insurers must implement robust data governance frameworks that can accommodate diverse regulations across jurisdictions. This creates operational complexity but also helps ensure high data protection standards globally.

REGULATORY COMPLIANCE AS A STRATEGIC IMPERATIVE

Collectively, these regulations highlight the significant compliance challenges faced by modern insurers. Insurers must thoroughly integrate regulatory obligations into their operational frameworks. A strong compliance strategy goes beyond simply meeting legal requirements; it involves proactive cybersecurity governance, risk management, incident preparedness, and transparent privacy practices (Romanosky, Hoffman, & Acquisti, 2014). The regulatory environment is dynamic and evolves quickly in response to new threats, technological advancements, and changing public expectations. As a result, insurers must remain vigilant, responsive, and strategic in their approaches to cybersecurity and privacy. They should view these efforts as essential investments in building long-term trust, resilience, and competitive advantage.

CYBERSECURITY STANDARDS AND FRAMEWORKS: NATIONAL INSTITUTE OF STANDARDS AND TECHNOLOGY AND INTERNATIONAL ORGANIZATION FOR STANDARDIZATION

Due to the complexity of the cybersecurity landscape and the strict regulatory environment, insurers increasingly rely on established cybersecurity standards and frameworks for effective risk management, compliance, and resilience. Two globally recognized frameworks that are particularly prominent and useful within the insurance industry are the National Institute of Standards and Technology (NIST) Cybersecurity Framework (CSF) and the International Organization for Standardization (ISO) Information Security Management Standards.

NATIONAL INSTITUTE OF STANDARDS AND TECHNOLOGY

The NIST, an agency of the US Department of Commerce, developed the NIST CSF in response to increasing cyber threats and the need for standardized risk management practices across various industries (NIST, 2018). Initially designed for critical infrastructure sectors, the NIST CSF has since gained widespread adoption across diverse sectors, including financial services and insurance, due to its flexible yet robust approach to cybersecurity management (Shackelford et al., 2015).

The NIST CSF is organized around five core functions that comprehensively manage cybersecurity: Identify, Protect, Detect, Respond, and Recover (NIST, 2018).

The Identify function helps organizations, particularly insurers, understand their cybersecurity risks by focusing on asset management, the business environment, and risk assessment. The Protect function outlines the necessary safeguards to deliver critical services consistently through secure practices. This includes access control, employee training, and data security protocols (NIST, 2018).

The Detect function requires continuous monitoring and anomaly detection to identify cybersecurity incidents quickly. The Respond function involves creating and implementing response plans, which include incident analysis, mitigation activities, and communication strategies. Finally, the Recover function assists organizations in returning to normal operations after an incident, focusing on recovery planning and incorporating improvements based on lessons learned (NIST, 2018).

NIST publishes Special Publications (SP) that offer insurers detailed guidance on cybersecurity. NIST SP 800–53 provides comprehensive security and privacy control baselines tailored to help organizations develop specific cybersecurity programs (NIST, 2020). In addition, NIST SP 800–39 and SP 800–30 outline methodologies for structured risk assessment and management, which are essential for identifying and mitigating threats in complex digital environments (NIST, 2012; NIST, 2011).

Insurance organizations utilize the NIST framework and its guidance to improve risk visibility, strengthen control environments, and demonstrate cybersecurity maturity to regulators, clients, and partners. As cybersecurity risks change, insurers often depend on these standards to continuously enhance their security strategies, aligning their cybersecurity efforts with business objectives and regulatory compliance requirements (Shackelford et al., 2015).

INTERNATIONAL ORGANIZATION FOR STANDARDIZATION

Alongside the NIST framework, the ISO offers internationally recognized standards for information security and privacy management. ISO/International Electrotechnical Commission (IEC) 27001 and ISO/IEC 27002 are particularly influential, as they provide the foundation for Information Security Management Systems (ISMS) that organizations worldwide, including insurers, use to enhance their security practices (Humphreys, 2016).

ISO/IEC 27001 outlines the requirements for establishing, implementing, maintaining, and continually improving an ISMS. The standard requires organizations to systematically assess information security risks and implement controls to mitigate those risks. By following a structured process of risk assessment, treatment planning, implementation, and regular review, ISO/IEC 27001 enables insurers to adopt a systematic, repeatable, and demonstrable approach to managing cybersecurity threats and vulnerabilities (Calder & Watkins, 2019).

ISO/IEC 27002 offers detailed best practices and guidance on selecting, implementing, and managing security controls, complementing ISO/IEC 27001. It addresses various areas, including human resource security, access management, cryptography, physical and environmental security, and incident management. This comprehensive resource helps insurers develop cybersecurity programs tailored to their organizational needs and regulatory requirements (Humphreys, 2016).

Recognizing the growing importance of privacy, ISO introduced ISO/IEC 27701—a privacy extension to ISO 27001. This standard is designed to help organizations establish Privacy Information Management Systems. It guides insurers on effectively managing personal information and ensuring compliance with global privacy regulations such as GDPR and CCPA (Calder & Watkins, 2019). By incorporating privacy directly into their information security frameworks, insurers can systematically address regulatory requirements, enhance consumer trust, and proactively manage privacy risks.

COMPARATIVE ANALYSIS AND PRACTICAL IMPLEMENTATION

Although the NIST and ISO frameworks share the goal of strengthening organizational cybersecurity, each comes with unique advantages and implementation considerations. The NIST CSF is highly flexible, allowing insurers to customize their approaches based on specific risk profiles and regulatory contexts. This flexibility makes it especially appealing in jurisdictions without mandated cybersecurity frameworks (Shackelford et al., 2015). On the other hand, ISO frameworks offer globally recognized certifications, which provide credibility and assurance to international stakeholders and clients. Certification to ISO 27001, particularly, can act as a competitive differentiator, signaling strong cybersecurity and privacy management capabilities (Calder & Watkins, 2019).

Many insurers use a hybrid approach by integrating elements from NIST and ISO standards. For instance, a US-based insurer may adopt the NIST CSF to align with regulatory requirements while pursuing ISO 27001 certification to support international business operations and demonstrate its security maturity to external stakeholders. Additionally, insurers often draw on detailed guidance from ISO 27002 and NIST SP in complementary ways. By combining the specific security practices and controls recommended by each framework, they aim to achieve a high level of cybersecurity maturity (Humphreys, 2016; Shackelford et al., 2015).

Adopting these cybersecurity standards goes beyond just complying with regulations or managing risks. It represents a strategic choice that shows insurers understand the importance of cybersecurity and privacy for their operational resilience and long-term competitiveness. Insurers that successfully implement and integrate these standards showcase their readiness to tackle evolving threats, commitment to protecting customer data, and proactive approach to risk management—traits increasingly valued by regulators, customers, and market participants.

CYBER RISK MANAGEMENT IN INSURANCE ORGANIZATIONS

In today's digital environment, managing cyber risk is not just an operational necessity but a strategic requirement for insurance organizations. As insurers increasingly rely on technology-driven systems for underwriting, claims processing, customer engagement, and administrative tasks, their vulnerability to cyber threats grows correspondingly. The vast amounts of personal, medical, and financial data that insurers collect make them appealing targets for sophisticated cyberattacks. This situation underscores the critical need for comprehensive cyber risk management strategies (Biener, Eling, & Wirfs, 2015; Marotta & McShane, 2018).

ASSET IDENTIFICATION AND RISK MAPPING

Effective cyber risk management starts with a comprehensive asset identification process. This includes creating a complete inventory of information technology systems, software applications, digital platforms, networks, databases, cloud resources, and third-party service providers (Whitman & Mattord, 2018). For insurers, this process goes beyond basic cataloging; it involves thoroughly evaluating each asset's role within the organization, its dependencies, and its vulnerabilities. For example, insurers must identify critical systems such as underwriting platforms, claims management systems, customer portals, mobile applications, and cloud-hosted solutions that store personally identifiable information, PHI, or sensitive financial data.

After completing a detailed inventory, insurers engage in risk mapping to clarify the relationships and interdependencies among their assets. Risk maps clearly visualize potential vulnerabilities, showing how a breach in one area, such as a compromised claims database, can lead to broader systemic failures. These failures might impact customer data privacy, regulatory compliance, and the organization's reputation (Peltier, 2016). By highlighting these connections, insurers can effectively prioritize resource allocation and develop targeted risk mitigation strategies to address the most critical vulnerabilities.

COMPREHENSIVE THREAT MODELING AND RISK ASSESSMENT

Insurers are facing a progressively sophisticated landscape of cyber threats. This includes advanced persistent threats (APTs), ransomware attacks, phishing schemes, and insider threats. To address these diverse challenges effectively, insurers must implement comprehensive threat modeling practices. These practices systematically identify potential threat actors, their likely attack vectors, and the expected impact of successful cyber incidents (Shostack, 2014).

Insurers often rely on established threat modeling methodologies, such as the STRIDE model, to evaluate and document potential cyber threats across their infrastructure. This model categorizes threats into six areas: spoofing, tampering, repudiation, information disclosure, denial of service, and elevation of privilege (Shostack, 2014).

Alongside threat modeling, structured risk assessment methods help insurers quantify and prioritize cybersecurity risks. By utilizing frameworks like NIST SP 800–30 and ISO 27005, insurers can thoroughly evaluate the likelihood of threats, the vulnerabilities of assets, and the potential financial, regulatory, and reputational impacts associated with these threats (NIST, 2012). These assessments typically employ qualitative techniques and expert-driven analyses, increasingly incorporating quantitative models to determine precise levels of risk exposure. By combining qualitative and quantitative approaches, insurers gain valuable insights that inform their cybersecurity investments and strategic decision-making.

INCIDENT PREPAREDNESS AND RESPONSE PLANNING

As cyber breaches are increasingly seen as inevitable rather than just theoretical possibilities, insurers must focus on thorough incident preparedness and response planning. Comprehensive incident response plans (IRPs) are essential to cyber resilience strategies, as they clearly outline the roles, responsibilities, procedures, escalation paths, and communication plans to follow during cyber incidents (Killmeyer, 2016). Insurers often conduct scenario-based tabletop exercises that simulate ransomware attacks, data breaches, or insider threats. These exercises are designed to test IRPs' effectiveness, identify gaps, and improve organizational readiness.

Rapid and coordinated response capabilities are crucial for insurers, as their reputations rely heavily on trust and reliability. Incident response teams, typically led by experienced CISOs, must be ready to quickly contain cyber incidents, assess damages, and initiate recovery actions. Effective communication with regulators, customers, business partners, and law enforcement agencies is key to successful cyber incident management. This approach helps minimize potential reputational harm and regulatory consequences (Killmeyer, 2016).

CYBER INSURANCE AS STRATEGIC RISK TRANSFER

An increasingly important aspect of insurers' cyber risk management programs is the strategic risk transfer through cyber insurance policies. Traditionally, insurers provided cyber insurance to other industries; however, the growing scale and complexity of cyber risks have led many insurers to obtain their cyber coverage. Cyber insurance policies typically cover costs related to data breach responses, regulatory fines, forensic investigations, business interruption losses, notification expenses, and third-party liability claims that arise from cybersecurity incidents (Biener et al., 2015).

Obtaining appropriate cyber insurance coverage can be challenging due to the constantly changing threat landscape, unclear coverage exclusions, and the lack of standardized risk quantification models. Insurers must thoroughly assess their cybersecurity posture, threats, regulatory obligations, and financial resilience to choose policies that effectively address their unique risk profiles. Comprehensive cyber risk assessments can guide insurers in determining coverage limits, selecting deductibles, and negotiating policies, ensuring they achieve optimal protection and cost efficiency in their cyber risk transfer strategies.

CONTINUOUS SECURITY MONITORING AND IMPROVEMENT

Continuous cybersecurity monitoring is essential for insurers' defensive strategies in an environment characterized by rapidly evolving threats. Advanced security operations centers equipped with real-time threat intelligence, anomaly detection systems, and AI-driven analytics allow insurers to proactively identify potential threats (Whitman & Mattord, 2018). Continuous monitoring also enables the rapid detection and containment of cyberattacks, minimizing their potential damage.

Insurers routinely perform penetration testing, vulnerability scanning, and red-team exercises to thoroughly evaluate their system defenses against simulated cyber-attacks. The insights gained from these activities drive ongoing enhancements in security controls, incident response capabilities, and staff training. Additionally, regular security audits and compliance assessments ensure that insurers' cybersecurity practices stay aligned with evolving regulatory requirements and industry standards, thereby maintaining strong cyber defenses.

EMBEDDING CYBERSECURITY INTO ORGANIZATIONAL CULTURE

Effective cyber risk management necessitates integrating cybersecurity awareness and best practices into the core culture of insurance organizations. Employee behavior is one of the most significant risk factors in cybersecurity, as many cyber incidents occur due to human errors, negligence, or targeted social engineering attacks (Hadlington, 2017). To address these risks, insurers implement comprehensive cybersecurity education programs that focus on raising awareness about phishing attacks, promoting secure password practices, outlining proper data handling procedures, and establishing clear incident reporting protocols.

Leadership is crucial in creating a culture that prioritizes cybersecurity. This involves allocating dedicated resources, communicating clearly, and actively participating in cybersecurity initiatives. When leaders emphasize the importance of cybersecurity, employees at every level become more engaged and vigilant, significantly lowering the organization's vulnerability to cyber threats. Insurers are increasingly aware that cybersecurity resilience relies not only on technical defenses but also on human vigilance, highlighting the necessity of comprehensive efforts to integrate cybersecurity into the organizational culture (Hadlington, 2017).

STRATEGIC ALIGNMENT AND GOVERNANCE

Effective cyber risk management goes beyond just technical and operational measures; it also involves strategic organizational alignment and governance. Insurers that successfully manage cyber risks incorporate cybersecurity considerations into their overall strategic planning, decision-making processes, and corporate governance structures. Executive-level oversight, through dedicated cybersecurity committees or board-level reporting, enhances accountability within the organization. This ensures that cybersecurity receives the necessary attention and investment, reflecting its strategic importance.

Insurers establish clear governance structures to ensure accountability for cybersecurity decisions. This approach fosters collaboration among cybersecurity, legal, compliance, and operational teams while also aligning with organizational goals and regulatory requirements. By strategically integrating these elements, insurers not only fulfill regulatory expectations but also effectively manage cyber risks. This safeguards customer trust, maintains operational stability, and sustains a competitive advantage.

PRIVACY BY DESIGN AND DATA GOVERNANCE

As insurers increasingly utilize data-intensive technologies, such as big data analytics, AI, and the IoT, concerns about privacy have risen significantly. Modern insurance practices involve extensive collection, storage, and analysis of personal data, which heightens the risks of data breaches, misuse of sensitive information, and violations of consumer privacy rights. To effectively address these challenges, insurance organizations have adopted frameworks like privacy by design (PbD) and implemented comprehensive data governance practices. This approach integrates privacy considerations directly into their operational processes and organizational cultures (Cavoukian, 2019; Solove & Hartzog, 2014).

UNDERSTANDING PRIVACY BY DESIGN

PbD was introduced by Ann Cavoukian in the 1990s and emphasizes the importance of integrating privacy considerations into the design and operational processes of systems, products, and business practices. This approach treats privacy as a fundamental aspect from the beginning, rather than just an afterthought for compliance (Cavoukian, 2019). PbD is based on seven core principles:

1. Proactive rather than reactive measures
2. Privacy as the default setting
3. Privacy embedded into design
4. Full functionality (positive-sum approach)
5. End-to-end security
6. Visibility and transparency
7. Respect for user privacy

These principles collectively promote the proactive management of privacy risks right from the start of technological initiatives, rather than dealing with issues only after they arise (Cavoukian, 2019).

In the insurance domain, PbD mandates that organizations integrate privacy considerations into creating new products and systems. This includes customer-facing applications, underwriting algorithms, telematics devices, and data-sharing platforms.

For example, when insurers develop telematics-based auto insurance products that utilize data from vehicle sensors and GPS tracking, privacy protections must be built into data collection, storage, and analysis processes, rather than being added later. Similarly, when using AI-driven underwriting or claims systems, insurers must proactively address potential risks such as algorithmic bias, unauthorized data disclosures, and unclear data processing practices. It is crucial to ensure transparency and fairness throughout these processes.

DATA GOVERNANCE: FRAMEWORK AND PRACTICES

Effective data governance is essential to an insurer's data privacy strategy. It entails having well-defined processes, roles, standards, and controls to ensure data is accurately, securely, and compliantly managed throughout its entire lifecycle (Ladley, 2019). In the insurance sector, strong data governance includes activities such as data acquisition, quality management, security measures, compliance oversight, and continuous monitoring and auditing.

A well-structured data governance framework typically includes the appointment of data stewards, privacy officers, and governance committees responsible for overseeing data practices throughout the organization. For insurers, data stewards ensure that data collected through digital channels, IoT devices, and customer interactions meets quality and compliance standards. On the other hand, privacy officers are responsible for ensuring compliance with relevant privacy regulations such as GDPR, CCPA, and HIPAA. They manage internal policies, training programs, and breach response protocols (Ladley, 2019).

Clear roles and responsibilities within a data governance framework facilitate accountability and collaboration across departments, including IT, legal, compliance, and business operations. Such cross-functional coordination is particularly critical within insurance, where regulatory complexities, data interdependencies, and the sensitivity of customer information necessitate rigorous and cohesive governance approaches (Ladley, 2019).

DATA MINIMIZATION, ANONYMIZATION, AND CONSENT MANAGEMENT

Data minimization, anonymization, and informed consent management are essential to PbD and effective data governance. Data minimization means collecting and retaining only the information necessary for specific business purposes, reducing exposure to unnecessary privacy risks (Solove & Hartzog, 2014). For insurers, this could involve limiting data collection to essential information needed for underwriting or claims processing. By doing so, they can decrease the amount of personal data at risk in the event of potential breaches.

Data anonymization and pseudonymization are essential techniques insurers use to protect sensitive customer information. Anonymization makes data unidentifiable, while pseudonymization allows insurers to process data securely without directly identifying individuals. This reduces privacy risks while retaining analytical value (Solove & Hartzog, 2014). These techniques are especially valuable when insurers use advanced analytics and AI-driven processes, enabling thorough data analysis while safeguarding customer privacy.

Informed consent management is crucial for insurers operating within complex regulatory frameworks like GDPR and CCPA. Insurers need to ensure that consumers clearly understand what data is being collected; how it will be used, shared, and stored; and the options available for opting out or requesting data removal (Tikkinen-Piri, Rohunen, & Markkula, 2018). Comprehensive consent management platforms help facilitate transparent interactions with consumers, enabling insurers to effectively manage consumer preferences and regulatory obligations simultaneously.

IMPLEMENTING PRIVACY IMPACT ASSESSMENTS

Privacy impact assessments (PIAs) are crucial tools within the PbD framework. They enable insurers to proactively identify, assess, and mitigate privacy risks before implementing new technologies or processes. A PIA typically involves systematically evaluating proposed initiatives to ensure they comply with regulatory requirements, adhere to privacy best practices, and meet consumer expectations (Cavoukian, 2019). Insurers often use PIAs to examine new products or technology deployments, such as telematics programs, health-related wearables, or AI-driven underwriting systems, ensuring that privacy considerations are thoroughly and proactively addressed.

For instance, an insurer that uses a mobile application to provide personalized health advice based on data from wearable sensors would conduct a PIA to identify potential privacy risks. These risks may include unauthorized data disclosure, excessive data collection, or inadequate consent processes. The findings from the PIA would inform necessary privacy enhancements, such as implementing additional user consent mechanisms, enhancing data encryption, or providing clear privacy disclosures. These measures would ultimately strengthen consumer trust and ensure compliance with regulatory requirements (Cavoukian, 2019).

BUILDING A PRIVACY-FOCUSED ORGANIZATIONAL CULTURE

Successfully embedding privacy into insurers' operations requires cultivating an organizational culture deeply committed to privacy principles and best practices in data governance. Insurance organizations should go beyond simply complyin g with regulations; they must integrate privacy training into their values, norms, and daily operational processes. Employees at all levels—from senior executives to frontline claims adjusters—must understand and embrace their roles in protecting customer privacy, demonstrating consistent vigilance and accountability in handling personal data.

Leadership is essential in fostering a culture that prioritizes privacy. Organizational leaders should regularly emphasize the strategic importance of privacy and data governance. This includes allocating resources to privacy initiatives, visibly supporting projects focused on privacy, and ensuring that staff are held accountable to high privacy standards (Hadlington, 2017). A strong, privacy-oriented organizational culture allows insurers to proactively address changing privacy expectations, maintain customer trust, and navigate complex regulatory environments.

By implementing PbD principles, strong data governance, thoughtful data handling practices, and proactive PIAs and cultivating a privacy-focused organizational culture, insurers can effectively manage the complex relationship between technological innovation and privacy obligations. Addressing privacy concerns is not just about meeting compliance requirements; it is a strategic opportunity for insurers to distinguish themselves through transparency, trust, and consumer-centric data practices. This approach fosters a competitive advantage and resilience in a global market increasingly sensitive to privacy issues.

ARTIFICIAL INTELLIGENCE AND CYBERSECURITY RISKS IN INSURANCE

As the insurance industry undergoes digital transformation, AI technologies have become powerful tools for streamlining processes, improving risk assessment accuracy, detecting fraudulent activities, and enhancing customer experiences. However, AI also introduces unique cybersecurity and privacy risks alongside these significant benefits. Given the complexity of AI systems and their growing importance in insurance operations, it is essential for insurance organizations to thoroughly understand these risks and develop proactive management strategies (Bostrom & Yudkowsky, 2014; Brundage et al., 2018).

ARTIFICIAL INTELLIGENCE ADOPTION IN INSURANCE OPERATIONS

The use of AI in the insurance industry has rapidly increased in recent years. Insurers now employ AI-driven algorithms to automate underwriting decisions, streamline claims processing, detect fraudulent activities, and enhance customer interactions through virtual assistants and chatbots (Balasubramanian, Libarikian, & McElhaney, 2018). Machine learning models analyze large datasets to identify patterns that human analysts might overlook, significantly improving risk assessment and pricing accuracy.

Telematics-based insurance offerings use AI to analyze driving behavior data, allowing for dynamic premium adjustments based on risk levels. Additionally, AI-driven virtual assistants improve customer service by promptly and accurately addressing policy inquiries, processing claims, and managing account requests. This increases operational efficiency and boosts customer satisfaction (Balasubramanian et al., 2018).

ARTIFICIAL INTELLIGENCE–SPECIFIC CYBERSECURITY RISKS

Integrating AI technologies into insurance operations creates unique cybersecurity vulnerabilities that differ significantly from traditional IT systems. These vulnerabilities encompass adversarial machine learning, model manipulation, data poisoning, and the exploitation of AI-driven automated decision-making processes.

ADVERSARIAL MACHINE LEARNING ATTACKS

Adversarial machine learning attacks involve deliberately manipulating data inputs to deceive AI algorithms. Cyber adversaries create carefully crafted, deceptive inputs often nearly indistinguishable from legitimate data. They aim to mislead AI systems and trigger incorrect decisions (Goodfellow, Shlens, & Szegedy, 2015). These adversaries may exploit vulnerabilities in the insurance industry by making subtle yet deceptive alterations to data used in underwriting or claims assessment processes. For instance, attackers could introduce slight modifications to digital images submitted as proof of damage, thereby misleading automated claims processing algorithms into approving fraudulent claims.

Adversarial attacks pose significant risks to underwriting accuracy and pricing fairness. Insurers that depend on automated risk assessments may unintentionally underprice policies or approve coverage based on manipulated risk data, resulting in considerable financial losses. Therefore insurers must establish robust safeguards to address these emerging threats, including adversarial attack detection algorithms and continuous monitoring of their models (Papernot et al., 2017).

DATA POISONING AND MODEL MANIPULATION

Data poisoning contaminates the datasets used to train AI systems by intentionally introducing false or misleading information. This manipulation can undermine the accuracy and reliability of the models (Steinhardt, Koh, & Liang, 2017). Insurers rely heavily on historical claims and policyholder data for predictive analytics, so contaminated datasets can severely impair model performance, compromise predictive accuracy, and lead to biased or incorrect outcomes. For example, if auto insurance telematics data is poisoned, it could distort risk profiles, resulting in inaccurate premium calculations or flawed underwriting decisions.

Attackers can manipulate existing AI models by injecting false feedback, which can gradually retrain the systems to serve malicious goals. For example, this model manipulation could bias AI-driven underwriting algorithms to approve high-risk insurance policies, ultimately increasing an insurer's overall exposure without immediate detection. To counteract these risks, insurers must implement adequate model validation, conduct data integrity checks, and establish robust governance frameworks to maintain confidence in AI-driven processes (Steinhardt et al., 2017).

EXPLOITATION OF AUTOMATED DECISION-MAKING PROCESSES

AI systems designed for automated decision-making are significant targets for cybersecurity threats because of their critical roles in operations. Attackers who exploit AI-driven automation can quickly disrupt entire business operations. For example, sophisticated phishing schemes may deceive AI-powered virtual assistants into disclosing sensitive customer information, initiating fraudulent financial transactions, or bypassing security protocols (Brundage et al., 2018).

Such attacks take advantage of the inherent trust in automated systems, leading to significantly greater potential damages than traditional cyberattacks. Insurers must acknowledge the limitations of these automated systems, continuously assess their vulnerabilities, and establish contingency plans to address failures or compromises in AI-driven processes quickly.

PRIVACY RISKS ASSOCIATED WITH ARTIFICIAL INTELLIGENCE IN INSURANCE

AI-driven technologies present significant privacy concerns. Insurers' dependence on extensive customer data can lead to unauthorized disclosures or misuse of sensitive information, resulting in regulatory violations and a loss of customer trust (Tikkinen-Piri, Rohunen, & Markkula, 2018).

ALGORITHMIC BIAS AND DISCRIMINATORY PRACTICES

One significant privacy risk associated with AI in the insurance industry is algorithmic bias, which can occur due to biased training datasets or flawed model designs. AI-driven underwriting or claims assessment processes might unintentionally discriminate against specific customer segments based on race, gender, age, or socioeconomic status, primarily when relying on historical datasets that reflect existing societal biases (Barocas & Selbst, 2016). These discriminatory practices violate fairness principles and could also breach regulatory requirements, such as GDPR or CCPA. This exposes insurers to significant legal, financial, and reputational risks.

To effectively manage algorithmic bias, it is essential to conduct thorough data validation, ensure clear model transparency, and regularly audit AI systems for fairness. Insurers should implement privacy-preserving techniques, such as differential privacy or federated learning, to reduce discriminatory outcomes and safeguard sensitive individual information (Barocas & Selbst, 2016).

EXCESSIVE DATA COLLECTION AND SURVEILLANCE RISKS

The data-intensive nature of AI increases risks associated with excessive data collection and invasive surveillance. For example, AI-driven telematics and wearable devices continuously collect personal data streams, raising the risk of privacy violations if mishandled. Overcollection or inappropriate processing of personal data can lead to a loss of customer trust, violations of regulatory frameworks, and significant legal and regulatory penalties for insurers (Solove & Hartzog, 2014).

To tackle privacy concerns, insurers should follow key principles such as data minimization, obtaining explicit consent, ensuring transparency, and limiting data use to specific purposes. Implementing thorough PIAs, effective consent management systems, and clear privacy policies will enable insurers to manage the privacy risks associated with AI more effectively (Cavoukian, 2019).

REGULATORY AND ETHICAL CONSIDERATIONS FOR ARTIFICIAL INTELLIGENCE IN INSURANCE

Insurance regulators are increasingly focusing on AI-driven processes, highlighting the importance of transparency, fairness, and accountability. Regulatory frameworks such as the GDPR in Europe, along with emerging guidelines like NYDFS AI regulations, require insurers to ensure that their AI-driven decisions are explainable, auditable, and fair. Insurers using AI systems must meticulously document their data sources, algorithms, model validation processes, and risk management protocols to demonstrate compliance with regulations and uphold ethical standards (Tikkinen-Piri et al., 2018).

Insurers have important ethical responsibilities to prevent harm caused by AI, ensure fairness, and maintain transparency and accountability. Organizations should adopt AI ethics frameworks that establish clear guidelines and governance structures to continually monitor and audit AI-driven processes. Independent ethical oversight boards, transparency reports, and third-party audits are essential tools for effectively managing the complex ethical landscape of AI in the insurance industry.

ARTIFICIAL INTELLIGENCE RISK MANAGEMENT AND MITIGATION STRATEGIES

To effectively manage cybersecurity and privacy risks driven by AI, insurers should implement integrated risk management strategies. This includes establishing comprehensive AI governance frameworks, continuously monitoring AI models, utilizing advanced threat detection techniques, and adopting proactive privacy measures. Effective governance requires clear accountability structures and well-defined roles and responsibilities for overseeing AI. Additionally, it is essential to have validation procedures, conduct regular audits, and establish incident response mechanisms to address AI-related threats (Steinhardt et al., 2017).

Continuous model monitoring is crucial to identify model drift, prevent adversarial attacks, and spot data anomalies ahead of time. Insurers should utilize automated monitoring systems, cybersecurity tools tailored for AI, and strong incident detection protocols to ensure rapid responses to mitigate AI-related incidents quickly.

Insurers should promote collaboration among cybersecurity professionals, data scientists, privacy officers, legal experts, and risk managers. This interdisciplinary approach ensures thorough and multidimensional management of AI-related risks. By fostering teamwork, insurers can responsibly leverage AI's transformative potential while proactively addressing its inherent challenges.

CASE STUDIES OF CYBERSECURITY AND PRIVACY BREACHES IN INSURANCE

Cybersecurity and privacy breaches in the insurance industry have significant consequences, extending beyond immediate financial losses to severe reputational damage and a long-term decline in consumer trust. By analyzing real-world cases, insurance organizations can gain valuable insights into their cyber vulnerabilities, identify systemic weaknesses, and develop more effective and proactive cybersecurity and privacy strategies.

CASE STUDY 1: ANTHEM DATA BREACH (2015)

The Anthem breach, which was discovered in 2015, stands as one of the largest cybersecurity incidents in the history of healthcare and insurance. Anthem, one of the largest health insurers in the United States, experienced a significant cyberattack that compromised nearly 80 million customer records. This breach included personal identification details, health information, social security numbers, and financial data (McCoy & Perlis, 2018).

The breach was attributed to advanced cyber attackers who initially gained access through targeted phishing emails sent to employees. After obtaining entry, the attackers escalated their privileges and moved laterally across Anthem's networks, exfiltrating large amounts of sensitive data. Although medical records were not directly accessed, the attackers acquired extensive personal information that could be used for identity theft, fraud, and long-term privacy threats (McCoy & Perlis, 2018).

The incident led to significant legal, regulatory, and financial consequences for Anthem. Investigations revealed major deficiencies in Anthem's cybersecurity practices, including poor access controls, inadequate encryption methods, and ineffective intrusion detection systems. As a result, Anthem agreed to pay $115 million to settle class-action lawsuits related to privacy violations and regulatory noncompliance. Additionally, the company incurred considerable expenses for customer notifications, credit monitoring, and cybersecurity remediation efforts (Romanosky, Hoffman, & Acquisti, 2014).

The Anthem breach highlighted important cybersecurity lessons for insurers. It underscored the necessity of having strong employee training programs to combat phishing threats, implementing strict network segmentation to prevent lateral movement within networks, and establishing rigorous data encryption practices. Furthermore, the breach emphasized the importance of developing comprehensive incident response plans and having rapid notification protocols in place to reduce regulatory and reputational damage after cyber incidents.

CASE STUDY 2: CNA FINANCIAL RANSOMWARE ATTACK (2021)

In March 2021, CNA Financial, one of the largest insurance carriers in the United States, suffered a significant ransomware attack that highlighted the increasing cybersecurity risks faced by insurers. Cyber attackers employed the Phoenix CryptoLocker ransomware to encrypt critical systems at CNA, which disrupted claims processing, policy issuance, and internal communications (Gandel, 2021).

The attackers demanded a substantial ransom in cryptocurrency for the decryption keys. Due to the severity of the operational disruption, CNA Financial reportedly paid around $40 million to regain access to its systems and data, making it one of the largest known ransom payments at that time (Gandel, 2021). This incident revealed critical vulnerabilities in CNA's cybersecurity posture, including inadequate detection capabilities, insufficient backup and recovery strategies, and weaknesses within remote working infrastructures. These issues were further exacerbated by the increased reliance on remote technologies during the COVID-19 pandemic.

In addition to the immediate financial losses, CNA experienced considerable operational disruptions, damage to its reputation, heightened regulatory scrutiny, and increased premiums for cyber insurance. The incident also had a wider impact, leading to greater awareness and elevated spending on cybersecurity across the insurance industry. The CNA breach highlighted the urgent need for effective ransomware defense measures, which include strong endpoint detection and response systems, comprehensive data backups, and well-developed incident response planning that can quickly restore critical services without succumbing to ransom demands.

CASE STUDY 3: FIRST AMERICAN FINANCIAL DATA EXPOSURE (2019)

First American Financial, a leading title insurer in the United States, faced a major privacy breach in 2019 when around 885 million sensitive customer documents were accidentally made available online because of misconfigured security settings. These documents included financial records, mortgage information, social security numbers, and other highly sensitive personal data. This incident represents one of the largest privacy breaches in the financial services sector (FTC, 2020).

The breach was primarily caused by a basic cybersecurity misconfiguration. An error in the web application allowed unauthorized access to sensitive documents without the necessary authentication, revealing serious shortcomings in governance and oversight. While no specific malicious actor was identified, the breach posed significant privacy risks for customers, leaving them vulnerable to potential identity theft, financial fraud, and unauthorized surveillance (FTC, 2020).

Regulatory authorities, including the Securities and Exchange Commission and the NYDFS, conducted extensive investigations into First American Financial. As a result, the company faced regulatory enforcement actions and agreed to significant settlements due to deficiencies in its cybersecurity management practices. This incident underscored the critical importance of rigorous cybersecurity governance, along with regular vulnerability scanning, penetration testing, and strict security configuration controls. Furthermore, the breach highlighted insurers' substantial privacy responsibilities, particularly concerning the secure and ethical management of sensitive customer data.

CASE STUDY 4: AVIVA PHISHING INCIDENT (2017)

In 2017, Aviva, one of the largest insurance providers in the United Kingdom, fell victim to a significant phishing attack that led to unauthorized access to employee email accounts. The attackers impersonated senior executives in targeted phishing emails, tricking several employees into revealing their email credentials. As a result, these compromised accounts exposed the personal information of thousands of customers, including sensitive financial data and personal identifiers (ICO, 2017).

Investigations revealed major deficiencies in employee cybersecurity awareness and training. Many employees struggled to identify phishing indicators, highlighting the human vulnerabilities present in cybersecurity strategies. Regulatory authorities, particularly the UK Information Commissioner's Office, criticized Aviva for its inadequate employee education, lack of effective phishing mitigation strategies, and poor access management practices (ICO, 2017).

In response to the incident, Aviva launched extensive cybersecurity training programs, introduced multifactor authentication controls, and enhanced their monitoring capabilities. This situation underscored the critical need for insurers to prioritize cybersecurity efforts on human factors. It highlighted the importance of comprehensive employee awareness, simulated phishing exercises, strong authentication mechanisms, and clear security policies to minimize vulnerabilities associated with social engineering attacks.

LESSONS LEARNED FROM CYBERSECURITY AND PRIVACY INCIDENTS IN INSURANCE

These cybersecurity and privacy breaches in the insurance industry collectively provide important insights and reveal recurring vulnerabilities that require focused attention:

- Human factors and employee training: Many cybersecurity incidents exploit human vulnerabilities, highlighting the need for continuous, targeted employee training to reduce risks associated with phishing, social engineering, and credential compromise.
- Robust technical controls: Effective cybersecurity necessitates a multilayered approach to technical defenses, including endpoint protection, network segmentation, stringent encryption standards, and secure system configurations to prevent data breaches and reduce the impact of cyber incidents.
- Incident response and recovery capabilities: Effective incident response planning significantly mitigates the impact of cybersecurity breaches. Insurers should routinely test their IRPs through simulations and tabletop exercises, continuously improving their ability to respond to emerging threats.
- Proactive privacy and data governance: Insurers need to implement proactive privacy measures by integrating PbD principles into their technological developments, performing thorough PIAs, and effectively managing sensitive data through strong data governance frameworks.
- Regulatory compliance and communication: Clear and open communication with regulators, customers, and stakeholders is crucial following cybersecurity incidents. Adhering to regulatory requirements, promptly notifying of incidents, and implementing transparent crisis communication strategies help reduce regulatory repercussions, lessen reputational damage, and build lasting customer trust.

These real-world case studies highlight the crucial need for thorough cybersecurity and privacy management in the insurance industry. Insurers must continuously improve and enhance their security measures by learning from past breaches. This proactive approach enables them to anticipate future threats and develop robust cybersecurity frameworks that protect essential data, maintain operations, and uphold customer trust.

EMERGING TRENDS AND FUTURE CHALLENGES

The rapidly changing digital landscape continuously reshapes the dynamics of cybersecurity and privacy in the insurance industry. New technologies, evolving regulations, and emerging cyber threats present unique challenges that insurers must proactively address to maintain operational resilience, ensure regulatory compliance, and preserve customer trust. Understanding and anticipating these developments is crucial for insurers aiming to stay competitive and effectively manage cybersecurity and privacy risks in the coming years (Biener, Eling, & Wirfs, 2015; Marotta & McShane, 2018).

ZERO TRUST ARCHITECTURE: THE NEW SECURITY PARADIGM

Traditional cybersecurity models often depended on perimeter-based defenses, under the assumption that internal networks were trustworthy once users or devices passed initial authentication. However, due to increasingly sophisticated cyber threats and the rise of remote work, insurers are now adopting the zero trust architecture. This model is based on the principle of "never trust, always verify" (Kindervag, 2010). Zero trust demands strict authentication and continuous monitoring at every stage, operating under the assumption that any device, network, or user could be compromised at any moment.

For insurers, adopting a zero trust approach includes implementing multifactor authentication, micro-segmenting networks, enforcing strict identity and access management, and utilizing continuous monitoring through AI-driven analytics. Transitioning to a zero trust architecture enhances insurers' ability to mitigate risks associated with ransomware attacks, credential theft, and insider threats. This approach significantly reduces the attack surface and allows for the rapid detection of anomalous activities (Kindervag, 2010).

Adoption can present various challenges, such as technological complexity, employee acceptance, and potential friction in user experiences. Successfully addressing these challenges requires comprehensive strategic planning, strong executive sponsorship, employee training, and phased implementation tailored to the specific operational environments of insurers.

QUANTUM COMPUTING THREATS TO CYBERSECURITY

Quantum computing poses a significant cybersecurity threat to the insurance industry. It utilizes the principles of quantum mechanics to perform computations at speeds far surpassing those of classical computers. This advancement presents a serious risk to the traditional cryptographic encryption methods that insurers depend on for protecting data and ensuring transaction security (Mosca, 2018).

Cryptographic algorithms that currently secure sensitive data for insurers, such as Rivest–Shamir–Adleman and elliptic curve cryptography encryption, could be compromised quickly by sufficiently powerful quantum computers. This exposure poses a significant risk, as it could allow malicious actors to access the most sensitive information held by insurers. As a result, insurers face an urgent need to strengthen their cybersecurity measures against quantum threats. Key preparations include adopting quantum-resistant encryption algorithms, updating critical systems and data to meet quantum-safe cryptographic standards, and regularly reassessing their cryptographic resilience (Mosca, 2018).

Insurers must take proactive steps to address quantum risks by collaborating with cybersecurity researchers, regulators, and technology vendors. Delayed responses may result in catastrophic data breaches, severely undermining customer trust and affecting competitive positioning.

INNOVATIONS IN PRIVACY-PRESERVING TECHNOLOGIES

Privacy-preserving technologies are evolving rapidly, providing insurers with effective tools to safeguard sensitive consumer data while still being able to perform necessary analyses. Techniques like differential privacy, federated learning, and homomorphic encryption allow insurers to securely process large datasets, ensuring compliance with regulations and maintaining consumer trust (Dwork & Roth, 2014).

Differential privacy introduces statistical noise into datasets, preserving individual privacy by making it difficult to extract reliable information about specific individuals. At the same time, it allows insurers to obtain accurate aggregate insights (Dwork & Roth, 2014). Federated learning enables insurers to train machine learning models on distributed datasets without the need for centralized data collection. This approach minimizes the risks associated with data breaches and unauthorized disclosures. Homomorphic encryption allows for computations to be performed on encrypted data, enabling insurers to process sensitive information without needing to decrypt it. This significantly reduces the risk of exposure (Gentry, 2009).

The widespread adoption of advanced privacy technologies faces several practical challenges, including computational complexity, implementation costs, and regulatory acceptance. Insurers need to invest in ongoing research, foster industry partnerships, and collaborate with regulators to promote the broader deployment and integration of methods that preserve privacy.

REGULATORY FORECASTING AND ANTICIPATED POLICY SHIFTS

As cybersecurity threats continue to evolve, insurance regulators worldwide are increasingly focusing on cybersecurity and privacy protections. Insurers should prepare for more stringent regulatory requirements, heightened reporting obligations, and increased oversight concerning data protection and AI-driven decision-making.

New regulatory trends suggest that insurers may soon be required to disclose their cybersecurity preparedness, comply with specific standards for AI explainability and fairness, and improve their privacy management practices to align with global frameworks similar to the GDPR (Tikkinen-Piri, Rohunen, & Markkula, 2018). For example, insurers may experience heightened regulatory scrutiny regarding the disclosure of cybersecurity incidents, necessitating prompt reporting, thorough documentation, and clear communication with customers and regulators.

Actively engaging with regulatory developments by participating in consultations, regulatory forums, and industry collaborations helps insurers stay ahead of compliance challenges. Investing in flexible and adaptive compliance frameworks allows insurers to quickly adjust to changing regulatory expectations, ensuring they maintain operational agility and a competitive edge.

EVOLVING RANSOMWARE THREATS AND ADVANCED PERSISTENT THREATS

Ransomware attacks are increasingly targeting insurance companies for financial gain and the theft of sensitive data. These attacks are rapidly evolving, becoming more sophisticated, widespread, and frequent. Cybercriminals exploit the heavy reliance of insurers on digital systems, using ransomware to disrupt operations, demand significant ransom payments, and steal sensitive customer information for further exploitation (Marotta & McShane, 2018). Double ransom attacks are increasingly common. In this scam, cybercriminals first carry out a traditional ransomware attack, during which the victim pays to have their data recovered. However, after receiving payment, the attackers then demand a second payment to prevent the public release of that stolen data. This tactic effectively extorts the victim for a second time.

APTs are sophisticated and targeted cyber operations often sponsored by state actors, posing significant risks to organizations. APTs aim to secretly infiltrate insurers' systems and remain undetected for long periods, during which they extract sensitive intellectual property, financial data, or customer information. To defend against APTs, organizations need strong threat intelligence capabilities, advanced endpoint detection, continuous monitoring, and comprehensive incident response strategies.

Insurers need to proactively improve their cyber defense capabilities, maintain strong backup and recovery strategies, and continuously refine their IRPs. They should also consider sharing threat intelligence and collaborating with cybersecurity coalitions and government organizations to gain insights into emerging threats and effective defensive strategies.

THE RISE OF CYBER-PHYSICAL SYSTEMS AND INTERNET OF THINGS VULNERABILITIES

The growing use of cyber-physical systems and IoT devices in insurance operations has created significant cybersecurity vulnerabilities. Connected vehicles, smart buildings, wearable health devices, and home automation systems give insurers unprecedented access to consumer behavior data, which enhances the accuracy of risk assessments. However, these interconnected devices often lack strong security measures, making them vulnerable entry points for cyber attackers who seek unauthorized access or data theft (Whitman & Mattord, 2018).

Insurance companies must thoroughly evaluate the security measures of IoT devices that are part of their products. They should implement strict cybersecurity controls and establish comprehensive vulnerability management protocols. To reduce risks associated with interconnected cyber-physical systems, it is essential to adopt enhanced security standards for IoT devices, along with strong data encryption, effective identity management, and ongoing vulnerability assessments.

BUILDING FUTURE CYBERSECURITY TALENT PIPELINES

Insurers are currently facing a significant shortage of talent in cybersecurity expertise. To effectively tackle future cybersecurity challenges, it is essential to develop strong talent pipelines. This involves emphasizing ongoing education, professional certifications, and continuous skill development. Insurers should proactively invest in partnerships with educational institutions, create internal training programs, and promote career pathways within the fields of cybersecurity and privacy.

As the cybersecurity and privacy landscapes continue to evolve rapidly, insurers must focus on attracting, developing, and retaining skilled cybersecurity professionals. This is essential for enhancing their resilience, operational effectiveness, and strategic agility. By prioritizing talent development, insurers can ensure they have the necessary capabilities to proactively respond to emerging threats, regulatory changes, and technological advancements.

To effectively address emerging trends and future challenges, insurers need to proactively manage evolving cybersecurity and privacy risks. By embracing advanced technologies, engaging robustly with regulatory frameworks, implementing proactive risk management strategies, and focusing on continuous talent development, insurance organizations can thrive amidst increasing cybersecurity complexities. This approach will help them protect consumer trust and maintain a competitive edge in a rapidly changing digital landscape.

CONCLUSION: BUILDING RESILIENT CYBERSECURITY AND PRIVACY PROGRAMS

In today's world, where digital infrastructure is essential to almost every aspect of the insurance industry, managing cybersecurity and privacy risks has become critical. These concerns are no longer just technical issues; they are essential for building institutional trust, ensuring financial sustainability, and maintaining regulatory compliance. As insurers transition into data-driven organizations, they must fundamentally reevaluate their security and privacy strategies to address the challenges posed by an interconnected and increasingly hostile threat landscape.

This chapter has examined the complex landscape of cybersecurity and privacy within the insurance industry. It covered regulatory requirements, operational frameworks, AI-related vulnerabilities, and emerging technological challenges. The discussion emphasized that insurers need to go beyond merely complying with regulations. Instead, they should implement integrated, proactive, and forward-thinking strategies that anticipate risks, enhance institutional resilience, and uphold the trust placed in them by both policyholders and regulators.

The adoption of industry standards like the NIST CSF and ISO/IEC 27001 gives insurers a solid operational foundation. However, technical controls alone are not enough. To create resilient cybersecurity programs, organizations need to engage in continuous threat modeling, conduct real-time risk assessments, implement adaptive governance, and foster a cultural shift throughout the organization. Cybersecurity involves more than just securing systems; it is about building an organization that can withstand, respond to, and learn from adversarial disruptions.

Privacy should be viewed as a strategic asset rather than a limitation. By implementing strong data governance, following PbD principles, and adopting accountability-driven practices, insurers can shift privacy from a compliance burden into a competitive advantage and a foundation for customer trust. Investments in transparency, consent management, and ethical data handling are no longer optional; they are essential elements of building digital trust in an increasingly skeptical and regulated environment.

The use of AI presents both significant opportunities and complex risks for insurers. As they leverage AI to enhance efficiency and improve decision-making, it is crucial for them to remain aware of potential issues such as algorithmic bias, the need for explainability, the risk of adversarial manipulation, and the importance of data integrity. To address these challenges, insurers should establish AI governance frameworks, conduct regular ethical reviews, and adopt a human-in-the-loop approach that balances automation with necessary oversight.

Insurers are facing a convergence of significant challenges: the growing threat of ransomware, the disruptive potential of quantum computing, the expansion of cyber-physical systems through the IoT, and the global rise of complex privacy regulations. Addressing these issues requires strategic foresight, ongoing investment in talent and infrastructure, and collaboration across the industry.

Cyber resilience in the insurance industry relies on leadership that recognizes cybersecurity and privacy as essential components of organizational credibility and long-term value creation, rather than merely technical functions. It is crucial for boards of directors to engage with cyber risk at a strategic level. Executives must align security and privacy initiatives with business innovation, while frontline staff should operate with awareness, discipline, and a sense of shared responsibility.

Resilient insurers will be those that view cybersecurity and privacy as ongoing, collective capabilities integrated into every system, decision, and interaction. The future of insurance will belong to institutions that not only help manage risk for others but also demonstrate a strong command over the digital risks they face themselves.

AI DISCLOSURE

During the preparation of this work the author(s) used Grammarly to correct grammatical errors and enhance readability. After using this tool/service, the author(s) reviewed and edited the content as needed and take(s) full responsibility for the content of the publication.

REFERENCES

Balasubramanian, S., Libarikian, A., & McElhaney, D. (2018). *Insurance 2030—The impact of AI on the future of insurance*. McKinsey & Company. https://www.mckinsey.com.

Barocas, S., & Selbst, A. D. (2016). Big data's disparate impact. *California Law Review*, *104*(3), 671–732. https://doi.org/10.2139/ssrn.2477899.

Biener, C., Eling, M., & Wirfs, J. H. (2015). Insurability of cyber risk: An empirical analysis. *The Geneva Papers on Risk and Insurance—Issues and Practice*, *40*(1), 131–158. https://doi.org/10.1057/gpp.2014.19.

Bostrom, N., & Yudkowsky, E. (2014). The ethics of artificial intelligence. In K. Frankish & W. Ramsey (Eds.), *The Cambridge Handbook of Artificial Intelligence* (pp. 316–334). Cambridge University Press.

Brundage, M., Avin, S., Clark, J., Toner, H., Eckersley, P., Garfinkel, B., & Amodei, D. (2018). *The malicious use of artificial intelligence: Forecasting, prevention, and mitigation*. https://arxiv.org/abs/1802.07228.

Calder, A, & Watkins, S (2019). IT governance: An international guide to data security and ISO27001/ISO27002 (6th ed.). Kogan Page.

Catlin, T., Lorenz, j., Münstermann, B., Olesen, P., & Ricciardi, V. (2017). Digital disruption in insurance: Cutting through the noise. https://www.mckinsey.com/industries/financial-services/our-insights/digital-disruption-in-insurance.

Cavoukian, A. (2019). Privacy by design: Origins, meaning, and prospects for assuring privacy and trust in the information era. In K. W. Bowyer & M. J. Burgoon (Eds.), *Privacy, Big Data, and the Public Good* (pp. 211–220). Cambridge University Press.

Chander, A., Kaminski, M. E., & McGeveran, W. (2021). Catalyzing privacy law. *Minnesota Law Review*, *105*, 1733–1804.

Deloitte. (2021). 2021 insurance industry outlook. https://www2.deloitte.com/us/en/pages/financial-services/articles/insurance-industry-outlook.html.

Dwork, C., & Roth, A. (2014). The algorithmic foundations of differential privacy. *Foundations and Trends in Theoretical Computer Science*, *9*(3–4), 211–407. https://doi.org/10.1561/0400000042.

FTC. (2020). *First American Title Company settlement*. Federal Trade Commission. https://www.ftc.gov/news-events.

Gandel, S. (2021). CNA reportedly paid $40 million in ransom to hackers. *CBS News*. https://www.cbsnews.com.

Gentry, C. (2009). *A fully homomorphic encryption scheme*. Stanford University. *PhD dissertation*. https://crypto.stanford.edu/craig.

Goldman, E. (2021). An introduction to the California Consumer Privacy Act (CCPA). Santa Clara Law Digital Commons. https://doi.org/10.1016/j.future.2010.12.006.

Goodfellow, I. J., Shlens, J., & Szegedy, C. (2015). Explaining and harnessing adversarial examples. *International Conference on Learning Representations (ICLR)*. https://arxiv.org/abs/1412.6572.

Gostin, L. O., Halabi, S. F., & Wilson, K. (2018). Health data and privacy in the digital era. *JAMA*, *320*(3), 233–234. https://doi.org/10.1001/jama.2018.8374.

Greenleaf, G. (2012). Global data privacy laws: Forty years of evolution. *Privacy Laws & Business International Report*, *115*, 10–13.

Hadlington, L. (2017). Human factors in cybersecurity; examining the link between Internet addiction, impulsivity, attitudes towards cybersecurity, and risky cybersecurity behaviors. *Heliyon*, *3*, (7)e00346. https://doi.org/10.1016/j.heliyon.2017.e00346.

Humphreys, E. (2016). *Implementing the ISO/IEC 27001 information security management system standard* (2nd ed). Artech House.

ICO. (2017). *Aviva data breach report*. UK Information Commissioner's Office. https://ico.org.uk.

Janger, E. J., & Schwartz, P. M. (2002). Gramm-Leach-Bliley Act: A new approach to information privacy. *New York University Law Review*, *78*, 1618–1664.

Killmeyer, J. (2016). *Cybersecurity incident response: How to contain, eradicate, and recover from incidents*. Apress.

Kindervag, J. (2010). *No more chewy centers: Introducing the Zero Trust model of information security*. Forrester Research.

Ladley, J. (2019). *Data governance: How to design, deploy, and sustain an effective data governance program* (2nd ed.). Academic Press.

Marotta, A., & McShane, M. (2018). Cybersecurity in the insurance industry: The real risks. *Risk Management and Insurance Review*, *21*(1), 57–68. https://doi.org/10.1111/rmir.12098.

McCoy, T. H., & Perlis, R. H. (2018). Temporal trends and characteristics of reported cases of data breaches involving health information. *JAMA*, *320*(12), 1282–1284. https://doi.org/10.1001/jama.2018.9363.

McGraw, D. (2013). Building public trust in uses of Health Insurance Portability and Accountability Act de-identified data. Association. Journal of the American Medical Informatics, 20(1), 29–34.

Mosca, M. (2018). Cybersecurity in an era with quantum computers: Will we be ready? *IEEE Security & Privacy*, *16*(5), 38–41. https://doi.org/10.1109/MSEC.2018.053761606.

NIST. (2011). *SP 800–30: Guide for conducting risk assessments*. National Institute of Standards and Technology. https://doi.org/10.6028/NIST.SP.800–30r1.

NIST. (2012). *SP 800–39: Managing information security risk*. National Institute of Standards and Technology. https://doi.org/10.6028/NIST.SP.800–39.

NIST. (2018). *Framework for improving critical infrastructure cybersecurity (Version 1.1)*. National Institute of Standards and Technology. https://nvlpubs.nist.gov/nistpubs/CSWP/NIST.CSWP.04162018.pdf.

NIST. (2020). *SP 800–53 Rev. 5: Security and privacy controls for information systems and organizations*. National Institute of Standards and Technology. https://doi.org/10.6028/NIST.SP.800–53r5.

Papernot, N., McDaniel, P., Goodfellow, I., Jha, S., Celik, Z. B., & Swami, A. (2017). Practical black-box attacks against deep learning systems using adversarial examples. *Proceedings of the 2017 ACM on Asia Conference on Computer and Communications Security*, 506–519.

Peltier, T. R. (2016). *Information security risk analysis* (3rd ed). CRC Press.

Rejda, G. E, & McNamara, M. J. (2021). Principles of risk management and insurance (14th ed.). Pearson.

Romanosky, S., Hoffman, D., & Acquisti, A. (2014). Empirical analysis of data breach litigation. *Journal of Empirical Legal Studies*, *11*(1), 74–104. https://doi.org/10.1111/jels.12035.

Scassa, T. (2020). Privacy law and re-identification. *Canadian Journal of Law and Technology*, *18*(1), 1–24.

Shackelford, S. J., Souter, A., & McNeal, G. S. (2015). The cybersecurity risk management framework: A comparative analysis. *Connecticut Insurance Law Journal*, *22*(1), 1–38.

Shostack, A. (2014). *Threat modeling: Designing for security*. Wiley.

Skinner, C. (2019). Digital human: The fourth revolution of humanity includes everyone. Marshall Cavendish International.

Solove, D. J., & Hartzog, W. (2014). The FTC and the new common law of privacy. *Columbia Law Review*, *114*(3), 583–676.

Steinhardt, J., Koh, P. W., & Liang, P. (2017). Certified defenses for data poisoning attacks. *Advances in Neural Information Processing Systems*, *30*.

Tikkinen-Piri, C., Rohunen, A., & Markkula, J. (2018). EU General Data Protection Regulation: Changes and implications for personal data collecting companies. *Computer Law & Security Review*, *34*(1), 134–153. https://doi.org/10.1016/j.clsr.2017.05.015.

Voigt, P., & Von dem Bussche, A. (2017). *The EU General Data Protection Regulation (GDPR): A practical guide*. Springer.

Von Solms, R., & Van Niekerk, J. (2013). From information security to cybersecurity. Computers & Security, 38(97–102). https://doi.org/10.1016/j.cose.2013.04.004.

Whitman, M. E., & Mattord, H. J. (2018). *Principles of information security* (6th ed). Cengage Learning.

Zissis, D., & Lekkas, D. (2012). Addressing cloud computing security issues. Future Generation Computer Systems, 28(3), 583–592. https://doi.org/10.1016/j.future.2010.12.006.

CHAPTER

Regulation, ethics, and responsibility in insurance technology

9

CHAPTER OUTLINE

INTRODUCTION: TECHNOLOGY, TRUST, AND THE SOCIAL CONTRACT OF INSURANCE

Insurance is fundamentally a promise—an agreement based on trust, regulatory oversight, and a mutual understanding of risk. This promise has depended on human judgment, legal contracts, and actuarial expertise for centuries to provide financial protection during uncertain times. However, this foundational promise is being redefined as the insurance industry rapidly digitizes, introducing algorithmic underwriting, automated claims processing, and behavioral pricing. The rise of insurance technology (InsurTech) has introduced new efficiencies, but it has also raised significant questions about fairness, accountability, transparency, and regulation.

Unlike many other industries, where technological disruptions are often viewed through the lenses of convenience or cost, the stakes in insurance are much more personal. When an artificial intelligence (AI)-driven model denies a customer's claim or charges a higher premium based on unclear data inputs, the consequences go beyond financial inconvenience. They call into question the insurer's role as a crucial social safety net. This makes the ethics and regulation of InsurTech not just operational issues but essential matters of public trust.

Technology is not neutral. Algorithms reflect the biases in their data, the assumptions made by their designers, and the goals of the institutions that deploy them. In

Insurance Technology. DOI: https://doi.org/10.1016/B978-0-443-43972-8.00008-0

the insurance industry, where historical data is used to predict future losses and set prices, these design choices can reproduce and amplify existing social inequities. For instance, risk models may unintentionally penalize individuals from marginalized communities using proxy variables such as zip code, employment status, or education level (Eubanks, 2018). When machines make decisions without providing explanations or avenues for recourse, those insured's human dignity and agency are put at risk.

The regulatory frameworks traditionally governing the insurance industry were not designed to accommodate AI, big data, or blockchain technologies. Historically, insurance regulation has emphasized solvency, rate adequacy, and consumer protection, primarily in the context of human decisions. As digital tools become more widespread, regulators face a dual challenge: adapting existing rules to new technologies and ensuring that innovation does not outpace regulatory oversight. In response, some jurisdictions have introduced regulatory sandboxes and InsurTech charters, while others have expanded the scope of data protection laws and algorithmic accountability statutes to encompass insurance products.

Regulation alone is not enough to guarantee ethical practices in InsurTech. Ethical considerations must be integrated into these technologies' design, implementation, and governance. This encompasses various issues, including explainability, consent, fairness, and the right to appeal decisions. Moreover, it raises more profound philosophical questions: Should insurers use genetic data in underwriting? Should customer behavior be monitored in real time to adjust pricing? Are certain risks, such as climate exposure, suitable for private insurance?

At the intersection of these issues, there is a growing movement toward responsible innovation in insurance. This framework balances technological advancement with social responsibility, legal compliance, and ethical foresight. It encourages insurers, regulators, technologists, and consumers to work together in creating systems that are not only efficient but also fair and just.

This chapter provides an in-depth exploration of InsurTech's regulatory and ethical dimensions. It begins by outlining the current regulatory landscape and identifying key legal issues associated with algorithmic decision-making, digital data, and decentralized platforms. The chapter then examines the ethical considerations that insurers must address when designing and deploying intelligent systems. A section on regulatory technology (RegTech) introduces emerging tools and platforms that aim to modernize regulatory compliance and risk oversight. Case studies illustrate instances where regulation and ethics have clashed or aligned with InsurTech innovation in real-world scenarios. Finally, the chapter concludes with guiding principles for creating more accountable, inclusive, and human-centered insurance systems in the digital age.

As insurers move through the 21st century, they must do more than adopt new technologies. They must also rethink the principles of fair insurance, clear communication, and responsible action. By doing this, they will meet changing regulations and reaffirm the essential social contract that underpins insurance: to protect individuals, not just manage risks.

THE REGULATORY LANDSCAPE OF INSURANCE TECHNOLOGY

The insurance industry has always been heavily regulated. Insurers must adhere to a framework of laws and oversight that includes capital requirements, product approvals, rate filings, and market conduct examinations. These regulations ensure financial solvency, protect consumers, and maintain market stability. However, introducing digital technologies into nearly every aspect of the insurance value chain—such as pricing, underwriting, distribution, claims processing, and customer engagement—has created challenges that many traditional regulatory frameworks were not designed to handle. Consequently, the regulatory landscape is transitioning to adapt to innovations like algorithmic decision-making, big data analytics, blockchain-based smart contracts, and AI.

Historically, insurance regulation in the United States has been managed at the state level, with each state having its insurance department. The National Association of Insurance Commissioners (NAIC) has played a crucial role in developing model laws and promoting uniformity across states. However, insurers often have to navigate a complex patchwork of state-specific requirements. This system functioned reasonably well in a predigital era, when product innovation was slow and insurers primarily operated within state boundaries. However, in the digital age, where InsurTech startups can launch nationally through direct-to-consumer platforms and global reinsurers use AI-powered underwriting tools across borders, this decentralized approach can hinder innovation and create uncertainty in compliance.

Regions have started experimenting with new frameworks in response to the need for innovation alongside consumer protection. One effective mechanism that has emerged is regulatory "sandboxes." Popularized by the United Kingdom's Financial Conduct Authority, these sandboxes allow companies to test new products or technologies in a controlled environment under the supervision of regulators (Zetzsche et al., 2017).

In the United States, several states—including Arizona, Utah, and Kentucky—have introduced their insurance sandboxes. These initiatives provide temporary exemptions or streamlined processes for novel products while implementing consumer safeguards, such as informed consent and disclosure requirements. These sandboxes have proven appealing to startups developing usage-based insurance, blockchain-based peer-to-peer models, and AI-driven underwriting platforms.

Around the world, various jurisdictions have adopted proactive approaches to InsurTech. For example, Singapore and Hong Kong have developed comprehensive strategies through their monetary authorities. These strategies include innovation offices, fast-track licensing, and integration of RegTech. The European Union established stringent data privacy and algorithmic transparency standards with its General Data Protection Regulation (GDPR). This regulation mandates that consumers be informed when automated decision-making significantly impacts them and allows them to request a human review. This directly affects insurers that utilize automated underwriting systems or algorithmic claims triage.

These emerging models indicate a shift in regulatory philosophy. Instead of focusing solely on static compliance, modern insurance regulation is increasingly concerned with dynamic oversight—the ability to monitor and evaluate systems that learn and evolve. This is especially important in machine learning, where models are regularly retrained with new data, potentially changing their behavior without explicit human intervention. This poses a dilemma for regulators: how to maintain regulatory clarity and protect consumers while also allowing the flexibility that innovation demands.

One approach to addressing this dilemma is to emphasize algorithmic accountability. Regulators in various jurisdictions have issued guidelines on the responsible use of AI and data in financial services. For example, the NAIC has developed a model bulletin on AI that encourages insurers to adopt fairness, transparency, privacy, and auditability in designing and deploying AI systems (NAIC, 2020). In Europe, the proposed AI Act aims to regulate high-risk AI systems, including those used in insurance. This legislation requires impact assessments, risk classifications, and documentation of data provenance and model performance (European Commission, 2021).

As new regulations are introduced, substantial uncertainty exists regarding how existing laws apply to emerging technologies. For example, insurance antidiscrimination laws were created with human underwriters in mind, not neural networks. If trained on biased historical data, can an AI system be held accountable for discriminatory decisions? Should insurers be allowed to use social media data or GPS tracking to determine policy prices, and if so, what constitutes informed consent? What legal status do smart contracts hold in claims processing without human intermediaries? These are not merely theoretical questions; they underscore many legal gray areas where insurers, consumers, and regulators must navigate new interpretations of fairness, privacy, and responsibility.

The concept of regulatory lag—the idea that technology advances more quickly than the laws designed to govern it—has become a primary concern in InsurTech. Insurers find themselves facing two significant risks: the risk of failing to comply with changing regulations and the risk of stagnation caused by overly cautious legal departments. To address these challenges, some firms are investing heavily in RegTech, a rapidly growing sector focused on automating compliance processes, enhancing transparency, and improving risk management. RegTech not only streamlines internal operations but also fosters more effective communication with regulators, a topic that will be explored in greater detail later in this chapter.

At the same time, regulators are increasingly leveraging technology to enhance their capabilities. The rise of supervisory technology (SupTech) allows regulators to utilize data analytics and AI to conduct market surveillance, identify systemic risks, and detect emerging trends in real time. For example, by aggregating anonymized telematics data, a regulator could observe industry-wide shifts in driving behavior that may indicate underpricing in specific segments of auto insurance. This ability to oversee companies and algorithms signifies a significant evolution in the regulatory function.

One area experiencing rapid development is the global convergence of insurance regulation, particularly regarding data governance and digital ethics. Although countries have different legal frameworks, there is an increasing consensus on key principles, such as the right to data privacy, the necessity for algorithmic transparency, and the prohibition of unjustified discrimination. International organizations like the International Association of Insurance Supervisors and the Organisation for Economic Co-operation and Development have issued guidelines that promote responsible innovation in insurance and encourage regulatory coordination across borders (IAIS, 2021). These efforts are essential in a world where InsurTech companies operate globally and digital risks, such as cyberattacks or widespread data breaches, do not recognize national boundaries.

The regulatory landscape for InsurTech is undergoing significant changes and facing various challenges. Innovation prompts regulators to reassess long-standing beliefs about measuring, pricing, and managing risk. Insurers are evolving from financial intermediaries into data-driven technology companies, necessitating reevaluating oversight mechanisms. As regulators aim to find the right balance between fostering innovation and protecting consumers, they need to engage more deeply with the relevant technologies, collaborate with the industry, and anticipate emerging tools' ethical and legal implications before they become widely adopted.

The most forward-thinking insurers will not simply wait for regulatory mandates in this environment. Instead, they will take a proactive approach by embracing principles of responsible innovation. They will embed compliance into their technological development processes and view regulation not as a constraint but as a framework for building public trust. By doing so, they can help shape a future where InsurTech is innovative, efficient, but also equitable, transparent, and accountable.

KEY LEGAL AND COMPLIANCE ISSUES IN INSURTECH

As insurance companies increasingly adopt digital platforms, data-driven personalization, and AI, they are navigating a complex and ever-changing legal landscape. While the foundational legal principles of insurance, such as contract law, fiduciary responsibility, and consumer protection, remain relevant, the rise of algorithmic decision-making and digital data introduces new layers of legal uncertainty and regulatory scrutiny. The key compliance issues facing InsurTech firms today are not just technical; they are intricately linked to how data is collected, interpreted, and utilized in automated systems that impact real people's lives and financial futures.

One of the most significant legal challenges in InsurTech is data privacy and consent. Traditionally, insurers have relied on structured, first-party data collected during underwriting, claims processing, and customer interactions. However, many InsurTech platforms now incorporate third-party data sources, such as social media activity, geolocation information, telematics, credit history, and behavioral or biometric data. While these additional data sources can enhance the accuracy of underwriting and customer profiling, they also raise important questions about what constitutes informed consent and the limitations on data usage.

In places like the European Union, data protection laws such as the GDPR impose strict requirements on collecting, storing, processing, and sharing personal data. Under the GDPR, individuals can access, correct, and delete their data. They can also object to certain forms of automated processing, especially those that have legal consequences or significant effects on them (Voigt & Von dem Bussche, 2017). For insurance companies that use machine learning to deny policy applications or settle claims, these regulations may create a legal obligation to provide explanations and allow for human review.

In the United States, the privacy regulatory environment is more fragmented than in other regions. No national privacy law is equivalent to the GDPR. However, several states, including California, Colorado, and Virginia, have implemented privacy laws granting consumers rights over their data.

The California Consumer Privacy Act (CCPA) and its successor, the California Privacy Rights Act, provide residents with several important rights: the right to know what data is being collected, the right to opt out of the sale of their data, and the right to request its deletion. For InsurTech companies operating nationally or globally, navigating these overlapping legal frameworks is challenging and essential, mainly since their business models often depend on dynamic data aggregation and AI-driven personalization.

The issue of discrimination and algorithmic bias is closely tied to data privacy. Insurance inherently involves differentiating between risks by charging higher premiums to individuals or properties deemed higher risk. However, when machine learning models are trained on historical data that reflects past biases, they can replicate or even worsen existing inequalities. For instance, a model that uses inputs like credit scores, ZIP codes, or occupation may unintentionally disadvantage applicants from marginalized communities, even if it does not explicitly consider race, gender, or ethnicity. Such practices could violate state and federal antidiscrimination laws, including the Fair Housing Act, the Equal Credit Opportunity Act, and various state insurance statutes.

The legal system has not yet fully addressed the complexities of algorithmic decision-making, but regulators are beginning to pay attention. In 2022, the Colorado Division of Insurance implemented regulations requiring insurers to use external consumer data and algorithms in life insurance to demonstrate that these systems do not lead to unfair discrimination (Colorado Department of Regulatory Agencies, 2022). This regulation marks a significant shift in how regulators perceive the relationship between technology and fairness in underwriting. Similar regulations may arise in auto and health insurance, where the fairness of rating variables is increasingly being scrutinized.

A key area of legal concern is transparency and explainability in automated decision-making. Traditionally, insurance decisions—such as whether to underwrite a policy, how to assess risk, or whether to approve a claim—were made by human professionals. Their reasoning could be reviewed and audited. However, with the emergence of algorithmic systems, particularly complex models like gradient boosting machines or deep neural networks, it has become challenging to understand the logic behind specific decisions. This lack of clarity erodes customer trust and poses legal risks if a decision is contested in court or examined by a regulator.

The legal concept of procedural fairness—meaning that decisions affecting individuals must be made based on transparent, consistent, and reviewable procedures—applies even in automated contexts. Therefore insurers must be ready to document how their algorithms function, how input variables are chosen, and how decisions can be explained to consumers and regulatory bodies. Failing to do so could result in regulatory sanctions, civil lawsuits, or damage to their reputation.

Smart contracts and blockchain applications in the insurance industry raise important legal questions. A smart contract is a self-executing program encoded on a blockchain that automatically enforces the terms of an agreement. These tools are increasingly used in parametric insurance, where payouts are triggered by objective events, such as a rainfall index exceeding a certain threshold or a flight being delayed beyond a specified time. While they offer efficiency, smart contracts also raise legal enforceability, jurisdiction, and available recourse concerns.

Traditional insurance contracts are interpreted within a framework of legal context and equitable principles. For instance, courts may consider factors such as intent, ambiguity, and the doctrine of utmost good faith. In contrast, smart contracts execute automatically based on coded logic, leaving little room for discretion. If an error occurs, such as an oracle providing incorrect weather data or a compromise in the blockchain, it becomes unclear who is liable or whether traditional insurance laws apply. Some jurisdictions, like Arizona and Tennessee in the United States, have recognized smart contracts as legally binding, but comprehensive legal frameworks are still lacking (Werbach & Cornell, 2017). As blockchain-based insurance expands, compliance, contract law, and consumer protection issues will become increasingly pressing.

The rapid pace of change in the InsurTech sector presents compliance vulnerabilities beyond individual technologies. Insurers developing AI tools or digital platforms may prioritize speed to market and innovation at the expense of thorough risk assessments and legal reviews. This can lead to unintentional violations of advertising standards, unjust claims practices, or improper data usage. In response, many regulators are encouraging companies to adopt a compliance-by-design approach. This means embedding legal reviews into the software development lifecycle and treating compliance as a continuous, cross-functional responsibility, rather than just a postdeployment auditing task.

Litigation risk is an increasing concern as algorithmic decision-making becomes more prevalent. Courts are beginning to encounter cases related to automated insurance denials, disputes over claims involving machine-generated decisions, and accusations of discriminatory pricing practices driven by algorithms. The legal standards for these cases are still developing, and courts often face challenges in making decisions based on technical evidence, particularly when proprietary algorithms or confidential data are involved. Therefore insurers must be prepared to defend their models in technical, legal, and public contexts, where transparency and fairness are crucial.

In conclusion, the legal and compliance landscape for InsurTech is becoming increasingly complex, dynamic, and significant. The digitization of insurance operations introduces new technological and legal risks that insurers must manage proactively. Key concerns include data privacy, discrimination, transparency, contract enforceability, and operational compliance across different jurisdictions.

While some companies may see regulation as a burden, the most forward-thinking organizations view it as a guide; it helps them build trust, ensure accountability, and navigate digital transformation with integrity. As the insurance industry evolves, the legal frameworks and compliance strategies that support it must also adapt, ensuring that innovation does not compromise justice or consumer rights.

ETHICAL CONSIDERATIONS IN ALGORITHMIC INSURANCE

As the insurance industry increasingly integrates sophisticated technologies—particularly AI, predictive analytics, and behavioral modeling—into its operations, it encounters regulatory scrutiny and significant ethical questions. The insurance sector has always been morally complex, as it asks individuals to trust that their needs will be addressed during times of loss and uncertainty while also managing risk on a population scale to ensure financial stability. The digitization of these functions does not eliminate the underlying ethical dilemmas; instead, it amplifies them and introduces new challenges.

Ethical considerations in algorithmic insurance revolve around several key themes: fairness, transparency, autonomy, accountability, and social responsibility. These themes become increasingly challenging to maintain as insurers transition from human-centric decision-making to model-driven processes. This shift often results in limited visibility into decisions and who is responsible for their outcomes.

Fairness is one of the most debated ethical issues in algorithmic insurance. Traditionally, insurers have used risk-based pricing, which involves charging higher premiums to individuals perceived to be more likely to incur losses. However, the digital age has significantly expanded the data types used to assess and differentiate individuals. This has led to the creation of "hyperpersonalized" pricing systems that, while potentially sound from an actuarial perspective, may seem unfair or exclusionary to consumers.

For example, consider a scenario where an algorithm determines that a single mother living in a high-crime neighborhood, with a long commute and an irregular work schedule, poses a higher risk for auto insurance. As a result, she may find herself priced out of coverage entirely, despite having no history of making claims. The ethical concern in this case is not about the accuracy of the model itself, but rather about the societal impact resulting from its implementation (O'Neil, 2016).

The issue becomes even more significant when models incorporate behavioral and biometric data, such as fitness tracker results, GPS locations, and social media sentiment analysis. These tools blur the line between risk assessment and surveillance. Suppose policyholders are constantly monitored and penalized for their sleep habits, step counts, or driving routes. In that case, they may view insurance as not a protective service but an invasive control system. In this context, fairness goes beyond simply avoiding discrimination; it necessitates a reevaluation of the ethical boundaries surrounding personalization itself.

Transparency, which refers to the ability to understand how decisions are made, is a crucial ethical principle increasingly challenged in the era of machine learning. In the past, traditional underwriting and claims decisions could be explained, even if not perfectly, by referring to underwriting guidelines, actuarial tables, or adjuster notes. However, algorithmic systems—particularly those that utilize neural networks or ensemble models—are often regarded as "black boxes" because their internal processes remain unclear, even to their developers. This lack of transparency undermines informed consent and weakens policyholders' ability to contest or appeal a decision. When a policyholder is denied coverage or their claim is flagged as suspicious by an algorithm, they deserve more than just a numerical score; they deserve a clear and understandable explanation.

To tackle this issue, some insurers are beginning to implement explainability frameworks, such as Shapley Additive Explanations or Local Interpretable Model-Agnostic Explanations, which provide post hoc interpretations of model decisions. However, these tools have limitations, particularly regarding their ability to capture the broader context in which the model operates. In an ethical sense, transparency extends beyond merely making models technically interpretable; it involves ensuring that systems are understandable, contestable, and communicable to nonexperts (Burrell, 2016). This is crucial for consumer protection and maintaining trust in a product like insurance, which is often intangible.

Autonomy is an important ethical consideration that deserves attention. Insurance traditionally focuses on managing risk, but technology now allows for behaviors to be nudged, influenced, or even coerced under the pretense of reducing risk. For example, an auto insurance company might use real-time telematics to assess drivers based on their braking patterns, cornering speeds, and phone usage. While this approach can lead to safer driving and fewer claims, it also raises concerns about behavioral control. When discounts are linked to specific behaviors, the distinction between encouraging safety and infringing on individual autonomy becomes blurry. This issue resembles health insurance models that reward consistent physical activity or penalize confident dietary choices. Are customers being empowered to make better decisions, or are they monitored and subtly directed by unseen algorithms?

The ethics of accountability add complexity to the issue. When humans make decisions, accountability is generally straightforward: we can identify an underwriter, an adjuster, or a manager and hold them responsible. However, accountability becomes less clear in systems where algorithms trained on historical data make decisions. Who is responsible when an AI model discriminates? Is it the data scientist who designed the model, the executive who authorized its use, or the organization as a whole? Ethical accountability requires that organizations take responsibility for the tools they employ, including the biases in training data, the assumptions embedded in algorithms, and the real-world consequences of automated actions (Zliobaite, 2017).

As insurers increasingly rely on third-party vendors and ready-made AI solutions, the chain of accountability becomes longer and more fragmented. Many InsurTech firms license algorithmic platforms developed by external providers, often with limited ability to audit or modify the underlying code. This can lead to "black-box outsourcing," where insurers delegate critical functions to algorithms they do not fully understand or control. Ethically, this raises significant concerns. Responsibility cannot be outsourced—especially when it involves decisions that affect people's financial protection, livelihoods, and peace of mind.

Ethical considerations in algorithmic insurance must prioritize social responsibility. Historically, insurance has played a crucial role in stabilizing society by pooling risk and distributing losses. This practice enables economic activity, supports recovery, and promotes resilience. However, if technology is employed in ways that fragment risk pools, exclude high-risk individuals, or worsen social inequalities, it undermines the very purpose of insurance. For instance, if machine learning allows insurers to identify highly unprofitable microsegments and then refuse to offer them coverage, the system shifts from protection to exclusion. This undermines the social contract of insurance and raises important questions about whether specific technological capabilities should be limited for public welfare.

The rise of peer-to-peer platforms and decentralized risk pools, such as blockchain-based insurance decentralized autonomous organizations, adds complexity to the ethical landscape. While these advancements offer the potential for greater transparency and efficiency, they also pose risks by eliminating essential institutional safeguards, such as regulatory oversight, capital reserves, and mechanisms for resolving disputes, that protect policyholders from systemic failures. In these contexts, ethical considerations extend beyond individual choices to the very structure of the system: Who establishes the rules? Who benefits from the system's design? Moreover, who is excluded?

Ethical governance in algorithmic insurance goes beyond simple compliance checklists or fairness audits. It demands prioritizing long-term impact over immediate profit or technical efficiency. This involves engaging with diverse stakeholders, conducting thorough impact assessments, establishing oversight boards, and promoting a culture of ethical reflection within the organization. Additionally, it is important to recognize that not all innovations are inherently beneficial; some technology applications, even if technically feasible and legally permissible, may still be ethically inappropriate.

In summary, the ethical challenges associated with algorithmic insurance are significant, complex, and deeply impactful. These challenges go beyond bias and explainability, including profound concerns about autonomy, responsibility, and justice. As insurers develop more advanced systems, they must also prioritize ethics, creating systems that not only predict risk but also promote fairness, that do not just optimize outcomes but also respect individuals, and that aim to serve market interests and the public good.

EMERGING REGULATORY TECHNOLOGIES IN INSURANCE

As insurers increasingly adopt complex digital tools—ranging from AI-powered underwriting engines to decentralized smart contracts—the regulatory frameworks designed to govern these technologies are experiencing significant strain. Regulators are tasked with overseeing systems that are dynamic, adaptive, and often difficult to understand. At the same time, insurers are facing growing compliance challenges as they attempt to navigate evolving regulations while maintaining operational efficiency. In response to this situation, a new category of technological solutions has emerged: RegTech.

RegTech, at its core, involves the use of technology, especially advanced analytics, machine learning, and automation, to ensure compliance with regulations and manage regulatory risks. Although the concept gained prominence in the post-2008 banking sector, where financial institutions faced a surge of new rules following the global financial crisis, its importance in the insurance industry has become increasingly apparent. In many ways, the insurance sector has experienced similar challenges: traditional, paper-based regulatory processes are proving inadequate in a landscape characterized by algorithmic pricing, real-time claims handling, and cross-jurisdictional data flows.

RegTech serves as a valuable tool for insurers and is emerging as a significant capability for regulators as well. For companies in the insurance industry, RegTech facilitates the automation of compliance tasks, enables real-time monitoring, and streamlines reporting functions. On the regulatory side, the related field of SupTech empowers supervisory bodies to efficiently ingest, analyze, and respond to market activities. Together, RegTech and SupTech are beginning to transform the landscape of regulatory interactions—not just by digitizing existing processes but by fundamentally redefining what regulation entails in the era of intelligent systems.

In the insurance industry, one of the most immediate applications of RegTech is automated compliance monitoring. Traditional compliance workflows often rely on periodic audits, manual checklists, and retrospective data reviews. However, with the increasing volume and speed of digital transactions—especially in direct-to-consumer models—these methods are no longer adequate.

RegTech platforms can be integrated directly into underwriting, claims, and customer engagement systems to monitor real-time actions, flagging any deviations from regulatory requirements as they happen. For example, a RegTech system might analyze call center transcripts using natural language processing to verify that representatives comply with disclosure requirements during sales conversations. Additionally, an algorithm that dynamically prices policies based on customer behavior can be complemented by a RegTech layer that checks for the use of prohibited variables or practices that could lead to adverse selection.

Another significant application of RegTech is in reporting and regulatory filings. Insurers must submit a large amount of data to state and federal regulators, including financial statements, product approvals, and market conduct data. These filings are often compiled from various systems, which requires complex reconciliation and interpretation. RegTech tools can automate the extraction, transformation, and submission of the necessary data, reducing errors and speeding up reporting cycles. Some platforms even simulate regulatory scenarios, such as stress tests or capital adequacy assessments, allowing insurers to proactively assess their compliance status before submitting.

Machine learning is increasingly important in risk and compliance analytics, especially for identifying emerging trends and potential misconduct. Similar to how insurers use predictive models to detect fraud or forecast claims, these techniques can also be applied to internal compliance data to foresee regulatory violations. For instance, by analyzing patterns in underwriting decisions, a RegTech system could detect subtle changes in approval rates for specific demographic groups, prompting a fairness audit. Additionally, by examining metadata in system logs, a platform might identify unauthorized access to sensitive customer information, which would help ensure compliance with data privacy laws such as the GDPR or the CCPA.

RegTech goes beyond just analytics; it also includes tools known as regulatory interpretation engines. These engines assist insurers in understanding and applying regulatory texts. They often use natural language processing to analyze legislation, align it with internal policy frameworks, and identify potential areas of misalignment. Some tools enable compliance officers to ask questions about regulations in plain language—such as "Are we allowed to use credit scores in pricing in State X?"—and receive structured, context-aware responses. Additionally, some platforms integrate regulatory libraries directly into software development pipelines, allowing product teams to assess whether new features may pose regulatory risks before launching them in the market.

In more advanced applications, RegTech is being utilized to integrate compliance into smart contracts and automated processes. For instance, a smart contract can automatically execute a payout based on a specific weather trigger in parametric insurance. RegTech layers can be added to ensure these parameters meet state-level regulatory requirements regarding clarity, coverage limits, and consumer disclosures. As insurers explore blockchain-based models to enhance transparency and trust, the capability to embed regulatory obligations directly into decentralized systems may become a crucial design feature.

The rise of real-time regulatory dialogue, supported by machine-readable rules and shared data infrastructures, is equally transformative. Traditionally, regulators received information through periodic reports, often with significant delays. With RegTech, insurers can establish secure, ongoing data channels that allow regulators to monitor selected metrics or flags as they change over time. This approach, sometimes called "continuous compliance," shifts regulatory oversight from a static, backward-looking function to a dynamic and collaborative one. It also provides a more nuanced understanding of systemic risk, enabling regulators to identify emerging threats, such as market-wide pricing anomalies or algorithmic drift, before they can harm consumers.

Regulators are also adopting SupTech tools to improve their supervisory capabilities. These tools include dashboards that track solvency positions in real time, anomaly detection systems that identify outlier firms or products, and AI-driven reviews of rate filings and product disclosures. SupTech allows regulators to monitor firms and the behavior of algorithms used throughout the industry. For instance, a supervisory agency might employ clustering algorithms to group similar pricing models submitted by insurers and then pinpoint outliers whose behavior requires closer examination.

While the RegTech movement holds great promise, it also faces significant challenges. One major issue is interoperability, which connects different systems, standards, and regulatory requirements across various jurisdictions. For example, insurance is often regulated at the state level in the United States. As a result, a RegTech solution that complies with regulations in one state may not meet the requirements of another.

Another challenge is interpretive ambiguity. Many regulatory rules are designed to be flexible, allowing for professional judgment in their application. Incorporating this ambiguity into automated systems can be difficult, as overly rigid interpretations may hinder innovation or lead to unnecessary alerts.

Another concern is the potential for regulatory capture by design. Suppose large insurers or technology vendors create proprietary RegTech platforms that shape how regulations are interpreted or enforced. In that case, there is a risk that compliance will favor the capabilities of these dominant players. Smaller firms may struggle to adopt or integrate these tools, resulting in an uneven playing field. This issue is particularly relevant in an industry where legacy systems and budget constraints often hinder digital transformation.

There are important ethical considerations to keep in mind. Automating compliance can create a false sense of security; just because a tool indicates that a system is compliant does not mean it is. Ultimately, compliance is a human responsibility. RegTech should be regarded as an enabler, not a substitute for critical thinking, professional judgment, and ethical leadership. Regulators and insurers should invest in the governance of RegTech to ensure that these tools are transparent, auditable, and designed with the public interest in mind.

The direction is evident. As innovation accelerates and regulation becomes more complex, RegTech will play a crucial role in the insurance compliance landscape. Insurers who view RegTech as a cost center may struggle to keep pace. In contrast, those that adopt RegTech as a strategic advantage—enhancing agility, building trust, and fostering collaboration with regulators—will be better positioned to thrive in the evolving digital marketplace.

In many ways, RegTech is the answer to the paradox of modern insurance: how to maintain strong oversight without slowing innovation, how to build systems that are both automated and accountable, and how to scale ethical practices in a data-rich, algorithmic world. For an industry that depends on trust, the integration of RegTech may not just be a technical evolution—it may be a moral imperative.

CASE STUDIES IN REGULATORY AND ETHICAL CHALLENGES

The ethical and regulatory complexities surrounding InsurTech are real and increasingly evident in disputes, investigations, and lawsuits. As insurers implement AI, algorithmic pricing models, biometric tools, and telematics on a large scale, the limits of legality and fairness are being challenged in the public sphere. These case studies illustrate the consequences of acting quickly without sufficient ethical safeguards or regulatory oversight. They also reflect the changing expectations of courts, regulators, and consumers regarding digital insurance.

One of the clearest examples of how regulatory concerns can escalate quickly occurred during the 2021 controversy involving Lemonade, a US-based digital insurer known for using AI and automation. In its promotional materials and blog posts, Lemonade emphasized using facial recognition and emotion-detection software to help process claims. This revelation led to public backlash and raised concerns among privacy advocates regarding using biometric data without explicit consent. In response, Lemonade quickly backtracked, clarifying that its technology did not reject claims based on facial expressions. Despite this clarification, the incident sparked inquiries from multiple state regulators and privacy watchdogs about whether using biometric tools violated state biometric information privacy acts or consumer protection laws.

Although no formal enforcement action was taken, the Lemonade case is a cautionary tale about the lack of transparency in claims automation and the ethical risks associated with data-driven personalization. It also signals to insurers that transparency is now essential, especially when using sensitive data sources that the public may not fully understand.

While Lemonade has managed to avoid litigation, other insurance companies have not been as fortunate. A recent ongoing class action lawsuit against State Farm (2022–24) claims that the company's use of telematics data has led to unexplained premium differences among drivers in similar situations. The plaintiffs argue that the algorithm applies inconsistent standards, which violate consumer protection laws and fail to provide adequate explanations. Although the case is still in the discovery phase, it highlights a growing trend: as consumers become more aware of how algorithms influence pricing and claims, they are increasingly challenging digital insurance decisions in court, often with regulatory support.

Connecticut's Insurance Department has initiated a 2023 investigation into the potential discriminatory effects of data-driven auto insurance pricing models. The investigation is focused on whether algorithms that use factors such as credit scores, occupation, and geographic location unfairly impact minority and low-income communities. The department has requested that insurers provide detailed documentation regarding their data sources, modeling methods, and procedures for testing fairness. This action is part of a broader regulatory trend aimed at ensuring algorithmic transparency, especially in models that influence pricing or access to insurance coverage.

A significant legal development in this area is Colorado Senate Bill 21–169, which became law in 2021 and entered its enforcement phase in 2023. This legislation requires life insurers that utilize external consumer data and predictive models to demonstrate that their systems do not lead to unfair discrimination. As a result, Colorado regulators now expect insurers to conduct formal bias testing, perform explainability assessments, and maintain documentation to show compliance with antidiscrimination laws. Notably, this law shifts the burden of proof—insurers are now required to affirmatively prove that their practices are fair, rather than assuming fairness unless a complaint arises.

This law establishes a precedent that other jurisdictions may soon adopt. It marks a new phase of regulation, treating algorithmic decision-making as a regulated product, subject to the same scrutiny as traditional rate filings or policy forms. In practice, this means that insurers must develop internal capabilities not only to build machine learning models but also to audit, defend, and explain these models to external stakeholders.

One area where ethical and regulatory boundaries are being challenged is the use of genetic, behavioral, and biometric data in underwriting. Currently, no US state permits health or life insurers to use genetic testing results for pricing decisions. However, some InsurTech startups have begun exploring partnerships with health platforms and DNA testing companies. Legal experts caution that even the indirect use of genetic or familial data, such as family medical history obtained from a digital intake form, might violate laws like the Genetic Information Nondiscrimination Act. These uncertainties highlight how innovative data sources often outpace the legal frameworks intended to govern them.

As the legal system evolves, courts are starting to address cases that not only focus on outcomes, such as denied claims or pricing disputes, but also on the design and structure of the algorithms themselves. Legal scholars predict that future litigation may involve discovery requests for source code, training datasets, and performance metrics. This raises important issues regarding trade secret protection and the explainability of models. Insurers must now be ready to defend their models not only in terms of statistical validity but also regarding ethical considerations and legal defensibility.

Even when litigation is avoided, regulators are taking a stronger stance in guiding ethical practices. For instance, the New York Department of Financial Services has issued guidance regarding the use of AI and machine learning in underwriting. This guidance emphasizes the importance of transparency, nondiscrimination, and consumer recourse. Similarly, California's Department of Insurance has conducted public hearings to discuss whether and how AI tools should be regulated under existing unfair discrimination statutes. These initiatives reflect a growing awareness that governance must evolve alongside technology and that regulators should play an active role in shaping what responsible innovation looks like.

Although these examples originate from the United States, similar actions are being taken in international jurisdictions. In the European Union, the proposed

AI Act aims to classify insurance underwriting tools as "high-risk AI systems." This classification would subject these tools to predeployment conformity assessments and postmarket monitoring. If this legislation is passed, insurers would be required to disclose their algorithmic processes, conduct bias audits, and provide explanations for automated decisions that significantly impact consumers. These provisions align with the existing rights under the GDPR concerning automated decision-making but expand their scope to explicitly include risk assessment and pricing within the insurance sector.

These cases and legal developments highlight a significant convergence between regulatory enforcement and ethical scrutiny. They indicate that insurers can no longer view technology as a neutral infrastructure or simply as tools for efficiency. Every algorithm decision—such as which data to use, how to preprocess it, which variables to prioritize, and how outcomes are communicated—has moral and legal implications. When these systems fail, the consequences extend beyond financial losses; they undermine trust, lead to litigation, and attract regulatory attention.

These cases emphasize the increasing expectation that insurers must take a proactive approach to identifying and addressing ethical risks, rather than reacting only after lawsuits or enforcement actions occur. It is no longer enough to wait for these events. Leading insurers are establishing internal ethics review boards, forming algorithmic fairness teams, and implementing third-party audit protocols. They are now mapping the risk lifecycle in terms of loss ratios and considering reputational, regulatory, and moral exposures.

As digital insurance continues to evolve, these case studies provide valuable insights. They highlight the real-world implications of algorithmic decision-making, the consequences of taking ethical shortcuts, and the necessity for a stronger alignment between innovation, regulation, and public values. Additionally, they demonstrate that effective regulation can serve as a partner in innovation rather than merely a limitation. For insurers aiming to lead responsibly in the digital age, the focus should be on embracing scrutiny by designing systems that merit it.

BUILDING RESPONSIBLE INSURANCE INNOVATION FRAMEWORKS

The challenges facing the insurance industry in the digital age include issues such as algorithmic discrimination, data privacy breaches, and regulatory uncertainty. These challenges highlight the urgent need for new governance models. As AI, predictive analytics, and real-time data streams become central to insurance operations, companies must go beyond merely complying with regulations as a reactive measure. Instead, they should integrate ethical considerations and regulatory responsiveness directly into their innovation processes. In this context, developing a responsible insurance innovation framework is not just about avoiding harm; it involves proactively designing systems that are fair, transparent, and aligned with the long-term interests of both customers and society.

A responsible innovation framework starts with the understanding that technology is not inherently value neutral. Each data pipeline, algorithm, or automation protocol carries underlying assumptions about risk, value, and human behavior. These assumptions influence outcomes in ways that may not be immediately apparent upon deployment. Therefore responsible innovation necessitates intentional governance structures that identify ethical risks early in the design process and maintain ongoing oversight throughout the technology's lifecycle.

A fundamental component of this framework is the establishment of multidisciplinary design and governance teams. Instead of relying solely on product managers and data scientists for innovation, leading insurers are now involving professionals from various fields, including legal, compliance, ethics, actuarial science, customer advocacy, and even sociology, in their development processes. These teams are responsible for examining the broader implications of new technologies before they are introduced to the market. They address questions of fairness, transparency, consent, and consumer impact not after the fact, but from the very beginning.

A vital element in project planning is the incorporation of ethical impact assessments. These assessments should complement technical risk evaluations and business case modeling. Before launching an AI-based claims triage tool or a behavior-based pricing model, for example, insurers should conduct an impact assessment that addresses several key questions: Who is most likely to be adversely affected by this system? What biases might be present in the training data? How will the system communicate its decisions to customers? What rights will users have to contest outcomes, and what mechanisms for redress will be available?

These assessments can be modeled after similar tools used in other industries, such as Data Protection Impact Assessments under the EU's GDPR or health technology assessments in the public health sector. In some instances, regulators may eventually mandate these reviews; in others, innovative companies may adopt them to differentiate themselves competitively and build trust with their customers.

Insurers should establish internal review boards or governance committees dedicated to overseeing algorithmic decision-making in addition to formal assessments. These bodies function as internal regulators by reviewing proposed models, identifying ethical concerns, and providing guidance or approval before deployment. Ideally, they operate independently from the teams that create the models to maintain objectivity. Their responsibilities typically include conducting fairness audits, evaluating explainability, and ensuring compliance with regulatory requirements.

Governance structures alone are insufficient for fostering responsible innovation. It is essential to promote a change in organizational culture. Leaders must consistently convey that ethics, fairness, and consumer trust are core values rather than optional add-ons. This cultural shift can be reinforced through employee training programs, incentive structures, and internal communications. Data scientists and software engineers should be supported in developing models that are both high performing and interpretable, as well as just. Achieving this may require retraining, revising performance metrics, or redefining what success means in product development.

Part of this cultural transformation involves moving from a mindset focused on minimum compliance," What do we need to do to avoid penalties?"—to a purpose-driven mindset: "What kind of insurance system do we want to build, and how can technology help us achieve that?" In this context, regulatory engagement becomes a collaborative effort rather than a confrontational one. Many leading insurers now cultivate proactive relationships with regulators by sharing their development roadmaps, participating in working groups, and even codeveloping principles for the responsible use of AI. Regulatory sandboxes, pilot programs, and public comment processes provide structured opportunities to test innovations in partnership with oversight bodies.

Transparency is a fundamental aspect of responsible innovation. Insurers should prioritize clear communication with consumers regarding the use of technology in pricing, underwriting, and claims. This involves providing straightforward disclosures about data sources, explaining algorithmic decisions, and creating accessible pathways for appeal or redress. The goal is not only to meet legal requirements but also to build understanding and trust. If a policyholder is denied coverage based on a predictive model, they should not simply receive a denial letter; they should also receive a clear explanation that helps them understand the decision, respond to it, and feel heard.

This commitment to transparency also applies to public accountability. Insurers have the option to publish summary reports of their algorithmic audits, fairness evaluations, or findings from ethics reviews. These reports demonstrate a genuine commitment to responsible innovation and encourage public dialogue. Some companies are even experimenting with algorithmic "nutrition labels" that explain how a model operates, the data it utilizes, its limitations, and how consumers can appeal its decisions. Although these disclosures are currently voluntary, they may become standard practice as regulatory expectations evolve.

Technology procurement and partnerships with third-party vendors are key components of a responsible innovation framework. Many insurers depend on external suppliers for analytics platforms, data feeds, or AI services. These relationships can lead to ethical and regulatory vulnerabilities if the tools used are not fully understood or are not subject to auditing. A strong framework should include vendor due diligence, requirements for model validation, and contractual obligations related to explainability, bias testing, and data privacy. Insurers must ensure that ethical accountability extends beyond their own organizational boundaries.

A responsible innovation framework must include continuous monitoring and iteration. Ethical and regulatory risks change as models are updated, data evolves, and consumer expectations shift. Static compliance documents or one-time fairness audits are inadequate. Instead, insurers should consider algorithmic systems as dynamic products that require routine revalidation, drift detection, and postmarket reviews. This approach should include collecting customer feedback, tracking dispute outcomes, and auditing real-world performance against established fairness and accuracy goals.

Some companies are creating automated dashboards to monitor ethical key performance indicators, such as the fairness of outcomes across different demographic groups, rates of appeals or overrides, and disparities in pricing or claims approvals. These systems allow for a proactive approach to emerging issues and ensure internal accountability for the ethical performance of technology.

In summary, creating a responsible innovation framework is not a one-time effort; it requires a long-term commitment from the organization. This process involves rethinking our processes, policies, and incentives to ensure that innovation benefits not only shareholders but also policyholders, communities, and society as a whole. It encourages insurers to view regulation as a foundation for developing more trustworthy, resilient, and human-centered systems, rather than as an obstacle. Additionally, it demands a new type of leadership—one that is equally comfortable with data ethics and actuarial data and that envisions the future of insurance not solely in terms of profits, but also in terms of principles.

CONCLUSION: GOVERNANCE, ACCOUNTABILITY, AND THE FUTURE OF FAIR INSURANCE

The insurance industry is on the brink of significant transformation. Technologies such as AI, predictive analytics, digital platforms, and blockchain are reshaping the landscape. As a result, the institutions, tools, and assumptions that have governed risk for over a century are being redefined. Despite the acceleration in the pace and precision of insurance operations brought about by these advancements, the core purpose of the industry remains the same: to provide protection, build resilience, and promote social and financial security.

This chapter has examined the legal and ethical challenges posed by InsurTech, as well as the emerging strategies to address them. It began by establishing the foundation of the discussion in the social contract of insurance—a trust-based agreement that technology should enhance rather than undermine. We explored the evolution of regulatory frameworks, which are increasingly adapting to algorithmic systems, data-driven underwriting, and new models of automation. Through case studies and legislative developments, we observed how regulators, courts, and consumers are responding to these changes with increasing demands for transparency, fairness, and explainability.

The key point of this discussion is that algorithmic decision-making poses not only a technical challenge but also a moral and societal one. When pricing models reinforce historical biases, or when claims systems deny coverage without justification, the harm goes beyond financial implications—it also affects ethical standards and reputations. In an industry that relies on long-term relationships and public trust, these failures can lead to consequences that extend far beyond mere short-term cost savings.

We also investigated the impact of emerging technologies, such as RegTech and SupTech, on modernizing oversight and compliance functions. These tools have significant potential to help manage regulatory complexities while promoting more agile, real-time, and collaborative governance approaches. However, their implementation must be approached with caution, ensuring transparency, interoperability, and equitable access for firms of all sizes.

The way forward involves not choosing between innovation and accountability, but rather integrating both. Insurance leaders need to adopt new governance models that incorporate ethics, legal compliance, and public responsibility into their development processes. They should invest in impact assessments, algorithmic audits, diverse design teams, and continuous monitoring systems. Additionally, it's essential to foster organizational cultures that prioritize long-term trust over short-term gains.

The future of fair insurance will largely depend on shared responsibility among all stakeholders. Regulators need to move beyond rigid rulebooks and engage more proactively with the technical aspects of modern insurance. Consumers should be equipped with the tools and rights necessary to understand and question algorithmic decisions. Additionally, the insurance industry must recognize its role not only as a risk manager but also as a steward of equity in an increasingly digitized society.

There are no perfect models—only improved systems that are built incrementally and thoughtfully. Achieving fairness in insurance cannot be accomplished through code alone; it requires judgment, dialogue, and a willingness to acknowledge the complexities involved. However, by adopting a framework of responsible innovation, insurers can create systems that are not only faster and smarter but also more just and resilient.

Ultimately, technology will keep advancing. The key question is whether our values will evolve alongside it and if we can create an insurance industry that not only addresses the risks we encounter but also embodies the kind of world we aspire to protect.

AI DISCLOSURE

During the preparation of this work the author(s) used Grammarly to correct any spelling or grammatical errors. After using this tool/service, the author(s) reviewed and edited the content as needed and take(s) full responsibility for the content of the publication.

REFERENCES

Burrell, J. (2016). How the machine 'thinks': Understanding opacity in machine learning algorithms. *Big Data & Society*, *3*(1), 1–12. https://doi.org/10.1177/2053951715622512.

Colorado Department of Regulatory Agencies. (2022). *Regulation 10-1-1: Governance and risk management framework requirements for life insurance algorithms and predictive models*. https://doi.colorado.gov/insurance/rules-regulations.

Eubanks, V. (2018). *Automating inequality: How high-tech tools profile, police, and punish the poor*. St. Martin's Press.

European Commission. (2021). *Proposal for a regulation on a European approach for artificial intelligence (Artificial Intelligence Act)*. https://eur-lex.europa.eu/legal-content/EN/TXT/?uri=CELEX:52021PC0206.

IAIS (International Association of Insurance Supervisors). (2021). *Issues paper on the use of big data analytics in insurance*. https://www.iaisweb.org/page/supervisory-material/issues-papers.

NAIC (National Association of Insurance Commissioners). (2020). *Principles on artificial intelligence*. https://content.naic.org/cmte_ex_ai_wg.htm.

O'Neil, C. (2016). *Weapons of math destruction: How big data increases inequality and threatens democracy*. Crown Publishing Group.

Voigt, P., & Von dem Bussche, A. (2017). *The EU General Data Protection Regulation (GDPR): A practical guide*. Springer International Publishing. https://doi.org/10.1007/978-3-319-57959-7.

Werbach, K., & Cornell, N. (2017). Contracts ex machina. *Duke Law Journal*, *67*(2), 313–382. https://scholarship.law.duke.edu/dlj/vol67/iss2/3/.

Zetzsche, D. A., Buckley, R. P., Arner, D. W., & Barberis, J. N. (2017). Regulating a revolution: From regulatory sandboxes to smart regulation. *Fordham Journal of Corporate & Financial Law*, *23*(1), 31–103.

Zliobaite, I. (2017). Measuring discrimination in algorithmic decision making. *Data Mining and Knowledge Discovery*, *31*, 1060–1089. https://doi.org/10.1007/s10618-017-0506-1.

CHAPTER

From innovation to implementation: Operationalizing insurance technology

10

CHATPER OUTLINE

Insurance Technology. DOI: https://doi.org/10.1016/B978-0-443-43972-8.00015-8

The insurance industry, traditionally known for its conservative approach and reliance on outdated systems, is entering a transformative era driven by technological innovation. Advancements in artificial intelligence, big data, decentralized systems, and behavioral analytics present insurers with unprecedented opportunities and complex challenges in implementation. Despite the increasing number of technological innovations introduced in the insurance sector, a persistent gap remains between ideas and execution, specifically between generating innovative solutions in innovation labs and successfully implementing them on an enterprise scale (Bughin et al., 2017; McKinsey & Company, 2020).

This chapter focuses on the essential journey from innovation to implementation. While the previous chapters in this textbook have examined the theoretical foundations and practical applications of specific technologies such as blockchain, machine learning, and cybersecurity, this chapter addresses the "how" of transformation—specifically, how insurers identify, test, and integrate new technologies into their existing processes and operating models. Doing so bridges the gap between creative experimentation and successful operation. The chapter provides a structured framework highlighting the institutional capabilities, regulatory environments, and cultural factors that can support or hinder innovation deployment.

Innovation in the insurance sector has evolved beyond traditional research and development departments and infrequent technology upgrades. Today, many leading insurers are setting up dedicated innovation labs and forming partnerships with external accelerators and incubators. These initiatives promote continuous idea generation, rapid prototyping, and agile experimentation. These labs provide a controlled environment for testing new technologies, business models, and customer experiences. At the same time, governments and regulatory bodies are implementing regulatory sandboxes—frameworks that allow insurers and startups to pilot innovations within defined compliance and consumer protection boundaries (Arner, Barberis, & Buckley, 2017). These two models—innovation labs and regulatory sandboxes—create a powerful dual-track innovation engine, allowing for both disruptive and incremental changes to be explored and assessed before full implementation.

Launching a pilot program and scaling it across an organization are fundamentally different processes. Many promising technologies that thrive in innovation labs struggle to transition into full production due to organizational inertia, compliance challenges, outdated IT infrastructure, and misaligned incentives. The risk-averse culture of the insurance industry, while necessary for safeguarding solvency and maintaining consumer trust, can often impede the adoption of agile processes, cloud-native tools, or customer-centric design thinking. Consequently, many companies find themselves in what is known as "pilot purgatory," where promising projects remain stuck in the proof-of-concept stage, unable to demonstrate their business value or secure the necessary investment for full-scale implementation (BCG, 2022).

The aim of this chapter is twofold. First, it seeks to clarify the structures and best practices associated with generating innovation in the insurance sector, including using labs, accelerators, and sandboxes. Second, it examines how insurers can develop the organizational capacity and governance mechanisms needed to transition from innovation to execution. This includes moving from testing a chatbot in a regulatory sandbox to deploying a company-wide AI claims platform, simulating cyber risk models in an incubator, and integrating these models into comprehensive underwriting procedures across the enterprise.

Drawing on global case studies, industry frameworks, and academic research to provide readers with a comprehensive understanding of how insurers can make innovation scalable, sustainable, and aligned with their strategic goals, it emphasizes the importance of digital readiness, leadership support, agile talent strategies, and cross-functional collaboration as essential transformation enablers.

Ultimately, the chapter argues that innovation is not just about creativity or technology but about effective delivery. In a market characterized by rapid change, evolving customer expectations, and competition from nontraditional sources, the true differentiator will not be who can generate the best ideas, but who can execute those ideas at scale with speed, integrity, and foresight.

INNOVATION LABS AND INCUBATORS IN INSURANCE

As the digital economy progresses, traditional insurance companies increasingly acknowledge the importance of creating structured environments for experimentation. These settings allow for testing new technologies, ideas, and business models without the constraints of everyday operations or regulatory risks. Innovation labs and incubators have become essential tools to facilitate this, providing a "safe space" for creativity and iterative development within or alongside established insurance organizations (Deloitte, 2020).

THE ROLE OF INNOVATION LABS IN INSURANCE

Innovation labs are specialized units, either internal or external, focused on researching, developing, and prototyping new technologies and solutions. Their primary responsibilities typically include ideation, experimentation, and testing, but often do not extend to full-scale deployment. These labs are designed to be agile, interdisciplinary, and entrepreneurial, to challenge conventional thinking and explore the viability of transformative ideas.

In the insurance sector, innovation labs serve several strategic purposes:

- Accelerating Product Development: Labs can quickly prototype insurance models based on usage, tools for AI-enabled fraud detection, or mechanisms for dynamic risk pricing before committing to enterprise-wide implementation.
- Talent Development and Cultural Change: Labs frequently create an innovative culture within risk-averse organizations by empowering cross-functional teams, promoting failure as a learning tool, and enhancing digital fluency across business units.
- External Collaboration: Innovation labs often connect insurers and startups, acting as entry points for venture scouting, open innovation initiatives, and codevelopment partnerships (Berendt et al., 2021).

INTERNAL VERSUS EXTERNAL INNOVATION STRUCTURES

Insurance companies typically choose between three organizational models for innovation labs:

- Internal Innovation Labs: These are in-house facilities that are fully integrated into the company's operations. Examples include Aviva's Digital Garage and AXA's Kamet Ventures. The advantages of internal labs include alignment with strategic goals and ease of integration; however, they can also experience bureaucratic inertia and limited exposure to external ideas.
- External Innovation Labs and Accelerators: Many insurers collaborate with established innovation hubs like Plug and Play Insurtech, BCG Digital Ventures, or MIT's Sandbox Innovation Fund. These partnerships provide better exposure to emerging tech ecosystems but may lack institutional knowledge and direct integration capabilities.
- Hybrid Models: Some companies use a hybrid approach, maintaining internal innovation hubs while engaging with external accelerators and venture partnerships. This strategy enables both breadth and depth in sourcing innovation.

The chosen organizational model often depends on the insurer's innovation maturity, market position, and digital ambition. Large multinational insurers may operate multiple innovation units across regions, while midsized carriers may benefit more from forming external partnerships or participating in consortia-based experimentation.

EXAMPLES OF INNOVATION LABS IN PRACTICE

- Lloyd's Lab (United Kingdom): Lloyd's Lab, operated by the Lloyd's of London insurance market, is a global accelerator for insurance technology (InsurTech) startups. The lab offers selected startups access to data, mentorship, and insurance experts, enabling them to codevelop solutions that tackle real-world market challenges. Successful projects have included catastrophe modeling platforms, parametric solutions, and AI-driven claims estimation tools (Lloyd's, 2022).
- Aviva Digital Garage (United Kingdom and Canada): Aviva's internal innovation hub emphasizes customer-centric design and digital product development. Known as The Garage, this hub has spearheaded the creation of mobile-first policy management tools and AI-powered chatbots directly integrated into Aviva's consumer platforms. Additionally, it acts as a catalyst for cultural change by introducing agile coaches and digital design experts to improve internal workflows (Aviva, 2021).
- Kamet Ventures (AXA Group): Kamet is an InsurTech incubator for AXA and is an independent venture studio. Unlike traditional accelerators, Kamet creates

and develops startups from the ground up, often taking a majority ownership stake until the startups reach commercialization. This approach enables AXA to foster external innovation while retaining strategic control over high-value results (Kamet Ventures, 2023).

SUCCESS FACTORS AND RISKS

While innovation labs provide a promising pathway for transformation, their impact is not guaranteed. Several success factors and common pitfalls have emerged from academic studies and industry evaluations:

- Executive Sponsorship: Strong support from the C-suite and clear mandates are crucial. Labs that lack direct executive alignment often encounter resource limitations and reduced influence.
- Integration Pathways: Laboratories must be connected to operational units. Failing to establish transparent handoff processes between laboratories and IT/business teams often results in "innovation theater," where promising pilots are never scaled.
- Metrics and Governance: Labs should be assessed based on learning velocity, validated hypotheses, and market alignment, not merely on the number of prototypes created. Establishing clear innovation key performance indicators (KPIs) is essential to justify ongoing investment.

The primary risk is the misalignment between the innovative goals of innovation labs and the cautious, compliance-focused nature of traditional insurance companies. Without a deliberate effort to connect these two perspectives, innovation labs may become isolated units that lack relevance within the larger organization (Bughin et al., 2017).

REGULATORY SANDBOXES AND CONTROLLED TESTING ENVIRONMENTS

In the highly regulated insurance industry, innovation must navigate a complex landscape of compliance requirements, consumer protection rules, solvency mandates, and national legal systems. While these regulations are designed to maintain market integrity and public trust, they can sometimes stifle experimentation and discourage the adoption of disruptive technologies. To address these challenges, governments and regulators worldwide have begun implementing regulatory sandboxes—frameworks that allow innovators to test new products and services in a controlled environment with direct oversight from regulators. These sandboxes have proven especially valuable in financial services, where noncompliance costs are high and systemic risks can quickly escalate.

ORIGINS AND PURPOSE OF REGULATORY SANDBOXES

The concept of a regulatory sandbox was first introduced by the United Kingdom's Financial Conduct Authority (FCA) in 2015. It aimed to lower barriers to entry for fintech startups while ensuring consumer protection and maintaining regulatory oversight (Zetzsche et al., 2017). This idea quickly gained popularity, especially among jurisdictions looking to attract investment and encourage innovation in heavily regulated financial markets.

At its core, a regulatory sandbox provides a supervised environment where companies can:

- Test a new product, service, or delivery mechanism with real customers
- Operate under a reduced regulatory burden (e.g., temporary waivers or modified compliance)
- Collect performance data and consumer feedback
- Collaborate with regulators to understand how existing rules might apply or need to evolve

By providing temporary relief or flexibility from specific requirements, such as capital reserves, licensing, or reporting obligations, sandboxes allow innovators to explore new business models without bearing a commercial launch's complete cost and legal risks.

SANDBOX DESIGN IN THE INSURANCE SECTOR

In the insurance context, regulatory sandboxes are typically designed to support experimentation with:

- Usage-based insurance and telematics products
- On-demand microinsurance for travel, gig work, or event-specific coverage
- Parametric insurance solutions tied to environmental data triggers
- AI-driven underwriting or fraud detection tools
- Smart contract–based claims processing

The sandbox framework typically includes the following features:

- Time-bounded operation (e.g., 6 to 12 months)
- Predefined customer group and use case scope
- Risk mitigation plans, such as consumer disclosures or opt-in provisions
- Real-time or retrospective supervisory reporting
- Exit conditions that define what happens after the sandbox period (e.g., full licensing or discontinuation)

Participation is typically open to startups and established companies, but the regulatory flexibility granted can differ by jurisdiction. Some sandboxes allow only minimal relief from regulatory requirements, while others offer more substantial exemptions if specific risk controls are implemented.

GLOBAL EXAMPLES OF INSURANCE SANDBOXES

Many countries have now adopted or adapted sandbox models to their local insurance markets:

- United Kingdom—The FCA Sandbox is a significant framework that has supported over 700 applications since it began. Notable use cases in insurance include digital identity verification for claims and blockchain-based marine cargo insurance (FCA, 2022).
- Singapore—Monetary Authority of Singapore operates a traditional sandbox and a "sandbox express" to accelerate low-risk innovation. Insurers have utilized this platform to test blockchain smart contracts and remote underwriting models for life insurance.
- United States—State-based sandboxes: Arizona was the first US state to establish a fintech sandbox in 2018, followed by Utah and Wyoming. The National Association of Insurance Commissioners has also looked into creating frameworks to unify sandbox activities across states. However, adoption remains fragmented due to the decentralized regulatory system.
- United Arab Emirates—Dubai International Financial Centre FinTech Hive hosts an innovation sandbox for insurers and reinsurers to explore AI risk modeling and distribute embedded coverage through super apps.
- India—The Insurance Regulatory and Development Authority of India focuses on financial inclusion and microinsurance, particularly targeting rural populations and agricultural risks using mobile-first technologies.

These examples illustrate the variety of sandbox structures and regulatory philosophies. Some prioritize consumer safety, while others emphasize competitiveness and market modernization. Most share a common goal: to foster agile and accountable innovation.

STRATEGIC BENEFITS OF SANDBOX PARTICIPATION

For insurers and InsurTechs alike, participation in a regulatory sandbox offers several advantages:

- De-risked Testing Environment: Firms can validate assumptions about demand, feasibility, and compliance with reduced financial and legal exposure.
- Regulatory Learning: Participants gain early insights into how their innovations will be regulated postsandbox, helping them plan for commercialization.
- Brand and Investor Credibility: Sandbox approval signals that a regulator views the innovation as viable and safe, increasing trust among investors, partners, and consumers.
- Faster Time to Market: The structured timeline of sandbox participation encourages rapid iteration and disciplined development cycles.

For regulators, sandboxes provide a way to learn about regulations, offering insights into new technologies before drafting or updating policies. They also enable regulators to observe market changes and pinpoint areas where existing laws might be too strict or outdated.

INTEGRATION CHALLENGES AND ORGANIZATIONAL PREPAREDNESS

While regulatory sandboxes have significant potential, they are not a cure-all. Various limitations and risks need to be addressed.

- Lack of Scaling Pathways: Innovations tested in the sandbox must still overcome the insurer's internal bureaucracy, IT limitations, and compliance procedures to scale—a challenge many underestimate.
- Sandbox Exit Ambiguity: Without clear regulatory guidance after the sandbox phase, some firms are uncertain, approved for testing, but unsure about commercial deployment.
- Uneven Regulator Capacity: In some jurisdictions, regulators may lack the technical expertise or resources to engage effectively with rapidly evolving innovations.
- Innovation Equity Gaps: Larger companies with compliance teams and regulatory connections are often better equipped to succeed in sandbox applications than smaller startups.

Organizational readiness is essential for insurers participating in sandboxes. Legal, IT, actuarial, and business teams must work together from the beginning to maximize the insights gained during testing. Furthermore, involving a regulatory affairs team during and after the sandbox phase can significantly improve the transition to market.

TOWARD GLOBAL HARMONIZATION AND REGULATORY COLLABORATION

A noticeable trend in sandbox design is cross-border harmonization. As the insurance industry becomes more digital and data driven, companies operate across multiple jurisdictions and need clear guidelines spanning these borders. In response, organizations such as the Global Financial Innovation Network (GFIN) have been established to explore multijurisdictional sandbox programs. These programs enable companies to simultaneously conduct tests in several countries under coordinated supervision (GFIN, 2020).

These developments could eventually result in establishing international regulatory frameworks for insurance innovation, similar to the Basel standards used in banking. In the meantime, insurers need to focus on compliance agility by developing internal frameworks that enable them to quickly adapt to various sandbox models, legal systems, and policy expectations.

THE FUTURE OF REGULATORY SANDBOXES IN INSURANCE

Looking ahead, regulatory sandboxes are likely to evolve from one-time test beds into ongoing innovation platforms. Regulators are experimenting with:

- Thematic sandboxes focused on environmental, social, and governance, climate risk, or AI ethics.
- Supervisory technology that automates sandbox oversight through application programming interfaces and real-time dashboards.
- Collaborative ecosystems where insurers, tech firms, and academics cocreate standards and tools within sandbox environments.

The future of sandboxes will likely involve closer collaboration with industry associations and research institutions. This could facilitate long-term studies on innovation outcomes and the effectiveness of regulations.

Ultimately, sandboxes are more than just tools for enabling risk-taking; they are mechanisms for cocreating a safer, more equitable future for the insurance industry that is responsive to emerging risks. Combined with a robust organizational strategy and frameworks for scaling after the sandbox phase, they become essential drivers of transformation.

FROM SANDBOX TO SCALE: SUCCESS METRICS, PILOT TRANSITIONS, AND INNOVATION FUNDING

The transition from an innovation pilot to a scalable enterprise solution is one of the most challenging stages in the technology adoption lifecycle, particularly in the insurance industry. This sector often faces obstacles such as legacy systems, regulatory complexities, and a conservative approach to change, which can hinder progress. While innovation labs and regulatory sandboxes provide valuable environments for testing, the results are often limited to prototypes and proofs of concept that do not reach full deployment.

RETHINKING SUCCESS IN INSURANCE INNOVATION

In traditional insurance settings, project success is measured by immediate financial returns, operational efficiency, or regulatory compliance. However, these metrics often fall short for early-stage innovations, where outcomes are uncertain and benefits can be intangible or realized only in the long term. To avoid superficial assessments, insurers must adopt learning-based metrics that evaluate success based on what has been validated or disproven, rather than solely on what has been developed (Ries, 2011).

Key metrics at this stage might include:

- Customer validation: Did users find the product desirable or helpful during testing?
- Technical feasibility: Did the prototype function reliably in the test environment?
- Operational fit: Was the innovation compatible with claims, underwriting, or service workflows?
- Regulatory soundness: Could the innovation be deployed under current compliance conditions or with minimal remediation?
- Scalability potential: Can the solution handle increased transaction volume, geographical expansion, or multichannel deployment?

The emphasis should be on qualitative insights and readiness indicators, rather than solely on feature delivery. For example, suppose an innovation lab demonstrates that customers prefer submitting claims through a chatbot and that the bot answers questions with 90% accuracy. In that case, the value lies in the insight gained and the following direction, not just the chatbot itself.

INSTITUTIONALIZING PILOT-TO-PRODUCTION PIPELINES

Creating a repeatable process for scaling innovation is essential. Successful insurance companies often integrate innovation pipelines into their digital transformation initiatives, ensuring they align with the organization's strategic planning. This alignment guarantees that innovation is not isolated but is connected to the needs of different business units and their KPIs.

A typical structure used by insurers is the five-stage innovation funnel:

- Ideation and Selection—Generation and vetting of ideas aligned with strategic needs
- Prototype and Test—Development of a basic working model for feasibility assessment
- Pilot Execution—Deployment in a constrained, often regional or product-specific environment
- Scale Readiness—Assessing integration needs, training, security, compliance, and performance
- Full Deployment—Enterprise-wide rollout with support infrastructure and KPIs

These pipelines typically incorporate stage gates—decision points where cross-functional stakeholders evaluate whether the innovation is ready to advance or needs to pivot. Insurers that do not clearly define these gates risk halting promising innovations or scaling solutions that have not been thoroughly tested, resulting in unsuccessful deployments and wasted resources.

ORGANIZATIONAL CHAMPIONS AND INNOVATION BRIDGE ROLES

The human element is crucial for successful scaling. Innovations cannot achieve scale without organizational champions—leaders who advocate for the project, secure the necessary resources, and bridge cultural and technical gaps. While champions often emerge from digital strategy teams, many insurers are formalizing this role through "digital translators." These professionals are fluent in both technical innovation and insurance operations.

These individuals ensure compliance teams are involved from the beginning, that claims or underwriting leaders recognize the pilot's potential, and that IT and security departments are prepared to support integration. Even technically sound solutions can struggle to gain internal acceptance without this human framework.

INNOVATION FUNDING MODELS: FROM INTERNAL CAPITAL TO VENTURE CAPITAL ENGAGEMENT

An essential yet frequently neglected aspect of scaling innovation is funding. Traditional capital budgeting processes are not well suited for emerging technologies, which develop more rapidly than annual planning can accommodate. Therefore insurers must adopt agile financing models that promote flexibility and experimentation while maintaining fiscal discipline.

Internal Innovation Funding Strategies:

- Innovation Capital Funds: Funds allocated for digital transformation initiatives are managed by a central digital office or innovation committee, disbursed according to milestone achievements.
- Stage-Gated Funding: Similar to venture capital funding, projects receive incremental resources upon achieving validation milestones, such as a working prototype, positive Net Promoter Scores (NPS) from the pilot, and compliance approval.
- Skunkworks and Shadow Budgets: In more risk-tolerant organizations, innovation teams might have discretionary budgets to pursue small-scale initiatives without formal governance, a structure that accelerates early experimentation.

External Funding and Venture Engagement:

- Corporate Venture Capital: Many large insurance companies, including Munich Re (through Digital Partners), AXA (via AXA Venture Partners), and American Family Insurance (through AF Ventures), have established internal venture capital arms to invest in InsurTech startups that align with their strategic objectives (KPMG, 2021).
- Strategic Partnerships: Insurers frequently collaborate with accelerators or venture capitalists to gain early access to technologies and ensure effective

integration pathways. For instance, Plug and Play InsurTech partners with numerous insurers to codevelop and test startup solutions.
- Venture Builders and Innovation Studios: Some insurers invest in startups through external studios, such as Kamet Ventures (AXA) or BCG Digital Ventures, gaining partial ownership of innovations that address specific business challenges.

These mechanisms enable insurers to scale successful internal projects and tap into external innovations that can be integrated into their core business. Insurers frequently assess build, buy, and partner strategies during the pilot scaling phase, weighing factors such as control, speed, and cost.

THE RISK OF INNOVATION THEATER

Despite the availability of various frameworks and funding tools, many innovation initiatives still struggle to succeed. A significant challenge is what is known as "innovation theater," which refers to activities like labs, hackathons, and demo days that create an illusion of innovation without delivering measurable business results (Pisano, 2019). This issue is particularly pronounced when there are unclear criteria for return on investment (ROI), a lack of strategic alignment, or insufficient commitment to integrating innovations into the business.

To mitigate this risk, successful insurers:

- Tie innovation goals directly to core business KPIs (e.g., improved loss ratio, reduced claims processing time).
- Assign executive sponsors with authority to drive cross-functional buy-in.
- Establish internal innovation accounting practices to track progress, value creation, and scalability potential over time.

To successfully scale innovation, organizations need more than just creative ideas and functional prototypes; they also require robust funding mechanisms, operational readiness, and cultural alignment. A clear strategy is essential to transition pilot projects into sustainable and scalable solutions. Without this, insurers risk becoming trapped in fragmented transformation, where isolated successes do not lead to meaningful progress for the organization as a whole.

OPERATIONALIZING INNOVATION: CORE CHALLENGES

Transforming traditional insurance companies through innovation is often a slow and complex process. Although ideation, pilot testing, and strategic alignment typically receive a lot of focus, the crucial stage—operationalizing innovation—can be the most challenging. During this phase, insurers encounter numerous obstacles, including outdated technology, regulatory challenges, internal resistance, talent shortages, and unclear governance. These issues are not just administrative or technical; they are deeply ingrained in the insurance industry's culture, which values stability, predictability, and caution over disruption, agility, and experimentation.

At the heart of this struggle is a cultural paradox. Innovation inherently brings uncertainty and requires a willingness to accept failure. However, most insurance organizations are designed to minimize uncertainty; their focus has traditionally been on quantifying and hedging against risk rather than embracing it. As a result, the drive for innovation often faces resistance from the very institutional structures that initially contributed to the resilience of insurers.

Middle managers may worry about workflow disruptions or their relevance within the organization. Underwriters might distrust algorithmic models that challenge established actuarial practices. Compliance teams often perceive new products as potential regulatory liabilities. Meanwhile, executive leadership, pressured by the need to meet quarterly financial targets, may find it difficult to justify long-term investments in technologies that do not offer immediate returns. This cultural friction hinders the spread of new ideas, even when pilot programs demonstrate clear customer value.

A recurring issue in the transition from innovation to implementation is "pilot purgatory." Many innovation initiatives that appear successful in controlled settings struggle to move into live business environments. Despite completing proofs of concept and receiving positive user feedback, these initiatives are often abandoned just before production. This happens due to misalignment with operational processes, lack of sufficient support, or integration-related technical challenges.

Innovation teams frequently work physically and functionally in isolation from core departments. This separation can create misunderstandings: the innovation team may underestimate the complexities involved in integration, while operations might overlook the long-term strategic importance of the pilot project. To overcome this divide, it is essential to establish coordination and a shared understanding that innovation is not optional—it is critical for survival.

The situation is complicated by the outdated technology stack that many insurers still depend on. Many core systems are built in COBOL or other obsolete programming languages and are essential for policy administration, claims processing, and financial accounting. While these systems are stable, they are also brittle and challenging to integrate with modern cloud-native or API-driven applications. Efforts to incorporate new tools into these legacy environments often lead to long delays, high costs, and an increased risk of downtime. Consequently, many promising innovations fall victim to technical debt, not because of a lack of strategic direction, but because the existing infrastructure cannot support them without significant reengineering.

To address this challenge, some insurers have adopted a two-speed IT architecture. This approach consists of a flexible front-end stack built on top of existing core systems, allowing for innovation. These digital layers are created using microservices and containerized applications, enabling insurers to experiment with new distribution channels, user interfaces, and underwriting logic without overhauling the entire system.

While this method provides a practical way to move forward, it also presents challenges related to data synchronization, version control, and the eventual migration to more modern platforms. Ultimately, the long-term solution involves core modernization, which, while capital intensive, is a necessary transformation that lays the groundwork for sustained innovation.

Beyond technology, regulatory constraints further complicate the transition from pilot programs to full production in the insurance industry. Insurance is one of the most regulated sectors globally, with strict rules governing pricing, disclosures, solvency, data privacy, and consumer protection. As innovations emerge, such as AI-based risk assessments, dynamic pricing models, or embedded insurance offered through third-party apps, they often encounter legal gray areas. Regulators may not be prepared to address these developments, resulting in delays, uncertainty, or even outright prohibition.

For example, in the United States, the state-based regulatory system creates a patchwork of requirements, making it incredibly challenging to scale a digital insurance product across state lines. A parametric flood product tested successfully in California may face significant resistance in Florida due to differing disclosure requirements or interpretations of consumer protection laws.

Some insurance companies have been embedding compliance personnel into their innovation teams to reduce regulatory friction from the beginning. This collaborative method, often called codesigning compliance, allows legal concerns to be addressed in an iterative rather than reactive manner. It also enables compliance teams to understand the innovation's value proposition better, leading to more constructive oversight. Insurers are increasingly engaging with regulators through informal dialogues, innovation offices, or participation in regulatory sandboxes. These approaches help build trust and provide opportunities to educate regulators about emerging technologies before they reach scale, ultimately reducing the gap between innovation and regulation.

Talent is a crucial aspect of operationalization, and it is often an underestimated factor. Implementing new technologies—especially AI, blockchain, or cloud-native solutions—requires skills typically not developed within insurance organizations. Recruiting data scientists, cybersecurity experts, cloud architects, and software engineers is challenging due to stiff competition from more glamorous sectors like technology and finance. Even when organizations successfully hire technical talent, they face a new problem: integrating these individuals into established organizational cultures. Many data scientists, for example, may find themselves underutilized or isolated because business functions do not know how to translate their outputs into actionable strategies.

Many existing employees struggle with the digital skills necessary to participate in innovation initiatives. For instance, underwriters may not fully grasp how gradient boosting models work, claims handlers might feel threatened by automation tools, and actuarial teams could be skeptical of neural networks due to their lack of interpretability. These skill gaps can hinder efforts to implement new technologies effectively. To address this issue, some insurers have introduced internal upskilling programs, innovation bootcamps, and cross-functional training initiatives to develop a digitally literate workforce. Additionally, some organizations have created "digital translator" roles—professionals who understand the business and the technology. These individuals help bridge communication gaps between the innovation and execution teams.

Governance structures play a crucial role in fostering or hindering innovation. Without clear ownership, funding, and oversight, many initiatives struggle due to uncertainty. Projects may be duplicated across departments, or even worse, they may be approved without adequate alignment with the broader strategic roadmap. Leading insurers are addressing this issue by establishing centralized innovation councils or steering committees that evaluate and prioritize innovation investments. These committees typically include stakeholders from strategy, operations, IT, risk, and compliance, ensuring a comprehensive perspective on the project's viability. They may also implement stage-gate processes requiring teams to demonstrate specific outcomes or conduct risk assessments before moving on to the next development phase.

Operationalization does not end with deployment. One of the most overlooked challenges is measuring and demonstrating the value of innovation over time. Unlike traditional business lines, where KPIs such as combined or loss ratios are well established, innovation efforts often require new metrics. These might include customer effort scores, improvements in time to market, fraud reduction through automation, or customer retention driven by digital engagement. In some instances, the value of innovation may be more strategic than financial, for example, entering a new market or forming a partnership with a tech platform that opens up future distribution channels.

Metrics should be adapted to fit the maturity and purpose of the innovation. A minimum viable product (MVP) should not be expected to meet the same profitability standards as a fully developed product. Similarly, experiments that test hypotheses may not achieve high uptake but can still provide valuable insights. Acknowledging and communicating this distinction is important to maintain executive support and build stakeholder confidence.

Insurers must recognize that operationalizing innovation is an ongoing, iterative process, not a one-time event. Markets change, technologies develop, and customer expectations evolve. Innovations that are successful today may require reengineering in the future. Therefore establishing cultural and structural agility is crucial for any innovation program. When insurers incorporate adaptability into their operational framework, they position themselves to embrace innovation and generate it continuously and responsibly.

In summary, implementing insurance innovation is a complex challenge that requires alignment across multiple dimensions, including technical, cultural, regulatory, and strategic aspects. It demands more than a vision; it necessitates execution excellence, collaboration across different functions, and the courage to question long-held assumptions. Companies that successfully navigate this intricate transition will survive in a digital-first future and take the lead in it.

MEASURING INNOVATION IMPACT AND VALUE REALIZATION

As insurers invest in innovative infrastructure, partner with InsurTech startups, and launch experimental pilots, they face a persistent challenge: accurately and credibly measuring the value these efforts deliver. Unlike traditional insurance projects, which often produce clear and timely outcomes, such as reduced loss ratios or increased policy volumes, innovation programs yield more ambiguous results. The value of these initiatives may be realized in stages, take nonfinancial forms, or emerge in areas that are difficult to quantify, such as customer experience, internal agility, or long-term market positioning.

Without reliable measurements, innovation can be dismissed as a luxury expense rather than recognized as a strategic growth driver. Therefore developing strong innovation metrics and frameworks for realizing value is not just a performance issue but essential for survival. Executive sponsors, shareholders, and regulators increasingly expect innovation to be tied to measurable outcomes. However, many insurers do not have the systems, methodologies, or cultural mindset needed to assess innovation in a consistent and disciplined manner.

REFRAMING INNOVATION METRICS: BEYOND RETURN ON INVESTMENT

Traditional financial metrics such as ROI, internal rate of return, and payback period often prove inadequate when assessing innovation. These metrics assume clear costs and predictable cash flows—conditions rarely present in early-stage experimentation. Applying these metrics too early or rigidly can stifle creativity, jeopardize promising projects, and drive innovation teams to concentrate on low-risk, incremental improvements instead of pursuing transformational opportunities.

To tackle this issue, insurers should implement a portfolio-based innovation accounting model. This method categorizes innovation efforts into three categories: core, adjacent, and transformational, and evaluates each based on relevant criteria. For example, a core automation project might be assessed using metrics related to operational efficiency, such as the reduction in average claims processing time. On the other hand, a transformational parametric product would be evaluated based on factors like time to market or customer engagement during testing. These metrics are not inferior to financial KPIs; instead, they are more suitable for the specific phase and goals of the innovation initiative.

A significant shift in perspective is recognizing validated learning as a valid outcome of innovation. Even if a pilot project does not scale successfully, it can provide strategic value by challenging assumptions, identifying regulatory obstacles, or revealing incorrect market hypotheses. When these insights are documented and shared, they contribute to institutional memory and help lower the costs associated with future mistakes.

CATEGORIES OF INNOVATION VALUE

Innovation value in insurance can be broadly segmented into four domains:

- Customer Impact: Innovations that enhance the customer experience, such as self-service claims portals, usage-based pricing models, and personalized underwriting engines, can be evaluated using metrics like NPS, customer satisfaction, engagement frequency, and reductions in complaints. In digital channels, metrics such as click-through rates, time spent on the platform, and bounce rates provide quantitative insights into improvements in user experience.
- Operational Efficiency: While automation, workflow digitization, and AI-powered tools may not directly boost revenue, they can significantly decrease loss adjustment expenses, minimize manual errors, and enhance human resource allocation. Metrics to measure these improvements could include process throughput, case resolution time, or reductions in cost per transaction.
- Strategic Enablement: Some innovations can open up future opportunities by entering new markets, forming new partnerships, or enhancing capabilities (e.g., through blockchain record-keeping or embedded insurance integrations). These innovations are often best assessed using proxy metrics such as participation in the ecosystem, the development of partnerships, or increased potential for cross-selling.
- Organizational Capability: Innovation maturity is a valuable asset. Investing in digital literacy, cross-functional teams, agile governance, and a culture that embraces quick failures enhances long-term adaptability. Measures of this investment can include employee participation in innovation programs, the number of MVPs delivered each quarter, and internal readiness assessments.

STRUCTURING AN INNOVATION METRICS FRAMEWORK

Insurers are creating structured frameworks to measure innovation, aligning projects with business objectives, and monitoring performance over time. One such model is the Innovation Accounting Framework (Blank, 2013), which adapts lean startup principles for larger organizations. This framework introduces layered metrics that are connected to:

- Inputs (funding, people, time)
- Outputs (MVPs, pilots, prototypes)
- Outcomes (learning, deployment, customer uptake)
- Impact (cost savings, revenue, market share)

This hierarchy enables innovation leaders to show early traction, even when financial impacts remain uncertain. It also aids in distinguishing meaningful projects from less valuable ideas, ensuring that attention is focused on those with greater strategic significance.

Many insurers enhance their offerings with innovation dashboards—real-time reporting tools that display initiative status, resource utilization, milestone tracking, and impact metrics. These dashboards, frequently aligned with innovation councils or steering committees, foster transparency and support informed decision-making.

BENCHMARKING AND MATURITY MODELS

Leading insurers increasingly conduct innovation maturity assessments as part of their measurement practices. These assessments evaluate an organization's innovation culture, governance, infrastructure, and capability development, comparing them against industry peers and ideal frameworks. One notable model used for this purpose is the Digital Insurance Maturity Framework, which assesses innovation across several dimensions:

- Digital leadership and vision
- Customer-centric design practices
- Agile execution models
- Technology and data readiness
- Talent and upskilling strategies
- Ecosystem and partnership activity

Results are generally used to prioritize capability-building initiatives and inform investment strategies. Sometimes, companies utilize third-party assessments to validate their innovation trajectories for boards, regulators, or investors.

FEEDBACK LOOPS AND ITERATIVE LEARNING

Measurement should be dynamic rather than static. Effective innovation ecosystems incorporate continuous feedback loops utilizing quantitative and qualitative data to inform iterations and scaling efforts. Conducting customer interviews, employee retrospectives, usability tests, and pilot debriefs can provide actionable insights that might not be captured in dashboards.

It is important for measurement systems not to focus exclusively on success stories. Documenting and reflecting on failures is vital for fostering an antifragile culture of innovation. A failed pilot that leads to future success is a valuable investment rather than a sunk cost.

For example, a global reinsurer evaluated its failed blockchain initiative not only by the resources spent but also by the disproven assumptions, the partnerships that were tested, and the governance lessons learned. These insights directly influenced the development of its next project: a decentralized claims verification platform that successfully achieved operational scale.

ALIGNING METRICS WITH STRATEGIC INTENT

One of the most crucial principles in measuring innovation is alignment. Metrics should align with the organization's strategic objectives rather than simply creating the appearance of innovation. For instance, an insurance company focused on cost efficiency should prioritize automation and process optimization metrics. On the other hand, a company aiming for growth through new markets should concentrate on metrics such as speed to market, partner integrations, and user acquisition.

Innovation for its own sake seldom secures long-term investment. However, when leaders can illustrate how innovation aligns with core objectives—profitability, retention, resilience, and differentiation—it becomes justifiable and essential.

This requires careful narrative framing. Stories should complement quantitative results. For example, how did a chatbot improve claims satisfaction? How did a machine learning model reduce underwriting bias? How did a digital platform enable brokers to sell new products remotely during a crisis? These stories humanize the numbers and help stakeholders understand the real-life impact of innovation.

SUSTAINING INNOVATION THROUGH STRATEGIC EXECUTION

Sustaining innovation is fundamentally different from initiating it. While generating ideas and launching pilot projects can often be accomplished through enthusiasm and short-term investments, maintaining momentum and integrating innovation into the core of a legacy insurance company requires a deliberate strategy, cultural adaptation, and structural support. Without sustainability, execution can lead to short-lived experiments, disjointed initiatives, and ultimately a loss of credibility in the innovation process. To avoid these pitfalls, insurers must adopt strategic execution as the bridge between novel thinking and long-term competitive advantage.

A key requirement for sustaining innovation is achieving institutional alignment. Innovations confined to a lab or innovation office often struggle to gain traction outside their initial environment. Insurers must integrate their innovation efforts with broader business strategies, core systems, and enterprise processes to ensure scalability and resilience. This integration involves both technical and organizational aspects. Strategy teams should link innovation KPIs to overall corporate goals, while business unit leaders should be empowered to co-own the outcomes of innovation initiatives. When innovation is viewed not as a separate activity but as an enabler of transformation, it becomes embedded in the organization's operating rhythm.

One essential aspect of successful innovation is maintaining leadership continuity and securing executive sponsorship. Leaders at the executive level play a crucial role in demonstrating the importance of innovation, allocating necessary resources, and addressing internal resistance. However, changes in leadership or shifting priorities can quickly hinder progress. To protect against this, some insurance companies establish formal governance structures, such as Innovation Advisory Boards or Digital Transformation Offices. These structures help ensure that innovation efforts remain consistent even during leadership transitions. They provide continuity, strategic guidance, and a dedicated space for balancing innovation risks and operational stability.

Change management is essential for the success of any initiative. Even the best-designed solutions can fail if they do not include efforts to prepare people and processes for adoption. Legacy organizations often encounter significant inertia, where existing workflows, incentive structures, and cultural norms resist new technologies. To sustain innovation, it is important to address these human factors directly. Communication strategies should present innovation not as a disruption but as an evolution, focusing on value creation, employee empowerment, and long-term resilience.

Training programs, innovation bootcamps, and digital fluency workshops are crucial in helping employees across various departments understand new tools and their relevance. Involving employees early in the design and testing phases fosters greater buy-in and uncovers valuable operational insights. This participatory approach aligns with the principles of human-centered design, which prioritize what is technologically feasible and strategically desirable and what is practical and meaningful for those who will use it daily.

Resource flexibility is crucial for sustaining innovation. Traditional budget cycles, procurement protocols, and inflexible staffing models can hinder the agility to develop ideas from MVPs to enterprise-wide platforms. Leading companies are implementing more adaptable funding models, such as rolling innovation budgets, milestone-based investments, and venture-style capital reserves. These approaches facilitate iterative scaling and reduce the bureaucratic delays that often slow innovation. Furthermore, insurers are exploring using internal incubators or venture studios that operate semiautonomously while remaining accountable for overarching enterprise goals.

Engaging with ecosystems enhances sustainability in the insurance sector. No insurer operates in isolation; many promising innovations arise from partnerships with startups, academic institutions, and technology vendors. By actively participating in InsurTech ecosystems, insurers can access new ideas, specialized skills, and alternative business models. However, maintaining these relationships requires established governance protocols, shared KPIs, and clear integration pathways. Strategic alliances should be viewed not as simple transactions with vendors but as collaborative platforms for creating mutual value.

One notable example is Munich Re's Digital Partners division, which collaborates with early-stage InsurTech companies to codevelop scalable products. This approach integrates innovation into the insurer's strategic distribution and underwriting efforts while providing external entrepreneurs with capital, reinsurance capacity, and access to the market. By fostering these ongoing partnerships, insurers enhance their innovation capabilities beyond internal research and development, creating a dynamic innovation network.

Metrics and measurements also play a crucial role in supporting sustainability. As mentioned in the previous section, the value of innovation needs to be regularly assessed and communicated. Sustaining innovation requires making progress visible—not only to executives but to the entire organization. Tools like dashboards, quarterly innovation reviews, and storytelling about successful deployments help reinforce momentum and demonstrate that innovation is not just an abstract concept, but something tangible and impactful.

Sustaining innovation is crucial to building the capacity for continuous adaptation. This entails fostering a culture of organizational agility—the ability to respond quickly and clearly to changing market conditions, customer expectations, and technological advancements. Agility is not just a result of technology stacks or lean methodologies; it is a mindset strengthened through iterative planning cycles, empowered teams, and decentralized decision-making. In agile organizations, innovation becomes a routine part of operations rather than an exceptional occurrence.

To sustain innovation, legacy insurers need to evolve their identity. They must transition from viewing themselves as merely risk-averse administrators of policy contracts to becoming dynamic providers of risk solutions. This shift allows exploring new business models, including usage-based pricing, embedded insurance, parametric triggers, and preventative risk services. Additionally, it transforms innovation from a departmental initiative into a shared responsibility that involves product development, actuarial science, compliance, IT, and customer experience.

Innovation sustainability is not limited to a specific program, product, or platform. Instead, it refers to an insurer's ability to consistently generate, embrace, and expand new ideas in line with its mission and the realities of the market. By focusing on strategic execution—encompassing governance, culture, talent, partnerships, and infrastructure—insurers can transform innovation from a delicate experiment into a lasting source of resilience and growth.

BUILDING A CULTURE OF CONTINUOUS INNOVATION

A sustainable innovation strategy is not just about processes, technologies, or even leadership support; it is fundamentally rooted in organizational culture. To foster a culture of continuous innovation, organizations must create an environment that encourages exploration, normalizes experimentation, and promotes adaptive learning. This cultural transformation is essential and challenging in the insurance industry, where risk aversion and regulatory compliance have traditionally shaped behaviors.

At the heart of an innovation-driven culture is a fundamental shift in mindset: a willingness to embrace uncertainty and iterate quickly. Insurance professionals are trained to assess, mitigate, and price risks, but this expertise can sometimes lead to resistance to change. To foster a culture of innovation, leadership must demonstrate openness to new ideas, accept failures in low-stakes environments, and encourage curiosity. This approach does not mean discarding rigor or accountability; instead, it involves shifting the default attitude from "prove it first" to "test it thoughtfully."

One of the most effective ways to encourage this shift is by fostering psychological safety. Teams are more likely to experiment and share unconventional ideas when they feel secure enough to fail. Research by (Edmondson, 1999) shows that psychological safety is strongly linked to learning behaviors and team performance, particularly in dynamic environments. For insurers looking to promote innovation, creating these environments requires intentional efforts, such as rewarding learning from failed projects, recognizing process improvements alongside revenue growth, and ensuring that all employees feel their voices are valued, regardless of rank.

Leadership behavior plays a crucial role in shaping organizational culture. Senior executives must do more than sponsor innovation programs; they must also embody the values of experimentation and continuous improvement. This involves participating in innovation workshops, publicly supporting agile teams, and sharing stories of successful and unsuccessful innovations as important learning experiences. When leaders normalize iterative processes and embrace learning from failure, it reduces stigma and accelerates cultural adoption throughout the organization.

Another important cultural factor is the democratization of innovation. Often, innovation is limited to specialized teams, such as labs, accelerators, or digital units, which can be isolated from the rest of the organization. While these teams play a valuable role in focused experimentation, innovation must become a shared responsibility across the organization. Leading insurance companies accomplish this by encouraging frontline employees to identify process inefficiencies, suggest product ideas, and propose new data sources for risk evaluation. Some organizations have set up internal idea platforms or "innovation marketplaces" where employees can submit concepts and compete for resources. Others conduct periodic hackathons or sprints that bring together cross-functional teams to address business challenges creatively.

Initiatives like these are not merely symbolic—they empower employees and create a grassroots movement for change. For instance, Allianz's "Global Innovation Challenge" invites teams worldwide to collaborate on solutions for strategic issues. Winning ideas are awarded funding, mentorship, and opportunities for scaling. This approach has led to the development of new services and fostered a sense of shared ownership and pride in innovation among employees.

Incorporating innovation into learning and development programs is essential. Continuous innovation demands ongoing upskilling. Insurance professionals must cultivate new competencies in data science, behavioral economics, customer journey design, and regulatory technology. Providing structured learning paths—through online platforms, in-house academies, or partnerships with universities—ensures employees are well equipped to make meaningful contributions to innovation efforts.

Insurers are increasingly recognizing the importance of diverse perspectives in fostering innovation. Teams of individuals with different professional backgrounds, demographics, and cognitive styles are more likely to produce creative and thorough solutions. By forming inclusive innovation teams that combine actuarial experts with designers, developers, and behavioral scientists, organizations can gain richer insights and identify potential risks that may be overlooked in more homogeneous groups.

To support cultural practices effectively, it is crucial to reconsider performance management and incentive structures. If KPIs and bonus systems only reward stability and efficiency, innovation will inevitably take a backseat to maintaining the status quo. Insurers must implement recognition and reward mechanisms that celebrate idea generation, experimentation, and cross-functional collaboration. Metrics such as the number of new ideas tested, customer problems resolved, or process improvements piloted should be included in performance evaluations, alongside traditional measures like revenue growth or policy count.

Celebrating small wins is essential. Innovation is rarely a straightforward or dramatic process; instead, it develops from a series of modest improvements accumulating into a significant impact. Sharing success stories within the organization, through newsletters, town halls, or internal social media, allows employees to see what is possible and inspires them to replicate these successes. These stories also make innovation more relatable, demonstrating that it is achievable by real teams within the organization, rather than just theoretical visionaries.

Cultural change takes time and consistency. A single hackathon or one-off pilot project will not transform an entire organization. Creating a culture of continuous innovation requires sustained commitment, clear messaging, and reinforcement across various platforms. This process is a marathon, not a sprint, but it offers lasting benefits regarding resilience, adaptability, and relevance in the fast-evolving insurance industry.

Insurers that successfully adopt this culture are not merely reacting to disruption but leading it. They create organizations where innovation becomes a part of everyday practice rather than a standalone initiative. In these environments, employees are empowered to enhance existing processes, envision new possibilities, and confidently navigate future challenges.

CONCLUSION—FROM LABS TO LEADERSHIP

The transition from innovation labs and regulatory sandboxes to comprehensive execution and leadership within the insurance industry is intricate and vital. What starts as isolated experimentation in a controlled environment must develop into a transformative integration that redefines how insurers operate, engage with customers, and deliver value in a digital landscape. This chapter has examined this journey's structural, strategic, and cultural aspects, highlighting not only the significance of generating ideas but also the importance of disciplined implementation.

Innovation labs and sandboxes serve as essential launchpads for development. They offer safe environments to test hypotheses, collaborate on solutions, and navigate regulatory uncertainties. Their actual value, however, lies in their ability to generate actionable insights, quickly create prototypes, and reduce risks associated with the unknown. For insurers, these spaces are not final destinations but catalysts for developing new capabilities, identifying unmet needs, and speeding up institutional learning.

Without clear pathways to scale and sustain innovations, even the most promising pilot projects may end up as stalled initiatives or isolated proofs of concept. Strategic execution is crucial in bridging this gap. It involves embedding innovation into the strategic agenda, aligning resources effectively, building cross-functional teams, and adopting flexible performance metrics. Effective execution ensures that innovation is not just a one-time event but an ongoing process that can adapt to changing customer demands, evolving technologies, and emerging risks.

The chapter highlights that sustaining innovation is primarily a cultural effort. While technology and capital are important, they alone are not enough. What sets leading insurers apart is their ability to promote psychological safety, encourage learning, democratize creativity, and develop lasting innovation capabilities. In these environments, employees proactively initiate change instead of waiting for instructions on what to improve.

Measurement and governance serve as essential frameworks for managing innovation responsibly. Organizations can take calculated risks while maintaining accountability by adopting a balanced portfolio approach, supported by relevant metrics and adaptable dashboards. Leadership must ensure that innovation meets short-term optimization objectives and supports long-term strategic positioning and societal relevance.

As insurance companies move from experimentation to transformation, strong leadership becomes essential. Leaders need to promote innovation not just as a business necessity but as a fundamental value and a lasting commitment. They should exemplify curiosity, foster resilience, and link vision with execution. The organizations they lead should evolve beyond merely insuring risks and become creators of new possibilities.

Ultimately, the success of insurance innovation is not determined by the quantity of ideas generated but by the capacity to turn those ideas into real impact. This impact should enhance protection, broaden access, improve efficiency, and contribute to a more adaptive, inclusive, and resilient insurance industry. This transformation, from innovation labs to leadership roles, will define the next era of insurance technology.

AI DISCLOSURE

During the preparation of this work the author(s) used Grammarly to improve the readability of this chapter and to correct any grammatical mistakes made by the author(s). After using this tool/service, the author(s) reviewed and edited the content as needed and take(s) full responsibility for the content of the publication.

REFERENCES

Aviva. (2021). Aviva Digital Garage: Driving innovation through customer-centric design. https://www.aviva.com/innovation/digital-garage/.

Blank, S. (2013). Why the lean start-up changes everything. *Harvard Business Review*, *91*(5), 63–72.

Boston Consulting Group (BCG). (2022). Why many digital transformations fail—and how to flip the odds of success. https://www.bcg.com/publications/2022/why-digital-transformations-fail.

Bughin, J., Catlin, T., Hirt, M., & Willmott, P. (2017). Why digital strategies fail. https://www.mckinsey.com/capabilities/strategy-and-corporate-finance/our-insights/why-digital-strategies-fail.

Deloitte. (2020). Innovation in insurance: How insurers can build a culture of continuous innovation. https://www2.deloitte.com/us/en/pages/financial-services/articles/innovation-in-insurance.html.

Edmondson, A. (1999). Psychological safety and learning behavior in work teams. *Administrative Science Quarterly*, *44*(2), 350–383. https://doi.org/10.2307/2666999.

Financial Conduct Authority (FCA). (2022). Regulatory sandbox lessons learned report. https://www.fca.org.uk/publications/research/regulatory-sandbox-lessons-learned-report.

Global Financial Innovation Network (GFIN). (2020). Cross-border testing: Lessons learned and next steps. https://www.thegfin.com/publications.

Kamet Ventures. (2023). About Kamet Ventures: Building the future of insurance and health. https://www.kametventures.com/about.

KPMG. (2021). Pulse of Fintech H2 2021: Global analysis of investment in fintech. https://kpmg.com/xx/en/home/insights/2022/02/pulse-of-fintech-h2-2021.html.

Lloyd's. (2022). InsurTech and innovation at Lloyd's: Transforming the insurance value chain. https://www.lloyds.com/news-and-insights/press-releases/2022/05/insurtech-and-innovation.

McKinsey & Company. (2020). The insurance industry: Reimagining the customer experience. https://www.mckinsey.com/industries/financial-services/our-insights/the-insurance-industry-reimagining-the-customer-experience.

Pisano, G. P. (2019). The hard truth about innovative cultures. Harvard Business Review, 97(1), 62–71. doi:https://hbr.org/2019/01/the-hard-truth-about-innovative-cultures.

Ries, E. (2011). *The lean startup: How today's entrepreneurs use continuous innovation to create radically successful businesses*. Crown Publishing Group.

Zetzsche, D. A., Buckley, R. P., Arner, D. W., & Barberis, J. N. (2017). Regulating a revolution: From regulatory sandboxes to smart regulation. *Fordham Journal of Corporate & Financial Law,* 23(1), 31–103.

CHAPTER

Careers in insurance technology: Artifical intellegence and the future workforce

11

CHAPTER OUTLINE

Insurance Technology. DOI: https://doi.org/10.1016/B978-0-443-43972-8.00017-1

Historically, insurance careers were characterized by well-defined, hierarchical structures within established carriers, where employees specialized in actuarial analysis, sales, claims, or operations. While these roles remain integral to the industry, the shift toward digitalization, automation, and data-driven decision-making has catalyzed a need for professionals skilled in technology, analytics, and systems thinking. Positions such as digital underwriters, product designers, data engineers, cyber risk analysts, and customer experience architects are increasingly vital in supporting innovation and growth within legacy carriers and disruptive startups.

The modern insurance workforce must navigate a complex regulatory landscape influenced by global interconnectedness, data privacy laws, and the challenges posed by algorithmic decision-making. Professionals in governance, risk, and compliance (GRC) roles now need to know not only traditional insurance regulations but also cybersecurity standards, digital ethics, and guidelines for AI transparency. Consequently, the skills necessary for success in this field are becoming increasingly interdisciplinary, combining domain expertise with technological proficiency and a strong ethical framework.

Insurance technology (InsurTech) firms, many of which are startup ventures supported by venture capital, have changed the talent landscape of the insurance industry. These companies often prioritize agility, experimentation, and customer-centric design, contrasting with the more methodical approach of traditional insurers. As a result, they attract a different mix of talent, often from outside the insurance sector. InsurTechs frequently recruit engineers, designers, behavioral economists, and marketing professionals to create user-friendly interfaces, optimize digital distribution, and build predictive models using alternative data sources. The culture within these organizations typically mirrors that of broader tech startups, characterized by flatter hierarchies, rapid iteration cycles, and a strong emphasis on innovation. At the same time, established insurers adapt by creating innovation labs, forming partnerships with tech firms, and developing internal digital transformation teams. These initiatives have led to hybrid roles that blend traditional insurance knowledge with digital product management and software engineering capabilities. This convergence requires professionals to be fluent in insurance fundamentals and adaptable to the pace and style of modern technology development.

In educational settings, the increasing range of careers in the insurance industry highlights the need for a more comprehensive curriculum and better career advising. Students benefit most when they grasp the entire landscape of the field, which includes areas such as reinsurance, surplus lines, embedded insurance, platform partnerships, and the regulatory aspects of this field. The pathways to enter the industry have expanded beyond traditional roles like actuarial science or positions at local agencies. Nowadays, entry points may include internships at digital claims startups, capstone projects on algorithmic fairness, or participation in data analytics competitions concentrating on loss prediction models.

In addition to positions at carriers and startups, there are abundant opportunities in the intermediary and support sectors of the insurance industry. Consultancies, technology providers, regulatory agencies, and research institutes all play a crucial role in shaping the industry's infrastructure and future development. Careers in these fields necessitate a systems-level understanding of risk and resilience, and they often overlap with government policy, financial services, and international trade.

This chapter will examine the fundamental organizational functions within the insurance industry, different distribution models, and effective marketing strategies. We will also discuss the professional development pathways that shape career advancement and the changing relationship between automation and human judgment. Throughout the chapter, we will emphasize the significance of digital fluency, ethical awareness, and a dedication to continuous learning as essential for success in traditional insurance and InsurTech environments.

CORE FUNCTIONS IN INSURANCE ORGANIZATIONS

Insurance organizations—whether traditional carriers, reinsurance firms, mutual companies, or digital-focused InsurTech companies—function within a complex ecosystem that evaluates, assumes, manages, and transfers risk. Each organization has several key functional areas, each responsible for a distinct but interconnected set of activities that support the company's value proposition. Understanding these core functions is crucial for students preparing to enter the industry, as it clarifies potential career paths and illustrates how insurance companies provide security and continuity in an increasingly unpredictable world.

UNDERWRITING

Underwriting is a crucial and historically significant function in the insurance industry. It involves evaluating and selecting risks to determine which insurance applications will be accepted and under what terms. Underwriters assess risk using actuarial models, statistical data, and, more recently, advanced analytics and AI tools. Underwriters purchase risks from producers who sell those risks.

While traditional underwriting focused on predefined criteria and human judgment, modern methods increasingly utilize algorithmic models, natural language processing, and real-time behavioral data—such as telematics in auto insurance or wearable data in health insurance. The role of underwriters is evolving to include "digital underwriting" teams that work closely with data scientists and engineers. Together, they develop predictive risk engines that can automate or enhance underwriting decisions.

CLAIMS MANAGEMENT

The claims function is the customer-facing core of the insurance industry. When policyholders experience a loss, the claims team assesses the damage, verifies coverage, calculates indemnity, and arranges for payment or remediation. Claims professionals must balance empathy for the customer with adherence to policy compliance and fraud detection.

Increasingly, claims teams are adopting advanced tools such as image recognition, remote inspections, automated chatbots, and blockchain-based claims verification processes. InsurTech firms' key goal is achieving "straight-through processing" (STP), where simple claims can be assessed, verified, and paid out with minimal human intervention.

However, despite this trend toward automation, complex claims—such as those involving bodily injury, litigation-related losses, or catastrophic events—still require the expertise of skilled adjusters, legal knowledge, and effective communication.

PRODUCT DEVELOPMENT AND ACTUARIAL SCIENCE

Product development teams create new insurance offerings and modify existing products to respond to changing market conditions, customer needs, and emerging risks. These teams must balance market opportunities, profitability, regulatory compliance, and risk transfer strategies.

Actuarial professionals are closely linked to product development. They utilize statistical modeling and financial theory to analyze risk, set pricing, and forecast future loss ratios and reserve requirements. Actuarial teams are essential for capital allocation, solvency monitoring, and reinsurance strategies.

In recent times, there has been an increasing expectation for actuaries to collaborate with data scientists and leverage machine learning techniques to enhance traditional models. This shift has created a demand for professionals who can work across disciplines.

DISTRIBUTION AND MARKETING

Insurance distribution is the process of selling products to customers. Traditionally, this has been done through various channels, including captive agents (who represent a single insurance carrier), independent brokers (who sell products from multiple carriers), and wholesalers (who provide specialty lines and surplus coverage).

In recent years, distribution methods have expanded to include direct-to-consumer (D2C) digital platforms, embedded insurance models (bundled with products like ride-share apps or online retail purchases), and comparison marketplaces.

Marketing teams support distribution by creating brand narratives, conducting market research, optimizing customer acquisition processes, and increasingly managing data-driven campaigns that utilize behavioral targeting and customer segmentation algorithms.

Digital marketing in the insurance industry encompasses various strategies, including search engine optimization (SEO), content marketing, influencer collaborations, and A/B testing on landing pages to convert potential customers. Professionals pursuing careers in this field should be knowledgeable about marketing analytics, customer journey mapping, and data privacy laws such as the General Data Protection Regulation (GDPR) and the California Consumer Privacy Act (CCPA).

OPERATIONS AND POLICY ADMINISTRATION

Policy administration involves several key tasks, including issuing insurance policies, managing policy renewals, processing endorsements, collecting premiums, and maintaining customer records. Insurance operations include billing systems, customer service support, workflow automation, and compliance documentation. Careers in this field increasingly focus on process optimization, robotic process automation (RPA), and developing low-code or no-code platforms to enhance operational agility. Business analysts, operations managers, and customer success specialists are crucial in ensuring effective policy lifecycle management, particularly in high-volume environments like personal auto or renters' insurance.

INFORMATION TECHNOLOGY AND DIGITAL PLATFORMS

In traditional insurance companies and InsurTech startups, IT and digital infrastructure are crucial in enabling strategic growth and gaining a competitive advantage.

Technology teams are responsible for building and maintaining platforms that support quote generation, policy issuance, claims handling, and data analytics. The modern insurance technology stack includes cloud computing, application programming interfaces (APIs), cybersecurity, mobile-first design, and customer portals.

Insurers increasingly require software developers, development operation (DevOps) engineers, cybersecurity specialists, user experience/user interface (UX/UI) designers, and digital architects to create scalable and secure solutions. As software-as-a-service–based policy administration systems and third-party integrations become more widespread, a solid understanding of insurance data structures and regulatory compliance is essential for technology professionals.

GOVERNANCE, RISK, AND COMPLIANCE

Insurance is one of the most regulated sectors within financial services. GRC functions ensure companies operate legally, adhere to ethical practices, and protect consumers and shareholders. This function encompasses enterprise risk management, compliance monitoring, auditing, privacy enforcement, and regulatory reporting.

With the rising threats from cyber attacks, artificial intelligence (AI)-related risks, and pressures related to environmental, social, and governance issues, the importance of the GRC's role has increased. Professionals in this field typically have law, finance, or policy backgrounds and work closely with regulators, internal audit committees, and executive leadership.

STRATEGIC LEADERSHIP AND INNOVATION

At the strategic level, insurance organizations need strong leadership to guide transformation and manage disruption. This includes roles such as chief innovation officers, strategy consultants, transformation program leaders, and business development professionals. These leaders must navigate partnerships, mergers and acquisitions, InsurTech investments, and global market dynamics while effectively aligning stakeholders and resources. Innovation teams are often responsible for exploring new distribution models, developing AI governance frameworks, and testing blockchain applications through proof-of-concept pilots.

MARKETING AND DISTRIBUTION CHANNELS IN INSURANCE

The insurance industry holds a unique position in the global economy, providing products that are often legally required, financially essential, and frequently misunderstood by many consumers. Unlike tangible goods or straightforward financial services, insurance must be tailored to individual risks. It is also regulated to protect the public interest and requires clear communication to bridge the gap between uncertainty and financial security. Insurance is the oxygen of the free market.

How insurance products are marketed and distributed is not just a logistical choice; it reflects strategic, regulatory, and cultural decisions that influence customer experience, profitability, and accessibility across different markets. A deep understanding of these distribution mechanisms is crucial for students entering this field.

Insurance is rarely sold directly to consumers. Due to these products' complexity, intangibility, and long-term nature, effective distribution usually requires human guidance or advanced digital infrastructure. Over the past century, this landscape has evolved into a multitiered system that includes agents, brokers, managing general agents (MGAs), wholesalers, digital platforms, and D2C models. Each player serves a specific role in bringing insurance products to market, impacting product design, pricing, and customer relationship management.

PRODUCERS

Among the most traditional and still prevalent models of insurance distribution are captive agents. These individuals represent a single insurance company and offer only that company's products to consumers. Their knowledge is specialized and extensive, and they often receive significant training and marketing support and exhibit strong brand loyalty. Insurers like State Farm and Farmers Insurance have established extensive networks of captive agents serving local communities.

This model promotes brand consistency and centralized control but limits consumers' ability to compare policies from different insurers. Captive agents, by design, cannot provide quotes from competing companies, which reduces consumer choice. In contrast, independent agents represent multiple carriers and act as intermediaries, helping clients compare options across the market. These agents often work in smaller firms or local offices and play a crucial role in commercial insurance settings, where customization and risk evaluation are essential.

Unlike captive agents, independent agents operate under a model that rewards client-centered solutions and the ability to place challenging or unique risks with specialized carriers. Their compensation typically comes from commissions paid by insurers, which may be supplemented by profitability or premium volume bonuses. While they are still technically agents of the insurers they represent, their diverse product offerings give them more flexibility to advocate for their clients.

BROKERS

An important part of the distribution ecosystem is the broker. Unlike agents, who represent insurance companies, brokers work on behalf of policyholders. They advocate for their clients, seeking the best insurance coverage, pricing, and terms. Brokers are especially important in handling prominent commercial placements and navigating complex risk environments, including cyber risk, multinational liability, aviation, and reinsurance.

Brokers are regulated differently from agents in many jurisdictions, and their compensation structures can vary. They may be paid through client fees, commissions, or a combination. The largest brokers in the world—Marsh McLennan, Aon, and Willis Towers Watson—operate globally, serving major corporations and governments, and provide risk advisory and consulting services.

WHOLESALERS

As insurance risks have become more complex, specialized intermediaries have emerged to serve niche markets. Wholesalers and surplus lines brokers connect retail agents with carriers not operating in the standard, admitted market. These intermediaries work with excess and surplus lines carriers—insurers not licensed in a particular state but permitted to write policies for nonstandard risks.

Wholesalers do not interact directly with insured parties; instead, they help retail agents secure coverage for risks outside traditional underwriting guidelines. These risks may include coastal properties, cannabis operations, high-value art collections, or emerging technologies. These intermediaries ensure that risk transfer mechanisms remain flexible and inclusive.

MANAGING GENERAL AGENTS

MGAs are uniquely positioned within the insurance system. They are granted underwriting authority by insurance companies, allowing them to quote, bind, and sometimes manage claims without the insurer's direct involvement. Essentially, an MGA functions like a small insurance company, but is supported by another firm's capital and regulatory authority.

MGAs are often created to serve niche markets, such as antique vehicle collections, drone liability insurance, or policies for boutique business owners. They combine an insurance company's underwriting expertise with a broker's market agility.

The importance of MGAs has significantly increased in the digital age. InsurTech companies are now using the MGA structure to experiment with new underwriting models and introduce digital-first products to the market, without needing to build comprehensive insurance operations from the ground up.

DIRECT-TO-CUSTOMER PATH

The D2C model has also gained popularity, especially for standardized personal lines products such as auto, renters, and travel insurance. In this model, insurers interact directly with customers through online platforms or call centers, eliminating the need for agents or brokers. Companies like GEICO, Progressive, and Lemonade have effectively implemented D2C strategies to streamline the quoting and underwriting processes, utilizing automation and user-friendly interfaces.

The benefits of the D2C model include lower distribution costs and improved scalability. However, some drawbacks include a lack of personalization and advisory services. For specific segments of the population—particularly digital natives and price-sensitive shoppers—D2C is an appealing option. Conversely, its effectiveness diminishes in more complex or commercial risk scenarios.

EMBEDDED INSURANCE

One of the fastest-growing trends in insurance distribution is embedded insurance. This approach integrates insurance offerings into noninsurance products or services at the point of sale. For example, customers may purchase travel insurance while checking out with an airline or receive insurance coverage bundled with a ride-sharing or food delivery service.

While embedded insurance is not new—credit card fraud protection and extended warranties have been offered this way for decades—new technologies have significantly expanded its scope. InsurTech startups and digital platforms are increasingly collaborating with e-commerce, mobility, and gig economy companies to provide seamless, API-driven coverage that fits into the customer's digital journey. This method reduces friction in the buying process and introduces insurance to markets that have been previously underserved or uninsured.

INSURANCE MARKETING

These distribution mechanisms depend on effective marketing strategies to reach consumers, educate them about products, and differentiate brands. Traditional marketing in the insurance industry places a strong emphasis on brand trust, customer loyalty, and community involvement. Captive carriers often invest millions in nationwide campaigns and slogans—such as "Like a good neighbor, State Farm is there"—reinforcing reliability and familiarity. At the local level, agents sponsor community events, engage in outreach efforts, and build personal relationships to generate referrals and repeat business.

The digital transformation of marketing is significantly changing how insurance is discovered and evaluated. Digital marketing channels, such as Google Ads, Facebook campaigns, and SEO-optimized blog content, are now central to attracting and converting customers. Email marketing automation enables insurers and agencies to maintain long-term relationships by sending reminders, renewal prompts, and cross-sell opportunities based on behavioral data.

Comparison sites and aggregators such as The Zebra, Gabi, and Policygenius have simplified comparing quotes from various insurance providers, effectively commoditizing some types of insurance. While these platforms provide convenience, they may also promote a focus on price rather than value. This shift can undermine efforts to encourage long-term relationships and advisory-driven sales in the industry.

MARKETING REGULATIONS

Regulatory constraints play a significant role in shaping marketing strategies within the insurance industry. Both state and federal regulations are implemented to protect consumers from misleading advertisements and unethical sales practices. Insurers are required to disclose policy limitations, ensure their agents are properly licensed, and avoid prohibited sales tactics.

As the use of digital tools continues to grow, regulators are increasingly focusing on data usage, algorithmic decision-making, and privacy compliance. Additionally, international regulations such as the GDPR in the European Union add further complexity, especially for companies that operate across borders or utilize personal data for targeted marketing and personalization.

STUDENT OPPORTUNITIES

For students preparing to enter the insurance industry, understanding the complex distribution and marketing framework is essential. How insurance products reach customers directly impacts costs, access, transparency, and customer satisfaction. It also affects insurers' operational realities by influencing the types of risks they can underwrite, the data they can collect, and the scalability of their operations.

Careers in this field are diverse and expanding. Sales-oriented roles, such as agents and brokers, remain foundational, particularly in commercial and specialized markets. At the same time, there is an increasing demand for marketing professionals with expertise in customer segmentation, campaign analytics, and digital channel management.

There is an increasing demand for technologists and UX designers to support embedded insurance models and API integration. Professionals with hybrid skills—those who understand risk management, consumer behavior, and technology—will find opportunities to manage general agent strategies, develop partnerships, and pursue go-to-market roles within InsurTech firms.

Marketing and distribution are not secondary to the insurance industry; they are essential to its ability to fulfill its social and financial commitments. As technology changes how insurance is discovered, purchased, and serviced, the future of insurance distribution will rely on the industry's ability to maintain trust, ensure fairness, and meet customers where they are—whether through a neighborhood agent or a mobile app integrated into an e-commerce transaction.

ORGANIZATIONAL ROLES AND CAREER PATHWAYS IN INSURANCE AND INSURANCE TECHNOLOGY

Insurance organizations today function more like complex ecosystems than traditional linear factories. Previously, operations were divided into distinct silos—such as underwriting, claims, actuarial, and distribution—but now they work as a network of capabilities interconnected by data pipelines, cloud platforms, APIs, and governance frameworks. These systems must not only meet regulatory standards but also fulfill customer expectations. So, careers in insurance have expanded and evolved: traditional positions have been transformed by analytics and automation, and new roles have emerged at the crossroads of technology, risk, and customer experience (McKinsey & Company, 2021; Deloitte, 2023). It is crucial for students and early-career professionals to understand how these roles are connected and how one might navigate between them. This knowledge is essential for thriving in an industry where value creation increasingly relies on cross-functional fluency.

UNDERWRITING PATHWAY

Underwriting remains a crucial capability, but the practice has evolved beyond relying primarily on manual reviews of submissions and static rating tables. In personal lines, quick decision-making and prefilling processes depend on data enrichment, geospatial layers, and suitable credit-adjacent proxies. In commercial and specialty lines, digital submission intake, optical character recognition for schedules, and portfolio optimization tools assist underwriters in evaluating opportunities and directing their focus where their expertise can make a significant impact.

Today's underwriters act more as curators of valuable insights rather than mere collectors of documents. They are expected to analyze model outputs, question assumptions, and collaborate with product managers and data scientists when issues related to drift or calibration occur (Society of Actuaries, 2021). Career progression typically begins with underwriting assistant roles focusing on risk intake and documentation. From there, individuals may advance to associate underwriter positions for smaller accounts, ultimately specializing in specific segments, such as property catastrophe, casualty, cyber, or marine, where domain expertise and broker relationships become critical differentiators.

At senior levels, expertise in portfolio management and treaty structures is just as crucial as understanding individual risks. Leaders in underwriting are assessed based on their ability to maintain a healthy combined ratio, ensure quality growth, and uphold strong governance practices.

CLAIMS PATHWAY

Claims organizations have also experienced a significant transformation. First notice of loss can now come through a mobile app, an API from an ecosystem partner, or a sensor alert from an Internet of Things device. Simple claims adjudication may be automated using decision engines and image analytics, while more complex claims require collaboration among medical, legal, and subrogation specialists.

Today's claims professionals must balance empathy with analytical skills. They need to communicate clearly with policyholders while managing coverage interpretation, fraud analytics, reserve methodology, and litigation strategy. Early roles focus on coverage verification and customer communication. Mid-career opportunities expand into areas such as complex loss adjusting, special investigations, and bodily injury negotiation. Senior roles evolve to include claims strategy, vendor networks, catastrophe operations, and transformation programs aimed at redesigning end-to-end processes to improve cycle time and minimize leakage.

ACTURARY PATHWAYS

As automation continues to expand, human roles are shifting toward areas that require nuance and credibility, such as exception handling, fraud pattern discovery, and dispute resolution. Actuarial science, which has long been the quantitative backbone of the insurance industry, is also evolving. While traditional credibility theory and generalized linear models remain essential, actuaries are increasingly collaborating with data engineers and machine learning specialists. This partnership allows them to evaluate nontraditional variables, adjust loss cost projections due to regime changes, and quantify uncertainty in climate and cyber risk scenarios.

The tools used in actuarial work are transitioning from spreadsheet-centric workflows to code-based pipelines, incorporating version control and model documentation standards that enhance auditability and reproducibility. Early actuarial roles typically focus on pricing support, rate filings, and reserve analysis. As actuaries advance in their careers, they often move into areas such as product design, reinsurance strategy, capital modeling, and enterprise risk oversight.

PRODUCT MANAGEMENT PATHWAY

The most sought-after professionals in this field possess a combination of actuarial judgment and machine learning expertise, along with the ability to effectively communicate model decisions to nontechnical stakeholders and regulators. The emergence of product management has created a distinct career path that bridges underwriting economics, customer experience, and engineering execution.

Insurance product managers identify customer problems, translate regulatory and rating constraints into experience design, and prioritize tasks across various stages, including quoting, binding, issuing, endorsements, and claims. They must balance risk appetite and profitability with usability, managing the trade-offs between minimum viable product releases and state filing timelines, as well as operational readiness.

Effective product leaders are fluent in concepts such as loss ratio, lifetime value, and unit economics while also being adept at managing sprints, API contracts, and integration risks. Many come from backgrounds in consulting, analytics, or underwriting and acquire agile delivery and UX practices on the job. Others hail from consumer tech and learn about insurance constraints through close collaboration with actuarial and compliance teams (Boston Consulting Group, 2022).

DATA SCIENCE PATHWAY

Data science and analytics roles have significantly increased across carriers, MGAs, and InsurTech companies. Professionals in this field develop models for various purposes, such as predicting the likelihood of policy binding for marketing efforts, forecasting customer lifetime value for retention strategies, detecting fraud, estimating claims severity, and triaging underwriting queues.

What sets effective insurance data science apart is not only its technical sophistication but also an understanding of regulatory boundaries, fairness considerations, and the operational context in which models are implemented. Model risk management, which was once primarily a concept in banking, is now part of insurers' three-lines-of-defense frameworks. As a result, documentation, validation, monitoring, and explainability have become standard requirements for any model that impacts pricing, underwriting, or claims outcomes (McKinsey & Company, 2021).

Career paths in this field typically begin with analyst or junior data scientist roles focused on building features and conducting experiments. As professionals gain experience, they often progress to lead roles that oversee model lifecycles, ultimately advancing to analytics leadership positions where they establish enterprise standards and align roadmaps with overall strategy.

TECHNOLOGY PATHWAY

Data science represents the "what," while engineering signifies the "how." Software engineers, solution architects, and DevOps specialists are responsible for designing and maintaining the digital infrastructure that connects quoting, policy administration, billing, claims, data warehouses, and external partners. They modernize core systems using APIs and microservices, migrate infrastructure to cloud platforms, and implement continuous integration and deployment pipelines. These efforts reduce release cycles while maintaining control over the processes.

Meanwhile, cybersecurity engineers and architects work in parallel, guided by frameworks like the National Institute of Standards and Technology Cybersecurity Framework and ISO/IEC 27001. Their goal is to ensure that the confidentiality, integrity, and availability of sensitive data comply with internal policies and regulatory obligations. For technologists, the insurance sector is not a slow-moving industry but a field where reliability, scalability, and compliance are intertwined. Even minor deployment choices can have significant legal and financial repercussions (Deloitte, 2023).

CORPORATE RISK PATHWAY

GRC functions have transitioned from being viewed as a cost center to becoming a strategic enabler. Privacy officers are responsible for monitoring data processing and obtaining consent, ensuring alignment with regulations such as GDPR and CCPA. Additionally, they evaluate vendor contracts related to cross-border data transfers and retention schedules.

Compliance teams review various elements such as advertising practices, producer compensation, surplus lines protocols, and safeguards against unfair discrimination. They also collaborate with filing teams on rates and forms, work with model owners to ensure explainability, and conduct adverse impact testing.

Enterprise risk teams integrate insurance and operational risks into capital planning, including credit, market, liquidity, and cyber risks. They also maintain ownership of the risk appetite statement, while the internal audit team provides independent assurance of these processes.

Careers in these areas are well suited for professionals who enjoy interpreting regulations, establishing controls, and guiding product and engineering teams to "design for compliance" from the outset, rather than adding it as an afterthought (McKinsey & Company, 2021).

MARKETING AND DISTRIBUTION PATHWAY

Marketing and distribution careers now encompass local communities and networks, keywords, and click-through rates. Captive agent leaders focus on building a strong local presence and establishing trusted relationships. Independent agency principals offer tailored solutions from multiple carriers to address complex risks. Meanwhile, brokerage producers navigate placements with wholesalers and specialty markets.

Concurrently, digital growth teams manage performance marketing, SEO, affiliate partnerships, and relationships with aggregators. They analyze acquisition costs concerning customer lifetime value while ensuring compliance with disclosures and data usage regulations.

The most successful marketers in the insurance industry combine compelling storytelling about protection and resilience with rigorous experimentation. They work to incrementally improve landing pages and quote funnel conversion rates while adhering to constraints on personalization and eligibility (Deloitte, 2023).

OPERATIONS PATHWAY

Operations and policy administration serve as the essential connection that makes commitments achievable. Professionals in these fields design workflows, implement RPA when appropriate, and manage vendor networks for inspections, repairs, medical reviews, or catastrophe responses. Customer service and retention teams increasingly rely on journey analytics and next-best-action recommendations to identify cross-sell opportunities or save strategies that align with underwriting guidelines and regulatory fairness.

Leadership roles in operations attract talent capable of translating strategy into effective processes. This involves measuring service levels, improving quality, and reducing outcome variations while remaining mindful of the human needs behind each policy and claims.

REINSURANCE PATHWAY

Reinsurance and capital management offer a range of careers that combine financial engineering with risk assessment. Facultative underwriters evaluate individual risks that exceed primary underwriting appetites, while treaty underwriters structure long-term portfolios to stabilize the results for cedants. Catastrophe modelers analyze risks' frequency and severity using vendor models and internal assessments.

Additionally, capital solutions teams engage with insurance-linked securities to access alternative funding through catastrophe bonds and collateralized reinsurance.

Key skills for success in reinsurance include analytical rigor, negotiation abilities, and a global perspective. This industry sector provides a comprehensive view of entire portfolios for students interested in macro-risk and markets rather than focusing solely on individual accounts.

MANAGING GENERAL AGENT PATHWAY

The MGA and program administrator segment has become a thriving area for entrepreneurial careers. Since MGAs operate with delegated authority, professionals in this field engage with the entire lifecycle of insurance operations. This includes shaping underwriting appetites, establishing distribution partnerships, managing rating and rules engines, designing services, preparing bordereaux reports, and maintaining relations with reinsurers. Career advancement in this sector can be swift, especially for generalists with a solid understanding of revenue growth and loss ratio management. Many InsurTech companies opt for the MGA model to test new products before seeking full-stack carrier licenses, making these organizations an excellent environment for product managers, growth leaders, and engineers who wish to gain comprehensive exposure to the industry (Boston Consulting Group, 2022).

SPECIALITY LINES PATHWAY

Specialty domains provide additional pathways for career development. For example, cyber underwriting and incident response create hybrid roles requiring technical expertise and policy knowledge. Marine and energy insurance necessitate familiarity with logistics, engineering, and geopolitics. Parametric products involve data sourcing, trigger design, and educating clients about basis risk. Additionally, embedded insurance roles focus on partner management, API product strategy, and understanding customer experiences in noninsurance environments.

In each of these cases, achieving career success follows a consistent pattern: develop domain expertise that builds trust, combine it with data and technology skills that enhance insights, and communicate effectively across different functions.

GENERAL INFORMATION ABOUT CAREER PATHWAYS

Compensation structures vary significantly by role and channel, and understanding these incentives can help students choose paths that align with their motivations. In production-oriented roles within agencies and brokerages, compensation is often based on commission, with bonuses linked to growth and profitability. Captive agencies may offer a combination of base salary support and marketing allowances, while independent agencies trade job security for greater autonomy and a higher potential for earnings.

Carrier roles typically offer a mix of salary and annual and long-term incentives, which reflect overall company performance and individual objectives. Roles in analytics and engineering might include equity options in InsurTech companies or shared-success plans in MGAs. On the other hand, roles in GRC and operations focus more on stability and career progression through increased responsibilities, rather than on variable pay.

Across all sectors, compensation packages increasingly recognize the value of interdisciplinary expertise, rewarding individuals who can effectively bridge technical and commercial outcomes.

Geography and market structure significantly influence career opportunities in the insurance industry. The Lloyd's market in London operates with distinct roles—coverholders, syndicates, managing agents, and Lloyd's brokers—that differ from those in US admitted markets. Additionally, global carriers must navigate regional regulatory nuances that impact product filing, data management, and distribution agreements.

The rise of remote work has expanded career options, allowing data, product, and engineering teams to be distributed globally. However, positions requiring a physical presence—such as field adjusting, inspections, and community-based sales—still value local knowledge and networks. Cross-border experience is becoming increasingly valuable, particularly in reinsurance, specialty lines, and multinational programs.

Ethics and professionalism are essential components of every successful career in the insurance industry. As algorithms increasingly influence pricing, eligibility, and claims processes, professionals must know how these patterns can inadvertently impact protected classes or lead to unequal outcomes. Additionally, as marketing becomes more precise, teams should be careful not to overpersonalize their approaches, which could compromise fairness or violate privacy expectations. With rising cost pressures, claims leaders must balance reducing leakage and ensuring fair claims practices while empathizing with policyholders. These issues are not secondary; they are critical for maintaining the industry's social license to operate and for fostering trust with policyholders and regulators (McKinsey & Company, 2021).

Career mobility across various functions is more common than students might think. Underwriters often transition into product development or reinsurance roles, while claims leaders may move into fraud analytics. Actuaries can take positions in venture investing or corporate development, and engineers might shift into platform product management. The key factors for these transitions are curiosity and a willingness to learn the languages of related disciplines.

Rotational programs offered by insurance carriers and brokers can accelerate this mobility by introducing new graduates to underwriting, claims, analytics, and operations within their first 2 years of employment. In contrast, InsurTech companies offer a different type of rotation, characterized by the fast-paced nature of building and iterating quickly within small teams.

FOR MY STUDENTS—ADVICE FROM ME

For students planning their next steps, three habits can enhance career resilience. First, develop data literacy, regardless of your discipline. The ability to read a model, question a performance metric, and understand issues related to bias and drift will make you a better underwriter, claims leader, or marketer.

Second, practice effective stakeholder communication. Translating between actuarial details, engineering constraints, and customer impact is essential for influencing others in complex organizations.

Finally, cultivate sound judgment through studying cases and seeking mentorship. While technologies and trends may change, your ability to make informed decisions about risk, fairness, and the right trade-offs will remain a key differentiator in your career.

Organizational roles in insurance and InsurTech are expanding and increasingly overlapping around common skills: analytical rigor, technological fluency, regulatory awareness, and a focus on human-centered execution. The career paths in this industry are no longer straightforward escalators; they have transformed into lattices that reward interdisciplinary skills and ethical clarity. Students who grasp this evolving landscape and pursue careers at these intersections will discover an industry that is both stable and impactful and unexpectedly entrepreneurial and intellectually stimulating.

EDUCATION, LICENSING, AND PROFESSIONAL DEVELOPMENT

The insurance industry has always been credential driven, relying on technical expertise, trust, and compliance with regulatory standards. Unlike other fields where informal experience or soft skills can suffice, insurance professionals must demonstrate their competence through structured educational programs, professional designations, and licensing requirements. In today's InsurTech-driven landscape, while these traditional pathways remain important, they are increasingly supplemented by new forms of technical training, certifications in emerging technologies, and continuous learning platforms that promote the development of cross-disciplinary skills. For students preparing to enter the industry, this section offers a clear roadmap for understanding professional development and its significance.

ACADEMIC FOUNDATIONS

Universities have been instrumental in preparing the insurance workforce. Degree programs in risk management, actuarial science, finance, and business administration provide the foundational knowledge needed for underwriting, claims processing, and actuarial analysis careers. Specialized courses in insurance technology, data analytics, and cybersecurity have been added to curricula, reflecting the increasing integration of risk management and digital transformation.

Graduate-level programs, such as master's degrees in risk management, insurance technology, or business analytics, can give individuals a competitive edge when seeking leadership positions. Additionally, the academic environment offers students opportunities to partake in research, case competitions, and internships, which connect classroom theory with practical applications.

LICENSING REQUIREMENTS

Licensing is one of the most formal entry points into the insurance profession. In the United States, insurance agents and brokers must obtain licenses from state insurance departments before selling policies. Licensing ensures these professionals understand regulatory requirements, ethical obligations, and basic product knowledge.

The licenses are typically specific to the type of insurance sold, such as property and casualty, life and health, or surplus lines. Additionally, continuing education is required; producers must complete approved coursework during each licensing cycle to remain compliant.

Claims adjusters in many states also face similar licensing requirements, especially when handling auto, workers' compensation, or catastrophe claims. For professionals looking to work across state lines or internationally, reciprocal licensing agreements or designation-based waivers can help reduce barriers. However, the regulatory differences between states continue to be a significant aspect of the industry.

PROFESSIONAL DESIGNATIONS

In addition to licensing, professional designations highlight an individual's expertise and commitment to the field. For instance, the Chartered Property Casualty Underwriter (CPCU) designation is recognized worldwide as a symbol of technical and ethical excellence in property and casualty insurance. Other notable designations include the Associate in Risk Management (ARM), Certified Insurance Counselor, and Associate in Insurance, all of which are widely respected.

For actuaries, advancing through the Society of Actuaries exam systems or the Casualty Actuarial Society is a challenging yet rewarding journey that shapes the actuarial profession. Additionally, students interested in global practices can pursue qualifications such as those offered by the Chartered Insurance Institute in the United Kingdom or the Fellow of the Institute of Actuaries of India, both of which provide international recognition.

Although these programs often take years to complete, they offer structured learning, enhance professional credibility, and provide access to influential alum networks.

EMERGING CERTIFICATIONS IN TECHNOLOGY AND DATA

As the insurance industry has become more digital, certifications once considered unrelated to the field have gained significant relevance. Data science certifications from platforms like SAS, Microsoft, or Google Cloud are increasingly valuable for professionals in predictive analytics or machine learning models. Additionally, cybersecurity credentials such as Certified Information Systems Security Professional and Certified Information Security Manager are essential for those responsible for protecting sensitive policyholder data. Cloud infrastructure certifications from providers such as Amazon Web Services or Microsoft Azure are particularly beneficial for technologists modernizing insurance platforms. Unlike traditional designations focusing solely on insurance-specific knowledge, these credentials link professionals to broader technological ecosystems, offering a competitive advantage in cross-functional teams.

CONTINUING EDUCATION AND LIFELONG LEARNING

Insurance is a dynamic field that is constantly evolving. Regulatory environments change, new risks arise, and customer expectations shift. While continuing education has always been a regulatory requirement, it is also a strategic necessity. Professionals in the industry are expected to stay updated on global solvency frameworks, climate risk disclosure requirements, and advancements in AI explainability.

Today, there are numerous options for learning, including online platforms, webinars, micro-credentials, and corporate training programs that offer on-demand education. Many organizations encourage or require employees to participate in professional development plans and provide support through course reimbursements, study time allowances, and mentoring programs that facilitate knowledge transfer across generations.

MENTORSHIP, NETWORKING, AND INDUSTRY INVOLVEMENT

In addition to formal education, mentorship and professional networking are crucial for career development. Organizations such as the Risk and Insurance Management Society, the Society of Actuaries, and InsurTech associations offer conferences, webinars, and networking events that connect professionals with peers, regulators, and thought leaders. Participating in professional associations can provide early access to internships, scholarships, and mentorship opportunities for students. Engaging in these networks also helps professionals stay informed about industry trends, regulatory changes, and technological advancements.

GLOBAL CONSIDERATIONS

For those interested in international careers, the importance of education and professional development is heightened by the global nature of risk. Professionals working with multinational insurers, reinsurers, or brokers must understand local regulations and international standards, such as Solvency II in the European Union and International Financial Reporting Standard 17 in accounting. Obtaining designations and certifications that have international recognition can open doors across different jurisdictions. Moreover, global risk management issues, including climate resilience, cyber warfare, and pandemic response, highlight the necessity for ongoing, adaptive learning that crosses borders.

In summary, education, licensing, and professional development are the foundation for insurance and InsurTech careers. While traditional degree programs and professional certifications remain important, the industry now demands a broader range of skills, including data science, technology, and cybersecurity expertise. Achieving success in this environment requires obtaining initial credentials and a dedication to lifelong learning, ethical practices, and active professional involvement. For students, this entails preparing to engage in various forms of learning—academic, professional, technological, and experiential—that will adapt and evolve with the industry.

CAREER PATHWAYS IN AGENCIES, BROKERAGES, WHOLESALERS, MANAGING GENERAL AGENTS, AND CAPTIVES

Distribution is not just a means of delivering products to consumers; it is the vital core of the insurance industry. Without effective distribution, even the most advanced products can become inaccessible to those who need them. This reality has significant implications for students and early-career professionals: the distribution structure influences most entry-level and mid-career opportunities. Whether starting a career as a local agency producer, a broker at a multinational intermediary, or an underwriter working closely with an MGA, the distribution model shapes daily responsibilities and long-term career paths, compensation structures, and opportunities for specialization.

To comprehend careers in insurance, it is essential to understand the various channels through which insurance products are marketed and sold. These channels include agencies (both captive and independent), brokerages (retail and wholesale), MGAs, and captives. Each channel operates under its own regulatory framework, compensation system, and organizational culture, resulting in unique professional environments.

AGENCIES: THE LOCAL FOUNDATION OF INSURANCE CAREERS

Agencies are among the most prominent entry points into the insurance profession. For decades, the typical image of an insurance career has been that of an agency producer or owner serving local households and small businesses. Agencies can be categorized as either captive, representing only one insurer, or independent, representing multiple insurance carriers.

Career paths are closely tied to the sponsoring company in a captive agency. Professionals usually begin as producers or sales associates, building their client base through community engagement, cold calls, and referrals. Over time, successful producers may transition into agency ownership, receiving support through financing and marketing assistance from the parent insurer. Careers in captive agencies emphasize loyalty to the brand, mastery of product lines, and strong relationship-building skills. Although captive agents are limited to one carrier, they benefit from comprehensive training and solid infrastructure support, which provide a structured environment for learning sales fundamentals, underwriting guidelines, and claims processes.

Independent agencies prioritize autonomy and advocate for their clients. Career paths in these agencies are often more entrepreneurial. Agents must manage relationships with multiple insurance carriers, understand a wider range of product lines, and negotiate coverage options for their clients. The independent agency model rewards individuals with strong business skills and adaptability. Compensation typically comes from commissions, often supplemented by profit-sharing agreements with carriers.

Career advancement in independent agencies can involve starting an agency from scratch or joining established firms that appreciate producers who can attract new clients. These agencies also offer opportunities for specialization in areas such as commercial lines, employee benefits, or niche sectors like transportation and construction. For students, pursuing a career in independent agencies can provide valuable exposure to various risks and the chance to develop expertise across different carriers. However, this path may have less structural support than a captive agency setting.

BROKERAGES: FROM LOCAL ADVISORS TO GLOBAL INTERMEDIARIES

Agencies generally cater to individuals and small businesses, while brokerages focus on larger and more complex accounts. Brokers represent the insured rather than the insurer, which means their primary loyalty lies with the client. This shift in focus changes the skill set required for a career in brokerage. Rather than simply selling standard policies, brokers act as negotiators and consultants. They are responsible for creating risk transfer arrangements tailored to corporations, nonprofits, and government entities' specific needs.

At the local or regional level, careers in brokerage are similar to those in independent agencies, where producers focus on building relationships and securing coverage from various carriers. The work environment is highly specialized in larger brokerages, particularly global firms like Marsh, Aon, or Willis Towers Watson. Employees typically start in analyst or associate roles, supporting senior brokers by preparing submissions, analyzing policy terms, and benchmarking client coverage against industry standards. As they gain experience, they progress to client-facing positions as account executives, managing extensive corporate relationships and navigating complex placements involving multiple insurers.

Brokerage careers also open opportunities in consulting services such as risk management, actuarial analysis, employee benefits, and captive formation. Because of their size and scope, global brokerages offer rotational programs, international mobility, and access to cutting-edge data and analytics platforms. Students entering brokerage careers must be comfortable operating in a consultative capacity, balancing technical insurance knowledge with negotiation skills and client advisory services. The brokerage model also rewards specialization; professionals may become experts in industries such as energy, healthcare, or aviation, working on placements that require deep domain knowledge.

WHOLESALERS: GATEWAYS TO SPECIALTY MARKETS

Insurance wholesalers act as intermediaries between retail agents and insurance carriers, particularly for risks inappropriate for standard markets. Careers in wholesaling provide exposure to specialty lines, high-severity risks, and innovative underwriting solutions. Professionals in wholesale brokerages develop expertise in excess and surplus lines, which offer greater flexibility in pricing and policy language. However, this expertise also requires a thorough understanding of regulatory requirements to ensure compliance with surplus lines laws.

For students and young professionals, wholesaling presents a different dynamic than retail distribution. Instead of cultivating long-term relationships with individual policyholders, wholesalers build networks with agents and brokers to help them place hard-to-insure risks. Wholesalers often begin underwriting support roles, where individuals review submissions, liaise with insurance carriers, and assist in preparing quotes. Over time, they may advance to broker positions, where their success relies on technical expertise, responsiveness, and the ability to navigate specialized markets such as cyber liability, environmental liability, or high-value property.

The wholesale environment is typically fast-paced and transactional, demanding the ability to manage multiple submissions and complex negotiations simultaneously. For professionals with a strong interest in technical details and problem-solving, a career in wholesaling can be advantageous and places them at the forefront of risk management.

MANAGING GENERAL AGENTS: ENTREPRENEURIAL HYBRIDS

MGAs hold a distinct role in the insurance value chain. They are neither insurance carriers nor traditional intermediaries. Instead, they operate with delegated underwriting authority granted by insurers. This authority enables MGAs to quote policies, bind coverage, and, in some cases, manage claims on behalf of the carriers. They often focus on specialized markets or innovative products.

Careers in MGAs combine underwriting, product development, and distribution elements. Early-career professionals may begin as underwriting assistants or account managers, supporting the submission process and managing relationships with retail agents. Because MGAs often focus on niche markets, these professionals quickly develop expertise in specific risk categories, such as marine cargo, renewable energy, or gig economy liability. Mid-career opportunities include roles in product development, where professionals create coverage tailored to underserved markets, and distribution leadership, overseeing networks of agents and brokers.

The InsurTech movement has revitalized the MGA model. Many digital-first insurers, such as Hippo, NEXT Insurance, and Pie, started as MGAs to test their products and validate their business models before acquiring full carrier licenses. Careers within these companies are dynamic, combining insurance expertise with technological skills like API integration, customer experience design, and data-driven underwriting. For students with entrepreneurial aspirations, MGAs present some of the most exciting opportunities in the industry, as they offer the flexibility of a startup coupled with the financial support of established carriers and reinsurers.

CAPTIVES: RISK MANAGEMENT FROM THE INSIDE OUT

Captive insurance companies are entities created and owned by noninsurance organizations to manage risks. These companies are often established by large corporations, municipalities, or industry groups that aim to have greater control over their risk financing. Careers in captive insurance are appealing to professionals interested in corporate risk management, finance, and governance.

Professionals collaborate closely with the parent company's risk management and finance teams in a captive insurance environment to design programs that align with the organization's overall strategic objectives. The roles in this setting may include captive managers, actuaries, compliance officers, and claims administrators. Unlike agencies or brokerages, which focus on serving external clients, captive insurance professionals work internally, aligning risk financing with the corporate balance sheet.

Students interested in careers in captive insurance must be familiar with the terminology used in both insurance and corporate finance. Since captives are frequently based in specialized jurisdictions such as Bermuda, Vermont, or the Cayman Islands, professionals in this field may also need knowledge of international regulations and tax policies. A career in captive insurance values strong analytical skills, governance expertise, and the capability to communicate risk financing strategies to senior executives effectively.

CAREER DEVELOPMENT ACROSS CHANNELS

Each channel in the insurance industry—agencies, brokerages, wholesalers, MGAs, and captives—offers distinct opportunities. However, it is essential to recognize that the industry is highly interconnected. Professionals often move between these channels, utilizing their skills and relationships to explore new roles. For example, an agent might transition to become a broker, a wholesale underwriter could join an MGA, or a captive manager might shift into consulting. This fluidity highlights the importance of transferable skills for students, such as relationship management, technical insurance knowledge, regulatory awareness, and technological fluency.

The choice of career channel greatly influences compensation and work style. Roles in agencies often feature commission-based pay and a level of entrepreneurial independence. Brokerage positions may offer a combination of a base salary, performance incentives, and a focus on negotiation and advisory skills. Wholesalers and MGAs typically provide a salary plus bonus structure, rewarding technical expertise and support in distribution. Captive careers may resemble roles in corporate finance, offering stable salaries and opportunities for strategic influence within a single organization. Each career path presents trade-offs regarding stability, income variability, and potential for long-term growth.

The insurance distribution system can seem overwhelming and unclear for students and new professionals. However, it also offers many great career opportunities. Agencies provide a chance to build local relationships and develop entrepreneurial businesses. Brokerages offer pathways to global consulting and large-scale risk advisory work. Wholesalers and MGAs expose professionals to specialized risks and innovative product development. Captive insurance companies integrate insurance into corporate finance and risk management strategies.

Understanding these channels extends beyond merely knowing how insurance is sold; it involves comprehending the entire ecosystem of careers that supports the industry. The distribution model influences how risks are underwritten, products are priced, customers are served, and careers are developed. By mastering this landscape, students can position themselves to build rewarding and impactful careers in one of the world's most dynamic and significant industries.

THE ROLE OF AUTOMATION AND ARTIFICIAL INTELLIGENCE IN INSURANCE CAREERS

The insurance industry has always relied on data to operate effectively. Actuaries analyze past losses to predict future risks, underwriters evaluate applications against established guidelines, and claims adjusters assess damages to determine compensation. However, today's data landscape's scale, speed, and complexity far exceed what manual processes can manage. Advances in AI, RPA, and machine learning are not just supportive tools but fundamental forces reshaping the insurance workforce. This technological shift raises important questions for students and early-career professionals: What tasks are being automated? What skills remain uniquely human? Moreover, what new roles are emerging at the intersection of insurance and technology?

AUTOMATION IN TRADITIONAL FUNCTIONS

In underwriting, automation has transformed the role of entry-level professionals. Routine tasks such as data entry, rule checking, and preliminary pricing can now be handled by algorithms that rely on structured databases, external APIs, and predictive models. Automated underwriting platforms can issue instant approvals for simple risks, including auto, renters, and travel insurance. Consequently, today's underwriters spend less time processing standard submissions and can dedicate more time to complex risks, portfolio strategy, and refining algorithmic models. For students, this shift means that technical literacy—specifically, an understanding of how these models operate, the data they utilize, and their potential blind spots—has become as crucial as traditional risk evaluation skills.

In claims management, AI-driven tools are transforming the first notice of loss and damage assessment processes. Mobile apps allow policyholders to submit photos or videos, which are then analyzed by image recognition software to estimate damages. Chatbots handle routine customer inquiries, allowing human adjusters to concentrate on high-value or contested claims. Fraud detection increasingly relies on anomaly detection algorithms that identify suspicious patterns within large datasets. While automation reduces cycle times and improves efficiency, human adjusters remain essential for litigation, bodily injury, or customer advocacy cases. Claims careers now require a balance between empathy and technical oversight, ensuring that automation enhances fairness rather than undermines it.

Actuarial science and pricing have undergone significant transformations. Traditional actuarial models relied on relatively small datasets and linear techniques. In contrast, modern pricing strategies utilize machine learning algorithms to manage unstructured data, nonlinear relationships, and complex interactions. This shift does not diminish the role of actuaries; rather, it enhances it. Actuaries must now collaborate with data scientists, validate model outputs, and communicate model risk to regulators. Aspiring actuaries must be proficient in programming languages such as Python or R, familiar with cloud computing tools, and understand the principles of model governance. It is important to note that AI complements actuarial expertise, rather than replacing it.

EMERGING ROLES AND SKILLS

Automation is transforming existing roles and creating new ones. AI product managers oversee developing and deploying machine learning models in underwriting, claims, and marketing workflows. Model risk managers ensure that algorithms are transparent, auditable, and compliant with regulatory standards. Data engineers construct pipelines that provide clean and reliable data for analytical models. Ethics officers and compliance professionals monitor the fairness and explainability of AI systems, reflecting the increasing regulatory scrutiny of algorithmic decision-making in financial services. Numerous opportunities exist for students entering this field at the intersection of technology and insurance, provided they are willing to cultivate technical skills and domain knowledge.

Communication and interpretability skills are becoming increasingly valuable. A model can generate highly accurate predictions, but trust in the model is compromised if underwriters, brokers, regulators, or policyholders do not understand how those predictions are formulated. Professionals who can bridge the gap between the technical language of AI and the practical needs of risk management will be indispensable. This role as a "translator" is emerging as one of the most important niches in the industry.

SHIFTING THE HUMAN–MACHINE BALANCE

One of the key questions regarding automation in insurance careers is whether AI will replace or enhance human roles. The reality is complex. Repetitive, rule-based, and high-volume tasks—such as data entry, simple claims processing, and compliance checks—are likely to be fully automated. However, tasks that require empathy, judgment, negotiation, and creativity depend on human involvement. Therefore careers in insurance are evolving to focus on higher-order skills. Professionals will be expected to supervise, interpret, and guide AI systems rather than compete with them.

For instance, AI tools can score leads in distribution, automate outreach, and personalize marketing campaigns. However, building trust, explaining complex coverage, and negotiating tailored solutions still require human producers and brokers. In governance, automated compliance systems can identify anomalies, but regulators expect human professionals to apply ethical principles with sound judgment. Even in claims—where automation is most advanced—policyholders often seek the comfort of a human voice during stressful situations. Students should view AI not as a threat but as a collaborator; it can free them from repetitive tasks and allow them to concentrate on their careers' strategic, creative, and relational aspects.

THE FUTURE OF WORK IN INSURANCE

Automation will continue to drive the industry toward hybrid roles that combine technical and human skills. Professionals who will thrive in this environment understand AI's capabilities and limitations and can collaborate with algorithms while maintaining ethical responsibility. Career development will increasingly focus on essential competencies in digital fluency, data literacy, and ethical awareness. Organizations are already investing in reskilling programs to equip underwriters, claims adjusters, and marketers with the necessary tools to understand and effectively leverage automation.

For students getting ready to enter the workforce, the message is clear: AI and automation are not eliminating jobs in insurance; instead, they are transforming them. The most in-demand professionals will combine industry knowledge with the skills to oversee, explain, and innovate alongside intelligent systems.

SUMMARY

The insurance industry is built on people, processes, and relationships. While technology is transforming areas such as distribution, underwriting, and claims management, it is the careers of individuals working in agencies, brokerages, wholesalers, MGAs, and captives that bring the system to life and connect abstract risk models to real-world protection. Understanding these distribution channels involves more than just technical knowledge; it also provides insight into the organizational culture, regulatory environment, and customer engagement strategies that define the industry.

This chapter has highlighted that for students and early-career professionals, an insurance career is not a single path but a diverse array of opportunities. Some individuals may pursue the entrepreneurial journey of starting their own agency and building a client base through local connections. Others may excel in the brokerage sector, navigating complex risks and utilizing advanced negotiation and advisory skills in a global environment. Additionally, some may discover their passion in specialty markets, collaborating with wholesalers, MGAs, or captives. Creativity, innovation, and domain expertise are key to achieving career success in these areas.

Automation and AI are transforming the landscape of work in the insurance industry. Routine tasks are increasingly handled by machines, which allows professionals to concentrate on higher-level judgment, empathy, and ethical oversight. This change is not eliminating jobs but evolving them, requiring digital fluency, regulatory understanding, and effective communication across technical and interpersonal contexts. The future of careers in insurance lies in hybrid roles—positions that combine traditional functions with technological capabilities, enabling professionals to excel at the intersections of risk, data, and customer experience.

Professional development and credentialing are essential in an industry defined by trust and long-term commitments. These pathways are expanding, with traditional designations like CPCU or ARM coexisting alongside cloud certifications, data science credentials, and continuous learning platforms. These resources prepare professionals to navigate an ever-changing landscape. Lifelong learning, adaptability, and ethical clarity are now central to building resilience in organizations and individual careers; they are no longer optional.

The careers of tomorrow in the insurance industry will not be defined solely by a choice between "traditional" insurance and "InsurTech." Instead, they will be shaped by the ability to integrate the best aspects of both. This means combining the relationship-driven, trust-centered values that have anchored the industry for centuries with the data-driven, technology-enabled tools transforming how protection is delivered in the 21st century. For students, embracing this duality is essential for entering the industry and thriving within it.

AI DISCLOSURE

During the preparation of this work the author(s) used Grammarly to correct any spelling or grammatical mistakes. After using this tool/service, the author(s) reviewed and edited the content as needed and take(s) full responsibility for the content of the publication.

REFERENCES

Boston Consulting Group. (2022). *The future of insurance: New distribution and business models*. Boston Consulting Group. https://www.bcg.com/publications/2022/future-of-insurance.

Deloitte. (2023). *2023 Insurance industry outlook: Navigating talent, technology, and transformation*. Deloitte Insights. https://www2.deloitte.com/insights/us/industry/financial-services/insurance-industry-outlook.html.

McKinsey & Company. (2021). *The future of insurance: Technology-led transformation*. McKinsey & Company. https://www.mckinsey.com/industries/financial-services/our-insights/future-of-insurance.

Society of Actuaries. (2021). *The evolving role of the actuary in the age of data science*. Society of Actuaries Research Institute. https://www.soa.org/research/topics/actuary-and-data-science.

Glossary of commonly used terms

GLOSSARY OF INSURANCE AND INSURTECH TERMS

This is a small selection of commonly used terms in the insurance technology industry.

A

Actuary A professional who applies mathematical and statistical methods to assess financial risk in insurance and finance.

Adverse Selection The tendency of individuals with higher-than-average risk to purchase or renew insurance more frequently than those with lower risk.

Aggregate Limit The maximum amount an insurer will pay for all covered losses during a policy period.

Algorithmic Underwriting Automated underwriting process powered by data-driven models and machine learning to assess risk more efficiently.

API (Application Programming Interface) A software intermediary that allows two applications to communicate. In insurance, APIs enable integration between carriers, distributors, and platforms.

API Gateway A centralized access point to manage, route, and secure API traffic in digital insurance ecosystems.

B

Behavioral Analytics The analysis of user actions (e.g., app behavior, driving patterns) to detect fraud, personalize products, or adjust pricing.

Binding Authority Permission granted by an insurer to an agent or broker to underwrite and bind coverage on the insurer's behalf.

Blockchain A decentralized ledger technology used in insurance to improve transparency, automate claims (via smart contracts), and mitigate fraud.

Broker An insurance intermediary who works on behalf of the insured to find and negotiate coverage.

Insurance Technology. DOI: https://doi.org/10.1016/B978-0-443-43972-8.00010-9

C

Capacity The financial limit up to which an insurer or reinsurer is willing to underwrite risk.

Captive Insurance An insurance company created and wholly owned by a noninsurance business to insure its own risks.

Claim A request by the insured for payment or service under the terms of an insurance policy.

Cloud Computing The delivery of computing services via the internet offers scalability and flexibility to modern insurers.

Coinsurance A cost-sharing arrangement where the insured pays a specified percentage of the covered costs.

Contingent Business Interruption Coverage for income losses due to disruptions in a supplier's or customer's operations.

Cyber Insurance A form of coverage against digital threats such as data breaches, ransomware, or system outages.

D

Data Lake A centralized repository for storing large volumes of raw data, used in advanced analytics and machine learning applications.

Data Privacy Impact Assessment A systematic process to identify and mitigate privacy risks, especially under regulations like GDPR.

Declarations Page The portion of a policy summarizing coverage limits, policyholder details, and effective dates.

Deductible The amount the insured must pay out of pocket before insurance coverage begins.

Digital Twin A virtual representation of a physical asset or system used to simulate and manage risk.

E

Embedded Insurance A model in which insurance is included as part of a noninsurance product purchase (e.g., within a car rental or app checkout).

Exclusion A policy provision that removes coverage for specified risks, activities, or property.

Explainable AI AI models that provide transparent, interpretable results—critical for regulatory compliance in underwriting and claims decisions.

F

Factor Analysis of Information Risk Model A quantitative model used to evaluate and communicate information security risks in financial terms.

I

Indemnity Insurance Insurance that reimburses the insured based on the actual value of the loss versus parametric triggers.

InsurTech The convergence of insurance and technology is improving efficiency, expanding distribution, and enhancing customer experience.

Internet of Things A network of internet-connected devices (e.g., sensors, vehicles, wearables) used for real-time risk monitoring and pricing.

L

Loss Ratio A performance metric calculated as claims paid divided by earned premiums.

M

Machine Learning A branch of AI focused on building systems that learn from data to make predictions or decisions without being explicitly programmed.

Moral Hazard The idea is that insurance may incentivize riskier behavior because the financial consequences are transferred to the insurer.

O

Oracles (Blockchain) Trusted data feeds that transmit real-world information (e.g., weather, market data) to smart contracts on a blockchain.

P

Parametric Insurance Coverage triggered by a measurable event (e.g., wind speed, rainfall), paying a fixed amount rather than assessing actual loss.

Policyholder The person or entity who owns the insurance policy and has contractual rights to coverage and benefits.

Premium The amount the insured pays to the insurer for coverage.

R

Reinsurance Insurance for insurers. A method for managing risk exposure by transferring it to another insurer.

Retention The amount of risk retained by the insurer or policyholder before transferring risk to another party.

Risk Pooling Combining multiple risks to make losses more predictable and manageable through the law of large numbers.

S

Smart Contracts Self-executing contracts are written on a blockchain, where conditions and obligations are automatically enforced.

Synthetic Data Artificially generated data is used for training models when real-world data is limited or sensitive.

T

Telematics Technology that captures data (usually from vehicles) on driving behavior, speed, and location to assess risk more dynamically.

Third-Party Liability Coverage for claims made by individuals or entities not named in the insurance contract, typically arising from injury or damage.

U

Underwriting The evaluation of risk and determination of premium pricing and coverage terms based on applicant information and risk modeling.

AI DISCLOSURE

During the preparation of this work the author(s) used Grammarly to improve readability and correct grammatical mistakes. After using this tool/service, the author(s) reviewed and edited the content as needed and take(s) full responsibility for the content of the publication.

Appendix: Simple code snippet

APPENDIX A: CODE SNIPPETS FOR INSURANCE TECHNOLOGY APPLICATIONS

This appendix includes simplified code examples that demonstrate how key insurance technologies can be applied in practice. Each snippet corresponds with concepts discussed in the main chapters, providing readers with a foundation for experimentation, prototyping, or deeper exploration.

Note: These examples are for instructional purposes only and are not production-grade code.

A.1 BLOCKCHAIN SMART CONTRACT FOR PARAMETRIC PAYOUTS

Related Chapter: Blockchain and Distributed Ledger Technologies

This Solidity smart contract executes an automatic payout when rainfall exceeds a threshold, simulating a parametric flood insurance policy.

```
pragma solidity ^0.8.0;
contract RainfallInsurance {
address payable public policyholder;
uint public threshold;
uint public payoutAmount;
constructor(address payable_policyholder, uint_threshold, uint_
   payoutAmount) {
policyholder =_policyholder;
threshold =_threshold;
payoutAmount =_payoutAmount;
}
function triggerClaim(uint rainfallAmount) public {
if (rainfallAmount >= threshold) {
policyholder.transfer(payoutAmount);
}
}
}
```

Insurance Technology. DOI: https://doi.org/10.1016/B978-0-443-43972-8.00009-2

A.2 PARAMETRIC INSURANCE PAYOUT CALCULATION

Related Chapter: Parametric Insurance

This Python function calculates a fixed payout based on observed rainfall and a defined trigger threshold.

```
def calculate_payout(rainfall, threshold, coverage):
if rainfall >= threshold:
return coverage
return 0
```

A.3 FRAUD DETECTION USING LOGISTIC REGRESSION

Related Chapter: Machine Learning and Artificial Intelligence

This snippet shows a basic binary classification model using logistic regression to detect fraudulent claims.

```
from sklearn.linear_model import LogisticRegression
from sklearn.model_selection import train_test_split
X_train, X_test, y_train, y_test = train_test_split(features,
  labels, test_size=0.3)
model = LogisticRegression()
model.fit(X_train, y_train)
predictions = model.predict(X_test)
```

A.4 SHAPLEY ADDITIVE EXPLANATIONS MODEL INTERPRETABILITY FOR UNDERWRITING

Related Chapter: AI Explainability and Interpretability

SHAP helps interpret complex models by attributing feature contributions to predictions.

```
import shap
explainer = shap.TreeExplainer(model)
shap_values = explainer.shap_values(X)
shap.summary_plot(shap_values, X)
```

A.5 FACTOR ANALYSIS OF INFORMATION RISK–BASED RISK SIMULATION

Related Chapter: Cybersecurity and Privacy Risks

This code simulates loss exposure using a basic Monte Carlo method, consistent with Factor Analysis of Information Risk methodology.

```
import numpy as np
simulations = [np.random.normal(10000, 2000) for_ in range(10000)]
expected_loss = np.mean(simulations)
print(f"Expected Loss: ${expected_loss:,.2f}")
```

A.6 SIMULATED INTERNET OF THINGS DATA FOR USAGE-BASED INSURANCE

Related Chapter: Decentralized Insurance and Internet of Things

This example shows how telematics data might be collected and sent to an insurer's server.

```
import requests
data = {
"vehicle_id": "TX-7890",
"speed": 65,
"braking": 1.8,
"acceleration": 3.1
}
response = requests.post("https://api.insurance.com/telematics",
  json=data)
```

A.7 REPRESENTATIONAL STATE TRANSFER APPLICATION PROGRAMMING INTERFACE CALL TO ISSUE A NEW POLICY

Related Chapter: Digital Transformation

Illustrates how a digital insurance platform might receive new policyholder data via an application programming interface.

```
import requests
policy = {
"name": "John Doe",
"policy_type": "Auto",
"coverage": 50000,
"premium": 85.75
}
response = requests.post("https://api.insurer.com/policies",
  json=policy)
```

A.8 REGULATORY SANDBOX SUBMISSION IN JSON

Related Chapter: Regulation, Ethics, and Responsibility

This JSON structure simulates a sandbox application submission to a national insurance regulator.

```
{
"startup_name": "RiskEdge AI",
"technology": "AI-based Underwriting Assistant",
"use_case": "Real-time credit risk scoring for small business
  insurance",
"jurisdiction": "NAIC Sandbox, USA",
"requested_exemptions": ["automated decision review", "underwriting
  threshold limits"]
}
```

A.9 CLAIMS SEVERITY PREDICTION WITH LINEAR REGRESSION

Related Chapter: Machine Learning and AI

A regression model that predicts expected claim costs based on policyholder and event data.

```
from sklearn.linear_model import LinearRegression
model = LinearRegression()
model.fit(X_train, y_train)
claim_costs = model.predict(X_test)
```

A.10 TIME SERIES ANOMALY DETECTION FOR CLIMATE INDEXING

Related Chapter: Parametric Insurance

Using rolling averages to detect abnormal climate conditions.

```
import pandas as pd
df['rolling_avg'] = df['rainfall'].rolling(window=7).mean()
df['anomaly'] = df['rainfall'] > (df['rolling_avg'] + 10)
```

Case studies for classroom discussions or presentations

INTRODUCTION

The Case Study Compendium aims to connect theory with practice by providing concise and insightful examples of how technology is transforming the global insurance industry. While the main chapters of this textbook establish the conceptual and technical foundations of insurance technology (InsurTech), this compendium emphasizes real-world applications, showcasing how innovation manifests across various companies, regions, and areas of risk.

Each case study in this section is carefully chosen to highlight a unique aspect of InsurTech, including telematics, natural language processing (NLP), parametric triggers, and digital ecosystem models. Instead of providing exhaustive analyses, these narratives are designed to foster classroom discussion, encourage critical thinking, and prompt practical reflection on how technology is transforming the insurance industry.

FOR EDUCATORS

This compendium can be used as a standalone teaching tool or as a supplement to lecture materials. Consider assigning specific case studies as:

- Prereading for classroom discussion
- Basis for in-class breakout debates or roleplay
- Launch points for student presentations or policy critiques
- Prompts for short written reflections on strategy, ethics, or risk

Each case includes discussion questions to facilitate the exploration of business implications, regulatory tensions, and customer impact, making them ideal for engaging students in undergraduate, graduate, and executive programs.

FOR STUDENTS

You are encouraged to view these cases not as final stories, but as ongoing scenarios. What strategies were successful? What risks still exist? How might these companies adjust their models for different markets or in response to stricter regulations? These

Insurance Technology. DOI: https://doi.org/10.1016/B978-0-443-43972-8.00013-4

examples provide an opportunity to test your understanding, challenge your assumptions, and consider your own role in shaping the future of insurance.

CASE STUDY 1: LEMONADE'S ARTIFICIAL INTELLIGENCE–POWERED CLAIMS PLATFORM

Related Chapter: Machine Learning (ML) and Artificial Intelligence (AI) in Insurance **Company**: Lemonade Inc. **Technology Focus**: NLP, Deep Learning, Behavioral Analytics **Region**: United States

BACKGROUND AND CONTEXT

Founded in 2015, Lemonade has become a disruptive force in the US insurance market by offering fully digital insurance services for renters, homeowners, pets, and term life. The company has built its brand on principles of radical simplicity, transparency, and speed, challenging traditional insurance practices through AI-driven processes. Unlike legacy insurers that rely on human-based underwriting and claims adjustment, Lemonade's core operations—from quotes to payouts—are designed to function autonomously, minimizing human involvement.

The company has a distinctive business model: it keeps a fixed percentage of premiums to cover operational costs, donates unclaimed premiums to charitable causes through its annual "Giveback," and uses behavioral science to reduce fraud. This approach aligns financial incentives more closely with customer outcomes, and technology is essential for making it operationally effective.

TECHNOLOGICAL INNOVATION

At the core of Lemonade's claims strategy is an AI system called "AI Jim." This system automates the processes of claims triage, fraud detection, and, in many cases, payment execution. When a customer files a claim through the mobile app, AI Jim engages in real-time conversations using NLP and chatbots. It gathers photographic and video evidence, reviews policy details, and conducts fraud risk assessments.

The platform incorporates ML models trained on internal and external datasets, including:

- Claims histories
- Customer behavior patterns
- Textual sentiment and vocal tone analysis
- Image and video recognition for evidence validation

Lemonade claims that in some scenarios, AI Jim has resolved and paid legitimate claims in under 3 minutes, without any human intervention.

CHALLENGES FACED

Despite its technical successes, Lemonade faced several hurdles:

- Regulatory skepticism: State regulators initially expressed concern about automated decision-making and compliance with unfair claims practices laws.
- Fraud detection edge cases: While AI handles typical claims efficiently, edge cases with ambiguous data or subjective context require human review.
- Data limitations: In early deployments, the lack of rich training data hindered the AI's ability to detect nuanced patterns in fraud and sentiment.

Lemonade addressed these issues by implementing hybrid workflows where AI flags uncertain claims for manual review and by continuously training models on new customer data.

OUTCOMES AND MEASURABLE RESULTS

- Claims speed: Lemonade reported that about 30% of claims are handled automatically, with some settled in under 3 minutes.
- Operational efficiency: The company operates with significantly lower administrative overhead per policy compared to traditional insurers.
- Customer satisfaction: Lemonade's Net Promoter Score has remained notably high for a digital insurer, averaging in the 60s.
- Scalability: AI infrastructure allowed the company to expand into Germany, the Netherlands, and France with minimal local onboarding costs.

LESSONS LEARNED

Lemonade's model demonstrates the strong synergy between customer-focused product design and AI-driven automation. The company has shown that AI in insurance goes beyond backend functions; it can transform the entire customer journey, from obtaining quotes to receiving claims payouts. Additionally, it emphasizes the importance of trust, ethical guidelines, and human fallback systems in creating responsible insurance automation.

DISCUSSION QUESTIONS

- What are the strengths and weaknesses of Lemonade's approach to using AI in claims processing?
- How might regulators respond to fully autonomous claims adjudication?
- What types of risks emerge when AI becomes the first (or only) touchpoint in a high-stakes customer interaction?

CASE STUDY 2: ALLIANZ'S GEOSPATIAL MACHINE LEARNING FOR CLIMATE RISK

Related Chapter: Parametric Insurance and Climate Risk Analytics **Company**: Allianz SE **Technology Focus**: Geospatial Data, ML, Satellite Imaging, Climate Modeling **Region**: Global (with focus on commercial property underwriting in Europe and Asia)

BACKGROUND AND CONTEXT

Allianz SE, one of the largest insurers in the world, has long acknowledged the growing impact of climate risk on its underwriting processes. As climate-related disasters become more frequent and severe, traditional actuarial methods have struggled to accurately assess and manage risks, particularly for commercial property portfolios vulnerable to wildfires, flooding, and hurricanes.

To maintain underwriting profitability and stay ahead of emerging climate regulations in the EU and Asia-Pacific markets, Allianz has started integrating geospatial ML tools to better assess and manage physical climate risk exposures.

This initiative was part of a larger investment in digital risk engineering, aiming to transition from reactive claims management to proactive risk selection and mitigation.

TECHNOLOGICAL INNOVATION

Allianz developed a proprietary geospatial risk engine that blends satellite imagery, remote sensing data, historical loss records, and climate models to evaluate location-based exposures.

The engine leverages:

- Satellite imaging and terrain mapping to assess vegetation density, proximity to coastlines, or urban infrastructure
- ML-based classification models to segment risk zones for events like flash floods, coastal storm surge, or wildfire spread
- Dynamic updating of exposure scores based on real-time weather feeds and environmental sensors

For instance, when assessing a commercial warehouse in Southeast Asia, the system evaluates not only the insured property but also its surrounding environment, including nearby drainage infrastructure, elevation, recent rainfall history, and floodplain overlays.

The tool integrates smoothly into Allianz's commercial underwriting platform, providing underwriters with a visual heat map of physical climate risks, with a resolution of up to 50 m.

CHALLENGES FACED

- Data harmonization: Integrating heterogeneous satellite, Geographic Information System, and policyholder data required complex data normalization processes.
- Model interpretability: Convincing underwriters and regulators to trust the output of ML-based geospatial models required additional explainability modules.
- Global localization: Calibrating the system for local geography and climate data (e.g., Bangladesh vs. Germany) demanded country-specific modeling and regulatory engagement.

To address these concerns, Allianz built internal training programs for underwriters and partnered with academic researchers to audit and validate model performance.

OUTCOMES AND MEASURABLE RESULTS

- Improved underwriting accuracy: The engine contributed to more granular risk segmentation, reducing unexpected loss ratios in climate-prone zones.
- Faster turnaround: Automated geospatial scoring reduced property assessment times from weeks to hours.
- Strategic risk avoidance: Allianz declined or repriced high-risk properties that legacy models previously misclassified.
- Regulatory alignment: The tool helped Allianz meet EU disclosure standards under the Sustainable Finance Disclosure Regulation.

LESSONS LEARNED

Allianz's implementation showcases how combining physical geography with ML can modernize underwriting. It also emphasizes the need for AI tools to be transparent, auditable, and context aware, particularly in high-impact sectors such as property insurance.

This case also provides a glimpse of how insurers might transform into partners in climate risk management, assisting clients in adapting to hazards as well as providing insurance.

DISCUSSION QUESTIONS

- What ethical or legal considerations arise from using satellite surveillance in underwriting?
- How can insurers balance automation with human judgment in risk selection?
- Should insurers have a responsibility to share geospatial risk insights with policyholders or the public?

CASE STUDY 3: PROGRESSIVE'S SNAPSHOT PROGRAM AND TELEMATICS-BASED PRICING

Related Chapter: Internet of Things (IoT), ML, and Usage-Based Insurance **Company**: Progressive Insurance **Technology Focus**: Telematics, Real-Time Driving Data, Behavioral Scoring, ML **Region**: United States

BACKGROUND AND CONTEXT

Progressive Insurance, one of the leading auto insurers in the United States, is well known for its technology-driven approach to underwriting. As early as the 1990s, the company began experimenting with usage-based insurance. They believed that individual driving behavior would provide a more accurate and fair basis for pricing than traditional demographic factors such as age, ZIP code, or gender.

This vision was realized with the launch of Snapshot, a telematics program introduced nationally in 2011. Snapshot utilizes devices or mobile apps to monitor real-time driving behavior, providing data to ML models that calculate personalized discounts or surcharges. This initiative not only represents a pricing innovation but also serves as a behavioral science experiment, encouraging drivers to adopt safer habits through immediate feedback.

TECHNOLOGICAL INNOVATION

Snapshot captures and analyzes multiple driving variables, including:

- Hard braking
- Rapid acceleration
- Time of day driven
- Total mileage
- Phone usage (in mobile app version)

The telematics data is sent using a plug-in device (OBD-II dongle) or through smartphone sensors. This data is processed by Progressive's internal ML models to create a behavioral risk score that directly impacts pricing.

The algorithm uses regression and classification models to predict both the frequency and severity of claims by analyzing patterns from millions of policyholders. Additionally, Snapshot allows Progressive to update a driver's premium dynamically as risk signals change over time, rather than depending solely on static annual renewals.

Progressive added a mobile gamification feature to its app that rewards safe driving and allows users to compare scores, enhancing engagement and retention.

CHALLENGES FACED

- Data privacy concerns: Early adopters expressed skepticism about being tracked, particularly regarding how data would be used in claims decisions.
- Driver selection bias: Risk-averse or already-safe drivers were more likely to enroll, limiting the generalizability of the data pool in early models.
- Regulatory oversight: State insurance regulators demanded transparency in how telematics data influenced pricing and whether it introduced bias.

Progressive tackled these issues by releasing transparency reports, granting users explicit control over data sharing, and offering actuarially validated justifications for each variable used.

OUTCOMES AND MEASURABLE RESULTS

- High enrollment: Over 30% of new auto customers opt into Snapshot, significantly increasing Progressive's underwriting granularity.
- Improved segmentation: Snapshot helped separate high-risk and low-risk drivers more effectively, improving profitability and retention.
- Claims frequency reduction: Participants in Snapshot showed modest improvements in driving behavior, reducing claims rates for selected segments.
- Market differentiation: Snapshot positioned Progressive as a pioneer in behavior-based pricing, prompting competitors like Allstate (Drivewise) and State Farm (Drive Safe & Save) to launch similar programs.

LESSONS LEARNED

Snapshot demonstrates how insurers can transition from reactive to proactive risk management using IoT and data analytics. By leveraging real-time behavior, Progressive introduced a more equitable model that rewards good driving and reduces reliance on potentially discriminatory historical proxies.

The case also shows that technological innovation in insurance is not just about data, but also about designing user trust, navigating regulation, and delivering feedback that changes behavior.

DISCUSSION QUESTIONS

- How can insurers ensure that telematics programs don't unintentionally penalize drivers who live in high-risk areas or commute at night?
- Should behavioral risk scoring be shared with other stakeholders, such as regulators or law enforcement?
- What's the ethical balance between incentivizing safe driving and surveilling personal habits?

CASE STUDY 4: AXA'S USE OF NATURAL LANGUAGE PROCESSING AND IMAGE ANALYTICS IN CLAIMS AUTOMATION

Related Chapter: AI in Claims Management and Customer Service **Company**: AXA Group **Technology Focus**: NLP, Image Analytics, Conversational AI **Region**: Europe and Asia

BACKGROUND AND CONTEXT

AXA, a multinational insurance and asset management firm based in Paris, is leading the way in adopting AI to improve operational efficiency and enhance customer satisfaction. In a strategic move toward automation and digital transformation, AXA has invested in AI to optimize the claims handling process, especially in the areas of motor and travel insurance. In these sectors, processing speed and customer engagement are crucial differentiators.

In response to increasing customer expectations, heightened digital competition, and pressure to reduce administrative costs, AXA aimed to modernize its claims intake and assessment process. This involved minimizing human intervention, enhancing turnaround time, and ensuring consistent service across its global markets.

TECHNOLOGICAL INNOVATION

AXA integrated NLP and image analytics technologies into its claims workflows through the development of AI-powered virtual assistants and digital portals.

- NLP-Based Chatbots: These virtual assistants collect loss information via web or mobile chat, interpreting customer narratives in multiple languages. NLP is used to extract structured data (e.g., time, location, damage description) from unstructured input.
- Image Recognition Models: Customers submitting motor or travel insurance claims can upload images of vehicle damage, lost baggage, or travel documentation. Deep learning models classify and assess the images to determine claims validity, damage severity, and fraud risk.
- Multilingual Claims Engine: In regions like Singapore, Germany, and Spain, AXA deployed systems capable of interpreting claims written in local languages and dialects, ensuring faster adjudication in diverse regulatory contexts.

This technology stack allows for real-time claims triaging, directing complex cases to human adjusters while automatically approving straightforward, low-risk claims within minutes.

CHALLENGES FACED

- Training data diversity: NLP systems needed to be trained on varied, multilingual datasets across geographies. AXA invested in custom datasets and employed transfer learning techniques to overcome gaps in local language nuance.
- Image authenticity: Verifying that uploaded images were recent, relevant, and unedited required building metadata extraction tools and partnering with forensics vendors.
- Customer trust: There was initial reluctance among some policyholders to interact with bots rather than human adjusters, especially in high-stress situations like auto accidents abroad.

AXA addressed these issues by offering hybrid claims handling options, enhancing transparency regarding AI usage, and providing customers the choice to opt out if desired.

OUTCOMES AND MEASURABLE RESULTS

- Accelerated processing: In some markets, up to 45% of claims are now fully handled by AI systems, with processing times reduced by 60%.
- Cost savings: Automation allowed AXA to reduce manual workloads, reassign adjusters to higher-value tasks, and cut operational costs significantly.
- Enhanced customer experience: Surveys indicated improved satisfaction scores in travel claims, where response time is a critical factor.
- Global scalability: The system's multilingual NLP and modular architecture made it easy to roll out across markets, including France, Japan, and the Middle East.

LESSONS LEARNED

AXA's experience demonstrates that AI technologies need to be integrated thoughtfully into the customer journey. NLP and image analytics are effective tools, but their success relies on cultural sensitivity, user control, and human oversight. The insurer's proactive combination of automation and empathy illustrates how digital transformation can extend beyond mere cost-cutting to genuinely improve relationships with policyholders.

DISCUSSION QUESTIONS

- How can insurers ensure AI-generated decisions remain fair and explainable, especially across different cultures?
- What are the risks of overrelying on image-based evidence for claims adjudication?
- Could customers begin to "game" AI claims systems with fabricated or manipulated data?

CASE STUDY 5: FLOODFLASH AND SMART PARAMETRIC INSURANCE

Related Chapter: Parametric Insurance, IoT Integration, and Climate Resilience **Company**: FloodFlash Ltd. **Technology Focus**: IoT (Water-Level Sensors), Parametric Triggers, Smart Contracts **Region**: United Kingdom (expanding to the United States and Europe)

BACKGROUND AND CONTEXT

Flooding is one of the most damaging and frequent natural disasters in the United Kingdom, costing the economy billions of pounds each year. However, many businesses, particularly small and mid-sized enterprises, have difficulty obtaining affordable flood insurance. Traditional indemnity insurance models often lead to slow claims processing, unclear coverage terms, and high administrative costs due to complicated loss adjustments.

Founded in 2016, FloodFlash aimed to fill a gap in the insurance market by utilizing parametric insurance. This approach pays out based on measurable, predefined triggers instead of relying on assessments of damage after an event occurs. By emphasizing data, speed, and simplicity, FloodFlash pioneered a new insurance model that has redefined the way flood risk is transferred, making it more transparent and accessible.

TECHNOLOGICAL INNOVATION

FloodFlash combines IoT technology with parametric underwriting to deliver fast, data-driven coverage. Their core solution consists of:

- Smart water-level sensors are installed at the policyholder's property. These tamper-resistant devices record water levels in real time and transmit data over cellular networks to FloodFlash's cloud platform.
- Parametric triggers are set during underwriting—for example, a policyholder might specify that if floodwaters reach 0.5 m, they will receive a £30,000 payout.
- Automated claims processing begins the moment the sensor detects the threshold level. Because there is no need to verify physical damage or estimate repair costs, payouts are issued within hours, often directly to the insured's account.
- Smart contract logic, while not blockchain native, enables rapid execution of the policy without adjuster involvement.
- FloodFlash policies are customizable, letting clients choose both the trigger depth and payout amount to reflect their risk appetite and financial exposure.

CHALLENGES FACED

- Consumer education: Many clients were unfamiliar with parametric models and initially misunderstood the disconnect between actual damage and fixed payouts.
- Sensor deployment logistics: Ensuring proper installation, calibration, and tamper-proofing of devices at scale posed operational hurdles.
- Regulatory oversight: Some regulators questioned whether parametric models could be classified as insurance products under existing frameworks. FloodFlash worked closely with the UK's Financial Conduct Authority to validate the model.
- Basis risk: Because payouts depend on water level rather than actual loss, situations occasionally arise where clients experience damage but do not meet the trigger or vice versa. FloodFlash mitigates this by offering fine-tuned trigger settings and clear client education during the onboarding process.

OUTCOMES AND MEASURABLE RESULTS

- Rapid payouts: FloodFlash has settled claims within 24 hours, compared to weeks or months in traditional models.
- Market penetration: The company secured coverage for previously uninsurable businesses, especially those in high-risk flood zones turned away by traditional carriers.
- Client retention: High satisfaction among policyholders led to strong renewal rates, particularly among businesses where downtime due to flooding poses existential threats.
- Scalability: The model's automation and simplicity allow expansion to new geographies without needing massive claims infrastructure.

LESSONS LEARNED

FloodFlash demonstrates how parametric insurance models, enhanced by real-time data and the IoT, can significantly change the financial dynamics of insurance. The straightforward nature of "if this happens, then we pay that" policies is attractive to clients in high-risk areas, effectively addressing the liquidity challenges often associated with climate-related disasters.

Nonetheless, the case emphasizes the significance of managing basis risk and establishing clear expectations. It reinforces the idea that technological innovation should be paired with robust client education, regulatory collaboration, and transparent product design.

DISCUSSION QUESTIONS

- How does FloodFlash's model redefine the insurer–insured relationship?
- What are the ethical implications of fixed payouts when damage does not exactly align with sensor readings?
- Could parametric models work in other perils like wildfire, hail, or cyber risk?

CASE STUDY 6: SWISS RE AND THE DIGITAL ECOSYSTEM MODEL

Related Chapter: Digital Transformation, Ecosystems, and Platform Strategies **Company**: Swiss Re Group **Technology Focus**: Digital Ecosystems, Application Programming Interface (API) Integration, Data Marketplaces, Risk Intelligence Platforms **Region**: Global (notably Europe, North America, and Asia-Pacific)

BACKGROUND AND CONTEXT

Swiss Re, one of the largest reinsurance companies in the world, has established itself as a leader in insurance innovation. However, with rising competition from agile InsurTech startups and the increasing complexity of global risk environments, Swiss Re recognized the necessity of transitioning from a traditional reinsurance model to a digital ecosystem strategy.

Instead of merely underwriting large commercial and catastrophe risks, Swiss Re has developed a connected ecosystem that provides data-driven services, platform connectivity, and risk intelligence to primary insurers, startups, and even non-insurance companies in sectors like logistics and healthcare. This ecosystem-focused approach positions Swiss Re as a facilitator of innovation and resilience, not just as a reinsurer.

TECHNOLOGICAL INNOVATION

Swiss Re launched several key digital initiatives that form the foundation of its ecosystem:

- Swiss Re's Magnum and iptiQ Platforms: Magnum is an automated underwriting engine utilized by more than 100 life and health insurers worldwide. It analyzes data from medical records, wearable devices, and self-reported surveys to assess underwriting risk using AI-driven decision-making logic.
- Risk Data Services via API: Swiss Re has made its proprietary risk datasets accessible through API-based tools. This enables clients to integrate climate risk scores, catastrophe models, and mortality trends directly into their underwriting and portfolio analysis systems.

- Ecosystem Partnerships: Swiss Re collaborated with technology companies, government agencies, and startups to establish networks for data exchange and product experimentation. These collaborations focus on telematics, parametric reinsurance, and supply chain risk modeling.
- Digital Marketplaces: Swiss Re offers clients access to on-demand actuarial services, global hazard mapping, and ML tools through platforms like Life Guide and CatNet, all integrated into the client's systems via secure APIs.

CHALLENGES FACED

- Cultural transformation: Internally, Swiss Re had to retrain staff and shift from a contract-based mindset to a digital product and service orientation.
- Integration barriers: Many of Swiss Re's primary insurer clients used legacy systems that were not prepared to consume APIs or support real-time data flows.
- Platform competition: Competing with tech companies and newer platforms forced Swiss Re to accelerate innovation cycles without sacrificing its reputation for precision and prudence.

To address these challenges, Swiss Re established multidisciplinary digital labs, invested in cloud modernization, and adopted agile development frameworks to accelerate internal experimentation and enhance external delivery.

OUTCOMES AND MEASURABLE RESULTS

- Revenue diversification: By monetizing services, not just risk transfer, Swiss Re created new revenue streams through data subscriptions and platform access fees.
- Partner expansion: iptiQ now supports dozens of digital insurance brands, embedded into bank apps, retail stores, and mobile health platforms.
- Global recognition: Swiss Re has become a case study in how traditional incumbents can evolve into technology orchestrators, driving innovation across the value chain.
- Increased agility: The company reduced time to market for digital product launches and improved client onboarding for risk intelligence services.

LESSONS LEARNED

Swiss Re's evolution demonstrates that the future of insurance is collaborative, digital, and modular. Rather than competing directly with InsurTech companies, the reinsurer chose to become an enabler by providing the tools, data, and infrastructure needed by a diverse range of partners.

This method shows that insurers adopting platform thinking and ecosystem design can enhance efficiencies, innovate more rapidly, and establish themselves as key players in emerging risk environments.

DISCUSSION QUESTIONS

- How can other incumbents replicate Swiss Re's ecosystem strategy without losing their identity?
- What risks are introduced when insurers open their platforms and data to external partners?
- Should insurance companies focus more on product innovation or platform orchestration going forward?

AI DISCLOSURE

During the preparation of this work the author(s) used Grammarly to improve readability and correct any grammatical mistakes. After using this tool/service, the author(s) reviewed and edited the content as needed and take(s) full responsibility for the content of the publication.

Index

C

D

I

Q

R

S

Printed and bound by CPI Group (UK) Ltd, Croydon, CR0 4YY
14/09/2026
02216291-0006